101 Solutions for School Counselors and Leaders in Challenging Times

Stuart Chen-Hayes:

I dedicate this book to my husband, Dr. Lance Chen-Hayes, mom, Dr. Lois F. Hayes, and son, Kalani, who have provided countless hours of love, fun, far-flung adventures, fabulous food, and flexibility.

Melissa Ockerman:

I dedicate this book to my pinch-me-how-did-I-get-so-lucky family—Joseph and Barbara (my parents); Aaron, Denise, Jennifer, Maura, and Micah (my siblings and in-laws); and Jackson, Adam, Ethan, Megan, and Claira (my nieces and nephews)—who have taught me that it's a beautiful world but there's no place like home.

Erin Mason:

I dedicate this book to my husband, Chris Mason, because he is "ideas people"; he never ceases to stimulate my intellect and support its growth. Plus, he can grill up a tasty steak and make a mean margarita. Marrying him was the best idea I ever had.

101 Solutions for School Counselors and Leaders in Challenging Times

Stuart F. Chen-Hayes

Melissa S. Ockerman

E. C. M. Mason

CORWIN
A SAGE Company

CORWIN
A SAGE Company

FOR INFORMATION:

Corwin
A SAGE Company
2455 Teller Road
Thousand Oaks, California 91320
(800) 233–9936
www.corwin.com

SAGE Publications Ltd.
1 Oliver's Yard
55 City Road
London EC1Y 1SP
United Kingdom

SAGE Publications India Pvt. Ltd.
B 1/I 1 Mohan Cooperative Industrial Area
Mathura Road, New Delhi 110 044
India

SAGE Publications Asia-Pacific Pte. Ltd.
3 Church Street
#10–04 Samsung Hub
Singapore 049483

Acquisitions Editor: Jessica Allan
Associate Editor: Kimberly Greenberg
Editorial Assistant: Cesar Reyes
Marketing Manager: Stephanie Trkay
Project Editor: Veronica Stapleton Hooper
Copy Editor: Dan Gordon
Typesetter: Hurix Systems Private Ltd.
Proofreader: Sarah J. Duffy
Indexer: Jean Casalegno
Cover Designer: Candice Harman

Printed in the United States of America

Library of Congress Cataloging-in-Publication Data

Chen-Hayes, Stuart.
101 solutions for school counselors and leaders in challenging times / Stuart F. Chen-Hayes, Melissa S. Ockerman, E. C. M. Mason.

pages cm

Includes bibliographical references and index.

ISBN 978-1-4522-7447-8 (alk. paper)

1. Educational counseling—United States—Handbooks, manuals, etc. 2. School administrators—United States—Handbooks, manuals, etc. 3. Educational leadership—United States—Handbooks, manuals, etc. I. Title. II. Title: One hundred one solutions for school counselors and leaders in challenging times. III. Title: One hundred and one solutions for school counselors and leaders in challenging times.

LB1027.5.C45 2013

371.4'22—dc23

2013027232

This book is printed on acid-free paper.

13 14 15 16 17 10 9 8 7 6 5 4 3 2 1

Contents

Acknowledgments

We humbly and joyfully acknowledge our pre-K–12 school counseling clients/students, school counseling graduate students, school counseling alumni, school counseling site supervisors, pre-K–12 school counseling and college readiness counseling colleagues, and pre-K–12 building and district leader colleagues for your wisdom, care, and concern in helping shape our ideas and solutions. We gratefully honor and appreciate our school counseling leadership, social justice advocacy, and counselor education mentors: Dr. Mary Smith Arnold, Maureen Casamassimo, Dr. Catharina Chang, Dr. Reese House, Dr. Anita Jackson, Dr. H. George McMahon, Dr. James Moore, Dr. Fran Mullis, Dr. Pamela O. Paisley, Dr. Susan Sears, Gail M. Smith, and Dr. Joanne White; our Transformed School Counseling (TSC) initiative colleagues including Dr. Trish Hatch at the Center for Excellence in School Counseling and Leadership (CESCAL) and co-author of the *ASCA National Model: A Framework for School Counseling Programs*; Dr. Vivian Lee and Pat Martin of the National Office for School Counselor Advocacy (NOSCA), authors of the *Eight College and Career Readiness Counseling Components* and the strategic planning tool that are essential parts of the "Own the Turf Campaign"; Dr. Peggy Hines and Karen Crews of the National Center for Transforming School Counseling (NCTSC); and the 180-plus dedicated members of the Association for Counselor Education and Supervision (ACES) Transformed School Counseling/College Access Interest Network (TSCCAIN). Your collective wisdom and spirited pursuit of equity continue to inspire us. Thanks also to Tyler Wicks, DePaul University school counseling graduate assistant, for technological wizardry in formatting the CAFÉ (Change Agent for Equity) School Counselor Evaluation, and Debbie Ashley, CUNY Lehman College Adjunct Counselor Education faculty, for co-authoring the Ethical School Counselor Scenarios. We are indebted to our acquisitions editor, Jessica Allan, whose passion for good writing, independent publishing, and the best possible solutions for K–16 practitioners is exemplary. Finally, we thank the entire production team at SAGE/ Corwin and our book reviewers who gave many useful ideas and suggestions to strengthen *101 Solutions.*

Publisher's Acknowledgments

Corwin would like to thank the following individuals for taking the time to provide their editorial feedback and insight:

Charisza Santos
Lewis & Clark College
Graduate School of Education and Counseling
Portland, OR

Erin J. Vandermore
Elementary School Counselor
Chicago Public Schools
Chicago, IL

About the Authors

Stuart F. Chen-Hayes, PhD, is program coordinator and associate professor of counselor education/school counseling at Lehman College of the City University of New York. He is also a part-time dissertation chair for Oregon State University's Counselor Education/School Counseling PhD program. Stuart has middle school, college student affairs, sexuality, family and couple, community mental health, and addictions counseling experience, and he is an equity-focused school counseling program consultant in K–12 school districts. Stuart also taught at National-Louis University in Chicago and at National Changhua University of Education in Taiwan. He is a co-founder and past president of Counselors for Social Justice, a past president of the North Atlantic Region Association for Counselor Educators and Supervisors (NARACES), a past president of the Illinois Counseling Association, and on the editorial boards of the *Journal of Gay, Lesbian, Bisexual, and Transgender Issues in Counseling,* the *Journal of Counselor Preparation and Supervision,* and the *Journal of International Counselor Education.* Stuart has written and/or co-authored 50 refereed publications and three streaming videos, including *Equity-Focused School Counseling: Career and College Readiness for Every K-12 Student* (2009), and *Counseling LBGTIQ Youth in Schools and Families, Vols. 1, 2* (2000). He is a mentor for the Counselor Educator Transforming School Counseling Coalition and co-chairs a monthly Association for Counselor Education & Supervision (ACES) Transformed School Counseling/ College Access Interest Network (TSCCAIN). Stuart has delivered 225-plus school counseling and social justice education presentations.

He received his counseling and human development services PhD from Kent State University and counseling and counselor education MSEd from Indiana University.

Melissa S. Ockerman, PhD, is an associate professor in the counseling program at DePaul University. A proud Buckeye, she graduated with an MA in school counseling and PhD in counselor education from The Ohio State University. Dr. Ockerman has established a strong research agenda focusing on school counselor leadership, the efficacy of school counseling interventions, and systemic anti-bullying and school safety strategies. She appeared before the Congressional Black Caucus in Washington, DC, to discuss bipartisan anti-violence policies. She is a frequent presenter at local, state, and national conferences. In 2012, she was named the Illinois Counselor Educator of the Year. Dr. Ockerman currently holds executive positions in national and state professional organizations, including co-chair of the Association for Counselor Education and Supervision (ACES) Transformed School Counseling/College Access Interest Network, and vice president, counselor education, for the Illinois School Counseling Association (ISCA). Additionally, Dr. Ockerman is chair of the school counseling committee for the Illinois Safe Schools Alliance, a National Center for Transforming School Counseling (NCTSC) Counselor Educator Coalition fellow, and an Advisory Council member for the Evidence-Based Practice in School Counseling conference. Her passion for educating the next generation of transformed school counselors is matched only by her strong desire to dismantle the pervasive achievement gap in schools through innovative and effective evidence-based school counseling interventions.

E. C. M. Mason, PhD, is a career-long advocate for the school counseling profession. Erin's accomplishments and contributions to the field derive from her 13 years of experience as a middle school counselor in her home state of Georgia. A proponent for modeling and supporting professional involvement and productivity, Erin fuels her passion for school counseling through state and national leadership opportunities. Erin served in multiple positions for the Georgia School Counselors Association (GSCA), including being the Government Relations co-chair for several consecutive years, and she was the 2012–2013 president of the Illinois School Counselor Association (ISCA). At the national level, Erin served as a lead RAMP reviewer for the American School Counselor Association (ASCA).

She now serves as one of four mentors for the Transforming School Counseling (TSC) Counselor Educator Coalition and as an Advisory Council member for the Evidence-Based School Counseling Conference. As a presenter, scholar, trainer, and consultant, Erin's particular interests in school counseling lie in the areas of technology use, comprehensive program implementation and the professional identity development of school counselors. Erin is an assistant professor at DePaul University in Chicago and received her MEd, EdS, and PhD from Georgia State University.

Introduction

Budget cuts; grass-roots rebellion against high-stakes testing; corporate challenges to public education; calls for accountability and evaluation; increasing student-to-school counselor ratios; unemployment and underemployment; and achievement, opportunity, attainment, and funding gaps all illustrate inequity among learners and school resources creating and responding to challenging times in K–12 schools. Common Core Standards and Career-Technical Common Core Standards have been developed to create more students who are career- and college-ready for a global economy and challenge systemic inequities in education. However, effectiveness of these initiatives is unclear and some worry about a narrowing of the curriculum due to their presence. At the same time, K–12 educational leaders—including school counselors and school counselor candidates—navigate the waters of academic, career, and college readiness and personal/social competencies for every K–12 student, with many stakeholders unclear about school counselor roles and responsibilities, fewer financial and human resources, and increased international expectations for all students to succeed in postsecondary education and careers.

This book is for educational leaders including school counselors who desire equity for every student. It is for school counselors facing challenging odds, including the average school counselor to student ratio in the high 400s to 1 and increasing in many U.S. states. This book is designed to give everyone who leads in schools, including school counselors, multiple equity-focused solutions that work in elementary, middle, and high schools.

We cannot predict the future, but we can work to ensure that educators collaborate to eliminate inappropriate tasks for school counselors—for instance, discipline, bus and hall duty, testing, and other noncounseling activities—so that school counselors can deliver comprehensive school counseling programs that reach every student, every marking period, every year. For students who need more than annual planning and school counseling core curriculum lessons, there must be adequate time and space for group counseling for some students and individual counseling for other students.

Not every student needs counseling. Every student, does, however, need an annually updated **ACCESS/Accomplishments Plan** (Chen-Hayes, 2013), developmental school counseling core curriculum lessons, and other data-driven activities (digital and traditional) that cultivate academic, career, college readiness, and personal/social competencies to help them live their dreams. Every school leader needs to evaluate their school counseling program interventions and outcomes on equitable resources and experiences for every student using the **ACCESS Questionnaire** (Chen-Hayes, 2007), revised for *101 Solutions* with the latest American School Counselor Association (ASCA) Model changes and National Office for School Counselor Advocacy (NOSCA) eight college and career readiness counseling components.

School counselors need to be evaluated effectively and building/district leaders need an appropriate evaluation tool to successfully ensure that school counselors are on target to meet the needs of all students. We created the **Change Agent for Equity (CAFÉ) Model** to focus school counselors and other leaders on key school counselor skills needed to implement a school counseling program—advocacy, collaboration, cultural competency, leadership, technology, and equity assessment using data (Mason, Ockerman, & Chen-Hayes, 2013; Ockerman, Mason, & Chen-Hayes, 2013). In *101 Solutions,* we present the **Change Agent for Equity (CAFÉ) School Counselor Evaluation** for building, district, state/province, and national educators to assess equity-focused school counselor outcomes in 16 key areas (see Chapter 1).

Questions and Challenges for School Counselors and Other Leaders

In this book, we challenge outdated notions and use of dated "guidance counselor" and "guidance program" terminology since the profession has been "school counselor" and "school counseling" for over 60 years. We ask why so many public elementary, middle, and high schools staff school counselors primarily for personal-social issues and crisis intervention with too little career/college and academic counseling and competency development.

We question why too many independent schools don't staff any school counselors until high school, and then their sole focus is college readiness without equal time for academic, career, and personal/social competencies. We challenge why school counselors are being cut and ratios are climbing when research indicates exactly the opposite would better prepare more students for higher academic achievement in literacy and math (Wilkerson, Pérusse, & Hughes, 2013) and college and career readiness and success (Lapan, 2012).

Outdated K–12 school counseling practices and lack of an evidence-based school and college readiness counseling program are indefensible when the research clearly shows that students benefit from lower counselor-to-student ratios by having greater likelihood of college admissions and greater likelihood of academic success and future college graduation (Lapan, 2012). Every student in public, charter, and independent schools deserves annual academic, career, college readiness, and personal/social competencies delivered from a professional school counselor's evidence-based school counseling program.

Why Building and District Leaders Need to Hire, Evaluate, and Empower Equity-Focused School Counselors

School counselors who focus on equity are a key career- and college-readiness success strategy in schools and districts *when they are given the appropriate tools and time to bust barriers and close gaps!*

However, effective school counseling programs require effective school counselors who are equity-focused and identify themselves as change agents (Mason et al., 2013; Ockerman et al., 2013). Our earlier work on the CAFÉ model purposefully positions the identity of the school counselor as leader, advocate, collaborator, and change agent for equity as the linchpin of school counseling programs. Therefore, when hiring school counselors, administrators must screen for these identities (and their complementary attitudes, knowledge, and skills) during interviews. Rather than, or in addition to, traditional one-on-one interviews, administrators may wish to utilize group interview formats, data analysis activities, or school counseling classroom lesson instruction to assess candidates' application of knowledge and skill performance.

How Do School Counselor-to-Student Ratios at 250 to 1 or Lower Promote Equity?

Three decades of research shows that schools with fully implemented school counseling programs are more likely to have higher math and literacy skills at the elementary level (Wilkerson et al., 2013) and to graduate students from high school and have them enter and graduate from college (Lapan, 2012). Recent research (Hurwitz & Howell, 2013) indicates that more school counselors at lower ratios leads to closing the opportunity and attainment gaps, with more students applying for and gaining admission to college because there is more time to spend with students to assist them with the process.

School counselors are often the only school professionals educated with career development, college readiness, multicultural, and ethics coursework prior to school service (CACREP, 2009).

The Goal of 101 Solutions: Dream Makers and Barrier Busters

We do not have all the answers, but in our combined 59 years of professional experience in school counseling, college counseling, and counselor education, we offer 101 evidence-based and practical solutions. We envision all educators as dream makers and barrier busters, advocating for equitable outcomes for all students, and we are honored and excited to help you as practitioners and future practitioners to achieve that goal.

Every school counselor needs awareness, knowledge, and skills in 16 core key areas, and leaders must evaluate school counselors on their effectiveness in equity-focused school counseling program areas:

1. Leadership as change agents for equity
2. Educator and school counselor collaboration
3. Program assessment and accountability
4. Achievement gap solutions
5. Opportunity and attainment gap solutions
6. College and career readiness
7. Annual college and career readiness planning
8. School-family-community partnerships
9. Ethics
10. Cultural identity and language solutions
11. Technology
12. School-wide and multi-systemic intervention
13. Administrative, operational, and supervision solutions
14. Advocacy and public relations
15. Anti-violence, bullying, and safety solutions
16. Ability, disability, gifted/talented solutions

Chapter Overview

We have a chapter in each of these areas and have included solution success stories that highlight how practicing school counselors and school counselor candidates have had equity-focused success in each of them at elementary, middle, and high school levels in urban, suburban, and rural areas. *101 Solutions* is structured with the following chapters for ease of use by leaders and future leaders in school counseling:

Chapter 1: Leadership Solutions: Change Agents for Equity: This chapter highlights equity-focused leadership for school counselors and other leaders as the linchpin for all 101 solutions presented by us. It includes a new assessment for K–12 school counselors and other leaders in buildings, districts, and at the state or province level to evaluate school counselor performance, the **CAFÉ School Counselor Evaluation**.

Chapter 2: Educator and School Counselor Collaboration Solutions: This chapter demonstrates the critical need for school counselor-leader-educator collaboration in elementary, middle, and high school settings and provides practical and creative ways to collaborate.

Chapter 3: Program Assessment and Accountability Solutions: This chapter helps school counselors and other leaders with collecting, analyzing, and sharing critical data regarding school counseling interventions to promote comprehensive school counseling programs, equitable outcomes for students, and increased school counseling positions. It includes a revised version of the **ACCESS Questionnaire** for school counseling program assessment in buildings, districts, and at the state/province level.

Chapter 4: Achievement Gap Solutions: This chapter assists school counselors as equity-focused leaders in helping close achievement gaps with implementing, assessing, and sharing the outcomes of school counseling program planning and curriculum interventions for every K–12 student and group and individual counseling for some students annually.

Chapter 5: Opportunity and Attainment Gap Solutions: This chapter helps school counselors and other leaders ensure every student graduates from high school with equitable opportunities leading to a postsecondary diploma, thereby closing opportunity and attainment gaps via implementing, assessing, and sharing outcomes of planning and curriculum interventions for every

K–12 student and group and individual counseling for some students annually.

Chapter 6: College and Career Readiness Solutions: This chapter gives school counselors specific tools and multiple resources specific to six of the eight NOSCA Career and College Readiness Counseling components to help develop student college and career readiness skills K–12.

Chapter 7: Annual College and Career Readiness Planning Solutions: This chapter discusses academic planning interventions that help students succeed post high school and become successful world citizens with **ACCESS and Accomplishments Plans** and resources specific to two of the eight NOSCA Career and College Readiness Counseling components to help develop student college and career readiness skills K–12.

Chapter 8: School-Family-Community Partnership Solutions: This chapter introduces the school-family-community partnerships model and illustrates innovative ways to create collaborative partnerships with parents/guardians/caregivers, community agencies, and local businesses to improve student outcomes. A list of resources to challenge familyism is included.

Chapter 9: Ethics Solutions: This chapter assists school counselors and other leaders to implement an ethical decision-making tool and review key ethical issues focused on equity. A series of ethical case scenarios in schools based on composites of actual incidents showcases the need for school counselors and other leaders to constantly review and refer to codes of ethics including the ASCA *Ethical Code for School Counselors,* the American Counseling Association *Code of Ethics,* and the National Association for College Admission Counseling *Statement of Principles of Good Practice.*

Chapter 10: Cultural Identity and Language Solutions: This chapter helps school counselors and other leaders take an equity-focused advocacy and leadership role to challenge multiple oppressions in schools and target interventions to support culturally and linguistically diverse students individually and systemically. Hundreds of specific tools and websites focused on assisting school counselors and other leaders challenge multiple oppressions such as ageism, beautyism, classism, genderism, heterosexism, immigrationism, linguicism, racism, religionism, and sexism are included.

Chapter 11: Technology Solutions: This chapter addresses current issues and concerns about the use of technology by school counselors and other leaders and provides a substantial set of tools and resources for immediate use in building digital skills for optimal student success and strengthening school counseling programs.

Chapter 12: School-Wide and Multi-Systemic Intervention Solutions: This chapter discusses how school counselors and other leaders create and sustain systemic change and lead school-wide reform efforts such as Response to Intervention (RTI), maximize time, promote equity-focused school counseling interventions, and better serve all students.

Chapter 13: Administrative, Operational, and Supervision Solutions: This chapter helps school counselors and other leaders with specific administrative and operational challenges and options in schools and with how to maximize supervisory relationships in the building.

Chapter 14: Advocacy and Public Relations Solutions: This chapter identifies how school counselors and other leaders can best use advocacy and activism to promote their school counseling programs and ensure that internal and external publics are clear about the role of the school counselor and their results in promoting academic, career, college readiness, and personal/social competencies for every student. It addresses advocacy as central to daily practice for students and the school counseling profession.

Chapter 15: Anti-Violence, Bullying, and Safety Solutions: This chapter addresses bullying and cyberbullying and how school counselors and other building and district leaders proactively create and implement comprehensive anti-violence and anti-bullying programs for all students to feel safe and learn.

Chapter 16: Ability, Disability, and Gifted/Talented Solutions: This chapter helps school counselors and other leaders take an equity-focused leadership role in affirming students of diverse abilities, disabilities, and gifts/talents in K–12 schools. A list of resources to challenge ableism is included.

How to Make the Most of *101 Solutions*

This book is best read as a whole because themes, solutions, and resources overlap and connect between and across chapters. However, each chapter can be read on its own. Each of the 16 chapters provides the following elements:

- A brief overview of the topic
- Key words defined for each chapter and summarized in the glossary

- Key questions and answers (101)
- Solution Success Stories to highlight how those in the field have successfully addressed the topics (50)
- Digital and print resources to help the reader implement solutions (1,000-plus)

References

CACREP. (2009). *Council for the Accreditation of Counseling and Related Educational Programs 2009 Standards.* Alexandria, VA: Author. Retrieved from http://www.cacrep.org/doc/2009%20Standards%20with%20 cover.pdf

Chen-Hayes, S. F. (2007). The ACCESS Questionnaire: Assessing K-12 school counseling programs and interventions to ensure equity and success for every student. *Counseling and Human Development, 39,* 1–10.

Chen-Hayes, S. F. (2013). Empowering multiple cultural identities in college readiness and admission. In National Association for College Admission Counseling (Ed.), *Fundamentals of college admission counseling* (3rd ed., pp. 150–174). Arlington, VA: Author.

Hurwitz, M., & Howell, J. (2013). Measuring the impact of high school counselors on college enrollment. *College Board Advocacy & Policy Center research brief.* New York, NY: College Board. Retrieved from http://media.collegeboard.com/digitalServices/pdf/advocacy/policycenter/research-brief-measuring-impact-high-school-counselors-college-enrollment.pdf

Lapan, R. T. (2012). Comprehensive school counseling programs: In some schools for some students but not in all schools for all students. *Professional School Counseling, 16,* 84–88.

Mason, E. C. M., Ockerman, M. S., & Chen-Hayes, S. F. (2013). Change-Agent-for-Equity (CAFÉ) model: A framework for school counselor identity. *Journal of School Counseling, 11*(4). Retrieved from http://www .jsc.montana.edu

Ockerman, M. S., Mason, E. C. M., & Chen-Hayes, S. F. (2013). School counseling supervision in challenging times: The CAFÉ Supervisor Model. *Journal of Counselor Preparation and Supervision, 5*(2), *Article 4.* doi:http://dx.doi.org/10.7729/51.0024

Wilkerson, K., Pérusse, R., & Hughes, A. (2013). Comprehensive school counseling programs and student achievement outcomes: A comparative analysis of RAMP versus nonRAMP schools. *Professional School Counseling, 16,* 172–184.

1

Leadership Solutions

Change Agents for Equity

As a school counselor, how do you act as a leader for every student? At the heart of creating equity for every student K–12 is the capacity and potential for every school counselor to be a leader. That is why leadership as change agents for equity is the first chapter and a prevalent theme throughout the 16 chapters of *101 Solutions*.

Leadership is an ethical educational imperative for educators if the educational system is to gain traction on issues of access and equity found in the achievement and opportunity gaps that plague K–12 schools (American School Counselor Association [ASCA], 2010). School counselors and other leaders have an essential role as *change agents for equity* (Mason, Ockerman, & Chen-Hayes, 2013; Ockerman, Mason, & Chen-Hayes, 2013) in ensuring all students reach their academic, career, college, and personal/social goals (see Figure 1.1). However, solutions for making that happen have not always coincided in K–12 school pre-service training or staff development. Extensive research now tells us that fully implemented, comprehensive school counseling programs delivered by well-prepared school counselors are *essential* to student success, but there is a vast implementation gap across programs, schools, districts, and states (Lapan, 2012). Therefore, school counselors have an ethical impera-tive to lead equitable change and to be leaders providing the school counseling program every student needs and to do the justice and equity work that every student deserves (ASCA, 2010; Chen-Hayes & Getch, in press; Chen-Hayes & Ockerman, in press; Holcomb-McCoy & Chen-Hayes, in press; Stone, 2005).

In many ways, entities within the school counseling profession have worked at the national level to empower school counselors to be leaders and have served as models of leadership for equity by high-lighting and strengthening the positioning of school counseling within the vast field of education, including the ASCA, the National Center for Transforming School Counseling (NCTSC), the National Office for School Counselor Advocacy (NOSCA), the Center for Excellence in

Figure 1.1   Change Agent for Equity (CAFÉ) School Counselor
            Model

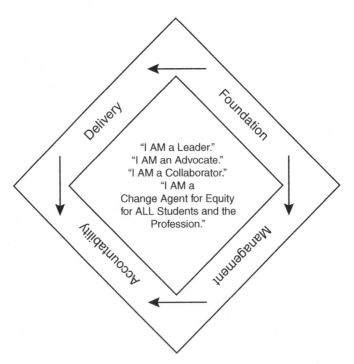

The program components are on the outer level radiating from the school counselor's professional identity. The CAFÉ model purports that school counselor professional identity comes first so that school counselors can generate equity-focused school counseling programs.

School Counseling and Leadership (CESCAL), and the Center for School Counseling Outcome, Research, and Evaluation (CSCORE). Even counselor educators are challenged to be role models of leadership and change agentry for their school counseling graduate students and to promote a consistent thread of leadership throughout the profession (McMahon, Mason, & Paisley, 2009; Ockerman, Mason, & Chen-Hayes, 2013). The bottom line is everyone in the profession of school counseling, whether educators, students, supervisors, or practitioners, must develop and implement leadership practices (ASCA, 2010, 2012; Dahir & Stone, 2012; DeVoss & Andrews, 2006; Dimmit, Carey, & Hatch, 2007).

Leadership is varied and can be learned. Leadership has evolved due to influences from various fields and disciplines including business, management, sociology, and psychology (Bush, 2003). While earlier definitions of leadership suggested that it was an inborn trait and thus only held by some people, leadership has matured to being considered a style to be honed or a skill that had to be learned. Beyond that, more recent definitions of leadership suggest that it is more complex and multifaceted. While school counselors possess some leadership skills, they have not been identified as such historically when leadership models were restricted to men with titles of power. Some of the skills that school counselors possess include knowing how to read people, being empathic and encouraging, and bringing a group to consensus. In schools where student success is a collaborative, ongoing effort and challenges arise, leaders of all types are critical to student success. Skills that school counselors may lack, such as creating a vision, managing policy, and purposefully challenging the status quo (Dollarhide, 2003; McMahon, Mason, & Paisley, 2009; Mason, 2010), can be learned. Having a basic understanding of various leadership styles and models can help school counselors and other leaders deepen their understanding of leadership in their own building and contribute to flexibility with the types of leadership in which they engage (Janson, 2009). Furthermore, school counselors who identify more strongly as leaders are more likely to report a fully implemented comprehensive school counseling program in their schools (Mason, 2010). Cooperation between various leaders in a school, specifically school counselors and administrators, significantly sets the tone for the way a school operates, including equity-focused practices in closing gaps such as equity audits that assess all policies and practices in the school on a continual basis to help close achievement, opportunity, and attainment gaps (Conley, 2010; Murray, 2011).

Key Words

Action Research: Research that is specific to a local school and is aimed at generating solutions not necessarily generalizable to larger populations

Annual Agreement: The ASCA National Model tool that delineates the school counselor's time spent in various tasks and the major function of the school counseling department; the agreement is to be co-constructed and agreed upon by school counselors and administrators

Authoritarian Leadership: Leadership that comes from one person who dictates what others are to do

Data-Based Decision Making: Decision making that is accomplished by reviewing critical data elements associated with the problem at hand, such as graduation rates, test scores, grades, and disciplinary or attendance rates

Democratic Leadership: Leadership that involves seeking the perspectives and feedback of those who are led

Distributed/Shared Leadership: Leadership that is shared within a group that makes decisions together with input from stakeholders

Equity: Fairness, justice, and ensuring that all students have the social capital and academic, career and college readiness, and personal/social competencies to reach their career/college dreams, facilitated by a school counseling program; some students need greater resources than others

Equity Audit: An assessment of all of a school's policies and practices and their effect on diverse cultural groups/identities within the school; this includes the master schedule, who takes rigorous courses, who receives career and college readiness counseling and planning, who graduates on time, who is over-credited and under-credited, and how school counselors and school counseling program resources are deployed for all students

Evidence-Based Practices: Interventions or strategies that are grounded in research and have publicly available data

Laissez-Faire Leadership: A leadership style in which leaders are vague and seemingly aimless, hands-off, and/or uninvolved

Leadership: Taking initiative to create positive change

Leadership Practices: Practices, either innate or learned, that create positive change

Outcome Research: Research that demonstrates the effectiveness of an intervention or program and suggests generalizability to larger populations

Program Assessment: The process of measuring a school counseling program's effectiveness, including process, perception, and outcome results; it typically includes regular pre- and post-tests, needs assessments, surveys, and questionnaires for various stakeholders including students, staff, families, and/or community members

School Profile: An overview of the school, including demographics, size, population, location, academic achievement strengths and gaps, and special programs

Servant Leadership: Leadership that has service as a core value and is carried out as a means to serve the greater good

Strategic Planning: Planning that is conducted in response to identified needs in a school and as a means to address those needs

Transformational Leadership: A type of leadership that empowers the leadership of others

Key Questions and Solutions

1. What does leadership in schools look like, and how can the CAFÉ School Counselor Evaluation assist?

Leadership, especially in schools, does not have to be defined by a title alone. In other words, principals and vice/assistant principals, and department chairs are not the only leaders in schools. Because of the multitude of tasks that need to be done and all of the stakeholders in schools that need to be served, it is critical that leadership is open to multiple forms and styles such as transformational leadership, servant leadership, shared leadership, distributed leadership, and so on (Northouse, 2004). Leadership can run the range from coordinating a canned food drive to chairing a committee, to initiating the implementation of a new school-wide program to close gaps, to presenting to colleagues on a relevant and timely topic.

All 50 U.S. states and countries around the world evaluating teachers and building leaders often lack appropriate evaluation tools for school counselors and school counseling programs. Few current national assessment tools for teachers mention school counselors. All too often, building leaders use teacher evaluation tools to assess school counselors but the jobs differ. It makes no more sense to evaluate school counselors with teacher evaluation tools than it does to evaluate teachers with school counselor evaluation tools. In school counseling, the current national evaluation tools are based on the ASCA National Model (ASCA, 2012) and include a school counseling program assessment, the school counselor performance appraisal, and the ASCA school counselor competencies. These tools assist administrators in understanding the types of activities school counselors should do to develop, deliver, and evaluate a comprehensive school counseling program with evidence-based outcomes. The one national evaluation tool for teachers that has a small component for assessing school counselors is *Enhancing Professional Practice: A Framework for Teaching* (Danielson, 2007), focused on increasing effective teaching using evidence-based practices. This model includes multiple other professions beyond teachers in schools, including school counselors. But challenging times call for greater solutions for equity and the school counselor's role in change agentry. We developed the CAFÉ School Counselor Evaluation to assess the 16 equity and change-agentry skills covered in *101 Solutions* (see Figure 1.2). We incorporate the complementary elements of the ASCA National Model school counseling program evaluation tools (ASCA, 2012), the NOSCA *Eight Components of College and Career Readiness Counseling*, and the *Framework for Teaching* rating categories (Danielson, 2007) to encourage individual school counselor assessment in additional areas.

2. What leadership models and strategies work best in K–12 schools?

There are many leadership models that have developed over time (Bennis, 1994; Bennis & Nanus, 1997; Bolman & Deal, 1991; Dollarhide, 2003; Kouzes & Posner, 2002; Northouse, 2004; Sergiovanni, 2000). The models of leadership that work best in schools are those in which leadership is shared beyond the principal; models such as distributed leadership, servant leadership, or transformational leadership (Sergiovanni, 2000). This type of leadership, which capitalizes on an individual's strengths and collaborative staff member relationship styles, has led to shared governance; shared decision-making, leadership, data, and inquiry teams; faculty councils; and student-managed peer disciplinary tribunals.

Northouse's (2004) definition identifies four interrelated ingredients prevalent across multiple theories of leadership: "(a) leadership is a process; (b) leadership involves influence; (c) leadership occurs within a group context; and (d) leadership involves goal attainment" (p. 3). Given that schools operate largely through group work (e.g., departments, academic teams, parent-teacher organizations) and that schools are highly goal-focused (e.g., attendance rates, graduation rates, academic achievement) a leadership structure that rests with a

Figure 1.2 CAFÉ (Change Agent for Equity) School Counselor Evaluation

School Counselor Name:

Date:

Evaluator Name:

School Name:

Directions: Rate the school counselor from 1 to 4 (unsatisfactory, basic, proficient, distinguished) in each area below:

1. *Leadership as Change Agents for Equity*	Rating			
Indicator	1 (Unsatisfactory)	2 (Basic)	3 (Proficient)	4 (Distinguished)
a. Demonstrates leadership by serving on school leadership, inquiry, and/or data teams				
b. Maintains active involvement in professional associations				
c. Initiates new programs and interventions to close achievement, opportunity, and attainment gaps				
d. Articulates personal equity-focused leadership activities				

(Continued)

Figure 1.2 (Continued)

	1 (Unsatisfactory)	2 (Basic)	3 (Proficient)	4 (Distinguished)
e. Assists with annual equity audits to assess school programs, policies, and practices with goals, objectives, and outcomes for change linked to the school's improvement plan				

2. Educator/School Counselor Collaboration

Indicator	Rating			
	1 (Unsatisfactory)	2 (Basic)	3 (Proficient)	4 (Distinguished)
a. Establishes or maintains a program advisory council				
b. Seeks the input and expertise of other educational professionals				
c. Co-plans or co-delivers program activities with other educational professionals				
d. Keeps current with academic instruction initiatives, and shares with staff the goals and outcomes of the school counseling program				

3. Program Assessment/Accountability

Indicator	Rating			
	1 (Unsatisfactory)	2 (Basic)	3 (Proficient)	4 (Distinguished)
a. Shares intervention results digitally and traditionally with all stakeholders				
b. Uses disaggregated school report card data to find gaps				
c. Uses School Improvement Plan and district goals to find gaps				
d. Aligns Interventions to school and district data				

e. Uses disaggregated data to target policies and practices for specific nondominant cultural groups including students of color: African American, Asian, Latino/a, Native American Indian/Pacific Islander, and mixed race students; low-income students (free/reduced lunch); bilingual students; students from nontraditional family types; students with nondominant immigration status; students with nondominant religion/spirituality/belief systems; LBGTIQ students; students with learning, emotional/behavioral, intellectual, physical, and/or developmental disabilities; gifted/talented students

4. Achievement Gap

Indicator	Rating			
	1 (Unsatisfactory)	2 (Basic)	3 (Proficient)	4 (Distinguished)
a. Delivers ASCA Student Standard academic competencies to all students				
b. Uses ASCA Closing the Gap Actions Plans and Results Reports				
c. Creates annual goals and objectives with measurable results of closing achievement gaps				
d. Monitors disaggregated school achievement data				

5. Opportunity/Attainment Gaps

Indicator	Rating			
	1 (Unsatisfactory)	2 (Basic)	3 (Proficient)	4 (Distinguished)
a. Delivers ASCA Student Standard career competencies to all students				

(Continued)

Figure 1.2 (Continued)

b.	Uses ASCA Closing the Gap Actions Plans and Results Reports			
c.	Creates annual goals and objectives with measurable results of closing opportunity gaps			
d.	Monitors disaggregated district high school graduation data to show who has attained college diplomas and what types of careers			

6. College and Career Readiness

Indicator	Rating			
	1 (Unsatisfactory)	2 (Basic)	3 (Proficient)	4 (Distinguished)
a. Demonstrates NOSCA 8 college and career readiness activities and interventions and outcomes in each area: College Aspirations, Academic Planning for College and Career Readiness, Enrichment and Extracurricular Engagement, College and Career Exploration and Selection Processes, College and Career Assessments, College Affordability Planning, College and Career Admission Processes, Transition from High School Graduation to College Enrollment				

7. Annual College/Career Readiness Planning

Indicator	Rating			
	1 (Unsatisfactory)	2 (Basic)	3 (Proficient)	4 (Distinguished)
a. Creates annual college and career plans with students				

Indicator				
b. Hosts parent/guardian events on college selection, admissions, and financial aid process and postsecondary options including 2-year, 4-year, and technical/trade schools and military and peace-making programs				
c. Creates opportunities for students to explore various postsecondary options on school grounds and at different college/career sites				

8. School-Family-Community Partnerships

Indicator	Rating			
	1 (Unsatisfactory)	2 (Basic)	3 (Proficient)	4 (Distinguished)
a. Develops/updates community resources guide				
b. Communicates both traditionally and digitally with parents/caregivers				

9. Ethics

Indicator	Rating			
	1 (Unsatisfactory)	2 (Basic)	3 (Proficient)	4 (Distinguished)
a. Maintains student/client confidentiality and educates all stakeholders on its importance and exceptions				
b. Uses an ethical decision-making model				
c. Distributes copies of the ASCA, ACA, and NACAC Codes of Ethics for all stakeholders in digital and traditional formats				
d. Consults with district attorney, other school counselors, social workers, psychologists, and Counselor Education faculty/supervisors				

(Continued)

11

Figure 1.2 (Continued)

10. Cultural Identity/Language

Indicator	Rating			
	1 (Unsatisfactory)	2 (Basic)	3 (Proficient)	4 (Distinguished)
a. Delivers cultural competencies in annual planning with students, classroom lessons, and other activities				
b. Delivers ASCA personal/social competencies to respect self and others				
c. Empowers all students to study at least two languages in school for cognitive and cultural gains				
d. Ensures bilingual students receive appropriate resources, supports, and rigorous coursework				
e. Implements affirmative school climate interventions and shares outcomes for students from multiple nondominant cultural groups such as age, ability/disability, appearance, ethnicity/race, gender, family type, gender identity/expression, immigration status, religion/spirituality/belief system, social class, and sexual orientation				

11. Technology

Indicator	Rating			
	1 (Unsatisfactory)	2 (Basic)	3 (Proficient)	4 (Distinguished)
a. Keeps current with legal and ethical issues related to schools' use of technology				

Indicator	1 (Unsatisfactory)	2 (Basic)	3 (Proficient)	4 (Distinguished)
b. Assists in developing or revising the school technology policies				
c. Utilizes various technology tools to engage and serve more students and families				
d. Annually updates school counseling program web page resources				

12. School-Wide/Multi-Systemic Intervention

	Rating			
Indicator	1 (Unsatisfactory)	2 (Basic)	3 (Proficient)	4 (Distinguished)
a. Takes a leadership role on school-wide committees (e.g., inquiry, data, school-based support, school counseling program advisory council)				
b. Connects school counseling program interventions and outcomes with school-wide academic, career/college readiness, and personal/social initiatives				
c. Collaborates with multiple internal school systems (master schedule, extracurriculars, access to rigorous coursework for all students) to create and sustain systemic change assisting all students				
d. Collaborates with multiple external systems (families, community organizations, businesses) to create and sustain systemic change assisting all students				

(Continued)

Figure 1.2 (Continued)

13. Administrative/Operational/Supervision

Indicator	Rating			
	1 (Unsatisfactory)	2 (Basic)	3 (Proficient)	4 (Distinguished)
a. Annually updates the SC/Administrator Agreement				
b. Reviews the school counselor evaluation tool regularly and with the administrator or evaluator				
c. Identifies the systemic structures in the school that may impede student success and offers potential solutions				
d. Serves as a source of school climate knowledge and expertise				
e. Provides evidence-based supervision for school counseling practicum and internship candidates				

14. Advocacy/Public Relations

Indicator	Rating			
	1 (Unsatisfactory)	2 (Basic)	3 (Proficient)	4 (Distinguished)
a. Identifies the needs of underserved populations and works to meet them				
b. Knows current legislation or policies impacting school counseling, education, and students				
c. Engages in advocacy by presenting data to stakeholders including school staff, families, school boards, district personnel, legislators				
d. Demonstrates one's own advocacy activities				

15. *Anti-Violence/Bullying/Safety*

Indicator	Rating			
	1 (Unsatisfactory)	2 (Basic)	3 (Proficient)	4 (Distinguished)
a. Delivers evidence-based anti-violence/bullying and safety programming in classroom lessons and school-wide activities to all students				
b. Educate parents/guardians, administrators, teachers, and all school staff on proactive anti-bullying strategies and the school's anti-bullying policies				
c. Advocates for students who feel unsafe				
d. Helps bullies develop healthy conflict resolution skills				
e. Delivers ASCA personal/social competencies on safety to all students				

16. *Ability, Disability, and Gifted/Talented*

Indicator	Rating			
	1 (Unsatisfactory)	2 (Basic)	3 (Proficient)	4 (Distinguished)
a. Collaborates with Special Education faculty and advocacy organizations				
b. Empowers families of students with varied abilities, disabilities, gifts/talents to advocate for their children's needs				
c. Ensures transition planning is effective and implemented annually for all students with IEPs				
d. Ensures IEPs and 504 plans are regularly updated and information on diagnosis and treatment plans is accurate and used in devising individual and group counseling services				

Source: Chen-Hayes, Ockerman, & Mason (2013).

single person, such as the principal, is less effective. However, each school is unique and there is no leadership model that is guaranteed to work in every school; the style of the principal has great impact on the culture and operations of a school (Leithwood, Louis, Anderson, & Wahlstrom, 2004; Marks & Printy, 2003; Reardon, 2011) and the school counseling program (ASCA, 2012).

3. How can school counselors be leaders if they don't see themselves as leaders?

Not all leaders shout from the soapbox. In fact, some of the best leaders are those who are thoughtful, observant, and listen more than they talk. Either way, leadership comes in all shapes, sizes, colors, and voices.

Consider some of the people who are considered effective leaders. What was it they said or did that is admired? Answering these questions can help highlight what is valued in a leader and perhaps what others would like to emulate. Getting comfortable as a leader can take more time for some than others but is more likely to develop when participating in leadership activities that are personally meaningful, such as starting a school counseling program advisory council (ASCA, 2012) or fighting to save school counselor jobs with evidence of school counselor success in helping close achievement and opportunity gaps (ASCA, 2010).

4. How can school counselors start being leaders?

Being a leader begins with identifying unique strengths and skills as a school counselor and educator. Leadership must come from a place of passion and drive. For school counselors, a large part of leadership comes from taking *initiative*. When school counselors take on a leadership role out of motivation, leadership will bring fulfillment, but when taking on a leadership role out of obligation or someone else's insistence, it will feel like a chore. Many school counselors and other educators are already leaders but do not realize it because they have assumed that leadership was associated with a specific title, office space, or salary.

Some ways to start or increase leadership roles in schools:

1. Be visible in and around the school whenever possible and connect professionally with school counselor, educator, staff, and administrator colleagues. A large part of leadership is the knowledge of who people are and understanding their specific roles.

2. Share expertise or knowledge that others in school would find helpful through mentoring, presentations, e-mails, or simple print materials for reference. School counselors often are the only ones in the building trained in career and college readiness counseling (see Chapters 6–7), ethics (see Chapter 9), and multicultural issues (see Chapter 10), so all three of these areas are ripe for staff development and taking on a leadership role.

3. Take on a new challenge. Leaders grow by pushing themselves outside of their comfort zones. Start by volunteering to pick up the slack for a colleague who must temporarily step aside, chair a committee, or introduce a new initiative to solve an equity-related achievement or opportunity gap in the school. For example, San Jose Superintendent Linda Murray used a collaborative leadership strategy including an equity audit to look at college preparatory course-taking patterns in her district disaggregated by race/ethnicity and gender. She found large discrepancies and created the vision and support that moved her district to making rigorous courses mandatory for every student in the district and shared the data of how gaps closed for underrepresented students once everyone was receiving rigorous courses preparing all students for career and college readiness (Murray, 2011).

Solution Success Stories

Story 1

Leadership can develop early in one's career. As a school counseling intern at a local public high school in the Midwest, Michelle became aware of the need for LBGTIQ students to feel welcome, safe, and valued in the community. Garnering support from some staff and administration approval but some resistance, she started the school's first Gay Straight Alliance (GSA). Along with a few key, passionate students, Michelle researched and invited in a local agency known for their advocacy for LBGTIQ populations, and she received training on starting the GSA and what to anticipate in the process. During the year, the GSA met regularly, marketed themselves to the school community, and sponsored several awareness-raising events. Michelle collected data on the impact of GSA involvement on students' grades and attendance and showcased this successful intervention prior to graduation with her master's degree in school counseling.

(Continued)

(Continued)

Story 2

An independent high school counselor in the Northeast, Terry, used his leadership skills to strengthen the profession and use of current terminology (ASCA, 2010, 2012). He challenged the use of the outdated term "guidance" and persuaded all on his school counseling team to use the term "school counselor." Other changes included adding "school counseling" to the name of the department, to office placards, and to the school's website so updated practices used in his school counseling program were reflected for all stakeholders with accurate terminology.

Story 3

A southwestern elementary school counselor, Felipe, designed a school counseling software program to not only track the school counselor's day-to-day responsibilities but calculate the percentage of academic, career, college readiness, and personal/social competencies being delivered daily/weekly by school counselors in an easy-to-read set of graphs and charts. He not only uses his creation but has shared it with several school counselor education programs across the country to disseminate an easy and effective way of monitoring school counselor time and outcomes in delivering academic, career, college readiness, and personal/social competencies to all students in a school counseling program.

Story 4

Several school counselor educators during a poster session at a recent Association for Counselor Education and Supervision (ACES) conference discussed the urgent need for a regular forum for monthly organizing and conversation about transforming school counseling and college readiness issues. Because of skyrocketing school counselor to student ratios, decreased public funding for school counselors, and threats to school counseling around the country, it was time to organize beyond a one-hour meeting at a biannual conference. As a result, two counselor educators, Melissa Ockerman and Stuart Chen-Hayes, were appointed co-chairs of the ACES School Counseling Interest Network and began a monthly network phone call in the fall of 2011 for all interested ACES counselor educators and supervisors. The network calls often feature a guest speaker, such as a representative of a national school counseling association, college counseling or career and college readiness advocacy groups, and other school counselor educators and school counseling site supervisors doing significant equity work in their states. Minutes from these calls are shared

(Continued)

on CESNET, the ACES Listserv for all counselor educators and supervisors. Often there are 20–30 persons on the monthly network calls, and to date, over 180 counselor educators and supervisors are part of the network. The new school counseling network was renamed the Transforming School Counseling and College Access Interest Network (TSCCAIN). They focus on the importance of counselor educators and supervisors using their leadership skills to teach and supervise with the principles of the National Center for Transforming School Counseling new vision of school counseling including closing achievement and opportunity gaps and creating college and career readiness skills in all K–12 students.

Resources

Digital

Center for Excellence in School Counseling and Leadership (CESCaL): www.cescal.org

Center for School Counseling Outcome, Research and Evaluation (CSCORE): www.umass.edu/schoolcounseling

Emergenetics: www.emergenetics.com

National Office of School Counselor Advocacy's Principal Counselor Relationship Toolkit: http://nosca.collegeboard.org/research-policies/principal-counselor-toolkit

The Leadership Challenge: www.leadershipchallenge.com/home .aspx

Print

Amatea, E., & Clark, M. (2005). Changing schools, changing counselors: A qualitative study of school administrators' conceptions of the school counselor role. *Professional School Counseling, 9,* 16–27.

American School Counselor Association. (2012). *The ASCA national model: A framework for comprehensive school counseling programs* (3rd ed.). Alexandria, VA: Author.

Baker, S. B. (2001). Reflections on forty years in the school counseling profession: Is the glass half full or half empty? *Professional School Counseling, 5,* 75–83.

Beesley, D., & Frey, L. L. (2001). Principals' perceptions of school counselor roles and satisfaction with school counseling services. *Journal of School Counseling, 4,* 1–27.

Bemak, F. (2000). Transforming the role of the counselor to provide leadership in educational reform through collaboration. *Professional School Counseling, 3,* 323–332.

Bennis, W. G. (1994). *On becoming a leader.* Cambridge, MA: Perseus.

Bennis, W. G., & Nanus, B. (1997). *Leaders: Strategies for taking charge.* New York, NY: HarperBusiness.

Bolman, L. G., & Deal, T. E. (1991). Leadership management and effectiveness: A multi-frame, multi-factor analysis. *Human Resource Management, 30,* 509–533.

Brooks-McNamara, V., & Torres, D. (2008). *The reflective school counselor's guide to practitioner research: Skills and strategies for successful inquiry.* Thousand Oaks, CA: Corwin.

Burns, J. M. (1978). *Leadership.* New York, NY: Harper & Row.

Chata, C. C., & Loesch, L. C. (2007). Future school principals' views of the role of professional school counselors. *Professional School Counseling, 11,* 35–41.

Chen-Hayes, S. F., & Getch, Y. Q. (in press). Leadership and advocacy for every student's achievement and opportunity. In B. T. Erford (Ed.), *Transforming the school counseling profession* (4th ed.). Boston, MA: Pearson.

Chen-Hayes, S. F., & Ockerman, M. S. (in press). Academic development and planning for college and career readiness K–12. In B. T. Erford (Ed.), *Transforming the school counseling profession* (4th ed.). Boston, MA: Pearson.

Clark, M., & Stone, C. (2001). School counselors and principals: Partners in support of academic achievement. *National Association of Secondary Principals Bulletin, 85,* 46–53.

Clemens, E. V., Milsom, A., & Cashwell, C. S. (2009). Using leader-member exchange theory to examine principal-school counselor relationships, school counselors' roles, job satisfaction and turnover intentions. *Professional School Counseling, 13,* 75–85.

Covey, S. R. (1992). *Principle centered leadership.* New York, NY: Free Press.

Curry, J. R., & Bickmore, D. (2012). School counselor induction and the importance of mattering. *Professional School Counseling, 15,* 110–122.

Curry, J. R., & DeVoss, J. A. (2009). Introduction to special issue: The school counselor as leader. *Professional School Counseling, 13,* 64–67.

Dahir, C. (2004). Supporting a nation of learners: The role of school counseling in educational reform. *Journal of Counseling and Development, 82,* 344–364.

Dahir, C. A., & Stone, C. B. (2009). School counselor accountability: The path to social justice and systemic change. *Journal of Counseling and Development, 87,* 12–20.

Dahir, C. A., & Stone, C. B. (2012). *The transformed school counselor.* Belmont, CA: Brooks/Cole.

Davis, T. (2005). *Exploring school counseling: Professional practices and perspectives.* Boston, MA: Lahaska Press.

DeVoss, J. A., & Andrews, M. F. (2006). *School counselors as educational leaders.* Boston, MA: Houghton Mifflin.

Dimmit, C., Carey, J., & Hatch, T. (2007). *Evidence-based school counseling: Making a difference with data-driven practices.* Thousand Oaks, CA: Corwin.

Dodson, T. (2009). Advocacy and impact: A comparison of administrators' perceptions of the high school counselor role. *Professional School Counseling, 12,* 480–487.

Dollarhide, C. T. (2003). School counselors as program leaders: Applying leadership contexts to school counseling. *Professional School Counseling, 6,* 304–308.

Dollarhide, C. T., Gibson, D. M., & Saginak, K. A. (2008). New counselors' leadership efforts in school counseling: Themes from a year-long qualitative study. *Professional School Counseling, 11,* 262–271.

Dollarhide, C. T., Smith, A. T., & Lemberger, M. E. (2007). Critical incidents in the development of supportive principals: Facilitating school counselor-principal relationships. *Professional School Counseling, 10,* 360–369.

Erford, B. T. (Ed.). (2012). *Transforming the school counseling profession.* Upper Saddle River, NJ: Prentice Hall.

Ford, A., & Nelson, J. (2007). Secondary school counselors as educational leaders: Shifting perceptions of leadership. *Journal of School Counseling, 5,* 1–27.

Gysbers, N. C. (2006). Improving school guidance and counseling practices through effective and sustained state leadership: A response to Miller. *Professional School Counseling, 9,* 245–247.

Herr, E. L. (2001). The impact of national policies, economics, and school reform on comprehensive guidance programs. *Professional School Counseling, 4,* 236–245.

Holcomb-McCoy, C. C. (2001). Exploring the self-perceived multicultural counseling competence of elementary school counselors. *Professional School Counseling, 4,* 195–201.

Holcomb-McCoy, C. C. (2005). Investigating school counselors' perceived multicultural competence. *Professional School Counseling, 8,* 414–423.

Holcomb-McCoy, C., & Chen-Hayes, S. F. (in press). Culturally competent school counselors: Affirming diversity by challenging oppression. In B. T. Erford (Ed.), *Transforming the school counseling profession* (4th ed.). Boston, MA: Pearson.

House, R. M., & Hayes, R. L. (2002). School counselors: Becoming key players in school reform. *Professional School Counseling, 5,* 249–257.

Janson, C. (2009). High school counselors' views of their leadership behaviors: A Q methodology study. *Professional School Counseling, 13,* 86–97.

Janson, C., Militello, M., & Kosine, N. (2008). Four views of the professional school counselor and principal relationship: A Q methodology study. *Professional School Counseling, 11,* 353–361.

Janson, C., Stone, C., & Clark, M. A. (2009). Stretching leadership: A distributed perspective for school counselor leaders. *Professional School Counseling, 13,* 98–106.

Johnson, J., Rochkind, J., Ott, A., & DuPont, S. (2010). *Can I get a little advice here? How an overstretched high school guidance system is undermining students' college aspirations.* San Francisco, CA: Public Agenda.

Kaplan, L. S. (1999). Hiring the best school counseling candidates to promote student achievement. *NASSP Bulletin, 83,* 34–39.

Katzenmeyer, M., & Moller, G. (2001). *Awakening the sleeping giant.* Thousand Oaks, CA: Corwin.

Keys, S. G., & Lockhart, E. (2000). The school counselor's role in facilitating multisystemic change. *Professional School Counseling, 3,* 101–107.

Kirchner, G., & Setchfield, M. (2005). School counselors' and school principals' perceptions of the school counselor's role. *Education, 126,* 10–16.

Kouzes, J. M., & Posner, B. Z. (2002a). *The leadership challenge* (3rd ed.). San Francisco, CA: Jossey-Bass.

Kouzes, J. M., & Posner, B. Z. (2002b). *Theory and evidence behind the five practices of exemplary leaders.* Retrieved from http://media.wiley.com/assets/463/74/lc_jb_appendix.pdf

Kouzes, J. M., & Posner, B. Z. (2003). *The leadership practices inventory: Self instrument* (3rd ed.). San Francisco, CA: Jossey-Bass.

Kouzes, J. M., & Posner, B. Z. (2004). *LPI Data 2004 .* Retrieved from http://www.leadershipchallenge.com/WileyCDA/Section/id-131362.html

Lapan, R. T. (2012). Comprehensive school counseling programs: In some schools for some students but not in all schools for all students. *Professional School Counseling, 16,* 84–88.

Leithwood, K., Louis, K. S., Anderson, S., & Wahlstrom, K. (2004). *How leadership influences student learning.* New York, NY: Wallace Foundation.

Leuwerke, W. C., Walker, J., & Shi, Q. (2009). Informing principals: The impact of different types of information on principals' perceptions of professional school counselors. *Professional School Counseling, 12,* 263–271.

Marks, H. M., & Printy, S. M. (2003). Principal leadership and school performance: An integration of transformational and instructional leadership. *Educational Administration Quarterly, 39,* 370–397.

Martin, P. J. (2002). Transforming school counseling: A national perspective. *Theory Into Practice, 41,* 148–153.

Mason, E. C. M. (2008). The relationship between school counselor leadership practices and comprehensive program implementation. *Counseling and Psychological Services Dissertations.* Paper 26. Retrieved from http://digitalarchive.gsu.edu/cps_diss/26

Mason, E. C. M. (2010). Leadership practices of school counselors and counseling program implementation. *National Association of Secondary School Principals Bulletin, 94,* 274–285.

Mason, E. C. M., & McMahon, H. G. (2009). Leadership practices of school counselors. *Professional School Counseling, 13,* 107–115.

McMahon, H. G., Mason, E. C. M., & Paisley, P. O. (2009). School counselor educators as educational leaders promoting systemic change. *Professional School Counseling, 13,* 116–124.

Northouse, P. G. (2004). *Leadership theory and practice* (3rd ed.). Thousand Oaks, CA: Sage.

Ockerman, M. S., Mason, E. C. M., & Chen-Hayes, S. F. (2013). School counseling supervision in challenging times: The CAFÉ Supervisor Model. *Journal of Counselor Preparation and Supervision, 5(2), Article 4.* doi:http://dx.doi.org/10.7729/51.0024

Paisley, P. O., & Hayes, R. L. (2003). School counseling in the academic domain: Transformations in preparation and practice. *Professional School Counseling, 6,* 198–204.

Paisley, P. O., & McMahon, H. G. (2001). School counseling for the 21st century: Challenges and opportunities. *Professional School Counseling, 5,* 106–115.

Pérusse, R., & Goodnough, G. E. (2004). *Leadership, advocacy and direct service strategies for professional school counselors.* Belmont, CA: Brooks/Cole.

Pérusse, R., Goodnough, G. D., Donegan, J., & Jones, C. (2004). Perceptions of school counselors and school principals about the National Standards for School Counseling programs and the Transforming School Counseling Initiative. *Professional School Counseling, 7,* 152–161.

Reardon, R. (2011). Elementary school principals' learning-centered leadership and educational outcomes: Implications for principals' professional development. *Leadership & Policy in Schools, 10,* 63–83. doi:10.1080/15700760903511798

Reynolds, S. E., & Hines, P. L. (2001a). *Guiding all kids: Systemic guidance for achievement in schools* (2nd ed.). Bloomington, IN: American Student Achievement Institute.

Reynolds, S. E., & Hines, P. L. (2001b). *Vision-to-action: A step-by-step activity guide for systemic educational reform* (6th ed.). Bloomington, IN: American Student Achievement Institute.

Ross, D., & Herrington, D. (2006). A comparative study of pre-professional counselor/principal perceptions of the role of the school counselor in public schools. *National Forum of Educational Administration and Supervision Journal, 23,* 1–18.

Ryan, T., Kaffenberger, C. J., & Carroll, A. G. (2011). Response to intervention: An opportunity for school counselor leadership. *Professional School Counseling, 14,* 211–221.

Saginak, K. A., & Dollarhide, C. T. (2006). Leadership with administration: Securing administrative support for transforming your program. *Journal of School Counseling, 4,* 1–19.

Senge, P. M., Cambron-McCabe, N., Lucas, T., Smith, B., & Dutton, J. (2012). *Schools that learn: A fifth discipline fieldbook for educators, parents, and everyone who cares about education.* New York, NY: Crown Business.

Sergiovanni, T. J. (2000). *Leadership for the schoolhouse. How is it different? Why is it important?* San Francisco, CA: Jossey-Bass.

Shillingford, M. A., & Lambie, G. W. (2010). Contribution of professional school counselors' values and leadership practices to their programmatic service delivery. *Professional School Counseling, 13,* 208–217.

Slater, L. (2005). Leadership for collaboration: An affective process. *International Journal of Leadership in Education, 8,* 321–333.

Stone, C. B., & Dahir, C. A. (2011). *School counselor accountability: A MEASURE of student success* (3rd ed.). Upper Saddle River, NJ: Pearson Education.

Zalaquett, C. P. (2005). Principals' perceptions of elementary school counselors' role and function. *Professional School Counseling, 8,* 451–457.

2

Educator and School Counselor Collaboration Solutions

A cardinal principle of education for stakeholders from Pre-K–12 students to parents and grandparents, and especially teachers and school counselors, is knowing how to "play well with others." Collaboration is essential to student success. Implementation of district-wide curricula and programming including federal, state, and local initiatives requires every school stakeholder to be on board. The collaboration of staff within a school is imperative for many issues including morale, school climate, operations, goal setting, program implementation, evaluation and testing, and ultimately student achievement (B. Johnson, 2003; Levine & Marcus, 2008; Williams, Prestage, & Bedward, 2001). Collaboration between school staff members is essential to the healthy, productive functioning of the school. Every staff member has a unique set of skills, training, background, and experiences with valuable insights and perspectives to the collective whole of a school (Thornberg, 2012). For school counselors to attend to the equity and social justice issues of academic success, career and college readiness, and personal/social success that arise in school counseling programs, strong collaboration and communication skills are a necessity (ASCA, 2010, 2012) including the use of ASCA student standards (Campbell & Dahir, 1997), school counselor competencies (ASCA, 2012), career and college readiness counseling components (College Board, 2010), and standards blending (Schellenberg, 2007; Schellenberg & Grothaus, 2009).

Key Words

ASCA School Counselor Competencies: The professional expectations of every school counselor in implementing a school counseling program that provides academic, career, and personal/social competencies to all students K–12

ASCA Student Standards: Originally called national standards, these were developed to outline the academic, career, and personal/social competencies each student is expected to learn from a school counseling program

Collaboration: The process by which school staff from various fields, disciplines, and roles come together to create solutions for issues that arise in their buildings

Common Core State Standards: Learning standards common across 45 of 50 states aligned with assessments attempting to ensure greater depth in teaching and learning with the outcome that every K–12 student is career and college ready

Professional Learning Communities: Formalized groups of school staff members, often across disciplines, engaged in ongoing, intentional, organized learning together for the benefit of understanding the needs of students and the school community

School Counseling Core Curriculum: The developmental classroom lessons school counselors plan, create, implement, and evaluate to deliver academic, career/college access, and personal/social competencies to all K–12 students in collaboration with teachers and other school leaders

School Counseling Program Advisory Council: A leadership group comprising stakeholders to include a teacher, school building leader, student, parent/guardian, and community member that advises school counselors on the goals, data, implementation, and evaluation of the school counseling program

Standards Blending: Demonstrating the school counseling program's effectiveness in academic success and closing achievement gaps by combining school counseling student standards delivered in school counseling core curriculum lessons with academic standards such as the Common Core State Standards for career and college readiness

Vertical Teaming: Staffing by educators within specific disciplines and districts or states to develop curricula, programs, and/or procedures sharing continuity and intentionality from one student level (elementary, middle school, high school) to another to ensure student academic success

Key Questions and Solutions

1. How can school counselors foster strong, synergistic working relationships between school counselors and teachers?

When school counselors and other school staff view their work as means to the same ends (student success) then collaboration has a ripe environment. Schools are often places of compartmentalization, where each staff member works individually without considering how it impacts or connects with others. McMahon, Mason, Daluga-Gunther, and Ruiz (in press) recommend conceiving of the school environment from an ecological or systems perspective where all persons and factors that operate within and around a school impact each other. Understanding different roles means staff support student needs without turf wars (Thornberg, 2012) and are effective in making systemic change for students' academic, career, and college readiness success (ASCA, 2012; Conley, 2010; Murray, 2011).

For school counselors who have been teachers, sharing this commonality with staff may increase credibility, particularly with veteran teachers and administrators. Many teachers may appreciate the school counselor who has experienced what it means to have a classroom and to work as a teacher, and may be more comfortable collaborating knowing there is that shared experience. On the other hand, school counselors who do not have a teaching background are far more prevalent as few states require teaching experience for school counselor certification/licensure. For non-teacher school counselors, it is important for current teachers and school counselors to recognize their separate but connected areas of expertise. School counselors employ their counseling, planning, and school counseling program development skills with teachers and staff to validate their unique concerns and shared challenges as partners in all students' academic success. Taking the time and energy to build rapport with staff and to educate others about the transformed role of the school counselor are essential skills for a school counselor; building collegial relationships with teachers and staff pays off when it is time to collaborate.

2. How can educational leaders collaborate for academic, career/college readiness, and personal/social competencies in students?

Considering that the goal of every staff member in a school is student success, the opportunities to collaborate are endless. Collaboration must, however, be encouraged and supported with time and resources by administration so that the value is evidenced throughout the school (Williams, Prestage, & Bedward, 2001). Given the demands and pressures on public school educators to produce and perform from district and federal mandates and for educators facing budgetary challenges, it is easy for the overarching goal of student success to get lost in isolation and compartmentalization. In these conditions, turf wars may evolve as staff members become more concerned about job security and job satisfaction. Keeping the goal of student success at the forefront while emphasizing the significance of each staff member's contribution is the charge of building leaders—both those with official titles and those, such as school counselors, who operate from informal leadership positions and with particular influence within the school community (see Chapter 1). Practices like vertical teaming and structures like professional learning communities create opportunities for collaboration across disciplines and for school counselors to share unique insights, observations, and school counseling program data in their capacity as "the eyes and ears of the school," as veteran school counselor educator and founding program director for the National Center For Transformed School Counseling, Dr. Reese House, often described their essential leadership role.

3. How can school counselors collaborate with teachers to deliver school counseling core curriculum lessons that address both Common Core academic standards and school ASCA student academic standards?

School counselors can be creative in finding connections between the ASCA Student Standards (ASCA, 2012; Campbell & Dahir, 1997) and standards like Common Core and district standards. The authors note that the Common Core standards are not without their detractors; some view them as narrowing the curriculum and having been developed by corporate and political interests over the needs of students with a lack of evidence of success prior to usage. However, the solution stories shared in this chapter provide helpful examples. Many teachers are delighted to share what they are teaching students and most welcome those who want to observe in the classroom or collaborate (Wood, 2012). For school counselors, nonevaluative classroom observation and teacher consultation help build rapport with staff and students and increase school counselor learning about course content and teaching styles. When school counselors approach teachers about collaborating, after becoming familiar with their courses and teaching styles, there is already a relationship built and less fear. Because teachers are heavily focused on academic content and rarely learned about the role of school counselors, school counseling programs, or ASCA Student Standards (ASCA, 2012; Campbell & Dahir, 1997) in their preservice education or staff development, they are often not aware of ASCA student standards addressing student knowledge of school and classroom skills such as note-taking, time management, emotion management, conflict resolution, and tying academic subjects in to future career and college readiness decisions. School counselors, by becoming familiar with K–12 course content and teaching and learning classroom environments, highlight where such ASCA Student Standards and competencies can apply, be taught, and be generalized by students. In discussing these opportunities for additional skill development in the context of learning academic standards, school counselors help teachers see the benefits of collaboration and the power of standards blending (Schellenberg, 2007; Schellenberg & Grothaus, 2009) to address the academic *and* developmental needs of students (Marlow, Bloss, & Bloss, 2000; Stringer, Reynolds, & Simpson, 2003).

4. How can school counselors best assist teachers with student behavioral issues and classroom management?

Similar to exploring course academic content through nonevaluative observation, school counselors can also use this use strategy to assess student behaviors and classroom management issues followed with teacher consultation and discussion. This is particularly important for school counselors without prior teaching experience, as they cannot speak from their own classroom teaching experience. Regardless, observing any teacher in a classroom is akin to coming into someone's home. Some teachers are protective of how their classroom has been established and are concerned that a school counselor asking to observe is being evaluative like administrators. Other teachers are more open and flexible about classroom observations. Here are suggestions for classroom observations and consulting with teachers about student behaviors and classroom management:

- Have casual conversations with teachers frequently and ask "How are your classes going?" so that they know you are interested in their work.
- Avoid lengthy public conversations and ask teachers to e-mail you if they want to talk in depth about a classroom issue.
- When setting up consultation appointments with teachers, make it convenient for them and offer to go to their room as they may feel more respected on their turf.
- Get to know teachers (and their students) to build trust before asking to observe in their classroom.
- Explain upfront why you are observing (to offer support and suggestions if desired) and that it is in no way a formal evaluation.
- Use behavioral checklists or rating scales for observing students and allow teachers to view these before and afterward.
- Schedule the observation at a time that is most convenient for teachers and remind them you are coming in; do not stop by unannounced.
- Using listening and attending skills when consulting with teachers, empathize and hear their concerns prior to offering suggestions.
- Ask solution-focused questions: How can I best help you? What do you think is working? What is not working? What do you want to see happen? If you had a magic wand, what would you change?

Solution Success Stories

Story 1

Karen, a middle school counselor in a rural school in the South grew more aware of the stress level of the special education teachers in her school due to new district mandates creating greater paperwork loads for them and a sudden influx of new special education students to the school. As a result, special education classrooms were over capacity and understaffed, behavior issues increased in frequency and intensity, and the teachers were visibly exhausted. In this large school with 4,000 students, the special education teachers often reported feeling isolated, unsupported, and often "forgotten" in large-scale, school-wide planning.

Based on her work with stress management for students, the school counselor created a stress management "small group" for interested teachers, one

(Continued)

morning a week for nine weeks, for a 30-minute period before teachers needed to be in their classrooms. Though the group was available to any teacher, the special education teachers were the ones who participated most frequently. The group was open; it was not necessary to come every time, and the participants varied from week to week.

Each session started with a general check-in from each member for sharing any particular successes or challenges from the week. Sometimes the check-ins became the content for group discussion, other times a guest speaker was brought in to present on a particular aspect of stress management, or an article, quote, or poem was shared. At the end of each session, the school counselor led the teachers through guided breathing and relaxation exercises.

Story 2

Barbara, a middle school counselor in the Southeast, based on the previous year's data, made it a goal one year to double the amount of time she spent in delivering school counseling core curriculum lessons. While many teachers in the school were willing to have her visit their classes periodically, they were not accustomed to more frequent visits. In an effort to win the teachers over, she began to review the standards for each subject area—math, language arts, science, and social studies—so that she could be knowledgeable about what they were teaching. As she reviewed the standards she began to see how some of the ASCA student standards (ASCA, 2012; Campbell & Dahir, 1997) could be incorporated and taught simultaneously with the academic subjects. Starting first with the math classes, she planned a lesson in consultation with the teacher that would incorporate calculating a class grade and a GPA with the concept of converting between fractions, decimals, and percentages. Once this was done in one math class, it caught on with others. Similarly, she designed lessons with the science teachers that incorporated stress management techniques with vocabulary and concepts about volcanoes and with social studies teachers that incorporated conflict resolution strategies with the study of the Civil War.

Story 3

Jennifer works in a midwestern middle school with approximately 1,100 students over three grade levels. The building leadership team had representation from every department with the exception of school counselors, so she spoke with her principal about this and was added to the team.

Jennifer's school is focusing on three main literacy strategies: read-aloud, talk-aloud, and think-aloud. Jennifer and other staff in her school meet once

(Continued)

(Continued)

a month all day to learn about the strategies, practice, share, and collaborate. The district also has instructional coaches who help with this process and assist as the staff members implement these strategies in the classroom.

Read-aloud is a strategy in which nonfiction text is used to support students in learning and understanding essential information in content areas. During her first read-aloud implementation, Jennifer worked with three of the literacy teachers to plan a lesson related to bullying and acceptance of others. In class, students were learning about fiction texts through a variety of ways, including reading several books that all tied into the areas of acceptance: *Star Girl* by Jerry Spinelli, *Maniac Magee* by Jerry Spinelli, *Freak the Mighty* by Rodman Philbrick, and *Surviving the Applewhites* by Stephanie S. Tolan; the timing of the lessons complemented the building-wide plans for Mix-It Up Day as well.

There were many positive outcomes of this collaboration process, according to Jennifer. First, being part of the building leadership team shows that professional school counselors are important, as all teachers are, and that school counselors care about instructional strategies, too. Using similar instructional strategies provides students with a common language that helps them understand content as well. Additionally, it was powerful to teach school counseling core curriculum content alongside literacy content. Making this connection to other curricular areas made the lesson more meaningful and relevant to the students because it did not seem like an add-on or something "extra." Jennifer found it was also a very time-efficient way to deliver the lesson to all students. The follow-up writing activity used by the teachers also provided Jennifer with the data needed to show whether or not the students were able to answer the essential questions for the lesson.

Jennifer shares this about the significance of educator and school counselor collaboration, "One of the barriers that I have found over the years in my work as a school counselor is that I do not have a teaching background. Oftentimes, professional development references concepts and skills to which I have not been exposed. It is important as a school counselor, in my opinion, to familiarize yourself with these concepts and skills. Because part of our time is spent in the classroom, we need to continue to improve our teaching skills as well. It is important to find a colleague that has the desire and willingness to work with you and then make it happen!"

Story 4

Catherine and Lisa, a middle school counselor and a high school English teacher in the Southwest, came together through a passion for postsecondary education and training and on the issue of student articulation. When their state began

(Continued)

training to implement the Common Core State Standards (CCSS), they used this as an appropriate and formal vehicle to allow for the integration of their individual professions. Using their expertise and experience, they developed a tool to illustrate the intersection of School Counselor professional standards and competencies, which they termed "Understanding Standards and Components: A Crosswalk for Collaboration."

Developing the crosswalk was essential to their collaborative process, as it focused their attention and provided a framework for their thoughts. Before they developed the crosswalk, they struggled with finding a balance between the teacher's and counselor's role in the classroom. The crosswalk, however, helped delineate each one's responsibilities and made clear the essential role they shared in the classroom, given that it is driven by the academic standards outlined in the CCSS and expands to include domains of growth, more specifically the ASCA student standards and NOSCA's Eight College and Career Readiness Counseling Components. This work fostered students' postsecondary aspirations and required them to imagine how they might use their new academic and personal skills in their future.

For the teacher, the crosswalk demands a multidimensional approach to lesson planning, going beyond the skills and texts required by the CCSS; for the counselor, this work allows for consistent and in-depth work in all domains, weaving students' insight and active reflection into their daily lives, even beyond the classroom. Together, they have continued to build a community of learners who are wholly supported and value education at any level.

Resources

Digital

ASCA National Standards for Students: http://static.pdesas.org/content/documents/ASCA_National_Standards_for_Students.pdf

ASCA School Counselor Competencies: www.schoolcounselor.org/files/SCCompetencies.pdf

Classroom Management Essentials (website, iPad app): www.classroommanagementessentials.com

Common Core Standards: www.corestandards.org

Edutopia: www.edutopia.org

Implementing the Common Core State Standards: The role of the school counselor (2012). Education brief from Achieve, College Summit, NASSP, NAESP. www.achieve.org/files/CounselorActionBrief_Final.pdf

Kansas State University Consultation and learning strategies for school counselors, special education teachers, and classroom teachers: http://coe.k-state.edu/departments/secsa/secsacollaboration.htm

Mix It Up Day: www.tolerance.org/mix-it-up/what-is-mix

Teaching Tolerance: www.tolerance.org

The IRIS Center: http://iris.peabody.vanderbilt.edu/resources.html

You Can Handle Them All (website, iPad app): www.disciplinehelp.com

Print

Brigman, G., Mullis, F., Webb, J., & White, J. (2005). *School counselor consultation: Skills for working effectively with parents, teachers and other school personnel.* Hoboken, NJ: Wiley

DuFour, R., Eaker, R., & Many, T. (2010). *Learning by doing: A handbook for professional learning communities at work.* Bloomington, IN: Solution Tree.

Goulet, L., Krentz, C., & Christiansen, H. (2003). Collaboration in education: The phenomenon and process of working together. *Alberta Journal of Educational Research, 49,* 325–340.

Hargreaves, A. (2001). The emotional geographies of teachers' relations with colleagues. *International Journal of Educational Research, 35,* 503–527.

Johnson, B. (2003). Teacher collaboration: Good for some, not so good for others. *Educational Studies, 29,* 337–350.

Levine, T. H., & Marcus, A. (2008). Closing the achievement gap through teacher collaboration: Facilitating multiple trajectories of teacher learning. *Journal of Advanced Academics, 19,* 116–138.

Marlow, L., Bloss, K., & Bloss, D. (2000). Promoting social and emotional competence through teacher/counselor collaboration. *Education, 120,* 668–674.

Mason, E. C. M. (2010, July/August). Leveraging classroom time. *ASCA School Counselor,* pp. 27–29.

Mason, E. C. M., & McMahon, H. G. (2009). Supporting academic improvement among eighth graders at risk of retention: A study using action research. *Research in Middle Level Education, 33.*

Noonan, K., Matone, M., Zlotnik, S., Hernandez-Mekonnen, R., Watts, C., Rubin, D., & Mollen, C. (2011). Cross-system barriers to educational success for children in foster care: The front line perspective. *Children and Youth Services Review, 34,* 403–408.

Ponec, D. L., & Brock, B. L. (2000). Relationships among elementary school counselors and principals: A unique bond. *Professional School Counseling, 3,* 208–217.

Senge, P., Cambron-McCabe, N., Lucas, T., Smith, B., Dutton, J., & Kleiner, A. (2012). *Schools that learn:* New York, NY: Crown Business.

Stauffer, S. D., & Mason, E. C. M. (2013). Addressing elementary teachers' stressors: Practical suggestions for school administrators. *Education Administration Quarterly.* doi:10.1177/0013161X13482578

Stringer, S. J., Reynolds, G. P., & Simpson, F. M. (2003). Collaboration between classroom teachers and a school counselor through literature circles: Building self-esteem. *Journal of Instructional Psychology, 30,* 69–76.

Thornberg, R. (2012). A grounded theory of collaborative synchronizing in relation to challenging students. *Urban Education, 47,* 312–342. doi: 10.1177/0042085911427735

Williams, A., Prestage, S., & Bedward, J. (2001). Individualism to collaboration: The significance of teacher culture to the induction of newly qualified teachers. *Journal of Education for Teaching, 27,* 253–267.

Wood, S. M. (2012). Rivers' confluence: A qualitative investigation into gifted educators' experiences with collaboration with school counselors. *Roeper Review, 34,* 261–274. doi:10.1080/02783193.2012.715337

3

Program Assessment and Accountability Solutions

We've all heard it before among our colleagues' conversations in the school counseling office, "What? Not another mandate that makes us use calculators! We're school counselors not math teachers! We hate math! Make it go away!" But data is not your typical four-letter word. In fact, being accountable is not as much about math or number-crunching as it is about ensuring equity-focused practices that affect *all* students and, in these challenging budget-tightening times, keeping our jobs.

As noted by Isaacs (2003), the profession of school counseling has been greatly affected by multiple influences seeking school counselor accountability. Within the profession, key movements such as the American School Counselor Association (ASCA) Student Standards (ASCA, 2012; Campbell & Dahir, 1997), the ASCA National Model framework for school counseling programs (ASCA, 2012), and the Transforming School Counseling Initiative place school counselor accountability practices at the forefront. Moreover, governmental mandates such as No Child Left Behind (NCLB) and the Blueprint for Reform: The Reauthorization of Elementary and Secondary Education

Act now set clear expectations for the collection, disaggregation, and analysis of data regarding educational outcomes for all students (Young & Kaffenberger, 2009). As such, school counselors must become avid users and consumers of data not only to be effective at their jobs but to keep them. While we share many concerns about the inappropriate aspects of grand scale government mandates for education and the over-focus on standardized testing and punitive approaches to educators and schools, we value evidence-based practice using data to show school counselor and school counseling program effectiveness is reaching all students, especially in ensuring all students are career and college ready. An essential part of the CAFÉ School Counselor Evaluation (see Chapter 1) is the school counselors' ability to be accountable and implement and evaluate a school counseling and college readiness program.

Key Words

Accountability: Being held responsible for one's work and the impact it has on stakeholders

Action Plan: A document that sets forth the objectives, resources needed, and persons responsible for enacting a desired outcome, such as the ASCA model tool to plan interventions to close gaps

Evaluation: A process used by an individual or group to determine progress or quality; evaluation is a key element in any improvement process

Needs Assessment: Activities designed to acquire information about stakeholder needs

Results Report: An ASCA Model tool that helps school counselors monitor the effectiveness of their interventions by documenting outcomes

School Counselor Performance Evaluation: Evaluating school counselors on their school counseling practices in personal/social, college/career, and academic domains and the impact that work has on their students and school community

Key Questions and Solutions

1. What is accountability and why do school counselors have to demonstrate it?

Now, more than ever, all educational professionals are being asked to demonstrate that they are helping to contribute to the success of students. In the era of increasing government accountability mandates, it is not enough to continue the status quo. School counselors have been called to move from the periphery into a leading role of dismantling the achievement gap and removing barriers to students' learning and well-being (Education Trust, 2003; Stone & Dahir, 2011). Underscoring the importance of this need and its integral role in shaping a comprehensive developmental school counseling program, *accountability* was chosen as one of the four main components of the ASCA National Model. Postulating that school counselors must articulate "how students are different as a result of the school counseling program," it is a professional obligation for school counselors to become data-driven advocates for their students and communities. Dimmitt (2009) highlighted the importance of accountability and its influence by noting, "demonstrating impact . . . can build social capital in the system as nothing else can" (p. 397). Thus, learning to speak the language of accountability becomes essential to school counselors' viability and long-term sustainability.

As stated by Stone and Dahir (2011), "Accountability requires systematically collecting, analyzing, and using critical data elements to understand the current achievement story for students, and to begin to strategize, impact and document how the school counseling program contributes toward supporting student success" (p. 214). School counselors must learn to determine their schools' unique needs, the interventions that will best aid in remedying those needs, and then determine how effective they are in implementing them by measuring the outcomes of their work. Martin and Robinson (2011) stated that in order for school counselors to be accountable change agents they must be able to prove that they are eliminating barriers to student success and academic achievement through a results-based school counseling program. Thus, the necessary first step to creating such a program is to examine existing critical data elements and designing and implementing a needs assessment for all stakeholders.

2. How can school counselors gather critical data from all stakeholders to demonstrate effectiveness?

All too often, school counselors continue to do something because that is the way they have always done it. Those days are past. Instead, school counselors must determine the needs of stakeholders through using readily available data and by creating and implementing needs assessments. Examining who is succeeding in one's school and, importantly, who is not is crucial to becoming an effective school counselor. Due to NCLB, all public schools must publish annual reports detailing the achievement of all students, including disaggregated data based on race/nationality, gender, socioeconomic status, and special educational needs. Reviewing existing data regarding the safety of students, discipline, dropout rates, Advanced Placement/International Baccalaureate (AP/IB) course enrollment patterns, and the college-going rate is the first step to determining a data-driven school counseling program. Utilizing this data to ask courageous questions—such as, "Why are African American males being suspended at greater rates than their peers?" "Why are there fewer low-income students enrolled in AP courses than their more advantaged classmates?" "What are the trends in college enrollment rates for our English language learners?"—lead to the important inquiry, "How does the school counseling program address these demonstrated gaps and create solutions to solve them?"

Additionally, school counselors should seek the voice of those they serve. Needs assessments provide an effective vehicle for accomplishing this task. New software makes it easy to create, distribute, and analyze needs assessments via online surveys. Hard copies should also be made readily available for students and parents/guardians/caregivers who do not have ready access to technology. Needs assessments should be simple, quick, and easy to interpret. School counselors can survey students at all grade levels, teachers, staff, and parents/guardians/caregivers regarding their perceived needs (academic, personal/social, and career/college), the severity and frequency of these needs using Likert scale items, as well as solicit ideas for solutions via open-ended questions. As cited by Baker and Gerler (2008), Kelly and Ferguson (1984) offer these helpful steps when designing a needs assessment:

A. Determine what you want to know.
B. Decide on the best approach for acquiring the desired information.
C. Develop survey items paying attention to language levels.
D. Have the items reviewed by colleagues, change the items as necessary, and then pilot-test them with a sample of children to determine the adequacy.
E. When the items are given orally to young children, the authors recommend

   ◦ Opening with an overview of the survey and its purpose,
   ◦ Explaining each item in detail and encouraging discussion to uncover misunderstandings,
   ◦ Reviewing the items to allow children to mark the ones they want to learn more about, and

○ Allowing children to review their answers if time permits to identify incorrect responses. (pp. 73–74)

In addition, Young and Kaffenberger's (2013) *Making Data Work* offers several examples of needs assessments that can be modified easily and used as a reference. Moreover, they offer guidelines for different data-collection methods and assist the reader in determining if quantitative (i.e., data expressed statistically) or qualitative data (data expressed through interviews, focus groups, case studies, etc.) would best answer their questions.

Once a data-driven need has been determined and evidence-based interventions have been implemented, school counselors must be diligent about evaluating their effectiveness. ASCA (2012) recommends that school counselors do this by developing three results reports: (1) School Counseling Core Curriculum Results Reports; (2) Small-Group Results Reports; and (3) Closing-the-Gap Results Reports. Specifically, the School Counseling Core Curriculum Results Report details the effectiveness and impact of the school counseling program while ensuring all students in the school are served. The Small-Group Results Report ensures that that small-group activities and interventions support the group goals and determines the impact and outcome of the small group. The Closing-the-Gap Results Report helps school counselors focus on creating, implementing, and measuring interventions designed to ensure equity and to remove historical barriers to access and academic success.

Moreover, ASCA (2012) recommended measuring the impact of interventions and effectiveness of school counseling programs and interventions via three types of data including process data ("what you did for whom"), perception data ("what do people think they know, believe, or can do"), and outcome data ("so what?": pp. 51–52). For example, let's say that a school counselor determines from existing discipline data that sixth-grade students need conflict-resolution skills and information about bullying. So she creates five classroom instruction lessons on bullying for sixth graders (process data) and following the intervention, 75% of sixth graders can properly identify at least three appropriate ways to respond to bullying (perception data). Examining outcome data, she notes a 25% decrease in bullying incidences since implementing the classroom instruction lessons for sixth graders. Utilizing all three types of data effectively paints a picture of the work being done and the measurable changes impacting students' academic, personal/social, and career/college success.

3. How do school counselors demonstrate accountability when teachers have to do so hourly?

Carey and Dimmitt (2012) reviewed six statewide school counseling outcome studies and found "school counselor data use influences positive outcomes for students but the specific outcomes achieved will be related to the state, district, and school priorities and supports" (p. 148). That is, school counselors must have clearly defined goals that align with local and state objectives and thus create data-driven interventions that are applicable to their students' needs. The researchers noted evidence that school achievement increased if schools focus their efforts in this area whereas interventions focused on school climate showed decreased suspension rates. Therefore, it is imperative that school counselors use data in meaningful and relevant ways based on the needs of their students.

Young and Kaffenberger (2013) offered four recommendations for school counselors related to the use of data and accountability. First, school counselors should identify program goals from which to base their comprehensive developmental school counseling program. In other words, these goals, based on student data and aligned with the school and district missions, should be the driving force behind the programmatic design and implementation. Second, school counselors at every level should be intentional about pairing scheduling duties with proactive academic and career/college counseling. That is, all school counselors should be advocating for challenging coursework for all students and be diligent about reviewing students' academic records to ensure equitable access to the curriculum. In the same vein, school counselors need to ensure that data is being utilized to bridge achievement gaps for historically marginalized populations. Again, using data to illuminate where these gaps exist and then creating meaningful programs to address these gaps is within the purview of the school counselor. Lastly, as addressed in more detail below and in Chapter 14, school counselors must consistently share their work with key stakeholders. These presentations should be based on data, should include summative and formative assessments, and should happen in a consistent, ongoing fashion.

4. What are the best school counseling program assessments?

Perhaps the most comprehensive and most widely known school counseling program assessment is the Recognized ASCA Model Program (RAMP). RAMP recognizes programs that demonstrate "how students are different as a result of what school counselors do" through the use of data-driven interventions and practices (ASCA, 2012). The RAMP application includes 12 components based on the ASCA National Model, including sections for all four quadrants (foundation, delivery, management, and accountability) and requires the submission of data-driven results reports demonstrating school counselor impact and effectiveness.

Tools like the School Counseling Program Implementation Scale (Carey & Elsner, 2006), the American School Counselor Association Readiness Survey, and the School Counselor Activity Rating Scale (Scarborough, 2005) can be utilized to help identify the nature of and extent to which school counseling services are implemented as well as how school counselors spend their time. School counselors can also use the *ACCESS (Academic development, Career development, College and postsecondary development, Emotional/personal development, Social/cultural development, and Skills) Questionnaire* (see Figure 3.1) to determine how they are utilizing their time and if it is intentionally directed toward equity-focused interventions in all three ASCA domains (Chen-Hayes, 2007) and college and career readiness (NOSCA, 2010).

Figure 3.1   The ACCESS Questionnaire (Revised, 2014)

The ACCESS Questionnaire is an equity-focused school counseling program needs assessment covering four school counseling program elements: (a) school counselor roles and professional identity; (b) school counseling program components; (c) college and career readiness interventions and closing gaps; and (d) multicultural and social justice equity interventions.

Section A: School Counselor Roles and Professional Identity

1. What percentage of time do school counselors devote to these tasks weekly?

   ____School counseling core curriculum lessons

   ____Group counseling sessions

   ____Individual counseling sessions

   ____Workshops for parents and guardians

   ____Staff development for teachers and administrators

   ____Academic, career, college, and personal/social planning with students

   ____Inquiry/data team meetings and planning with specific data to close achievement, opportunity, and attainment gaps

   ____Management and accountability activities for the school counseling program including action plans, results reports, and program assessment

   ____Classroom observations/individual consultations

   ____Paperwork

   ____Crisis

   ____Discipline

   ____Scheduling classes and class changes

   ____Other (List:_____)

   100% TOTAL

2. Based on Question 1, what *should* school counselors do, and how will this change?

3. What are school counselor competencies at this school (with evidence) in each of these areas?

   Scale: 1 = Unsatisfactory, 2 = Basic, 3 = Proficient, 4 = Distinguished

Figure 3.1

Plans, organizes, and delivers the school counseling program	1	2	3	4
Implements the school counseling curriculum for all students	1	2	3	4
Implements annual updated academic/career/ college/personal/social plan reviewed by student, teachers, and parent/guardian	1	2	3	4
Provides individual and group counseling, consultation, and referrals	1	2	3	4
Provides effective school counseling program management	1	2	3	4
Discusses program management system and action plans with administrators	1	2	3	4
Establishes school counseling program advisory council	1	2	3	4
Collects and analyzes data on school counseling program direction/emphasis	1	2	3	4
Regularly monitors every student's academic/ career/college readiness/personal/social progress	1	2	3	4
Analyzes data, time logs, and calendars to increase school counseling program efficiency for all students	1	2	3	4
Disseminates school counseling program results reports	1	2	3	4
Conducts yearly school counseling program assessments	1	2	3	4
Acts as student advocate, leader, collaborator, and systems change agent	1	2	3	4

4. How does the school counseling program incorporate and disseminate current ASCA, ACA, and NACAC codes of ethics?

5. What are the ethical/legal issues at the school and how do school counselors help resolve them?

6. What professional counseling associations do school counselors have current memberships in (with evidence), and if none, why?

____American School Counselor Association (ASCA)

____ASCA state branch

____American Counseling Association (ACA)

____ACA state branch

(Continued)

Figure 3.1 Continued

____National Association for College Admission Counseling (NACAC)

____NACAC state branch

____The College Board (institutional membership)

____Chi Sigma Iota (international counseling honorary)

____Other (List:_____)

7. How often do school counselors and supervisor(s) read the *Professional School Counseling* journal, and how else do they stay current on research?

8. What is the professional identity (i.e., degrees, certification, background, and experience) of the school counselor supervisor(s), and where do they access current research on school counseling programs?

9. How are school counselors and the school counseling program referred to at this school, and if outdated words are used, when will language shift to current terms?

Section B: School Counseling Program Components

10. Which of the following specific ASCA National Model components are fully implemented with evidence? (Check all that apply)

a. ASCA Model Foundation

____Mission and vision statements

____SMART goals

____ASCA Ethical Standards for School Counselors

____ASCA Student Standards

____ASCA School Counselor Competencies

b. ASCA Model Delivery System

____School counseling core curriculum classroom lessons for all students

____Individual/group student planning with all students

____Group and individual counseling, consultation, and referral

c. ASCA Model Management System

____Annual agreement

____School counseling program advisory council

Figure 3.1

_____School counseling program use of data and action plans

_____School counselor's use of time and calendars

d. ASCA Model Accountability

_____School counseling program results reports

_____School counselor performance appraisal

_____School counseling program assessment analysis

11. What percentage of these school counseling program services do all students at the school receive annually?

    School Counseling Core Curriculum lessons: _____% of students

    Group counseling: _____% of students

    Individual counseling: _____% of students

    Individual/group (ACCESS) planning: _____% of students

12. What percentage of school counseling core curriculum lessons delivered annually addresses each ASCA Student Standards domain and NOSCA components (total 100%)?

    Academic development: _____%

    Career development: _____%

    College readiness development:_____%

    Personal/social development: _____%

13. How are process, perception, and outcome data used to measure effectiveness in developing student competencies in school counseling core curriculum lessons?

14. What is the ratio of school counselors to students compared to the state/national average and how might it change?

15. What needs-assessment and strategic planning tools are used to monitor stakeholder needs and feedback about the school counseling program?

16. Which students receive few or no services, and how can all students receive academic, career/college readiness, and personal/social competencies?

17. What supports do students needing the greatest academic assistance receive (i.e., students with disabilities, bilingual students, students of color, poor/working-class students), and how are outcomes measured?

(*Continued*)

Figure 3.1   Continued

18. How is the school counseling program promoted (with evidence such as brochures, handouts, student/faculty handbooks, the school's website, bulletin boards, school report card, and school improvement plan)?

19. What are the greatest strengths and improvements needed for the school counseling program?

20. What professional development do school counselors receive each year, and what topics do school counselors want more often?

21. What percentage of staff development topics cover the school counselor's role in providing (1) academic development competencies, (2) career/college readiness competencies, (3) personal/social competencies, and (4) collaboration with parents and guardians?

Section C: College and Career Readiness Interventions and Closing Gaps

22. What are the school's student achievement, opportunity, attainment, and funding gaps, and with whom do school counselors collaborate to close gaps?

23. How do school counseling program staff advocate access, equity, and success for all students, including career and college readiness?

24. What school counseling program interventions in each of the NOSCA eight college and career readiness counseling components are provided to every student annually (with evidence):

    a. College Aspirations

    b. Academic Planning for College and Career Readiness

    c. Enrichment and Extracurricular Engagement

    d. College and Career Selection Processes

    e. College and Career Assessments

    f. College Affordability Planning

    g. College and Career Admission Processes

    h. Transition From High School Graduation to College Enrollment

25. What technologies do school counselors use to assist students, staff, and parents/guardians with career and college readiness?

Figure 3.1

26. How do school counselors lead in closing achievement and opportunity gaps (leadership/data teams; academic department meetings; school improvement plan; evaluating policies and procedures for equity)?

27. How do school counselors show evidence of closing achievement and opportunity gaps by improving student academic, career/college readiness, and personal/social competencies?

Section D: Multicultural and Social Justice Equity Interventions

28. What is the multicultural/social justice equity climate at the school, and how does the school counseling program support it?

29. How are multicultural and social justice equity awareness, knowledge, and skills of school counselors assessed?

30. How effective are school counseling program staff at providing equity interventions for the following underrepresented groups of students?

- Students of color (African Americans, African immigrants, Arabs, Asians, Latinas/os, Native American/Pacific Islanders/ indigenous, mixed race) [Equity issue: racism]
- Students with emotional, physical, developmental, intellectual, and/or learning disabilities and/or gifted/talented students [Equity issue: ableism]
- Students who qualify for free and reduced lunch (from poor and working-class families) [Equity issue: classism]
- Girls [Equity issue: sexism]
- Lesbian, bisexual, gay, two-spirit, and questioning students, and students perceived as LBGTIQ [Equity issue: heterosexism]
- Students under age 18 [Equity issue: ageism]
- Students from nondominant family types (single-parent, LBGTIQ parents, blended families, families of divorce, only children, adoptive, foster) [Equity issue: familyism]
- Students with nondominant appearances [Equity issue: beautyism]
- Bilingual students [Equity issue: linguicism]
- Students from nondominant religious, spiritual, or other belief systems (e.g., Buddhist, Jewish, Muslim, Hindu, Santerian, Sikh, Jain, earth-centered, atheist, agnostic) [Equity issue: religionism]

(Continued)

Figure 3.1 Continued

- Students with nontraditional gender identity/expression (gender-variant, transgendered, or transsexual) [Equity issue: genderism]
- Students who are noncitizens and recent immigrants [Equity issue: immigrationism]

31. Which issues in Question 30 are least addressed by school counseling program interventions?

32. What are the goals to increase multicultural and social justice equity interventions in the school counseling program?

33. How are multicultural and social justice equity issues addressed in school policies and procedures (e.g., course selection/access, staffing, curriculum, texts, teaching styles, mission/vision, goals, school improvement plan)?

34. Who are the greatest allies and blockers for multicultural and social justice equity interventions, and how can blockers become allies?

35. What additional information would you like to share?

Source: Chen-Hayes (2007, 2014).

5. What are the best ways to share program assessments and outcome data with stakeholders in and outside school?

While this is discussed more fully in Chapter 14, sharing information about school counselor accountability should be done routinely with other annual presentations regarding the school counselor's role to administrators, teachers, staff, parents/community members, and School Counseling Program Advisory Council members. Additionally, data can be shared in monthly newsletters, via the School Counseling department web page, brochures, and public relation materials. Both quantitative and qualitative data should be shared demonstrating the effectiveness of the program/interventions as well as the impact on student academic performance, emotional well-being, and career/college goals. Doing so helps galvanize support for the school counseling department and reinforces the active role of the school counselor.

As stated by Young and Kaffenberger (2013), "sharing why data are used as a catalyst to close achievement gaps and improve program services can lead to heightened parent and student awareness" (p. 74). Moreover, these researchers recommended that the concise use of charts and tables summarizing school counselor practices is appealing to school administrators. School counselors are wise to routinely create these types of reports and to share them liberally with stakeholders. Helping others to recognize the impact of school counselors' work, as evidenced through data, moves school counselors out of an ancillary position into one viewed as integral to student success and achievement.

Solution Success Stories

Story 1

Danielle is an elementary school counselor in the mid-Atlantic region. Creative solutions to gathering data are often necessary in schools with multiple grade levels or in which school counselors have large caseloads. Danielle sought to understand the needs of her students in a K–8 school but struggled with the limitations of needs assessments, especially when it came to younger grades. As a solution she started a practice called Minute Meetings. This practice involved targeting a particular classroom per day and collaborating with the teacher for permission to hold the meetings. On the agreed-upon day, Danielle set up two chairs in the hallway, and over the course of the day pulled each student from the classroom for a "minute meeting." The meeting was not intended to be counseling and was structured to screen for students that might need individual counseling or other interventions. Questions might include such things as students rating their happiness at school on a scale of 1 to 5 or responding to a fill-in-the-blank question like, "The hardest thing about school is _____." Often, the minute meetings took more than exactly one minute, but the practice enabled Danielle to connect with every student in a way that caused minimal disruption to the classroom and helped her assess the needs of students.

Story 2

Erin is a middle school counselor in the Southeast who used the principles of action research to intervene with eighth-grade students at risk of being retained the following school year. After assessing the need for a small-group intervention with eighth-grade teachers, Erin began an 18-week program called "The Game"

(Continued)

(Continued)

with 33 students. The title of the group, as well as ongoing language and metaphors such as referring to the group as a "team" were used because many of the involved students identified as athletes or as enjoying sports. The program included multiple interventions for all the targeted students including group counseling, individual counseling, advising, mentoring, and tutoring. "Pep rallies" were held at the end of each of the marking periods and "MVPs" and significant "stats" were recognized. At the end of the intervention, data showed that the majority of students' grades increased and of the 33 students, only 2 were retained.

Story 3

Francesca is a midwestern suburban high school counselor. "How I gathered data: A team of counselors and administrators collected achievement and achievement-related data during a data retreat over the summer two years prior to submitting our RAMP application. Data was retrieved from the school report card (including standardized test scores and graduation rates) and needs assessments administered to all students and staff, attendance and discipline data, student report cards, and pre/post surveys administered via a computer-based program called Naviance. Our most successful intervention was a program given to junior Latino students for our closing-the-achievement-gap project. The graduation rate of our Latino students in 2010 was 82.5%. Our department has noticed a gap from first-generation Latino students to second- and third-generation Latino students. Our goal has been to strengthen the resources given to these students, particularly juniors. Our school counseling department has taken on a large leadership role in closing the achievement gap. Programs we have facilitated include Latino Parent Nights, Multicultural Clubs, English language learner support groups, and freshmen and senior Latino Summit programs at our local community college. My counseling department's closing-the-achievement-gap project and the ISAC (Illinois Student Assistance Commission) college and career exploration program were delivered to our first-generation Latino students to increase course completion rates, increase subgroup ACT scores, and ultimately increase the number of first-generation Latino students graduating high school and applying to college. Also, our district and school goal is to see a minimum of six-point growth from the EXPLORE (eighth-grade standardized test) to the ACT (11th-grade standardized test). Our Latino subgroup has struggled to meet this goal; therefore, this group was formed to increase awareness of the relationship between academic growth and college and career readiness. A total of 20 Latino, first generation in college, junior students participated in the ISAC group for eight weeks. As a result, graduation rates rose from 82.5% in 2009/2010 to 91.4% in 2010/2011.

(Continued)

We had significant growth from the EXPLORE to the ACT among our Latino population. Immediately following this closing-the-gap intervention, junior students took the ACT. As a result, there was a composite 4.2-point growth and particularly a 4.9-point growth in English. This has increased by 1% from the previous year. Also, overall AP tests increased by 18.6%; 4% of Latino students from our group registered for an AP (Advanced Placement) class for the following year."

Story 4

Dr. Trish Hatch shares how school counselors can use the Flashlight Builder tool. Don't keep your school counseling success in the dark! School counselors-in-training at San Diego State University know that highlighting just *one* thing done well within the data-driven school counseling program can quite literally "shine a light" on the school counselor and the school counseling program. Using the Flashlight Builder package (www.cescal.org), fieldwork students collaborate with site supervisors to complete action plans, lesson plans, pre- and post-tests, cross-walks, and results reports for core curriculum and closing-the-gap intentional counseling interventions in their schools. They then use the Flashlight PowerPoint template to present their results-based work to stakeholders. As an example, two graduate students created, implemented, and evaluated their study skills curriculum and data-driven interventions with sixth-grade students in a Southern California middle school. Using the Flashlight Builder tools, they collected process, perception, and outcomes data demonstrating the impact of the curriculum lessons and small groups. They shared with the principal and faculty their results, which included increases in students' organizational and study skills, students' ability to access school supports, and importantly, substantial increases in students' homework completion rates and grade point averages. Thus, by focusing on designing, implementing, and evaluating curriculum and interventions in *one* focus area (study skills) and by making hard work "visible" through the use of the Flashlight PowerPoint, the students and school counselors "enlightened" stakeholders about one of the many ways school counselors, through evidenced-based programs, make a positive difference in the lives of children (Hatch, 2014).

Resources

Digital

Center for Excellence in School Counseling and Leadership (CESCAL): www.cescal.org

Center for School Counseling Outcome Research and Evaluation (CSCORE): www.umass.edu

Qualtrics: www.qualtrics.com

SurveyMonkey: www.surveymonkey.com

Print

American School Counselor Association. (2012). *The ASCA national model: A framework for school counseling programs* (3rd ed.). Alexandria, VA: Author.

Brooks-McNamara, V., & Torres, D. (2008). *The reflective school counselor's guide to practitioner research.* Thousand Oaks, CA: Corwin.

Carey, J., & Dimmitt, C. (2012). School counseling and student outcomes: Summary of six statewide studies. *Professional School Counseling, 16,* 146–153.

Dimmitt, C., Carey, J. C., & Hatch, T. (2007). *Evidence-based school counseling: Making a difference with data-driven practices.* Thousand Oaks, CA: Corwin.

Dimmitt, C., Carey, J. C., McGannon, W., & Henningson, I. (2005). Identifying a school counseling research agenda: A Delphi study. *Counselor Education & Supervision, 44,* 215–228.

Falco, L. D., Bauman, S., Sumnicht, Z., & Engelstad A. (2011). Content analysis of the *Professional School Counseling* journal: The first ten years. *Professional School Counseling, 14,* 271–277.

Kaffenberger, C., & Davis, T. (2009). Introduction to special issue: A call for practitioner research. *Professional School Counseling, 12,* 392–394.

Lapan, R. T. (2012). Comprehensive school counseling programs: In some schools for some students but not in all schools for all students. *Professional School Counseling, 16,* 84–88.

Mason, E. C. M., & McMahon, H. G. (2009). Supporting academic improvement among 8th graders at risk of retention: A study using action research. *Research in Middle Level Education, 33.*

Mason, E. C. M., & Uwah, C. J. (2007, Fall). An eight-step research model for school counselors. *The Georgia School Counselor Association Journal,* pp. 1–5.

Rowell, L. L. (2006). Action research and school counseling: Closing the gap between research and practice. *Professional School Counseling, 9,* 376–384.

Stone, C. B., & Dahir, C. A. (2011). *School counselor accountability: A MEASURE of student success* (3rd ed.). Boston, MA: Pearson.

Whiston, S. C., Tai, W. L., Rahardja, D., & Eder, K. (2011). School counseling outcome: A meta-analytic examination of interventions. *Journal of Counseling & Development, 89,* 37–55.

Young, A., & Kaffenberger, C. (2013). *Making data work* (3rd ed.). Alexandria, VA: American School Counselor Association.

4

Achievement Gap Solutions

School counselors and other leaders in schools play a critical role in ensuring the academic success of every student (American School Counselor Association [ASCA], 2010, 2012). It is essential to monitor data on academic success for every group of students to help close achievement gaps with school counseling program interventions (Hartline & Cobia, 2012; Holcomb-McCoy, 2007; Stone & Dahir, 2011; Young & Kaffenberger, 2013). In the past decade, strong correlational data has emerged showing the effects of fully implemented school counseling programs on the academic success and career and college readiness for students in Connecticut (Lapan, Whitcomb, & Aleman, 2012), Missouri (Lapan, Gysbers, Bragg, & Pierce, 2012), Nebraska (Carey, Harrington, Martin, & Hoffman, 2012), Rhode Island (Dimmit & Wilkerson, 2012), Utah (Carey, Harrington, Martin, & Stevenson, 2012), Washington (Sink, Akos, Turnbull, & Mvududu, 2008; Sink & Stroh, 2003), and Wisconsin (Burkhard, Gillen, Martinez, & Skytte, 2012). Achievement gaps, the difference in academic performance between cultural groups K–12 (Holcomb-McCoy, 2007; Holcomb-McCoy & Chen-Hayes, in press; R. S. Johnson, 2002), persist in the United States (Murray, 2011) although they have lessened at both the elementary and middle school levels. However, high school achievement gaps are wide and due primarily to the difference in resources in schools, including who gets the best teachers, the most intensive curriculum, and consistently high expectations and other learning supports for success (Conley, 2010; Holcomb-McCoy, 2007;

R. S. Johnson, 2002; Murray, 2011). Educational leaders *including* school counselors must partner with all stakeholders, especially teachers and students (Achieve, 2012), to ensure measures are taken to help close achievement gaps, particularly for students with whom schools have had the least success (ASCA, 2010).

Key Words

Achievement Data: Academic performance information about K–12 students derived from school report cards, school improvement plans, standardized testing, grades, career and college assessments, and state and national databases

Achievement Gap: The difference in academic performance between and across diverse cultural groups by ethnicity/race, gender, ability/disability, social class, language, and other cultural variables

Advanced Placement (AP): College-level course material taught in high school courses that offer the possibility of advanced standing in college courses and/or college credit if an exam is taken and passed with a certain score

ASCA Student Standards (Academic): The original three elements of what students should learn from a school counseling program in the academic domain are effective learning, academic preparation for postsecondary options, and relating academics to careers

Closing-the-Gap Action Plan: The ASCA Model planning tool to help close achievement (and opportunity and attainment) gaps

Closing-the-Gap Results Report: The ASCA Model planning tool that shows process, perception, and outcome data in closing achievement (and opportunity and attainment) gaps

Data-Based Decision-Making Models: Conceptual frameworks that assist school counselors in using information to make successful interventions K–12 that help to close achievement, opportunity, and attainment gaps

Disaggregated Data: Data that is pulled apart to look at differences by group, including grade level, gender, age, ability/disability, ethnicity/race, language, and social class (free and reduced lunch), and is used to identify inequitable policies and practices that can close gaps

EZAnalyze: Free software, developed by Dr. Tim Poynton for school counselors and leaders to use to collect, study, and disseminate data for school counselors, school counseling programs, and educators, that can easily be used to help close achievement gaps

International Baccalaureate: Pre-K–12 course curriculum framework offered for elementary, middle, intensive IB, and high school students focused on depth and breadth of learning using units of inquiry, theme-based learning permeating all course subjects throughout the year, and inquiry-based learning. The last two years of the high school program are known as the IB Diploma and passing intensive IB college-level content courses, based on essay exams, allows some students to enter college with course credit and/or advanced standing. The IB curriculum framework is taught worldwide and recognized internationally for developing critical thinking and international-mindedness. All students are expected to study at least one world language in addition to the language of instruction in the IB model with a focus on international learning.

School Counseling Core Curriculum: The developmental classroom lessons school counselors plan, create, implement, and evaluate to deliver academic, career/college access, and personal/social competencies to all students K–12 in collaboration with teachers and other school leaders

Standards Blending: Demonstrating the school counseling program's effectiveness in academic success and closing achievement gaps by combining school counseling student standards delivered in counseling core curriculum lessons with academic standards such as the Common Core State Standards for career and college readiness

Key Questions and Solutions

1. What can school counselors and school counseling programs do to help close achievement gaps in K–12 schools with underserved students—students of color, poor and working-class students, students with disabilities, bilingual/recent immigrant students, and LBGTIQ students?

The first item is where to find your school data to locate the achievement gaps for your school, district, and state disaggregated by cultural identity. Every school has achievement gaps—public, public charter, and independent. But the public schools in most states have published report cards and a mandated annual school improvement plan, both rich in data. However, all states differ in what they report, when, and how often. School counselors need to look at varied data points over time—grades, grade point averages, and standardized test scores are three places to begin. Once the data has been found, then it's time to collaborate with educator colleagues on what specific school counseling program interventions can be developed to help close the gaps. Major work is needed to guarantee every student receive academic planning annually from a school counselor who regularly monitors academic results for all student groups disaggregated by cultural variables (ASCA, 2012; Holcomb-McCoy, 2007; Stone & Dahir, 2011; Young & Kaffenberger, 2009). In addition, all students benefit from academic skill-building competencies from school counseling core curriculum lessons using the ASCA student standards (ASCA, 2012; Campbell & Dahir, 1997). After implementing two key interventions of academic planning for every student and school counseling core curriculum lessons for every student, particularly for students with whom those interventions are not successful, then it's time for intensive academic group counseling and if that is ineffective, individual academic counseling. Planning and school counseling classroom lessons serve the widest number of students fastest with the least school counselor time and energy when school counselor caseloads average close to 500 students. Group work is the next choice if groups are done with six to eight students, as research indicates a group of that size is as effective if not more so than individual counseling, and it is more time- and cost-effective for school counselors.

Next, savvy school counselors show evidence of their effectiveness by creating a closing-the-gap action plan with expected process, perception, and outcome data (ASCA, 2012) for a particular cultural group of students. Last, school counselors implement interventions to close the achievement gap and then share the process, perception, and outcome data in a closing-the-gap results report with stakeholders celebrating successes and redesigning interventions that were not successful (ASCA, 2012).

The ASCA national standards for school counseling programs (Campbell & Dahir, 1997) were renamed ASCA student standards (ASCA, 2012). The nine student standards include three academic standards (effective learning, academic preparation for careers/college, and relationship of academics to careers/college); three career standards (career exploration, achieve future career goals, and the relationship of personal qualities, education, and career); and three personal/social standards (understanding and respecting self and others, decision-making and achieving goals, and safety and survival skills). They also include specific competencies or learning objectives and measurable indicators of student success in demonstrating the competencies when they have been successfully learned (Campbell & Dahir, 1997).

2. How can school counselors develop needs assessment surveys for students, educational staff, and families that illuminate achievement gaps?

This is where use of the *school counseling program advisory council* (ASCA, 2012) is essential. If missing it's time to collaborate and build one to support the program and collaboratively monitor the school counseling program's role in interventions to close achievement gaps. The advisory council, comprised of key ally stakeholders (a teacher, parent/guardian, building leader, community leader, and current student or alumni), assist school counselors and the school counseling program in developing an annual achievement gap needs assessment/evaluation for students, families, and educators in the school and suggest and monitor specific achievement gap data points. There are also obstacles to be overcome in terms of the politics of achievement gaps. Although they are present in all schools, different stakeholders will react with interest, scorn, or fear depending on how they are presented. In a public school education climate where data can and is held against teachers and leaders by politicians in punitive ways, savvy school counselors want to be creative and collaborative in developing and responding to needs-assessment questions, understanding the political climate in their school, district, and state. Sample questions for needs assessment with each set of stakeholders related to achievement gap closure may include the following:

Educators and Staff

- What are the greatest achievement gaps with students at our school?
- Which groups of students are most and least successful?
- What strategies have been most successful in closing gaps in your classroom?
- What do you most need help with in closing an achievement gap?
- What is the easiest way to monitor achievement gap data and where do you need more help?

Parents and Guardians

- What are achievement gaps at our school and how can you find the data and monitor them?
- What can you do as a parent/guardian to help close achievement gaps?

- What are our teachers doing to help close achievement gaps?
- What are school counselors doing to help close achievement gaps?
- What are building leaders doing to close achievement gaps?

Students

- What are the achievement gaps at our school and how can students find and monitor them?
- What groups of students face the widest achievement gaps at our school?
- What can you do to help other students close achievement gaps?
- How do teachers help students close achievement gaps?
- How do school counselors help students with academic success and closing achievement gaps?
- What do high-achieving students do to be successful?
- Would you volunteer to tutor or be a study buddy?
- Would you like a tutor or study buddy?

3. What interventions to close the achievement gaps can school counselors implement with teachers in K–12 schools?

Promoting school counselors as partners in academic achievement and closing gaps through building a data-driven school counseling program is the most important skill based on school counseling research (ASCA, 2010, 2012). Academic achievement has been enhanced in schools with fully implemented school counseling programs, according to research studies in six states (Lapan, 2012). It is time for schools lacking them to start the process with the foundation of the ASCA Model (2012). Create a school counseling program mission, vision, and goals using a school counseling program assessment, closing-the-gap action plans and results reports, maintaining the school's data profile, and monitoring achievement data with the school counseling program Advisory Council (ASCA, 2012).

Intensity, depth, and breadth in learning are essential for student success across the United States to ensure the greatest possible post-secondary success outcomes (Conley, 2010; R. S. Johnson, 2002; Murray, 2011). As discussed in Chapter 7, all students need college preparatory and career development coursework including four years of intensive English, math, science, social studies, and a world language at the high school level to qualify for the widest range of selective college and career postsecondary options (Conley, 2010; Murray, 2011).

Common Core standards, adopted in most states, were designed to assist all public school and public charter school educators in providing students with greater rigor in teaching all students to be college and career ready. School counselors have an important role in assisting all stakeholders in understanding the importance of Common Core and focusing on specific academic subject areas in advocating for greater depth (Achieve, 2012). However, there is no evidence or research base demonstrating that Common Core standards will be effective, so it's imperative that school counselors watch how they are implemented in schools and monitor successes and concerns for students, faculty, and leaders throughout their implementation. School counselors can partner with teachers in blending school counseling core curriculum lessons (ASCA, 2012) using ASCA student standards (Campbell & Dahir, 1997) and competencies with common core standards as a partnership to close achievement gaps collaboratively in classroom instruction. This concept, *standards blending*, was developed by Rita Schellenberg (2008) and has been shown to close achievement gaps and increase student pro-social behavior (Schellenberg & Grothaus, 2009, 2011). School counselors can collaborate with an ally teacher and look at how both can use Common Core standards (and other intensive curriculum frameworks such as International Baccalaureate) and school counseling core curriculum lessons to close an achievement gap in the school as a team and share outcomes with all stakeholders.

4. How can school counselors collect and analyze data to ensure achievement-gap interventions serve all students?

There are multiple tools to assist school counselors in collecting data to close achievement gaps. Some of the most potent tools include the following data-driven decision-making models and assessments:

- ASCA Model's process, perception, and outcomes data (ASCA, 2012)
- E-Z Analyze: free software for school counselors and other educators to crunch data downloadable for Excel spreadsheets at www.ezanalyze.com

- MEASURE: Data-based decision-making model that encourages school counselors to focus on these easy-to-remember elements in closing gaps: Mission, Element, Analyze, Stakeholders-Unite, Results, Educate (Stone & Dahir, 2011)
- PLAN: ACT's early college readiness exam that can be used to assess academic subject strengths and areas to improve; it can be used by students and educators to shift instruction to assist students with more successful learning in high school, including preparation for ACT exam in the junior year of high school
- PSAT: The College Board's early college readiness exam that assesses academic knowledge strengths and improvements needed by students and educators for shifting instruction to assist students with successful learning in high school including preparation for the junior-year SAT exam

5. What evidence-based curricula help school counselors close achievement gaps and increase successful academic and social competencies?

Three counselor educators (Brigman & Campbell, 2003; Brigman, Webb, & Campbell, 2007) reported strong results in academic achievement and student social skills development with elementary and middle school students using their Student Success Skills curriculum: www.studentsuccessskills.com. In addition to the evidence-based Student Success skills curriculum, Springboard is the College Board's pre-AP instructional model starting in sixth grade focused on college-level curricula, high expectations, and expanded opportunities and access for all students using culturally responsive pedagogy and engaging students with problem-solving and critical thinking skills: http://springboardprogram.collegeboard.org/components.

Advanced Placement courses increase college-level curricular experiences and encourage students with successful passage of AP exams to enter and graduate from college. AP exam takers with appropriate scores can place out of numerous college courses and save money and time and demonstrate advanced skills. AP courses focus on one piece of the curriculum at a time and are usually multiple-choice exams that focus on memorization of content: http://apcentral.collegeboard.com/apc/public/courses/index.html.

Contrasting to AP courses are International Baccalaureate curriculum framework courses (www.ibo.org). Unlike AP classes usually found at the high school level, IB can be PreK–12 and focuses on project- and inquiry-based assessment and essay examinations for demonstration of learning and critical thinking. Students who complete the last 2 years of high school in an International Baccalaureate Diploma Program receive not only college-level course material but often credit and advanced standing at universities around the world as the IB diploma is an internationally recognized curriculum framework.

Both AP and IB have strengths and some schools in the United States offer students the chance to experience coursework with both. AP currently has a wider range of offerings in the U.S. public schools and a larger audience; IB was traditionally found in independent schools but in the past decade many urban public schools with large numbers of dual-language learners and recent immigrant families have chosen IB as a focus to increase success among culturally and linguistically diverse students with strong international connections. Study in two languages is expected throughout the duration of an IB program. However, more than any other achievement-gap strategy, there is still great inequity in terms of who is receiving access to AP and IB classes and who is not, based on ethnic/racial identity, social class, disability, and language identities across the United States. While many more schools are offering some AP classes and IB programs are on the rise, too many students have no access to these intensive college-level classes, and without intensive academic subject classes and successful performance on AP and IB exams, large groups of U.S. students do not have access to reaching their dreams until equity-focused school counselors and other leaders turn this around.

Solution Success Stories

Story 1

Jahaira, a northeastern urban elementary school counselor, closed the achievement gap for 1,600 poor and working-class students of African American and Latino/a ethnic and racial identities by increasing attendance with subsequent rises in grades and attendance. How? She devised a reward system in every classroom and made it a school-wide project for a year and collected pre- and post-baseline data to show how better attendance would not only reward classrooms but further school goals of improving math and English language arts grades with more students in class for instructional time. Her outcomes included substantial rises in attendance and higher average grades in all subjects across the school, and this convinced her principal to hire a second school counselor to lessen the caseload to one school counselor for 800 students.

(Continued)

(Continued)

Story 2

Emma, a suburban northeastern middle school counseling intern, struggled to find an achievement gap until she located a group of White upper-middle-class eighth-grade boys who saw themselves as "the bad kids" who were getting Cs. All of them had done well in elementary school, and there were no behavioral or personal/social concerns other than this group had decided it was cool to be "bad." She developed an academic achievement group to address student strengths and challenge them on their perceptions of what being "bad" was doing for their futures. After a 15-week period of group counseling intervention, all of the boys had raised their grades and reported specific skills in academic achievement that they could use in the classroom. Six months later, only one had to go to summer school and all enrolled in high school with a successful transition.

Story 3

Keyanna, an urban northeastern public high school college counselor, chose to close an achievement gap when looking at her school's data finding that most of the sophomores in one class of biology were failing. The teacher had great difficulty relating effectively to poor and working-class Latino/a and African American students, and the power struggles were unhelpful to students who had checked out on any hope of passing the class. The counselor used after-school counseling core curriculum lessons for all students (ASCA, 2012), group counseling for some students, and individual counseling for other students to build resilience and persistence skills with students from the biology class. After her three interventions in a 15-week period, the class pass rate rose by 33%, and those students did not have to retake the class in summer school.

Resources

Digital

9 Evidence-based Study Tips: http://bps-research-digest.blogspot .com/2010/09/9-evidence-based-study-tips.html

Academic Earth (free online courses): www.academicearth.org

Achieve (helping states raise academic standards and graduation requirements): www.achieve.org

ACT Question of the Day: www.act.org/qotd

The Algebra Project (using mathematics to ensure quality public school education for every child): www.algebra.org

Alternative Education Resource Organization: www.educationrevolu
tion.org

American Association of School Administrators (AASA): www.aasa
.org

American Diploma Project (35 states promoting aligned high school
standards, graduation requirements, and assessments): www
.achieve.org/adp-network

American Educational Research Association (AERA): www.aera.net

American Federation of Teachers (AFT): www.aft.org

American Library Association (ALA): www.ala.org

American Sign Language (ASL): www.handspeak.com

ASCD (empowering resources for how educators learn, teach, and
lead): www.ascd.org

Attendance Works (ensuring every district tracks chronic absence data
PreK–12 and successful interventions): www.attendanceworks.org

Banned Books Week (freedom to read and challenging censorship):
www.bannedbooksweek.org

Better World Books (worldwide literacy initiatives): www.betterworld
books.org

Big Picture Learning (innovative, personalized schools with authentic,
rigorous, relevant learning and assessment): www.bigpicture.org

Black History Pages: http://blackhistorypages.com

Bloom's Taxonomy of Learning (updated): www.odu.edu/educ/
roverbau/Bloom/blooms_taxonomy.htm

Books for Africa (ending Africa's book famine): www.booksforafrica
.org

BrainPop (digital media for K–12 students): www.brainpop.com

Brains.org (practical classroom applications of current brain research):
www.brains.org

Center for Advanced Research on Language Acquisition (CARLA):
www.carla.unm.edu

Center for Applied Linguistics (CAL): www.cal.org

Center for Excellence in School Counseling and Leadership (CESCAL):
www.cescal.org

Center for School Counseling Outcome Research and Evaluation
(CSCORE): www.umass.edu

Center for the Study of Race and Equity in Education: www.gse.upenn
.edu/equity

Chess in the Schools: http://chessintheschools.org

Class Size Matters: www.classsizematters.org

Common Core State Standards Initiative (preparing students for college and career): www.corestandards.org

Communities in Schools (empowering students to stay in school and achieve): www.communitiesinschools.org

Cool Math for Kids: www.coolmath4kids.com

Council of the Great City Schools: www.cgcs.org

Coursera (free online courses): www.coursera.org

Data Quality Campaign (using data to improve student achievement): www.dataqualitycampaign.org

Digital Learning Environments (tools and technologies for effective classrooms): www.guide2digitallearning.com

Early College High School Initiative: www.earlycolleges.org

Education Sector (advocacy for high-quality publicly financed K–12 education and resources for high-quality colleges): www.educationsector.org

The Education Trust (closing achievement and opportunity gaps K–16): www.edtrust.org

Educators for Social Responsibility: http://esrnational.org

Edudemic (free online courses): www.edudemic.com

EdX (free online courses): www.edxonline.org

Equal Opportunity Schools (identifying missing students to move into advanced courses [AP, IB] leading to increased student engagement and performance and closing achievement and opportunity gaps): www.eoschools.org

Equity Assistance Centers (race, gender, and national origin equity assistance to public schools): www.equityassistancecenters.org

Everyone Graduates Center: www.every1graduates.org

Excelencia! in Education (accelerating Latino/a student success in higher education): www.edexcelencia.org

EZ-Analyze and Time Tracker (data tools for educators): www.ezanalyze.com

Families and Advocates Partnership for Education (FAPE) (improving educational results for children with disabilities): www.fape.org

First Book (access to new books for needy children): www.firstbook.org

Flagway Campaign (practicing and celebrating learning math): www.typp.org/flagwaycampaign

Flashcard Machine: www.flashcardmachine.com

Flipped Learning: http://flipped-learning.com

Graduation Plans (grades 6–12): www.learnmoreindiana.org/K12academics/Requirements/Pages/GradPlan.aspx

HandsOn Science Partnership: http://handson1.tmdhosting960.com

Hemispheric Dominance Inventory/Brain-Based Learning Styles: http://frank.mtsu.edu/~studskl/hd/learn.html

High-Quality Decision Making (research-based ACIP model: alternatives, consequences, information, plans): www.careerkey.org/asp/your_decision/high_quality_decisions.html

How to Study: www.howtostudy.org

Illustrative Mathematics (Common Core standard examples of math lessons, projects, videos): www.illustrativemathematics.org

Implementing the Common Core State Standards: The Role of the School Counselor Action Brief: www.achieve.org/publications

Indykids! (a free paper for free kids): http://indykids.net

Institute for Mathematics and Education: www.ime.math.arizona.edu

Institute for Research and Policy on Acceleration: www.accelerationinstitute.org

International Model for School Counseling Programs: www.aassa.com/page.cfm?p=356

Intervention Central: Response to Intervention (RTI) resources: www.interventioncentral.org/home

Jumpstart (fostering skills for life-long learning in early childhood): www.jstart.org

Khan Academy (free lessons for anyone, anywhere): www.khanacademy.org

Kids Gardening: www.kidsgardening.org

Kids In Need Foundation (free school supplies): www.kinf.org

Kids' Zone (National Center for Educational Statistics for students): www.nces.ed.gov

Leading Success (online toolkit for educational leaders; College Board): www.leadingsuccess.org

Learning Forward (National Staff Development Council): www.learningforward.org

MIND Research Institute (K–12 math instructional software and systems): http://mindresearch.net

National Assessment of Educational Progress (NAEP) (USA K–12 report card): http://nces.ed.gov/nationsreportcard

National Association for Bilingual Education (NABE): www.nabe.org

National Association for the Education of Homeless Children and Youth: www.naehcy.org

National Association for the Education of Young Children (NAEYC): www.naeyc.org

National Association for Multicultural Education: http://nameorg.org

National Association of Elementary School Principals (NAESP): www.naesp.org

National Association of Independent Schools (NAIS): www.nais.org

National Association of Secondary School Principals (NASSP): www
.nassp.org

National Association of State Boards of Education: www.nasbe.org

National Center for Education Statistics: www.nces.ed.gov

National Center for Homeless Education: http://center.serve.org/
nche

National Center for Transforming School Counseling (NCTSC): www
.edtrust.org

National Center on Education and the Economy (researching the
world's best education systems): www.ncee.org

National Center on Response to Intervention (RTI): www.rti4success
.org

National Council for the Social Studies (NCSS): www.socialstudies.org

National Council of Teachers of English (NCTE): www.ncte.org

National Council of Teachers of Mathematics (NCTM): www.nctm.org

National Dropout Prevention Centers: www.dropoutprevention.org

National Education Association: www.nea.org

National History Day: www.nhd.org

National Institute for Learning Outcomes Assessment: www.learning
outcomesassessment.org

National Institute for the Study of Transfer Students: http://blog
.northgeorgia.edu/transferinstitute

National Numeracy Network: www.serc.carleton.edu/nnn/index
.html

National Science Teachers Association: www.nsta.org

National Summer Learning Association: www.summerlearning.org

Naviance: www.naviance.com/about

Next Generation Science Standards: www.nextgenerationscience.org

Open Educational Resources (OER) Commons: www.oercommons
.org

Partnership for Assessment of Readiness for College and Careers
(PARCC) (internationally benchmarked math and literacy assessments): www.parcconline.org

Plans of Study (16 career clusters and career pathways for advising
high school students' academic course selection): www.careertech
.org/career-clusters/resources/

Programme for International Student Assessment (PISA): www.oecd
.org/pisa/aboutpisa/

Progress in International Reading Literacy Study: http://nces.ed.gov/
surveys/pirls/

Quality Education is a Constitutional Right (QECR) (student-led movement amending the U.S. Constitution to ensure a high-quality education): www.qecr.org

Quizlet (flashcards and study games; English, español): http://quizlet.com; http://quizlet.com/blog/hablas-espanol

Radical Math (integrating social/economic justice): www.radicalmath.org

Read for the Record (Jumpstart) (early literacy for low-income preschool children): www.jstart.org

Read, Write, Think: The International Reading Association: www.readwritethink.org

Responsive Classroom (evidence-based academic and social success): www.responsiveclassroom.org

SAT Question of the Day: http://sat.collegeboard.org/practice/sat-question-of-the-day

Save Our Schools (supporting equitable public school funding; ending high-stakes testing for evaluation; family/community leadership in education policy formation; curriculum responsive to and including local communities; qualified and committed teachers in every school): www.saveourschoolsmarch.org

SchoolCounselorCentral.com (resources for school counselors to help close gaps including a graduation tracker and a personalized learning plan): www.schoolcounselorcentral.com

Science Buddies (science fair project ideas and STEM career descriptions): www.sciencebuddies.org

Scientist Interview Videos (National Academy of Sciences): http://nas.nasonline.org/site/PageServer?pagename=INTERVIEWS_by_subject

Student Success Skills K–12 (evidence-based school counseling curriculum for cognitive and social skills): www.studentsuccessskills.com

Study Guides and Strategies (multiple languages): www.studs.net

Study Habits Inventory: Which Study Skills Can You Improve? www.educationplanner.com/students/self-assessments/improving-study-habits.shtml

Teach-nology (support for educators' effective use of technology in teaching and learning): www.teach-nology.com

TED (free lectures): www.ted.com

Trends in International Mathematics and Science Study (TIMSS): http://nces.ed.gov/timss

United Opt Out National (ending corporate education reform and overemphasis on high-stakes testing in K–12 public schools): http://unitedoptout.com

Universal Design for Learning: www.celt.iastate.edu/teaching/udl.html

VARK Questionnaire (a guide to learning styles; multiple languages): www.vark-learn.com/english/page/asp?p=questionnaire

Whole Movement (folding the circle for information): www.whole
movement.com

The Young People's Project—Math Literacy and Social Change: www
.typp.org

Print

Barna, J. S., & Brott, P. E. (2011). How important is personal-social development to academic achievement? The elementary school counselor's
perspective. *Professional School Counseling, 14,* 242–249.

Bodenhorn, N., Wolfe, E. W., & Airen, O. E. (2010). School counselor program
choice and self-efficacy: Relationship to achievement gap and equity.
Professional School Counseling, 13, 165–174.

Bruce, A. M., Getch, Y. Q., & Ziomek-Daigle, J. (2009). Closing the gap: A
group counseling approach to improve test performance of African-
American students. *Professional School Counseling, 12,* 450–457.

Carey, J., & Dimmitt, C. (2012). School counseling and student outcomes:
Summary of six statewide studies. *Professional School Counseling, 16,*
146–153.

Carey, J., Harrington, K., Martin, I., & Hoffman, D. (2012). A statewide evaluation of the outcomes of the implementation of ASCA National Model
school counseling programs in rural and suburban Nebraska high
schools. *Professional School Counseling, 16,* 100–107.

Carey, J., Harrington, K., Martin, I., & Stevenson, D. (2012). A statewide
evaluation of the outcomes of the implementation of ASCA National
Model school counseling programs in Utah high schools. *Professional
School Counseling, 16,* 89–99.

Chen-Hayes, S. F. (2007). The ACCESS Questionnaire: Assessing K–12 school
counseling programs and interventions to ensure equity and success for
every student. *Counseling and Human Development, 39,* 1–10.

Cholewa, B., & West-Olatunji, C. (2008). Exploring the relationship among
cultural discontinuity, psychological distress, and academic achievement
outcomes for low-income, culturally diverse students. *Professional School
Counseling, 12,* 54–61.

Clemens, E. V., Carey, J. C., & Harrington, K. M. (2010). The School Counseling
Program Implementation Survey: Initial instrument development and
exploratory factor analysis. *Professional School Counseling, 14,* 125–134.

Dahir, C. A., Burnham, J. J., & Stone, C. (2009). Listen to the voices: School
counselors and comprehensive school counseling programs. *Professional
School Counseling, 12,* 182–192.

Dimmit, C., & Wilkerson, B. (2012). Comprehensive school counseling in
Rhode Island: Access to services and student outcomes. *Professional
School Counseling, 16,* 125–135.

Fitch, T. J., & Marshall, J. L. (2004). What counselors do in high-achieving
schools: A study on the role of the school counselor. *Professional School
Counseling, 7,* 172–177.

Hatch, T., & Chen-Hayes, S. F. (2008). School counselor beliefs about ASCA National Model school counseling program components using the SCPCS. *Professional School Counseling, 12*, 34–42.

Johnson, R. S. (2002). *Using data to close the achievement gap: How to measure equity in our schools.* Thousand Oaks, CA: Corwin.

Lapan, R. T. (2012). Comprehensive school counseling programs: In some schools for some students but not in all schools for all students. *Professional School Counseling, 16*, 84–88.

Lapan, R. T., Gysbers, N. C., Bragg, S., & Pierce, M. E. (2012). Missouri professional school counselors: Ratios matter, especially in high-poverty schools. *Professional School Counseling, 16*, 117–124.

Lapan, R. T., Gysbers, N. C., & Petroski, G. F. (2001). Helping seventh graders be safe and successful in school: A statewide study of comprehensive guidance and counseling programs. *Journal of Counseling and Development, 79*, 320–330.

Lee, V. V., & Goodnough, G. E. (2011). Systemic, data-driven school counseling practice and programming for equity. In B. T. Erford (Ed.), *Transforming the school counseling profession* (3rd ed.; pp. 129–153). Boston, MA: Pearson.

Miranda, A., Webb, L., Brigman, G., & Peluso, P. (2007). Student success skills: A promising program to close the academic achievement gaps of African American and Latino Students. *Professional School Counseling, 10*, 490–497.

Poynton, T. A., Carlson, M. W., Hopper, J. A., & Carey, J. C. (2006). Evaluating the impact of an innovative approach to integrate conflict resolution into the academic curriculum on middle school students' academic achievement. *Professional School Counseling, 9*, 190–196.

Sciarra, D. T. (2010). Predictive factors in intensive math course-taking in high school. *Professional School Counseling, 13*, 196–207.

Sink, C. A., Akos, P., Turnbull, R. J., & Mvududu, N. (2008). An investigation of comprehensive school counseling programs and academic achievement in Washington State middle schools. *Professional School Counseling, 12*, 43–53.

Sink, C. A., & Stroh, H. R. (2003). Raising achievement test scores of early elementary school students through comprehensive school counseling programs. *Professional School Counseling, 6*, 352–364.

Suh, S., & Suh, J. (2007). Risk factors and levels of risk for high school dropouts. *Professional School Counseling, 10*, 297–306.

Trusty, J., Mellin, E. A., & Herbert, J. T. (2008). Closing achievement gaps: Roles and tasks of elementary school counselors. *Elementary School Journal, 108*, 407–421.

Tucker, C., Dixon, A., & Griddine, K. (2010). Academically successful African American male urban high school students' experiencing of mattering to others at school. *Professional School Counseling, 14*, 135–145.

Villalba, J. A., Akos, P., Keeter, K., & Ames, A. (2007). Promoting Latino student achievement and development through the ASCA National Model. *Professional School Counseling, 12*, 272–279.

Walsh, M. E., Barrett, J. G., & DePaul, J. (2007). Day-to-day activities of school counselors: Alignment with new directions in the field and the ASCA National Model. *Professional School Counseling, 10,* 370–378.

Webb, L. D., & Brigman, G. A. (2006). Student success skills: Tools and strategies for improved academic and social outcomes. *Professional School Counseling, 10,* 112–120.

West-Olatunji, C., Shure, L, Pringle, R., Adams, T., Lewis, D., & Cholewa, B. (2010). Exploring how school counselors position low-income African American girls as mathematics and science learners. *Professional School Counseling, 13,* 184–195.

Young, A., & Kaffenberger, C. J. (2011). The beliefs and practices of school counselors who use data to implement comprehensive school counseling programs. *Professional School Counseling, 15,* 67–76.

5

Opportunity and Attainment Gap Solutions

School counselors and other leaders play a major role in closing both opportunity and attainment gaps in K–12 schools (American School Counselor Association [ASCA], 2010; Chen-Hayes, 2013; Holcomb-McCoy & Chen-Hayes, in press). While the United States has wide achievement gaps at the public high school level, public elementary and middle school gaps have narrowed. *Opportunity gaps* are the difference in which students, disaggregated by cultural group/identities, receive annual career and college readiness planning and counseling interventions, intensive coursework (including Advanced Placement courses, International Baccalaureate curriculum framework, and honors courses), the strongest teachers (teaching in-subject with longevity), and other experience and social capital that boost success in college and career with measurable outcomes (Holcomb-McCoy & Chen-Hayes, in press; Murray, 2011). Achievement and opportunity gaps have an additive effect demonstrated in college graduation rates. Many students are not graduating with diplomas from four-year colleges and universities and two-year college rates are worse. *Attainment gaps* are the difference in rates of students graduating with a college diploma (two-year or four-year) across different cultural groups when data is disaggregated by ethnicity/race, social class, ability/disability, language background, and gender (Holcomb-McCoy & Chen-Hayes, in press).

School counselors need to know how to find opportunity and attainment gap data and then use that data to help close the K–12 gaps that directly affect college graduation rates.

Interestingly, the two largest national surveys of middle and high school counselors from all 50 U.S. states (College Board, 2011a, 2012a) indicated strong support for school counselors taking responsibility and demonstrating accountability in key areas to help close opportunity and attainment gaps through changing their policies, practices, and school counseling program interventions (College Board, 2011a, 2012a). The ongoing challenge, according to the *2011 National Survey of School Counselors: Counseling at the Crossroads* (College Board, 2011a) and *2012 National Survey of School Counselors—True North: Charting the Course to Career and College Readiness* (College Board, 2012a), is that while many school counselors embrace the work, they don't always get the administrative support they need to make changes in their roles and responsibilities toward more work in closing opportunity and attainment gaps. Paradoxically, the more school counselors can use data to show the effectiveness of gap-closing work with opportunity and attainment gaps, the more they can off-load inappropriate school counseling tasks such as discipline, paperwork, and crisis-of-the-moment firefighting that impede closing gaps.

Key Words

ACCESS and Accomplishments Plans: Planning tool to help school counselors and school counseling programs close opportunity and attainment gaps by ensuring K–12 students get annual planning focused on academic, career, college-access, and personal/social competencies using the National Office for School Counselor Advocacy (NOSCA) 8 college and career readiness components and ASCA 9 student standards

ASCA Student Standards (Careers): The original three ASCA student standards for career development are (1) Career Exploration; (2) Achieve Future Career Goals; and (3) Personal Qualities, Education, and Career Relationship

Attainment Data: Information showing which students are graduating from undergraduate two-year and four-year colleges and universities with a diploma within four, five, or six years after enrollment, disaggregated by cultural group/identities

Attainment Gap: The difference in rates of students graduating with a college diploma (two-year or four-year) across different cultural groups when data is disaggregated by ethnicity/race, social class, ability/disability, language background, and gender

College Best Fit: The college that best suits each student on multiple variables—academic major(s), affordability, graduation rate, housing options, location, public/private, two-year or four-year, student activities/services, and so forth

College Results Online: The Education Trust's annually updated website that monitors college graduation rates with disaggregated data for all U.S. four-year colleges and universities

Common Data Set Initiative: Annual report by colleges and universities compiled by major educational publishers to ensure quality and accurate college information for informed decision making for students, families, and other stakeholders involved in high school to college transition

Disaggregated Opportunity and Attainment Data: K–12 college/career readiness and college graduation information categorized by cultural group that can indicate inequitable patterns across multiple data points that make the difference in college and career/technical program admission and graduation

Opportunity Data: Data points that indicate which students K–12 are given the social capital and college and career readiness competencies needed to successfully enter and complete four-year and two-year college, university, and career/technical programs

Opportunity Gap: The difference between disaggregated student cultural group/identities in access to annual career and college readiness planning and counseling interventions, challenging coursework (including Advanced Placement courses, International Baccalaureate curriculum framework courses, and intensive honors courses), the strongest teachers (teaching in-subject with longevity), and other experience and social capital that boosts success in college and career with measurable outcomes

Process, Perception, and Outcome Data for Opportunity and Attainment Gaps: The impact of a school counseling program intervention on moving an opportunity or attainment data point—such as increased attendance, fewer tardies, more students in challenging courses, more students graduating from two-year and four-year colleges and career/technical programs, higher grades, fewer behavioral incidents, every student completing a college/career/academic plan, all students taking PSAT and PLAN, and so forth

School Improvement Plan: School annual goals for improvement that should address achievement, opportunity, and attainment gap performance

StudentTracker: A software program designed to monitor college attainment rates for high school cohorts

Key Questions and Solutions

1. How can school counselors locate attainment gap data to better service K–12 students and families in closing attainment gaps?

In the past decade, public and independent college tuition and fees have skyrocketed (OECD, 2013). State governments have slashed expenses, usually by cutting aid to public colleges and universities, with the rationale that they could raise tuition to cover expenses instead. However, that has made affordability a challenge for a majority of families and strengthens the importance of school counselors taking a major role assisting families with successful selection of college and career/technical programs (NOSCA, 2010; O'Shaughnessy, 2012). Powerful variables to watch are college graduation rates and the cost savings for graduating on time from two-year and four-year colleges. The added expenses and additional barriers for students delaying college graduation annually beyond the targeted date include students whose financial aid runs out due to taking too many remedial courses at the community college level, leaving them no way to finish a 2-year degree let alone transfer to a 4-year institution. Rising tuition, book costs, additional college fees, and continuing inflation and poor job prospects keep many students from graduating from college on time if at all. College Results Online (www.collegeresultsonline.org) is free and annually updated by the Education Trust disaggregating four-year college and university graduation rates by ethnicity/race, gender, and social class and giving comparative data among similar types of institutions. Schools that have high graduation rates are an indicator of success and an indicator of how quickly students are able to graduate and save the money and stress of not obtaining a college degree with the concomitant loss of earning power. At the same time, flagship public universities and the most selective independent schools consistently have the highest graduation rates, reflecting the often greater financial endowments and other resources at these institutions compared to most colleges and universities. But the most interesting data is from some schools that are neither public flagships nor highly selective independents that have created strong college graduation cultures with data-monitoring systems to increase their student graduation rates.

A second tool for school counselors is fee-based but provides powerful data about high school students after they leave high school. StudentTracker is used to assist high schools (and other entities) to monitor their graduates' enrollment and graduation data from colleges and career/technical institutes. It can be used to better inform whole-school and school counseling program career and college readiness counseling policies, practices, and service delivery K–12. Data collection includes numbers of students enrolling in college, time to completion of degree, college persistence/graduation rates, attendance at in-state versus out-of-state schools, two-year versus four-year or career/technical schools, and attendance for students who have not graduated from high school. More information can be found at www.studentclearinghouse.org/high_schools/studenttracker.

2. What types of data are needed to plan interventions to eliminate opportunity gaps in K–12 schools?

Opportunity data are data points that indicate which K–12 students are given the social capital and college and career readiness competencies needed to successfully enter and complete two-year and four-year college, university, and career/technical programs. There are many excellent programs available to assist families with success prior to formal K–12 schooling. Jumpstart's Read for the Record, for example, promotes early literacy activities with college-student mentors who read books consistently with children in low-income neighborhoods to build early literacy skills. Full-time early childhood education programs are also key for three- and four-year-olds, as well as full-day kindergarten. While the United States has improved on closing gaps for elementary school students, less than 50% of all three-year-olds are in early childhood programs. This is a far cry from other developed nations that have upward of 75% or more three-year-olds in early educational experiences designed to boost their skills prior to formal schooling (OECD, 2013).

Examples of what school counselors can do K–12 to collect and monitor opportunity data (NOSCA, 2013) include information in K–12 schools showing

- student attendance rates;
- annual academic/career/college plans;
- career assessment completions;
- completion and submission of college and career/technical school applications;
- college admissions examination participation rates and scores (EXPLORE, PLAN, ACT; PSAT, SAT, SAT subject tests);
- college exploration program participation;

- college/career acceptance rates (two-year, four-year, career/ technical programs; numbers of early decision/early action acceptances);
- course enrollment and completion of Algebra 1 and other high-level math classes;
- dropout rates;
- promotion rates;
- enrichment experiences (summer bridge, TRIO programs, GEAR-UP, STEM);
- enrollment in and completion of college courses required for in-state public school admissions;
- extracurricular activities and leadership positions;
- completion of financial literacy/financial aid and planning experiences;
- completion of FAFSA;
- scholarship application completions/award rates;
- proficiency rates in state academic tests by academic subject, rigorous coursework enrollment patterns (AP, IB, and honors);
- placement of students with strongest teachers (teaching in-subject with longevity); and
- other experiences and social capital that boosts readiness for college admission through graduation and career success.

To get there, assess the school counseling program with the following questions:

- What percentages of students, disaggregated by cultural identities including ethnicity/race, free/reduced lunch, gender, language background, and ability/disability/gifted/talented identity, get annual career and college readiness planning and counseling interventions?
- What are the barriers for every student in taking challenging coursework in the school/district, such as tracking, minimum grade point averages or grades in prerequisite courses, teacher recommendations, having to take a qualifying exam for placement in a magnet or honor school, and so on, disaggregated by cultural identities?
- How is challenging coursework (including AP, IB, and honors) accessed by every student, not only those who ask for it or who have certain academic grades or prerequisite courses disaggregated by cultural identities?

- How are the strongest teachers with greatest longevity, teaching in-subject assigned to the full range of students (most struggling to most advanced disaggregated by cultural identities)?
- What percentages of students, disaggregated by cultural identities, attend school or off-campus annual career and college fairs?
- What percentages of students, disaggregated by cultural identities, participate actively in one or more extracurricular activities after school, on weekends, or online?
- What percentages of students, disaggregated by cultural identities, are involved in community service or service learning in school or after school?
- What percentages of students, disaggregated by cultural identities, are involved in school athletics/sports?

3. How can school counselors use data to create interventions on college aspirations and building a college-going culture, particularly in elementary and middle schools and early high school?

To start, the idea begins with assisting all stakeholders to examine their beliefs and strategies about career and college readiness. This can be done with a quick needs assessment asking teachers:

- In what part of the year and your classes would you like to build in career and college readiness activities to strengthen college aspirations?
- What resources and collaboration on planning and lessons with all students would you like from the school counseling program for inspiring students in your classes with a college-going culture?

Once responses are in hand, team and collaborate with all stakeholders to build college aspirations through school counseling core curriculum lessons in all subjects, career/college days, group work, and annual planning. To promote college and career readiness and gap-closing in addition to these activities, school counselors can use school counseling program websites, bulletin boards, brochures, and school counseling program mission/vision statements to give a clear message that everyone needs postsecondary education (ASCA, 2012; NOSCA, 2010). This helps build every student's belief in his or her

ability to succeed in college and other forms of postsecondary education. NOSCA provides elementary, middle, and high school guides
(NOSCA, 2013), giving examples of not only student and school interventions but interventions with multiple additional systems—district,
families, and the community—for the eight elements of college and
career readiness counseling, including building college aspirations
and a college-going culture (NOSCA, 2010). For example, in the curriculum, school counselors can team with subject teachers in these
classes:

- Arts: Promoting careers in the arts and what the academic
  expectations are in postsecondary career and college admissions, such as creating an admissions portfolio or video of one's
  dance, art, theater, singing, or instrumental music and emphasizing the importance of having backup and secondary careers
  because most arts positions are low paid.
- History: Promoting careers in history and occupations that
  often attract history majors and the necessary coursework to
  get into college for a history major—what difference in the
  world historians make and how this inspires college-going as
  well as the career paths of folks who study history and go on to
  other degrees and occupations, including education and legal
  careers.
- Literacy: Verbal and written expression and reading are essential college and career readiness skills. Focus on the careers that
  strong speakers and writers can follow and what they need on
  career/college paths. Who are inspiring literary figures and
  what were their career/college paths?
- Math: Focus on career and college paths for mathematicians
  and related careers. Share famous mathematicians and their
  career and college paths. Discuss the importance of math for
  careers that have the widest array of options and the top salaries and what important math courses are precollege (algebra,
  algebra 2/trigonometry, geometry, pre-calculus, calculus).
- Physical Education: Focus on career and college paths needed
  that include physical work, including athletics, physical education, and the importance of athletes having second careers
  because of a high percentages of injuries, limited playing time
  in most sports, and few athletes make a living in professional
  sports for a significant time.
- Science: Focus on career and college pathways for scientists in
  diverse areas of science: astronomy, biology (animal science

and botany), chemistry, engineering, the environment, geology, health, physics, robotics, and science education.

- Technology/Media: Focus on career and college pathways using technology such as computers, education, information technology, social media, and new media/technologies.
- World Languages: Focus on career and college pathways in K–20 education, hospitality, translation, international business, marketing, and other careers where fluency in more than one language is essential for success.

Murray (2011) and Conley (2010) provided stories of the San Jose city school district and a number of other schools that focused on opportunity and achievement gaps and made systemic decisions ensuring all students would be career and college ready, including requiring AP, IB, and other challenging courses for all students. These stories help highlight the possibilities for all schools to eradicate pervasive opportunity gaps that, if not resolved effectively, turn into attainment gaps.

It is equally important to focus on students and their families. It is especially critical to target workshops and interventions with students and families of first-generation college students early on to focus on discussing beliefs and values about college and whether it is realistic, achievable, and affordable, and to challenge myths and stereotypes about it at the same time. Savitz-Romer and Bouffard (2012) discussed the importance of a developmental approach to college access, especially for students from under-served communities who may not be motivated for college. Two outstanding texts for parents and guardians on college access and the college admissions process, focused on affordability, are *Admission Matters: What Students and Parents Need to Know About Getting Into College* (Springer, Reider, & Morgan, 2013) and *The College Solution: A Guide for Everyone Looking for the Right School at the Right Price* (O'Shaughnessy, 2012).

4. What should educational leaders including school counselors do to reduce opportunity and attainment gaps?

More than anything else, school counselors need supportive building leaders who allow them the necessary time to focus on career and college readiness, including sustained, relevant, and quality professional development to help close gaps (Hartline & Cobia, 2012). Following are resources for reducing opportunity and attainment gaps:

- NOSCA online resources include the Own the Turf campaign, an annual Destination Equity conference, free college and career readiness podcasts, and annual surveys of thousands of school counselors nationwide.
- The College Board includes annual regular update workshops for school counselors around the country that show how school counselors can use College Board materials in college and career readiness work with all students, including the *College Counseling Sourcebook* (College Board, 2012b).
- ASCA provides an annual national conference and state branch conferences with focus on helping school counselors provide school counseling program resources, including career and college readiness and implementing the ASCA National Model (ASCA, 2012).
- AVID (Advancement Via Individual Determination) provides evidence-based support for school counselors and other educators to implement their career and college readiness curriculum in elementary, middle, and high schools. AVID has strong results in placing students in eighth-grade algebra, completing college preparatory high school curricula, passing AP exams, and ensuring high school graduation and college admission for Latino/a and African American students across the United States compared to peers who have not been involved in AVID (www.avid.org/abo_dataandresults.html).
- Equal Opportunity Schools: This organization pairs with school districts to find students from nondominant backgrounds who are in their schools and eligible to take AP and IB courses but are not enrolled in them to raise student engagement and help close achievement, opportunity, and attainment gaps (www.eoschools.org).
- The National Association for College Admission Counseling (NACAC) provides an annual national conference, podcasts, print resources such as *Fundamentals of College Counseling* (NACAC, 2012), and state conferences for school and college counselors as well as annual college fairs for students and families.
- The National Career Development Association (NCDA) provides an annual national conference on career development and career counseling as well as many state branch conferences, print resources, and a large database of websites specific to career counseling.
- The National Center for Transforming School Counseling (NCTSC) provides focused professional training in closing

achievement and opportunity gaps for school counselors in rural, urban, and suburban districts and has hosted annual summer conferences or shoulder conferences for school counselors and school counselor educators.

In addition to the quality professional development listed above, school counselors and other educational leaders should work to reduce opportunity and attainment gaps through their everyday practices. Knowledge and dissemination of the Common Data Set, for example, is important for school counselors in advising students accurately about college selection. In addition, a key component of the ASCA Model (ASCA, 2012) school counseling programs is use of both a Closing-the-Gap Action Plan and a Closing-the-Gap Results Report. These interventions are created by analyzing and collecting data with the goal of finding specific populations that are being underserved within the school in terms of opportunity and attainment (ASCA, 2010). Based on this data, school counselors work with their educational leaders to formulate an intervention designed to decrease an opportunity gap, which is what K–12 schools can focus on most readily. Once data is collected about who is attaining a college diploma and who is not in the school, opportunity gaps can be targeted even more powerfully to assess which groups of students need more resources and more effective college-graduation success interventions. The opportunity gap intervention is then implemented and evaluated to determine process data (the number of students affected), perception data (what the students think, know, or can demonstrate), and outcome data (the impact).

Solution Success Stories

Story 1

School counseling intern Kristen met with her school counseling site supervisor at an urban northeastern elementary school that had seen budget cuts and a reduction in staff so that her site supervisor was the only school counselor, with a more than 1-to-600 school counselor-to-student ratio in the elementary school. Although the site supervisor had studied college access in her graduate program, she had no time to focus on this due to other urgent academic and personal/social issues facing her students. Bringing in the school counseling intern allowed the school counseling

(Continued)

(Continued)

program to target college readiness for the first time with elementary school students. But there was no way that they could reach all students in every grade. They decided that Kristen's focus should be fifth graders, and so Kristen was able to deliver college access/readiness in a series of lessons, groups, individual counseling, and planning activities over two semesters of internship. Kristen was able to reach every fifth grader with planning and multiple lessons and demonstrated closure of a college and career readiness opportunity gap with lessons and planning for all fifth graders; she also used group and individual counseling for some fifth graders and was able to show evidence of helping close an achievement gap with that set of interventions.

Story 2

A newly hired bilingual urban northeastern middle school counselor, Zuleika, came into a school that had never had a school counseling program and a student body facing large opportunity gaps that had never received any college-access or career readiness information. In her first year, she developed a school counseling program mission and vision, as well as goals for developing the school counseling program based on the ASCA National Model's nine Student Standards (ASCA, 2012; Campbell & Dahir, 1997) and NOSCA's eight college and career components (NOSCA, 2010). She created 17 lesson plans and targeted one achievement gap and one opportunity gap. For the first time, middle school students received college- and career-access counseling through her lessons and group and individual counseling. She demonstrated a 100% increase in career and college readiness planning and learning in her lessons in a school with an almost entirely second-generation Dominican, Mexican, and Puerto Rican student body.

Story 3

In an affluent Chicago suburban school, school counselors reviewed data related to the ACT exam and found that African American male students were earning much lower scores than their White male peers. The school counselors worked with their administrator to garner monies for an after-school ACT workshop that targeted this population. Upon completion of the workshop, participants retook the ACT exam and scored significantly higher, thus increasing their chances to get into a four-year college or university of their choice. This success story illustrates how examining data, with a particular focus on underserved populations, including young men of color, makes positive differences and a long-term impact on the lives of students.

Resources

Digital

(NOSCA 2) College and Career Exploration and Selection Processes

AVID (closing the achievement gap by preparing all students for college readiness and success): www.avid.org

Big Future (career and college exploration and planning tools): https://collegeboard.org

Bright Outlook (occupations expected to grow rapidly in the near and/or new/emerging fields): www.onetonline.org/find/bright?b=0&g=Go

Bureau of Labor Statistics (BLS): www.bls.gov

Career OneStop (career planning online tools): www.careeronestop.org

CollegeEd (College Board's grade 7–12 career and college planning program curricula): http://professionals.collegeboard.com/k-12/planning/collegeed

College.gov: (I'm going; English/español): www.college.gov

College Navigator (at National Center for Educational Statistics): http://nces.ed.gov

CTE (Career Technical Education): www.careertech.org

Employment Projections (information about the U.S. labor market 10 years in advance): www.bls.gov/emp/home.htm

Equal Opportunity Schools: www.eoschools.org

Job Corps (free education/training for youth, career and GED/high school diploma education): www.jobcorps.gov

Jumpstart (promoting early childhood education skills): www.jstart.org

KnowHow2GO (college access skills for grades 6–12): http://knowhowtogo.org

O*NET Online (career exploration and job analysis): http://online.onetcenter.org

Occupational Employment Statistics and Wage Estimates: www.bls.gov

Occupational Outlook Handbook (English/español): www.bls.gov

Read for the Record (recruiting college students to develop early childhood literacy skills in poor neighborhoods): www.jstart.org

The Real Game Series (research-based curriculum helping students and adults imagine the future they would love to achieve their dreams; grades 3–adult): www.realgame.org

Self-Directed Search (research-based electronic assessment discovering careers and college major[s] matching interests and abilities): www.self-directed-search.com

Step-by-Step College Awareness and Planning for Families, Counselors, and Communities (NACAC) (curriculum grades 7–12): www .nacacnet.org/PublicationsResources/Marketplace/student/ Pages/GuidingEducation.aspx?PF=1

Strong Interest Inventory (discovering interests, preferences, and personal styles for career and college-major decision making): www .cpp.com/products/strong/index.aspx

World-of-Work Map (how occupations relate to each other based on work tasks): www.act.org/world/plan_world.html

You Can Go! (College Board's college access information): http://you cango.collegeboard.org

(NOSCA 8) Transition to College Enrollment from High School Graduation

Campus Compact: www.compact.org

College Completion Agenda: http://completionagenda.collegeboard .org

College Unbound (using peer learning and authentic assessment to educate students in nonclassroom settings to achieve a college diploma): www.collegeunbound.org

First in the Family—Your College Years (audio slideshows of first-generation students about attending college and transition from high school): www.firstinthefamily.org/collegeyears/index .html

First in the Family—Your High School Years (resources about attending college from first-generation college students): www.firstinthefam ily.org/highschool/Introduction/html

Gateway to College (empowering high school students in danger of not graduating and dropouts to earn a college diploma and dual credit): www.gatewaytocollege.org/home.asp

National Academic Advising Association (NACADA): www.nacada .ksu.edu

National Institute for Learning Outcomes Assessment: www.learning outcomesassessment.org

National Institute for the Study of Transfer Students: http://blog .northgeorgia.edu/transferinstitute

National Survey of Student Engagement: nsse.iub.edu

StudentTracker (software program designed to help accurately gauge the college success of high school graduates): www.studentclear inghouse.org/high_schools/studenttracker

Young Men of Color Initiative (improving educational participation and college completion for young men of color): http://advocacy

.collegeboard.org/college-preparation-access/young-men-color-initiative and http://youngmenofcolor.collegeboard.org

Print

Auerbach, S. (2002). Why do they give the good classes to some and not to others? Latino parent narratives of struggle in a college access program. *Teachers College Record, 104,* 1369–1392.

Bryan, J., Holcomb-McCoy, C., Moore-Thomas, C, & Day-Vines, N. L. (2009). Who sees the school counselor for college information? A national study. *Professional School Counseling, 12,* 280–291.

Bryan, J., Moore-Thomas, C., Day-Vines, N. L., & Holcomb-McCoy, C. (2011). School counselors as social capital: The effects of high school college counseling on college application rates. *Journal of Counseling & Development, 89,* 190–199.

College Board. (2008). *Inspiration & innovation: Ten effective counseling practices from the College Board's Inspiration Award schools.* Washington, DC: Author.

College Board. (2012). *The college counseling sourcebook: Advice and strategies from experienced school counselors* (7th ed.). Washington, DC: Author.

Collins, D. E., Weinbaum, A. T., Ramon, G., & Vaughan, D. (2009). Laying the groundwork: The constant gardening for postsecondary access and success. *Journal of Hispanic Higher Education, 8,* 394–417.

Fitzpatrick, C., & Costantini, K. (2011). *Counseling 21st century students for optimal college and career readiness: A 9th–12th grade curriculum.* New York, NY: Routledge.

Gibbons, M. M., & Borders, L. D. (2010). A measure of college-going self-efficacy for middle school students. *Professional School Counseling, 13,* 234–243.

Gibbons, M. M., Borders, L. D., Wiles, M. E., Stephan, J. B., & Davis, P. E. (2006). Career and college planning needs of ninth graders—as reported by ninth graders. *Professional School Counseling, 10,* 168–178.

Griffin, D., & Farris, A. (2010). School counselors and collaboration: Finding resources through community asset mapping. *Professional School Counseling, 13,* 248–256.

Hossler, D., Schmidt, J., & Vesper, N. (1998). *Going to college: How social, economic, and educational factors influence the decisions students make.* Baltimore, MD: Johns Hopkins University Press.

Krell, M., & Pérusse, R. (2012). Providing college readiness counseling for students with Autism spectrum disorders: A Delphi study to guide school counselors. *Professional School Counseling, 16,* 29–39.

Lapan, R. T. (2012). Comprehensive school counseling programs: In some schools for some students but not in all schools for all students. *Professional School Counseling, 16,* 84–88.

Lapan, R. T., Gysbers, N. C., Bragg, S., & Pierce, M. E. (2012). Missouri professional school counselors: Ratios matter, especially in high-poverty schools. *Professional School Counseling, 16,* 117–124.

Lapan, R. T., Whitcomb, S. A., & Aleman, N. M. (2012). Connecticut professional school counselors: College and career counseling services and smaller ratios benefit students. *Professional School Counseling, 16*, 117–124.

Marisco, M., & Getch, Y. Q. (2009). Transitioning Hispanic seniors from high school to college. *Professional School Counseling, 12*, 458–462.

McKillip, M. E. M., Rawls, A., & Barry, C. (2012). Improving college access: A review of research on the role of high school counselors. *Professional School Counseling, 16*, 49–58.

Muhammad, C. G. (2008). African American students and college choice: A consideration of the role of school counselors. *NASSP Bulletin, 92*, 81–94.

National Association of College Admission Counseling. (2013). *Fundamentals of college admission counseling* (3rd ed.). Arlington, VA: Author.

National Office for School Counselor Advocacy. (2010). *Eight components of college and career readiness counseling*. Washington, DC: Author.

Ohrt, J. H., Lambie, G. W., & Ieva, K. P. (2009). Supporting Latino and African-American students in Advanced Placement courses: A school counseling program's approach. *Professional School Counseling, 13*, 59–63.

Perna, L., Rowan-Kenyon, H., Thomas, S., Bell, A., Anderson, R., & Li, C. (2008). The role of college counseling in shaping college opportunity: Variations across high schools. *Review of Higher Education, 31*, 131–159.

Savitz-Romer, M., & Bouffard, S. (2012). *Ready, willing, and able: A developmental approach to college access and success*. Cambridge, MA: Harvard Education Press.

Sciarra, D. T., & Ambrosino, K. E. (2011). Postsecondary expectations and educational attainment. *Professional School Counseling, 14*, 231–241.

Sciarra, D. T., & Whitson, M. L. (2007). Predictive factors in postsecondary educational attainment among Latinos. *Professional School Counseling, 10*, 307–316.

Smith, W. L., & Zhang, P. (2009). Students' perceptions and experiences with key factors during the transition from high school to college. *College Student Journal, 43*, 643–657.

Tang, M., Pan, W., & Newmeyer, M. (2008). Factors influencing high school students' career aspirations. *Professional School Counseling, 11*, 285–295.

Trusty, J., & Niles, S. G. (2003). High school math courses and completion of the bachelor's degree. *Professional School Counseling, 7*, 99–107.

Trusty, J., & Niles, S. G. (2004). Realized potential or lost talent: High school variables and bachelor's degree completion. *Career Development Quarterly, 53*, 2–15.

Turner, S. L., & Ziebell, J. L. C. (2011). The career beliefs of inner-city adolescents. *Professional School Counseling, 15*, 1–14.

6

College and Career Readiness Solutions

Common Core standards have been adopted in 45 U.S. states as a systemic strategy to promote career and college readiness through a narrowed curriculum focused on strengthening teaching and learning with a current focus on literacy and mathematics. While not everyone agrees about their effectiveness as there has been no prior research conducted on their efficacy, the effort attempts to boost stagnant college graduation rates, especially for students of color and poor and working-class students facing achievement, opportunity, and attainment gaps (Holcomb-McCoy & Chen-Hayes, in press). The high school level is especially targeted, as well as bilingual students and students with disabilities. The strategy seeks to narrow gaps facing K–12 students that cry out for creative and effective educational leadership and school counseling interventions for college and career readiness (Chen-Hayes, 2013; Chen-Hayes & Ockerman, in press; College Board, 2011a, 2012a; Conley, 2010; Hines, Lemons, & Crews, 2011; Murray, 2011). Too often achievement, opportunity, and attainment gaps are based in a funding gap—there is a lack of family wealth and opportunities for poor and working-class students that appears in grave inequities in educational resources and outcomes in U.S. K–12 public, public charter, and independent schools as well as college graduation rates (Chen-Hayes, 2013; Duncan & Murnane, 2011; Holcomb-McCoy & Chen-Hayes, in press). Wealthy families, who often live in wealthy communities with the best-funded schools, have the greatest resources and increasingly put more of those resources toward enrichment activities outside of school (Duncan & Murnane, 2011). Thus, a challenge for all school counselors and leaders is to adequately resource all students in schools, especially those who don't come from families with wealth and related economic assets.

School counselors and other educational leaders are in a key position to advocate as equity-focused change agents to challenge policies, practices, and school counseling programs to close opportunity and attainment gaps in the area of college and career counseling using the American School Counselor Association's (ASCA's) nine student standards—especially career and postsecondary standards and competencies (ASCA, 2012; Campbell & Dahir, 1997) and the National Office for School Counselor Advocacy (NOSCA) Eight Components of College and Career Readiness. Systemic interventions include building a college-going culture ensuring all students receive rigorous coursework and are engaged in extracurricular and enrichment activities starting in early elementary school. Moreover, all students and their families, particularly first-generation immigrant families and students without parents who have been to college, should have access to college and career exploration and affordability information and the college application and admissions processes starting in elementary school. Importantly, school counselors and building leaders should connect students with sustaining community resources to ensure a seamless transition into the world of work or postsecondary options. All solutions should be developmental in nature and equity-focused to guarantee every student is college and career ready.

Key Words

Career and Technical Education: The goal of CTE is to prepare students to gain entry-level employment in high-skill, high-wage jobs and/or to continue their education in their chosen career field.

Career Development: Understanding interests, skills, and personality strengths in the process of making successful transitions between grade levels to postsecondary options and the world of work

College Access: The activities engaged in by students, educators, and students' families that ensure students have the social capital and other resources to successfully pursue a college education

College and Career Readiness: The activities engaged in by students, educators, and students' families that ensure students have the academic, social, and career- and college-planning skills to successfully pursue a college education and/or career of their choice; *college ready* means the ability to begin college with the necessary skills and knowledge to be successful without having to take remedial coursework; *career ready* means one is able to enter the workforce with the requisite skills to be successful and advance in one's chosen profession

Common Career Technical Core Standards: The academic standards designed to ensure student success in postsecondary career and technical education (including college), which are focused on 16 career clusters and the academic pathways to reach them successfully

NOSCA Eight Components of College and Career Readiness Counseling: The essential tools that all elementary, middle, and high school counselors use to ensure college and career readiness skills by high school graduation

Key Questions and Solutions

1. What are the NOSCA Eight Components of college and career readiness counseling?

The eight NOSCA (2010) college and career readiness counseling components are as follows:

1. **College Aspirations:** Building a college-going culture K–12, including the persistence skills to meet challenges and build competencies necessary to enroll in and graduate from college/career/technical programs
2. **Academic Planning for College and Career Readiness:** Promoting K–12 preparation for all students, including planning and successful learning in challenging courses for college and career success
3. **Enrichment and Extracurricular Engagement:** Increasing school engagement K–12 for every student with varied extracurricular and enrichment experiences that include development of interests, talents, and leadership
4. **College and Career Exploration and Selection Processes:** Providing early and regular information and experiences allowing every student to make informed college/technical school and career choices

5. **College and Career Assessments:** Preparing for and partici-
    pating successfully in multiple career and college assessments
6. **College Affordability Planning:** Ensuring students and fami-
    lies receive early and accurate information about the cost of
    college and postsecondary education, payment options, and
    the processes for successful financial aid and scholarships
    with minimal or no debt
7. **College and Career Admission Processes:** Ensuring students
    and families have early and accurate information on career and
    college admission requirements and application procedures
8. **Transition From High School Graduation to College
    Enrollment:** Helping students successfully transition from
    high school to college with school and community resources to
    challenge barriers to enrollment.

As discussed in previous chapters, these components are fully
realized when school counselors utilize data-driven, equity-focused
practices to implement them in their school counseling programs
(ASCA, 2010, 2012). Done successfully, school counselors can help all
students accomplish their college and career dreams, but the goal is
to start early in elementary school with the first six components and
continue the focus throughout middle and high school with all eight
components (NOSCA, 2010).

2. How do school counselors implement and assess career and college readiness activities and evidence-based curricula in elementary schools?

Elementary school presents students with the awareness phase of
career development. Savvy school counselors and building leaders
start a college-going culture beginning in kindergarten. Since many
states now require annual or individual learning plans, adding or
creating an elementary-appropriate career and college readiness
component to these plans, supervised by school counselors, is an
easy way to build college-going culture and connect to students and
their families (Chen-Hayes, 2013). In addition to planning for all students, school counseling core curriculum is the other essential tool
that elementary school counselors can use in collaboration with
classroom teachers to ensure annual learning for students about the
world of work, the differences between a job and a career, and understanding how academic subject classes help shape interests, skills,
and values (Chen-Hayes & Ockerman, in press). Resources and curricula include the ASCA Student Standards (Campbell & Dahir, 1997)

in the career domain, NOSCA's guide for elementary school counselors implementing the NOSCA eight in elementary schools (College Board, 2010), and state and national sites with elementary-focused career development activities such as Career Cruising, Pathways, and Career Zone. Classroom lessons, ready-made worksheets, and online activities can also be found at *Paws in Jobland* (www.bridges .com/us/prodnserv/paws/index.html) and *Career Development and Exploration Resources for K–8* (www.missouricareereducation.org/ doc/sos2012winter/career-k8-resources.pdf). Elementary teachers, school counselors, and building leaders can team and collaborate to ensure that discussions of academic, college, and career development and their related competencies are done at every grade level annually and measured with assessments that indicate students' acquisition of career-related knowledge at their particular developmental level.

3. How do school counselors implement and assess college readiness activities and evidence-based curricula for all middle school students?

Middle school presents students with the exploration phase of career development. Playing off of the previous awareness phase in elementary grades, building leaders and school counselors can implement activities that expose students to career and college with more depth such as career and college fairs, career- and college-related guest speakers, and brief field trips to area colleges or partner companies. In some cases, partnering organizations, such as Junior Achievement, can provide ongoing lessons presented in the classroom to expose students to skills such as job interviewing, budgeting, and networking. Because the middle school learner is experiencing great change physically, socially, and emotionally, mentoring programs with area community-based partners can help support students in their identity development including planning for college and career options.

An abundance of career exploration websites and tools exists to engage the middle school student. Rather than deep focus on a few career or college options, middle school students should engage in exploring their unique abilities, interests, and values so that they understand what makes for a good match when exploring colleges and careers. Middle school students need help learning that while they may be particularly good at something, if they are not interested in it (or vice versa), this may impact their future job satisfaction and success.

4. How do school counselors implement and assess college readiness activities and evidence-based curricula for all high school students?

High school is a critical time for students as they must make decisions about their future path. Thus, it is imperative that school counselors and building leaders recognize this need and plan sequential and meaningful career programming in their schools. These programs should build upon the competencies that were gained in elementary and middle school and propel students to (1) build college/career awareness (i.e., expose students to a multitude of college/career opportunities); (2) foster career exploration (i.e., give students hands-on and virtual experiences beyond the classroom); (3) provide career assessment (i.e., help students learn about their values, interests, and competencies through assessments and surveys); and (4) engage in college/career planning (i.e., assist students in annual goal setting around achieving their dreams; Dahir & Stone, 2012).

To build college/career awareness it is advantageous for schools to consider annual college and career fairs that offer a multitude of options, including two-year and four-year colleges, trade schools, and military and peace-keeping opportunities. In addition, care should be taken to invite local guests who are culturally relevant and who challenge gender stereotypes. For example, exposing students to male nurses and female firefighters will broaden their perspectives and allow them to engage in healthy dialogues around these issues.

Given that many schools now require community service or service-learning hours, school counselors, building leaders, and internship coordinators should work together to guarantee these hours are meaningful for students. While a student may be able to earn hours in a variety of ways, schools should be intentional about helping students link their volunteer efforts to opportunities that will further their career goals and skills. For example, if a student is interested in working with animals and thinks he or she may want to pursue veterinary medicine, community service efforts should be directed toward local pet shelters and rescue societies. These endeavors help to foster relevant career exploration opportunities while simultaneously providing applicable hands-on experiences to further students' understanding of themselves in the world of work.

In this evolving technological age, a series of online career assessments are available to students for free or for a minimal fee. Some school districts may also purchase licenses to more comprehensive college/career software systems, including Naviance and statewide systems such as What's Next IL? and New York Career Zone. These career-planning tools help students to assess their values, skills, interests, and competencies based on traditional career assessments including the Meyers-Briggs Type Indicator, the Strong Interest Inventory, and Career Key. Students can then link the results of these assessments to careers that match their profile and further to postsecondary institutions that offer coursework in these specialty areas.

5. Where in the school day can school counselors put career and college readiness counseling components?

School counselors can make the most of classroom time by collaborating with teachers and aligning the ASCA student standards in the career domain with academic subject-area standards (Mason, 2010). For example, when students are studying civil or national battles and wars in social studies or history courses, deliver a companion lesson on conflict resolution that draws on and reinforces the vocabulary and concepts from the academic course. Another excellent option that more schools are moving toward is having school counselors teach a credit-bearing course focused on career and college readiness using their own curricula or ones developed by groups such as AVID. In addition to a dedicated course, school counselors can assist students with the following interventions and locations:

- All subjects
- Advisories
- Study halls
- Large-group activities
- School counseling core curriculum

6. What other duties can educational leaders delegate from school counselors so that career and college readiness is a primary role of school counselors K–12?

With budgetary concerns mounting, it is imperative to work *smarter* not *harder*. An efficient way to do this is for all stakeholders to work from their strengths and proven skill sets. School counselors have long been plagued with their desire to "pitch in and help" (Whiston, 2002) and thus have been relegated to tasks that take their attention away from important tasks such as ensuring all students are college and career ready. To work more effectively, it is wise for school counselors to collaborate with building leaders prior to the commencement of the school year to discuss their role and responsibilities. ASCA recommends this come in an annual agreement in which both parties negotiate and sign an agreement that clearly articulates the school counselor's caseload and responsibilities to students, parents, staff, community, and district (ASCA, 2012).

In these negotiations, care should be taken to discuss how school counselors can assist with relevant matters without doing clerical (e.g., data entry, stuffing envelopes) or supervisory (e.g., monitoring recess, buses, or the lunchroom) tasks that are better served by other qualified staff members. For example, rather than disciplining children, school counselors can work with children with behavioral issues through individual, small-group, and classroom lessons that focus on learning conflict resolution and building strong relationships. Similarly, school counselors can disaggregate and analyze testing data to better serve students rather than completing data entry of test scores or counting test booklets. ASCA provides a comprehensive list of inappropriate tasks for school counselors that serve as a valuable tool when determining on-the-job responsibilities for school counselors (see the following).

- Discipline
- Crisis
- Paperwork
- Recess
- Hall monitoring
- Bus duty
- Errands for building leaders
- Class coverage
- Standardized testing

Once the inappropriate tasks are removed, school counselors can focus on the four key interventions that should comprise 80% of the school counselor's day—direct service to students in planning/advising for all students, school counseling core curriculum lessons, and group and individual counseling (ASCA, 2012). By being a team player and sharing one's strengths, all work can be completed efficiently without taking away from the main task at hand—preparing students to be productive and capable world citizens.

7. How can school counselors use data and create interventions to assist families with college affordability?

Student debt is now greater in the United States than credit card debt. In the last decade, public colleges and universities and independent institutions have seen tuition skyrocket (O'Shaughnessy, 2012). Many public schools have focused on recruiting wealthier out-of-state students as states have boosted nonresident tuition the fastest. While there is plenty of financial aid available in the form of merit aid for students who are doing well in academics or other talents, need-based aid, or what is given to students who can't afford college (College Board, 2012), has stayed steady or declined concomitant with constant funding challenges facing public and independent institutions. With an ongoing global downturn, recent college graduates are jobless in many countries or in poorly paying hourly jobs that cannot help them meet their college loan repayments. School counselors can focus their energies on helping all stakeholders, especially students and families in the earliest elementary grades, with understanding the costs and benefits of college and postsecondary career/technical education, how to afford it with the least amount of debt, and how to avoid bankruptcy. This includes learning how to create a college savings plan and the various financial instruments, such as 529 plans, for doing so; the differences between scholarships, grants, work-study, federal loans, and private loans; and how institutions often drastically reduce the price of tuition from what is stated on their websites (College Board, 2012; O'Shaughnessy, 2012). Math teachers and school counselors can work closely to teach efficacy skills for students and families in financial planning and affordability for college and career education paths using a family's own data or projected data. Everyone needs to know about the Free Application for Federal Student Aid (FAFSA) and the importance of filing it early and annually. College cost calculators are another excellent tool. The federal government now requires net price calculators on every college or university website so that students and families can accurately estimate total costs of attendance, including tuition, room and board, and all other fees owed for college attendance.

8. What low-tech and high-tech leadership and advocacy strategies can school counselors use to promote K–12 career and college readiness skills especially for poor and working-class students, students of color, students with disabilities, and bilingual/recent immigrant students?

School counselors should consider using the following mediums to convey their college and career readiness messages to *all* students:

- Bulletin boards
- Brochures
- Newsletters
- Digital bulletin boards
- Digital brochures and newsletters
- School counseling program website
- Blogs

- Pinterest
- Glogster
- Smore
- Twitter
- LinkedIn

9. How can school counselors create vibrant career and technical education programs for all students with challenging postsecondary options that do not include four years of college?

The Southern Region Educational Board eloquently answers this question by asserting:

> We cannot identify which students will ultimately achieve academic success once all the components of a first-class high school education are in place. This is one of many reasons why we need to challenge every student to prepare for the highest levels of education possible. We do that by creating multiple paths to college and careers that keep academic and upper-level job options open. We should establish a high threshold that we expect most high school graduates to achieve, while recognizing the need for an even higher threshold for some. Educators must challenge themselves to take each student as far as possible—and educators must have the support and tools they need. (Bottoms, Spence, & Young, 2009, p. 2)

In recognition that boredom is the number one reason why students drop out of high school (Metropolitan Life, 2002), and that students of color and low-income students are dropping out and being offered challenging curriculum at unequal rates (Weiner & Hall, 2004), it is incumbent on educational leaders and school counselors to enroll all students in challenging coursework. This requires disrupting long-held beliefs about who can or cannot enroll in AP, IB, or honors courses and who has access to these course types in language arts, science, and mathematics. Given that employers believe 72% of new job entrants are deficient in their writing skills and 54% are deficient in their math skills (*Entrants to the 21st Century U.S. Workforce,* 2006), many schools must do a better job of preparing the future workforce. K–12 school counseling programs must guarantee that all students are held to high standards so that regardless of students' career and college choices, they contribute to the economy and lead productive and satisfying lives. Recognize that not everyone needs or desires a four-year college degree. Students can do well with two years of college and an associate's degree if they pick their course of study wisely in the building trades and technical fields, but all high school students now require postsecondary education.

Solution Success Stories

Story 1

Chris is a high school counselor in an urban school on the East Coast with 100% of students on free/reduced lunch from families of Puerto Rican, Dominican, Mexican, and African descent. Prior to his being hired, there was no career/college counseling until senior year and few students applied to, let alone attended, 2- or 4-year colleges or trade schools. In one year's time, using lessons derived from the *College Counseling Sourcebook* (College Board, 2012b) and NOSCA (2010), Chris delivered career/college readiness lessons to most students in sophomore and junior years and increased the numbers of seniors applying to and being accepted at 2-year and technical programs.

Story 2

Anthony was a school counseling intern in a Bronx high school that had students performing at a high level, getting career/college access while others didn't get any access until the very end of senior year. With the support of the school counselor site supervisor, he started with the class of juniors and did an all-class assembly with a co-leader who spoke in Spanish so that for the first time all juniors had career and college readiness lessons and a pathway to where they needed to go next—something never done systemically in that school with students performing below a B average.

Story 3

Kira, a high school counselor in a midsize city in the Northeast, was hired to do college counseling in a district with few resources and a primarily free- and reduced-lunch population of first-generation Latino/a students along with a few African American, White, and Asian students. A former college admissions counselor, she was able to give college and career planning to all students. She implemented a process of facilitating college counseling lessons early in a student's high school experience. Her data indicated significantly higher rates of student admission and attendance at four-year colleges than in prior years as well as greater numbers of students attending two-year colleges. She also achieved a significant rise in scholarship dollars attained through her developmental advocacy in early planning for college readiness for every student at the school in freshman and sophomore years rather than only for juniors and seniors who came by the office.

Resources

Digital
(NOSCA 1, 3–7, and Salary Websites)

**Note: For NOSCA 2 and 8 digital resources, see Chapter 7.

(NOSCA 1) College Aspirations

Advising Undocumented Students for College Admission: http://professionals.collegeboard.com/guidance/financial-aid/undocumented-students

America's Promise Alliance (ensuring all young people graduate from high school career and college ready via Grad Nation): www.americaspromise.org

Association on Higher Education and Disability: www.ahead.org/

AVID (closing the achievement gap by preparing all students for college readiness and success): www.avidonline.org

Big Future (career and college exploration and planning tools): https://collegeboard.org

Breakthrough Collaborative (motivating low-income middle and high school students toward college and careers): www.breakthroughcollaborative.org

Center for Student Opportunity (promoting college aspirations/access for all): www.csopportunity.org

Center for the Study of Race and Equity in Education: www.gse.upenn.edu/equity/

Character/Leadership-Building Assessment for College and Career Admission: www.educationplanner.com/students/self-assessments/character.shtml

College Board (English/español): www.collegeboard.com

College Bound Blog (higher education access issues): http://blogs.edweek.org/edweek/college_bound/

College Countdown Tips for Parents With Middle School Teens (NACAC): www.nacacnet.org

College Countdown Tips for Parents With High School Teens (NACAC): www.nacacnet.org

CollegeEd (College Board's grades 7–12 career and college planning program, curricula): http://professionals.collegeboard.com/K–12/planning/collegeed

College.gov (college access, planning) (English/español): www.college.gov

College Preparation Checklist (for students/families): http://studentaid.ed.gov/PORTALSWebApp/students/english/checklist.jsp

College Savings Initiative (increasing postsecondary education access and completion among low-income students via college savings plan reforms): http://collegesavingsinitiative.org/content/about-initiative

College Unbound (increasing accessibility and graduation rates for nontraditional college students): www.collegeunbound.org

College Workshops for Students Curriculum (grades 7–12; NACAC): www.nacacnet.org

Common Core State Standards Initiative (preparing students for college and career): www.corestandards.org

Counselors' Corner Blog: http://hscw-counselorscorner.blogspot.com/

Early College High School Initiative (combining academic rigor and time/money savings to motivate students compressing high school diploma completion and the first two years of college): www.earlycolleges.org

Elementary School Counselor's Guide to Implementing NOSCA's Eight Components of College and Career Readiness Counseling: http://media.collegeboard.com/digitalServices/pdf/advocacy/nosca/11b-4383_ES_Counselor_Guide_WEB_120213.pdf

Families, Counselors, and Communities Working Together for Higher Education (English/español): www.nacacnet.org

First in the Family—Your College Years (audio slideshows from first-generation students): www.firstinthefamily.org/collegeyears/index.html

First in the Family—Your high school years (resources about attending college from first-generation college students): www.firstinthefamily.org/highschool/Introduction/html

Gateway to College (empowering high school students, dropouts, and graduation-in-danger students to earn a college diploma and dual credit): www.gatewaytocollege.org/home.asp

GEAR-UP Partnerships (Gaining Early Awareness and Readiness for Undergraduate Programs): www2.ed.gov/programs/gearup/awards.html

High School Counselor's Guide to Implementing NOSCA's Eight Components of College and Career Readiness Counseling: http://media.collegeboard.com/digitalServices/pdf/nosca/11b-4151_HS_Counselor_Guide_web.pdf

KnowHow2GO (college access skills for grades 6–12): http://knowhowtogo.org

Lumina Foundation (increasing student postsecondary access and success): www.luminafoundation.org

Middle School Counselor's Guide to Implementing NOSCA's Eight Components of College and Career Readiness Counseling: http://media.collegeboard.com/digitalServices/pdf/advocacy/nosca/11b-4382_MS_Counselor_Guide_WEB_120213.pdf

My Future, My Way: First Steps Toward College (student aid on the web's middle school college planning site; English, español): http://studentaid.ed.gov/PORTALSWebApp/students/english/introducing.jsp?backURL=/gotocollege/collegefinder/advanced_find.asp&Language=en&returnurl=/students/english/introducing.jsp

National Association for College Admission Counseling (NACAC): www.nacacnet.org

National College Access Network (college equity and success for all students): www.collegeaccess.org

National College Advising Corps (recent college graduates advising students in underserved schools on college access): www.advisingcorps.org

National Office for School Counselor Advocacy (NOSCA) (promoting school counselors as leaders in college readiness, student achievement, and school reform): http://nosca.collegeboard.org/

Parent Involvement in Career and Educational Planning and College Access With Elementary, Middle, and High School Age Students: http://acrn.ovae.org/counselors/involvingparents.htm

Springboard (the College Board's pre-AP instructional model starting in sixth grade with high expectations and expanded access and opportunity): http://springboardprogram.collegeboard.org/components

Step-by-Step College Awareness and Planning for Families, Counselors, and Communities (NACAC; curriculum grades 7–12): www.nacacnet.org/PublicationsResources/Marketplace/student/Pages/GuidingEducation.aspx?PF=1

Students With Disabilities Preparing for College/Post-Secondary Education: Know Your Rights and Responsibilities: www2.ed.gov/about/offices/list/ocr/transition.html

TRIO Programs (McNair Scholars, Upward Bound, Talent Search for college access/readiness): www2.ed.gov

uAspire (college aspirations, affordability, and access for all students): www.uaspireusa.org

United We Dream (equitable access to higher education for all students regardless of immigration status): www.unitedwedream.org

You Can Go! (College Board's college-access information): http://youcango.collegeboard.org/

Young Lives on Hold: The College Dreams of Undocumented Students (pdf): http://professionals.collegeboard.com/guidance/financial-aid/undocumented-students

Young Men of Color Initiative (improving college completion for young men of color): http://advocacy.collegeboard.org/college-preparation-access/young-men-color-initiative and http://young-menofcolor.collegeboard.org/

(NOSCA 3) Enrichment and Extracurricular Engagement

AFS-USA (international and intercultural learning experiences): www.afsusa.org/

After-School Corporation (TASC) (giving all kids opportunities to grow through after-school and summer programs): www.tascorp.org

Alliance for Young Artists and Writers (identifies teens with exceptional artistic and literary talent): www.artandwriting.org

American Mathematics Competitions (AMC): www.amc.maa.org

American Model United Nations International (global perspectives for future leaders): www.amun.org

American Sign Language (ASL): www.handspeak.com

Association of Zoos and Aquariums: www.aza.org

The Camp Experts and Teen Summers (free summer camp and teen summer program advisory source): www.campexperts.com

ChessKids Academy (online lessons, quizzes, chess computers, and software help any school run a chess club): www.chesskids.com/

CIEE (international study for U.S. high school and college students and faculty and for international students in the United States): www.ciee.org/

City Year (tutoring and mentoring to help students graduate from high school): www.cityyear.org

Corporation for National and Community Service (AmeriCorps, Learn and Serve America, SeniorCorps): www.nationalservice.gov

Corps Network (strengthening the United States through service and conservation): www.corpsnetwork.org

Coursera (free online college classes): www.coursera.org

Dynamy (experiential education to challenge, support, and empower young people): www.dynamy.org

EdX (free online college courses): www.edxonline.org

Enrichment Alley (summer, school year, and gap-year activities): http://enrichmentalley.com/programs/search

First Lego League (an international robotics program for 9-to-14-year-olds): www.firstlegoleague.org

Harvard Family Research Project (strengthening families with complementary learning, family involvement, and out-of-school time information): www.hfrp.org

Indykids! (progressive print and online newspaper written and edited by and for fourth graders to eighth graders): www.indykids .net

International Education and Resource Network (iEARN): www.iearn .org

Johns Hopkins Center for Talented Youth: www.cty.jhu.edu

Key Club International (student-led organization providing service, character, and leadership development with caring and inclusiveness): www.keyclub.org

Khan Academy (free online academic lessons): www.khanacademy .org

KidsBowlFree.com (free bowling for children and caregivers; shoe rental additional): www.kidsbowlfree.com

KidsCamps.com (free Internet search for U.S. and international summer camps): www.kidscamps.com/

Kids Gardening: www.kidsgardening.org/

Language Games (free online language games): (Deutsch, English, español, française, italiano): www.languagegames.org

Little Kids Rock (bringing K–12 students music education when budgets are cut): http://littlekidsrock.org

MathCounts (enrichment club and competition promoting middle school mathematics achievement): www.mathcounts.org

Museums on Us (free admission to over 150 museums across the United States): http://museums.bankofamerica.com

National Academic Quiz Tournaments (organizes middle school, high school, and college quiz bowls): www.naqt.com/

National Association of Intercollegiate Athletics (NAIA) Eligibility Center (Division III): www.playnaia.org

National Collegiate Athletic Association (NCAA; Divisions I and II): www.ncaa.org

National Collegiate Athletic Association (NCAA) Clearinghouse/ Eligibility Center: web1.ncaa.org/ECWR2/NCAA_EMS/NCAA .jsp

National Forensic League (promoting middle and high school speech and debate activities): www.nflonline.org

National History Day: www.nhd.org

National Honor Society (NHS) and National Junior Honor Society (NJHS): www.nhs.us

National Institute on Out-of-School Time: www.niost.org

National Junior College Athletic Association: www.njcaa.org/

National Spelling Bee: www.spellingbee.com

National Summer Learning Association (supporting quality summer learning programs accessible to youth to close "summer loss of learning" and achievement gaps): www.summerlearning.org

Odyssey of the Mind (international competition providing creative problem solving for students K–college): www.odysseyofthemind.com

Outward Bound (inspiring character development and self-discovery and compassion for others of all ages): www.outwardbound.org

Peace Corps (promoting friendship and world peace): www.peacecorps.gov

PianoAdoption.com (finding a new home for all serviceable pianos): www.pianoadoption.com

Privatelessons.com (music teacher listings): www.privatelessons.com

Roadtripnation.org (curriculum empowering students to connect academics to real-world experiences): http://roadtripnation.org/

SAT Question of the Day: http://sat.collegeboard.org/practice/sat-question-of-the-day

Science Buddies (science fair project ideas and STEM career descriptions): www.sciencebuddies.org

Sea/mester (learn watermanship skills and ocean and earth science college credit in a program at sea): http://seamester.com

Students Against Destructive Decisions (SADD) (peer education in middle and high schools and colleges preventing underage drinking, substance abuse, impaired driving, teen violence, and suicide): www.sadd.org

True Colors: www.true-colors.com/content.php

What Kids Can Do (using media showing the power of young people when their ideas are taken seriously, especially youth marginalized by poverty, race, and language): www.whatkidscando.org

Where There Be Dragons (adventure, exploration, and knowledge educational program): www.wheretherebedragons.com

World Scholar's Cup (middle and high school students collaboratively problem solving using debate, writing, and public speaking): http://scholarscup.org

Writing for Peace: (essay contest for youth): www.writingforpeace.org

(NOSCA 4) College and Career Exploration and Selection Processes; ASCA Standards for (C1) Career Exploration, (C2) Achieve Future Career Goals, (C3) Personal Qualities, Education, and Career Relationship

10 Most Common College Admission Mistakes (Education Now): www.ednow.org/id30.html

322 Green Colleges: www.centerforgreenschools.org/greenguide

American Association of Community Colleges: www.aacc.nche.edu/

The Annapolis Group (130 top liberal arts colleges): http://college news.org/annapolis-group-member-colleges

Association for Career and Technical Education: www.acteonline.org

Big Future (career and college exploration and planning): https://col legeboard.org

Braintrack (10,000 higher education institutions in 194 countries): www.braintrack.com

Bright Outlook (occupations expected to grow rapidly and/or new and emerging fields): www.onetonline.org/find/bright?b=0&g=Go

Bureau of Labor Statistics (BLS): www.bls.gov

Campus Pride: (LBGTIQ student leaders): www.campuspride.org/

Cappex: (college search and matching where students present themselves digitally to colleges): www.cappex.com

Career and Education Calculators: http://finance.yahoo.com/calcula tor/index/

Career Cluster Search (discover occupations and then focus education plans on educational pathway necessary for a particular career): www.onetonline.org/find/career?c=0&g=Go

Career Cruising (digital career and college planning tools): http:// public.careercruising.com/us/en/products/

Career Decision-Making Tool: http://acrn.ovae.org/decision.htm

Career Guide to Industries: www.bls.gov/oco/cg/home/htm

Career Interest Game: http://career.missouri.edu/students/majors -careers/skills-interests/career-interest-game/

Career Key (research-based career and college major information and assessments): www.careerkey.org

Career Key Map of Career Clusters and Pathways: www.careerkey .org/asp/education_options/ck_map_career_clusters.html

Career OneStop (career planning online tools): www.careeronestop .org

Career Planning Internet Sites (National Career Development Association): http://associationdatabase.com

Career Readiness Partner Council (comprehensive vision of career readiness): www.careerreadynow.org

Career Resource Library: www.acinet.org

Career Technical Education (CTE) (16 career clusters, pathways, and curricula for a globalized workforce): www.careertech.org/

Career Videos (English, español): www.acinet.org/videos/COS_videos_by_cluster.asp?id=33,27,14,11,8,1&nodeid=28

Careers Out There (video interviews): http://careersoutthere.com

Catholic Colleges Online: www.catholiccollegesonline.org

Choosing a College Major Based on Interests and Personality Type (Holland codes): www.careerkey.org/asp/match_up_personality_to_college_majors.htm#personality

Christian College Guide: www.christiancollegeguide.net

College Board (English/español): www.collegeboard.com

College Board International (college study abroad information): http://international.collegeboard.org

CollegeData.com (narratives of 100 students' college searches and on-campus experiences after admission): www.collegedata.com

College Major Environments—Choosing the Best Fit (Holland codes/personality/environment fit): www.careerkey.org/asp/education_options/holland_college_major_environments.html

College Major-Personality Match Importance: www.careerkey.org/asp/education_options/personality_college_major_match_why_important.html

College Majors 101: www.collegemajors101.com

CollegeMeasures.org (informing and improving the decision-making process with two-year and four-year college data tools): www.collegemeasures.org

College Navigator (at National Center for Educational Statistics): http://nces.ed.gov

College Partnerships and Articulation Agreements (successful transfer-student transitions between two-year and four-year colleges): www.finaid.org/otheraid/partnerships.phtml

College Planning for Students With Disabilities: www.educationquest.org/swd.asp

College Portraits of Undergraduate Education: www.collegeportraits.org/

College Rankings (*Washington Monthly*) (social mobility—recruitment/graduation of low income students, research generated, and student community service): www.washingtonmonthly.com/col lege_guide/rankings_2010/national_university_rank.php

College Results Online (graduation rate database for four-year colleges): www.collegeresults.org

College Week Live (free online college fair): www.collegeweeklive.com

Colleges That Change Lives: www.ctcl.org

Common Data Set Initiative: (improving quality and accuracy of data for making college decisions): www.commondataset.org

Community College Research Center: www.ccrc.tc.columbia.edu/

Community College Survey of Student Engagement: www.ccsse.org

The Completion Arch—Measuring Community College Student Success: http://completionarch.collegeboard.org/?ep_ch=PR&ep_mid=10534038&ep_rid=41392751

CoolWorks (jobs in great places): www.coolworks.com

Council of Public Liberal Arts Colleges: www.coplac.org

Economic Value of College Majors Study, "What's It Worth?": http://cew.georgetown.edu/whatsitworth/

Employment Guide/Worker Rights for Young Workers: http://labor-studies.org/work-related/your-rights-on-the-job/your-rights-on-the-job/

Find the Best College for You: www.consumerreports.org/cro/resources/streaming/college-choices/final/college-choices.htm

Future Job Projections (USA): www.bls.gov/oco/oc02003.htm

Going to College (selecting a college and college life for persons with a disability): www.going-to-college.org/overview/index.html

Green Jobs: www.bls.gov/green/

High-Quality Decision Making: www.careerkey.org/asp/your_decision/high_quality_decisions.html

Hillel's College Search: Guide to Jewish Life on Campus: www.hillel.org

How to Write a Resume: www.howtowritearesume.net/resumebuilder.aspx

Information Interviewing (eight steps of career exploration): www.careerkey.org/asp/career_development/information_interviewing.html

International Association for Educational and Vocational Guidance (IAEVG) (Deutsch, English, español, français): www.iaevg.org

Job Corps (free education/training for youth, career and GED/high school diploma education): www.jobcorps.gov

Job-Hunt.org: www.job-hunt.org

Job Shadow (shadow real people's jobs online): www.jobshadow.com

Jobs for the Future: www.jff.org

LBGTIQ-Friendly Campus Climate Index (national listing of LBGTIQ-friendly campuses): www.campusprideindex.org

The More You Learn the More You Earn: www.educationplanner.com/ students/career-planning/explore-salary-pay/more-learn-more-earn.shtml

Multicultural Career Counseling Minimum Competencies: http:// associationdatabase.com/aws/NCDA/pt/sp/guidelines

My First Resume: www.careerkids.com/resumeSL.php

My Future, My First Steps Toward College: Student Aid on the Web's Middle School College Planning Site (English, español): http:// studentaid.ed.gov/PORTALSWebApp/students/english/ introducing.jsp?backURL=/gotocollege/collegefinder/ advanced_find.asp&Language=en&returnurl=/students/ english/introduc ing.jsp

National Association of Independent Colleges and Universities (includes UCAN profiles of most independent colleges): www .naicu.edu

National Career Development Association (NCDA) (Internet-based career planning resources): http://associationdatabase.com

National Career Development Guidelines: http://associationdatabase. com/aws/NCDA/pt/sp/guidelines

National Career Development Guidelines Activities for High School Students (digital educational games): http://acrn.ovae.org/ncdg/ ncdg_activities.htm

National Survey of Student Engagement (Annual report of undergraduates' college experience, use of time, and benefits from college attendance): http://nsse.iub.edu

Naviance (online course, college, and career planning): www.naviance .com/about

O*NET Online: Career exploration and job analysis: http://online .onetcenter.org

Occupational Employment Statistics and Wage Estimates: www.bls .gov

Occupational Outlook Handbook (English, español): www.bls.gov

Occupational Outlook Quarterly online: www.bls.gov/opub/ooq/ home.htm

Parents' Role in Career Development for Children and Youth: www .careerkey.org/asp/career_development/parents_role.html

Payscale (precise snapshot of the job market to make informed career decisions): www.payscale.com

Real Game series (research-based curriculum helping students and adults imagine the future they would love to achieve their dreams grade 3–adult): www.realgame.org/

Science Buddies (science fair project ideas and STEM career descriptions): www.sciencebuddies.org

Self-Directed Search (assessment discovering careers and college major(s) matching interests and abilities): www.self-directed-search.com/

SummerJobs.com: www.summerjobs.com

Vocational Schools Database: www.rwm.org

Women's College Coalition: www.womenscolleges.org

Work Colleges Consortium (liberal arts colleges integrating work, learning, and service): www.workcolleges.org

World-of-Work Map (how occupations relate to each other based on work tasks): www.act.org/world/plan_world.html

(NOSCA 5) College and Career Assessments

ACT (resources for education [college] and workplace success including the ACT exam taken in 11th grade for college admissions): www.act.org

ACT Explore (test of English, math, science, and reading done in seventh or eighth grade): www.act.org/explorestudent/tests/epas.html

ACT Plan (test of English, math, science, and reading done in 10th grade assisting with post-high school planning, ACT preparation, and measuring academic progress over time): www.actstudent.org/college/planuse.html

ACT Question of the Day: www.act.org/qotd/

Advanced Placement (AP) Exams: www.collegeboard.com/student/testing/ap/about.html

Career Interest Game: (based on Holland codes, a digital assessment of one's personality fit with specific work environments and careers): http://career.missouri.edu/students/majors-careers/skills-interests/career-interest-game/

Career Key (research-based career and college major information and assessments): www.careerkey.org

Career Key map of career clusters and pathways: www.careerkey.org/asp/education_options/ck_map_career_clusters.html

Career OneStop: Pathways to Career Success: www.careeronestop.org

College Board (English/español): www.collegeboard.com

Holland's Six Personality Types (RIASEC) (evidence-based research in assisting career exploration and college major selection): www.careerkey.org/asp/your_personality/hollands_6_personalitys.html

It's Not All About Money (career assessment focused on interests, good fit, work/life balance, fair compensation/benefits, opportunities to build skills and advance, and environment/setting): www.educationplanner.com/students/career-planning/find-careers/not-about-money.shtml

Let's Get Ready (empowering equal access and support for higher education with free SAT prep and college advising): www.letsgetready.org

The More You Learn the More You Earn: www.educationplanner.com/students/career-planning/explore-salary-pay/more-learn-more-earn.shtml

Myers-Briggs Type Indicator (understanding self and others for career, college, and leadership development and interpersonal success): www.cpp.com/products/mbti/index.aspx

National Center for Fair and Accurate Testing (FAIRTEST): www.fairtest.org

O*NET Online (career exploration and job analysis): http://online.onetcenter.org

Occupational Employment Statistics (and wages): www.bls.gov

Occupational Outlook Handbook (English, español): www.bls.gov

PSAT/NMSQT (Preliminary SAT/National Merit Scholarship Qualifying Test): www.collegeboard.com/student/testing/psat/about.html

SAT: www.sat.collegeboard.org

SAT Question of the Day: http://sat.collegeboard.org/practice/sat-question-of-the-day

SAT Subject Tests (demonstrating college readiness in specific subjects): http://sat.collegeboard.org/about-tests/sat-subject-tests

Self-Directed Search (discovering careers and college major[s] matching interests and abilities): www.self-directed-search.com/

Skills Search (identifying careers for exploration): www.onetonline.org/skills/

Strong Interest Inventory (discovering interests, preferences, and personal styles for career and college-major decision making): www.cpp.com/products/strong/index.aspx

Student Interest Survey for Career Clusters (English/español): www.careertech.org/resources/clusters/interest-survey.html

Transferrable Skills Survey: www.d.umn.edu/kmc/student/loon/car/self/career_transfer_survey.html

(NOSCA 6) College Affordability Planning

A Better Chance (increasing the numbers of well-educated young people capable of assuming positions of responsibility and leadership through College Preparatory Schools Program of 500 Better Chance Scholars at 300 schools): www.abetterchance.org

American Indian College Fund: www.collegefund.org

American Indian Higher Education Consortium (unifying voice of tribal colleges and universities [TCUs]): www.aihec.org/

Asian and Pacific Islander American Scholarship Fund: www.apiasf .org

Beware of College Preparation Services/Financial Aid/Fafsa/ Scholarship Scams and Fraud: www.fsa4counselors.ed.gov/ clcf/scams.html

Big Future (career and college exploration and planning tools [free]): https://collegeboard.org

Black Excel (the college help network for Black students and other students of color for college scholarships and access/admissions information): www.blackexcel.org

Career and education calculators (What is the value of a college education? Will I be able to pay back student loans? What is the feasibility of student loan repayment? When should I begin saving for a child's education? What are the advantages of 529 plans? What are the advantages of Coverdell ESAs? What will my loan payments be? How long until my loan is paid off? Will I be able to pay back my student loans? How much will I learn in my lifetime? Should I live on campus, off campus, or at home?) http://finance.yahoo .com/calculator/index/

College Affordability and Transparency Center (U.S. DOE) (annually updated data on net pricing of colleges and universities including tuition, room and board and all other fees minus financial aid awards): http://collegecost.ed.gov/catc/Default.aspx

CollegeData.com (free college match, college chances, admissions tracker, scholarship finder, net cost calculator, EFC contribution estimator, common application and universal common application grids, and great stories of what worked/didn't for college searches of almost 100 students with longitudinal excerpts of their year-by-year experiences in college): www.collegedata.com/

College Funding/Scholarships for Students With Disabilities: www .washington.edu/doit/Brochures/Academics/financial-aid .html

College InSight (making data on college affordability, diversity, and success easy to find, compare, and analyze): http:// college-insight.org

College Savings Initiative (includes video clip addressing the savings gap for poor/working class students and college completion, increasing postsecondary education access and completion rates among low-income students via innovative public policy and 529 college savings plan reforms): http://collegesavingsinitiative.org/content/about-initiative

College Savings Plan Network (a national nonprofit association dedicated to making college more accessible and affordable for families providing 529 college savings plan information from all states): www.collegesavings.org/index.aspx

College Scholarship Service (CSS)/Financial Aid Profile (College Board) (used primarily by private nonprofit schools in addition to the FAFSA to help determine a family's EFC [Expected Family Contribution]): http:// profileonline.collegeboard.com

College Solution Blog (Lynn O'Shaughnessy's college affordability and admissions tips site): www.thecollegesolution.com/tag/college -blog

Colleges With Free Tuition: www.finaid.org/questions/freetuition .phtml

Colleges With No-Loan Financial Aid for Low Income Students: www .finaid.org/questions/noloansforlowincome.phtm1

Colleges With Tuition Freezes, Tuition Cuts, and Level Tuition: www .finaid.org/questions/tuitionfreeze.phtml

Common Data Set Initiative (collaborative effort among higher education data providers to improve the quality and accuracy of data involved in students making college decisions): www.common dataset.org

Consumer Financial Protection Bureau Student Loan Complaint System (private loans and link for federal loans): https://help.con sumerfinance.gov/app/studentloan/ask

Education Sector (a hybrid institution formed at the intersection of public policy, research, and journalism creating independent analysis and innovative ideas—U.S. students deserve a high-quality, publicly financed education through high school and the financial help necessary to attend high-quality colleges and universities): www.educationsector.org

FAFSA (free application for federal student aid; English/español): www.fafsa.ed.gov

FAFSA Completion by High School (There is a strong correlation between FAFSA completion and college enrollment. Federal Student Aid provides high schools with current data about their FAFSA submissions and completions so that high schools can track their progress and help ensure students complete a FAFSA.

A completed FAFSA allows counselors to determine a potential student's eligibility for federal student aid—a key factor in families' college decisions.): http://federalstudentaid.ed.gov/datacenter/fafsahs.html

FAFSA Completion Guide for LBGTIQ Families: www.finaid.org/fafsa/lgbtfafsa.phtml

FAFSA FAQs for Students and Families: http://studentaid.ed.gov/PORTALSWebApp/students/english/faqs.jsp

Fastweb (free matching service for college scholarships, financial aid, loans): www.fastweb.com

Federal Aid First (site explaining why federal college loans are usually the best deal for borrowers [undergraduate, graduate Stafford loans—subsidized and unsubsidized—and PLUS loans for parents/guardians of dependent students and graduate students to help finance college] over private loans due to lower fixed interest rates and more flexible repayment schedules; also links to FAFSA and how to apply): www.federalstudentaid.ed.gov/federalaidfirst/

Federal Student Aid (how to prepare for college, what types of aid are available, who qualifies for aid, how to apply for aid, how to repay loans): www.studentaid.gov

Federal Student Aid Glossary: http://studentaid.ed.gov/glossary

Federal Student Aid Ombudsman Group (resolving disputes over direct loans, Federal family education [FFEL] program loans, guaranteed student loans, and Perkins loans): www.studentaid.ed.gov/repay-loans/disputes/prepare

Federal Student Financial Aid Information for School Counselors (online information for students and parents planning for college, career, and trade schools): www.fsa4counselors.ed.gov/PORTALS WebApp/cotw/main.jsp

FinAid (the smart student guide to financial aid): www.finaid.org

Financial Aid and Scholarship Wizard: (financial application deadlines, scholarship searches, expected family contribution and federal aid estimates, interpreting financial aid award letters): http://student aid2.ed.gov/getmoney/fin_aid_wizard/

Financial Aid for LBGTIQ Students: www.finaid.org/otheraid/lgbt .phtml/

Financial Aid Glossary: www.nslds.ed.gov/nslds_SA/SaGlossary.do

Financial Aid in Seven Easy Steps (NACAC): www.nacacnet.org

Financial Aid Letter.com (decodes the jargon of financial aid letters to compare financial aid packages): www.financialaidletter.com/index.html

Financial Aid Shopping Sheet: www.ed.gov/blog/2012/11/more -than-500-colleges-agree-to-adopt-financial-aid-shopping-sheet /?utm_source=dlvr.it&utm_medium=linkedin&goback= .gde_3956987_member_186266012

Five Ways Ed Pays (data-based benefits of college education): http:// advocacy.collegeboard.org/five-ways-ed-pays/home

Free College Applications (lists colleges and universities with no-fee applications): www.freecollegeapplications.com

Hispanic College Fund (funding for Latino/as): www.hispanicfund .org

Hispanic Scholarship Fund (Latino/a scholarships): www.hsf.net

"I Have a Dream" Foundation (empowers low-income children through higher education with guaranteed tuition support and col- lege/career success skills): www.ihaveadreamfoundation.org

Institute for College Access and Success (making higher education affordable): http://ticas.org

Latino College Dollars (scholarships; English, español): www.latinocol legedollars.org

Lumni (paying for college by committing a fixed percentage of future income for a set period): www.lumniusa.net

Managing Student Loans (borrower responsibilities, repayment, and postponing payment): www1.salliemae.com/after_graduation/ manage_your_loans/

Mapping Your Future (free college, career, financial aid, and money management for middle, high school, and college students; English, español): http://mappingyourfuture.org

MeritAid.com (free directory of $11 billion in merit scholarships avail- able to U.S. college students): www.meritaid.com

Money as You Grow (20 things kids need to know to lead financially smart lives): http:// moneyasyougrow.org

National Association of Student Financial Aid Administrators (NAFSAA): www.nafsaa.org

National College Finance Center (educating students and families about college financing): www.collegefinancecenter.org

National Merit Scholarship Corporation (all precollege students)/ National Achievement Scholarship Program (African American college students): www.nationalmerit.org/

National Student Loan Data System (U.S. Department of Education's cen- tral database for student aid): www.nslds.ed.gov/nslds_SA/

Point Foundation: (LBGTIQ college scholarships and support): www .pointfoundation.org

Posse Foundation (expanding the pool for colleges to recruit outstanding young leaders from diverse backgrounds at top colleges, seeking more welcoming environments): www.possefoundation.org/

Project Grad USA (college-access program for students in low-income areas with academic, community, and financial assistance): www.projectgrad.org

Project on Student Debt: http://projectonstudentdebt.org

Questbridge (supporting low-income students from high school through college to first job): http://questbridge.org/

ScholarPRO (scholarship search): www.scholarpro.com/

Scholarship Scams: www.ftc.gov

Scholarships.com (free college scholarship search and financial aid information): www.scholarships.com

Student Aid on the Web (Federal student aid—Expected Family Contribution [EFC] estimators, Scholarship/College Matching Wizard, grant, scholarship, and loan differences): http://studentaid.ed.gov

Student Loan Borrower Assistance Program: www.studentloanborrowerassistance.org

uAspire: (college aspirations, affordability, and access for all students): www.uaspireusa.org

UNCF: www.uncf.org

Work Colleges Consortium (integrating work, learning, and service in liberal arts colleges): www.workcolleges.org

Young Lives on Hold: The College Dreams of Undocumented Students (pdf): http://professionals.collegeboard.com/guidance/financial-aid/undocumented-students

(NOSCA 7) College and Career Admission Processes

Admission Options in Higher Education (NACAC) (free downloadable poster): www.nacacnet.org/PublicationsResources/Marketplace/student/Pages/AdmissionPoster.aspx

American Association of Collegiate Registrars and Admissions Officers (AACRAO): www.aacrao.org

College Admissions.411 (español): www.hitn.tv

College Admissions Process Guide for Parents (NACAC) (English/español): www.nacacnet.org

College Admissions Process Guide for Students, National Association for College Admission Counseling (NACAC) (calendar and checklist): www.nacacnet.org

College Admissions Process Students' Rights and Responsibilities (NACAC) (English/español): www.nacacnet.org

College Partnerships and Articulation Agreements (promoting successful transfer-student transitions between two-year and four-year colleges): www.finaid.org/otheraid/partnerships.phtml

College Summit (raising college enrollment): www.collegesummit.org

Common Application (one application for 450-plus institutions focused on holistic admissions for better access and equity in admission): www.commonapp.org

Common Data Set Initiative (improving the quality and accuracy of data involved in making college-going decisions): www.common dataset.org

Let's Get Ready (free SAT prep and college advising): www.letsget ready.org

Naviance (increasing student achievement with online course, college, and career planning): www.naviance.com/about

**For NOSCA Component 8, Transition from High School to College Enrollment Weblinks, See Chapter 7

Salary Links

Career Builder Salary: http:// Cbsalary.com

Careeronestop.org's Salary Information: www.careeronestop.org/ SalariesBenefits/SalariesBenefits.aspx

Collegegrad.com's Salary Information: www.collegegrad.com/ salaries/index.shtml

Indeed.com's Salary Search: www.indeed.com/salary

Monster.com's Salary and Benefits Information: http://career-advice .monster.com/salarybenefits/home.aspx

NACE Salary Survey 2012: www.mville.edu/images/stories/ Undergraduate_StudentLife/ServicesForStudents_CCD/PDFs/ NACE_Salary_Survey_April_2012_Full_Report.pdf

Pay Scale: www.payscale.com/

Salary.com: www.salary.com

Vault.com's Salaries and Compensation: www.vault.com/salaries.jsp

Wage web: www.wageweb.com

Print

Auerbach, S. (2002). Why do they give the good classes to some and not to others? Latino parent narratives of struggle in a college-access program. *Teachers College Record, 104,* 1369–1392.

Bryan, J., Holcomb-McCoy, C., Moore-Thomas, C, & Day-Vines, N. L. (2009). Who sees the school counselor for college information? A national study. *Professional School Counseling, 12,* 280–291.

Bryan, J., Moore-Thomas, C., Day-Vines, N. L., & Holcomb-McCoy, C. (2011). School counselors as social capital: The effects of high school college counseling on college application rates. *Journal of Counseling & Development, 89,* 190–199.

Ceja, M. (2004). Chicana college aspirations and the role of parents: Developing educational resilience. *Journal of Hispanic Higher Education, 3,* 338–362.

Chang, D. H. F. (2002). The past, present, and future of career counseling in Taiwan. *Career Development Quarterly, 50,* 218–225.

Chen-Hayes, S. F., Saud Maxwell, K., & Bailey, D. F. (2009). *Equity-based school counseling: Ensuring career and college readiness for every student* [DVD]. Hanover, MA: Microtraining Associates.

College Board. (2008). *Inspiration & innovation: Ten effective counseling practices from the College Board's Inspiration Award schools.* Washington, DC: Author.

College Board. (2012). *The college counseling sourcebook: Advice and strategies from experienced school counselors* (7th ed.). Washington, DC: Author.

Collins, D. E., Weinbaum, A. T., Ramon, G., & Vaughan, D. (2009). Laying the groundwork: The constant gardening for postsecondary access and success. *Journal of Hispanic Higher Education, 8,* 394–417.

De Leon, A. P. (2011). *A model prekindergarten through 4th year of college (P-16) individual graduation plan proposal.* Applied Research Projects, Texas State University-San Marcos. Retrieved from http://ecommons.txstate.edu/arp/364

Fallon, M. A. C. (2011, Spring). Enrollment management's sleeping giant: The net price calculator mandate. *Journal of College Admissions,* pp. 6–13.

Fitzpatrick, C., & Costantini, K. (2011). *Counseling 21st century students for optimal college and career readiness: A 9th-12th grade curriculum.* New York, NY: Routledge.

Gibbons, M. M., & Borders, L. D. (2010). A measure of college-going self-efficacy for middle school students. *Professional School Counseling, 13,* 234–243.

Gibbons, M. M., Borders, L. D., Wiles, M. E., Stephan, J. B., & Davis, P. E. (2006). Career and college planning needs of ninth graders—as reported by ninth graders. *Professional School Counseling, 10,* 168–178.

Horn, L., & Berktold, J. (1999). *Students with disabilities in postsecondary education: A profile of preparation, participation, and outcomes* (National Center for Education Statistics No. 187). Washington, DC: U.S. Department of Education.

Hossler, D., Schmidt, J., & Vesper, N. (1998). *Going to college: How social, economic, and educational factors influence the decisions students make.* Baltimore, MD: Johns Hopkins University Press.

Krell, M., & Pérusse, R. (2012). Providing college readiness counseling for students with Autism spectrum disorders: A Delphi study to guide school counselors. *Professional School Counseling, 16,* 29–39.

Lapan, R. T. (2012). Comprehensive school counseling programs: In some schools for some students but not in all schools for all students. *Professional School Counseling 16,* 84–88.

Lapan, R. T., Whitcomb, S. A., & Aleman, N. M. (2012). Connecticut professional school counselors: College and career counseling services and smaller ratios benefit students. *Professional School Counseling 16,* 117–124.

Lee, S. M., Daniels, M. H., Puig, A., Newgent, R. A., & Nam, S. K. (2008). A data-based model to predict postsecondary educational attainment of low-socioeconomic-status students. *Professional School Counseling, 11,* 306–316.

Marisco, M., & Getch, Y. Q. (2009). Transitioning Hispanic seniors from high school to college. *Professional School Counseling, 12,* 458–462.

McKillip, M. E. M., Rawls, A., & Barry, C. (2012). Improving college access: A review of research on the role of high school counselors. *Professional School Counseling, 16,* 49–58.

Muhammad, C. G. (2008). African American students and college choice: A consideration of the role of school counselors. *NASSP Bulletin, 92,* 81–94.

National Association of College Admission Counseling. (2013). *Fundamentals of college admission counseling* (3rd ed.). Arlington, VA: Author.

Ohrt, J. H., Lambie, G. W., & Ieva, K. P. (2009). Supporting Latino and African-American students in Advanced Placement courses: A school counseling program's approach. *Professional School Counseling, 13,* 59–63.

Oliva, M. (2004). Reluctant partners, problem definition, and legislative intent: P–20 policy for Latino college success. *Journal of Hispanic Higher Education, 3,* 209–230.

Perna, L., Rowan-Kenyon, H., Thomas, S., Bell, A., Anderson, R., & Li, C. (2008). The role of college counseling in shaping college opportunity: Variations across high schools. *Review of Higher Education, 31,* 131–159.

Perna, L, & Titus, M. A. (2005). The relationship between parental involvement as social capital and college enrollment: An examination of racial/ethnic group differences. *Journal of Higher Education, 76,* 485–518.

Sciarra, D. T., & Ambrosino, K. E. (2011). Post-secondary expectations and educational attainment. *Professional School Counseling, 14,* 231–241.

Sciarra, D. T., & Whitson, M. L. (2007). Predictive factors in postsecondary educational attainment among Latinos. *Professional School Counseling, 10,* 307–316.

Smith, W. L., & Zhang, P. (2009). Students' perceptions and experiences with key factors during the transition from high school to college. *College Student Journal, 43,* 643–657.

Tang, M., Pan, W., & Newmeyer, M. (2008). Factors influencing high school students' career aspirations. *Professional School Counseling, 11,* 285–295.

Torrez, N. (2004). Developing parent information frameworks that support college preparation for Latino students. *High School Journal, 87,* 54–59.

Trusty, J., & Niles, S. G. (2003). High-school math courses and completion of the bachelor's degree. *Professional School Counseling, 7,* 99–107.

Trusty, J., & Niles, S. G. (2004). Realized potential or lost talent: High school variables and bachelor's degree completion. *Career Development Quarterly, 53,* 2–15.

Turner, S. L., & Ziebell, J. L. C. (2011). The career beliefs of inner-city adolescents. *Professional School Counseling, 15,* 1–14.

7

Annual College and Career Readiness Planning Solutions

"Good school counselors have keen insight into which students (including which groups of students) are on a dead-end path, which students are en route to a solid high school education that will produce real choices, and which students are somewhere in between" (Hines, Lemons, & Crews, 2011, p. 2). This quote from *Poised to Lead: How School Counselors Can Drive College and Career Readiness*, asserts that school counselors are key players in assisting all students to reach their college and career dreams. Moreover, the American School Counselor Association (ASCA) student standards academic domain (ASCA, 2012; Campbell & Dahir, 1997) outlined the school counselor's proactive role in linking academics to the world of college and work in three standards:

Standard 1: Students will acquire the attitudes, knowledge and skills that contribute to effective learning in school and across the life span.

Standard 2: Students will complete school with the academic preparation essential to choose from a wide range of substantial postsecondary options, including college.

Standard 3: Students will understand the relationship of academics to the world of work and to life at home and in the community.

By strategically collecting, analyzing, and distributing data, school counselors become ambassadors of academic rigor helping all students reach their optimal career and college goals (ASCA, 2012; Hines et al., 2011). This chapter, aligned with the second component of the eight National Office for School Counselor Advocacy (NOSCA) college and career readiness counseling components (NOSCA, 2010), Academic Planning for College and Career Readiness, outlines what types of academic planning interventions are effective, why academic challenge is important, how to advocate for academic rigor, and what types of data are needed to help school counselors become college and career readiness champions for all students. Lastly, website resources for both academic planning for college and career readiness and for transitions from high school to college (the eighth NOSCA component) are also included.

Key Words

Carnegie Unit: A measure for the amount of time a student has studied a subject. Instruction that lasts 40–60 minutes 4–5 times a week, for 36–40 weeks, for a total of 120 hours annually, is one "unit" of high school credit.

College Knowledge: The ability to navigate the college search and application process

Core Academic Skills: Skills such as critical thinking, writing, and reading comprehension that transcend subject matter and allow students to be successful in a variety of fields

Free Application for Federal Student Aid (FAFSA): An application required by the federal government that determines the amount of federal financial assistance for which a student qualifies; used by many universities/colleges to determine scholarship and grant contributions.

Individual Student Planning: Ongoing systemic activities assisting the individual student in establishing personal goals and developing future plans, such as individual learning, graduation, and ACCESS/Accomplishments plans

Key Questions and Solutions

1. What types of academic planning interventions help students succeed after high school as successful world citizens?

In a study completed by research team Roderick, Nagoka, and Coca (2009), evidence for postsecondary success was determined by how well students were academically prepared and the coursework they completed. Specifically, they asserted that there are four key areas in which to focus skill development ensuring students are college ready: (1) content knowledge of specific subject areas; (2) "core academic skills" such as critical thinking and analysis; (3) executive functioning skills such as self-regulation, time management, and problem solving; and (4) "college knowledge" comprising of an understanding of how to navigate all facets of the college search and application process.

School counselors can be instrumental in all four areas. Specifically, they help all students gain access to advanced coursework and provide tutoring referrals and academic resources to be successful. School counselors must meet annually with all students to ensure that they understand their course choices, the value of challenging courses, and how courses relate to their specific career goals. Moreover, school counselors must be vigilant about assisting students with obtaining academic assistance either through school-sponsored academic tutoring and interventions or via community resources.

School counseling core curriculum should include both classroom instruction and group activities (ASCA, 2012) targeted at linking students' academics with their future career and college goals. Beginning early in a child's career, school counselors should present lessons centered on self-knowledge related to skills, interests, values, and learning styles. Small-group activities can complement these lessons and offer opportunities to visit colleges and career/technology centers. In order for students to navigate successfully the college search and application process, school counselors should provide learning and information sessions for parents/guardians as well. Part of these workshops should include hands-on instructions regarding completing the FAFSA and the financial aid process. Researchers found that students who had been accepted to a four-year institution and completed the FAFSA were 50% more likely to actually enroll in the institution than students who had been accepted but not completed the FAFSA (Roderick et al., 2009), making this a crucial component in school counselors' college-planning efforts.

2. With academic challenge among the most important factors in student academic success, how can school counselors convey this to all stakeholders?

Research indicates that adding just one Carnegie unit (i.e., 120 hours of course time) in intensive math more than doubles the likelihood of college completion (Trusty, 2004). Thus, it becomes incumbent upon school counselors to share the importance of academic challenge as it relates to future college success. Moreover, school counselors must be advocates for all students to have equitable access to rigorous course curriculum (College Board, 2010; Hatch, 2012). Therefore, this information must be shared routinely with students, parents, and teachers. Using all means possible, school counselors can share the value of challenging AP, IB, and honors courses while delivering classroom instruction via the school counseling program web page and through electronic and hard copy school counseling program newsletters to parents and students. Moreover, this topic should be discussed during teacher professional development days and departmental meetings. School counselors should work with department chairs to review the criteria for entrance into college preparatory classes and ensure entrance into these courses does not discriminate as historically fewer students of color, bilingual students, poor and working class students, and students with disabilities have had access to challenging courses in public schools.

3. In budget-challenged times, how do school counselors advocate for more honors, AP, and IB classes K–12?

It is paramount that school counselors communicate the fact that "by 2018, two-thirds (63%) of all jobs, and 90% of the higher paying jobs will require postsecondary education" (West Virginia Community and Technical College System, 2013) to all stakeholders. Therefore, advocating for challenging AP, IB, and honors courses, where students learn the critical thinking skills necessary for postsecondary success, is a professional obligation rather than an option. School counselors must become ambassadors of this knowledge, helping others link the importance of rigor to the relevance it has on students' life chances (Conley, 2010; Murray, 2011). School counselors can help interpret standardized test scores to advocate for students who may have been placed in lower-level courses so as to advance these students to courses commensurate with their skill level. To assist children and adolescents with increased academic expectations, school counselors should partner with department chairs and advanced upper-grade students to tutor and mentor students with this transition. Moreover, partnering with community agencies and local colleges to broker tutoring services is also advisable. School counselors cannot only help students get into challenging courses; they must ensure enough support to help them succeed.

4. What data do school counselors collect to advocate advanced coursework for all students?

Historically, not all students have had equal access to AP, IB, and honors courses. The Education Trust cites research demonstrating that

African Americans, Latinos, and Native Americans are less likely to be enrolled in college preparatory courses. For example, in 2003, only 22% of Latino students were enrolled in a full college prep track as compared to 39% of their White peers. To compound this issue, low-income students are less likely to attend schools that offer advanced-level math courses. Yet, children who successfully complete rigorous coursework will be successful in postsecondary education (Adelman, 2006; Greene, 2003). Therefore, school counselors must collect data that promotes challenging academic course planning for all students with necessary supports. Helpful data elements include the following:

- Advanced course enrollment and completion patterns (IB, AP, honors) disaggregated by race/ethnicity, free and reduced lunch status, language status, gender, and ability
- AP potential (see the free web-based research tool designed to help identify students likely to be successful in AP courses who may have been overlooked: http://professionals.collegeboard .com/k-12/prepare/appotential)
- State proficiency test scores disaggregated by race/ethnicity, free and reduced lunch status, language status, gender, and ability
- Departmental restrictions and guidelines that determine entrance into AP, IB, and honors courses
- College entrance exam scores (ACT/SAT) disaggregated by race/ethnicity, free and reduced lunch status, language status, gender, and ability
- Enrollment and completion patterns of two-year, four-year, and career/technical schools disaggregated by race/ethnicity, free and reduced lunch status, language status, gender, and ability
- Courses taught by highly qualified teachers

The data garnered from these indicators helps school counselors and other leaders paint a clear picture of who is succeeding in a school and who is not. Armed with this data, school counselors can begin to advocate for equitable access to challenging coursework for all students and the increased probability of students' future success.

5. How can school counselors prepare students for career and college readiness in academic planning and transitions from elementary to middle school, middle to high school, and high school to college/career/technical programs?

The Education Trust's motto, "College Begins in Kindergarten," is an excellent reminder that college and career readiness planning should start early in elementary school for all stakeholders—students, their families, teachers, and led by school counselors. NOSCA's (2010) eight career and college readiness components promote academic planning as a critical element for college and career success. They differentiate planning at all grade levels in three separate guides for school counselors—elementary, middle, and high school. But school counselors cannot do this work alone. All educators and family members need to have regular conversations with every student, starting in elementary school, about what it takes to reach one's career and college dreams via academic planning.

The dialogue has to begin early. Helping students make connections between their academic courses and enrichment are key to the future in terms of college and career majors. The ASCA Student Standards in the academic domain include this as a key competency for K–12 students (ASCA, 2012; Campbell & Dahir, 1997). While most people change college majors at least once, it is better for entering college students to have a strong idea of two or three top career clusters to help ensure attendance at a college with strong academic programs in each career cluster rather than a specific major. This can help with college choices early on so that students who may change their mind do not have to transfer to another college because their first choice did not offer other majors in which they were interested.

At the same time, school counselors need to access disaggregated data for schools to discover which students struggle with grades and social skills between elementary and middle school as well as between middle and high school. Then, school counselors need to look at the percentage of students who are graduating from high school, who are admitted to two-year and four-year colleges, and who go on to work or are unemployed or opt for the military, peace-making, or volunteer experiences or gap years. By examining these trends, school counselors can begin to make a difference in helping students make a smooth and sustainable transition into their next phase of life. This can be accomplished by creating school counseling curriculum lessons, sharpening annual planning tools like ACCESS/Accomplishments Plans (Chen-Hayes, 2013), and creating activities to foster assistance with transitions for students and families (see Figure 7.1).

6. How do school counselors use planning to lead and advocate for career and college readiness for our underserved students?

One of the benefits of technology is that anyone with a computer or smartphone access now has at their fingertips highly sophisticated planning tools for college and career access. Some of the best planning sites now not only offer in-depth college and career planning information but target sixth graders and up so students can check in annually to see exactly what they need to reach their future goals. In addition, many sites now offer engaging videos and digital recordings of culturally and linguistically diverse students sharing their experiences in college admissions and college life. The combination of strong planning sites that are free and realistic videos that reflect the diversity of today's K–12 and tomorrow's college population is shaping the future. Some of the best planning websites include *You Can Go, Big Future,* and *My Way* from the College Board, and *Know How to Go, You Can Go,* and *Big Future* focus videos on nontraditional students who are often first-generation college-goers. School counselors need to be structuring and monitoring use of websites with regular planning sessions and school counseling core curriculum lessons with students to keep the momentum going and help facilitate students' decision-making process throughout their entire academic career.

But what about families that don't have access to digital resources at home? School counselors can advocate "digital drop-in" hours or host events at school, the local library, or a community center so that students and family members can connect digitally to important school, academic, and college/career readiness information. Finally, it is critical to predict bumps in the road between the end of high school and the beginning of college. Many first-generation students encounter difficulties between the end of senior year and the start of college and school counselors must prepare them for how to be resilient and deal with the challenges in the summer before high school. School counselors can do this by having (paid) summer office hours and by connecting students to college student affairs offices and personnel over the summer that can smooth the transition between high school and college.

Various schools monitor planning data in different ways. Many states now require some form of career/college planning to be conducted annually by school counselors, but it is voluntary in most states, with little accountability to guarantee every student has an annual plan monitored beyond the individual school counselor or school counseling program. Yet waiting until high school is too late. Commercial programs like Naviance, in schools that can afford the program, have the capability of tracking some opportunity gap data, but school counselors have to use the program in an equity-focused manner. Too often it is a tool for competitive college admission and the career and college planning tools within it are not necessarily monitored to see which students are accessing them and which ones are not. Many districts have not been able to afford Naviance, but all students should have annual access to academic, career, college readinesss, and personal/social planning with a school counselor (Chen-Hayes, 2013). ACCESS/Accomplishments Plans (Chen-Hayes, 2013; see Figure 7.1) were developed as a key planning tool to help every K–12 student with their academic, career, college readiness, and personal/social goals and opportunities starting in kindergarten. Annual updates help to focus students on specific opportunity and attainment goals at elementary, middle, and high school levels, and language of the tools can be adjusted for younger elementary students (see Figure 7.1).

Figure 7.1   ACCESS and Accomplishments Plans

The ACCESS Plan: Goal-Setting to Reach Your Dreams!

The ACCESS Plan is used for K–12 student goal setting and includes topics from the American School Counselor Association (ASCA) nine Student Standards (academic, career, personal/social competencies) and the National Office for School Counselor Advocacy (NOSCA) eight College and Career Readiness Counseling Components.

Name:_____

Date: _____

Grade: K 1 2 3 4 5 6 7 8 9 10 11 12

Directions: Write or circle the appropriate letter for your responses under the question. Update your answers anytime with your school counselor, parent/guardian, teachers, and other important persons in your life.

1. What three things will you do this semester to improve academic skills?

    A.

    B.

    C.

2. What are the most challenging classes you can take to reach your career and college dreams?

3. How will challenging math, science, literacy, history, world language, and arts classes prepare you for your career and college dreams?

4. What three careers/jobs would you like?

    A.

    B.

    C.

5. To succeed in the three careers/jobs (from Question 4), what college/postsecondary education is needed?

    A.

    B.

    C.

(Continued)

Figure 7.1 Continued

6. To find a great career and college major, what are your greatest strengths, interests, and talents?

7. Who helps you think about graduating from college/postsecondary education?

   A. Parent/guardian

   B. Teachers

   C. School/college counselors

   D. Friends

   E. Siblings/other family members

   F. Clergy at place of worship

   G. Coaches

   H. Extracurricular activity leaders

   I. College visit representatives

   J. College fair representatives

   K. Other:_____

8. What can you do in school to reach your career and college dreams?

   A. Take the most rigorous courses (honors, AP, IB, college-preparatory) in high school.

   B. Research different careers and colleges early, as well as specific requirements for admission test scores, grades, required courses, activities.

   C. Develop a plan to pay for college with the least amount of debt for you and your family.

   D. Participate in depth in one or two extracurricular activities.

   E. Study or show fluency in at least one world language in addition to English.

   F. Participate in regular community service to make a difference and care for others.

   G. Participate in one or two arts programs at school and/or as extracurricular activities.

   H. Participate in depth in at least one sport or athletic activity.

   I. Know the particular hooks (legacy, athletics, special talents, cultural identities, etc.) that may increase college admissions at selective schools.

Figure 7.1

J. Update your ACCESS/Accomplishments plan annually with your school counselor, teacher, or parent/guardian.

9. What arts, extracurricular activities, leadership, sports, travel, and community service can you do to help reach your career and college dreams?

10. How will you explore careers and colleges to find the best fit?

   A. Explore possible college majors offered by various colleges and possible careers/jobs.

   B. Job-shadow someone.

   C. Attend a career/college fair.

   D. Visit potential colleges online via virtual tours or in person on campus tours.

   E. Understand admission requirements including applications, deadlines, essays, exams, recommendations, selectivity (from open admissions to highly selective), and transcripts.

   F. Understand different admission policies: early action, early decision, regular, and rolling admissions.

   G. Understand affordability and compare financial aid packages and non-loan support for the entire duration of your college experience.

   H. Consider geography: commuter school, living on campus, urban, suburban, rural, in-state, out-of-state, or international.

   I. Consider social life and student activities: residence halls, Greek life, athletics, student clubs, multicultural environment, arts opportunities, spirituality/religion.

   J. Consider size: Small (1,000 students or less), medium (1,000–5,000 students), large (5,000–10,000 students), or very large (10,000 or more students).

   K. Consider student supports: academic support/tutoring, counseling services, disability services, health services, media/library/technology services, and multicultural and LBGTIQ services.

   L. Consider type of college: two-year community, four-year public, four-year private not-for-profit, four-year private for-profit, or trade/technical/career school.

   M. Consider emphasis and mission of diverse colleges: career, liberal arts, research, and/or teaching.

(Continued)

Figure 7.1 Continued

11. What assessments (tests) will you need in middle or high school to reach your career and college dreams?

   A. Career Key

   B. Self-Directed Search

   C. Strong Interest Inventory

   D. Myers-Briggs Type Indicator

   E. ASPIRE (assessing K–12 learning)

   F. EXPLORE (eighth and ninth grades)

   G. PLAN (sophomores)

   H. ACT (juniors)

   I. PSAT (sophomores)

   J. SAT (juniors)

   K. SAT subject exams (high school)

   L. AP (Advanced Placement) course exams (high school)

   M. IB (International Baccalaureate) Diploma course exams (juniors and seniors)

   N. CLEP (College Level Examination Program)

   O. TOEFL (English language skills)

   P. Other:_____

12. How will you afford education for your career and college dreams with little or no debt for you and your family?

   A. Grants

   B. Scholarships

   C. Savings

   D. Expected family contribution

   E. Work-study

   F. Federal loans

   G. Other:_____

13. What will transitions be like for you between high school and college/career, and how can you prepare for bumps in the road that might block your college/career dreams?

Figure 7.1

14. How do you respect yourself and your cultural identities/languages, and how do you respect people with different cultures/languages?

15. What are your academic, career/college, and personal/social goals for the year and how will this affect career and college decisions?

16. How do you stay safe and keep others safe inside and outside of school including no bullying or violence in person and in cyberspace?

17. What else can you write about your academic, career/college, and personal/social goals for this semester?

The Accomplishments Plan: Making Dreams Come True

The Accomplishments Plan is used for K–12 student college and career planning and provides reflection for essays and recommendations for academic, career, and college goals.

Name:_____

Date:_____

Grade: K 1 2 3 4 5 6 7 8 9 10 11 12

Directions: Write an answer or circle the appropriate letter(s) for your responses under the question. Update your answers anytime in discussions with your school counselor, parent/guardian, teachers, and other important persons in your life.

1. What makes you unique?

2. What are your hobbies?

3. What are your three best personal qualities?

    A.

    B.

    C.

4. What are your chores at home?

5. What are your sports/athletics?

6. What are your arts activities?

    A. Animation/illustration/cartooning

    B. Band/orchestra/instrument: _____

(Continued)

Figure 7.1 Continued

C. Chorus/singing

D. Crafts

E. Creative writing

F. Dance

G. Graphic/web design

H. Painting

I. Photography

J. Theater

K. Other: _____

7. What are your extracurricular activities?

8. What are your after-school jobs?

9. What are your community service projects?

10. What languages do you speak and read?

11. What are your experiences with diverse cultures and international travel/study?

12. What are your leadership positions?

13. What awards/honors have you received?

14. What, if any, are your activities at a place of worship?

15. What are your three favorite academic subjects?

A.

B.

C.

16. What are your three top career/job choices?

A.

B.

C.

17. What are your three top potential college majors?

A.

B.

C.

Figure 7.1

18. What are your three top college choices and why?

   A.

   B.

   C.

19. Which adults would write the best recommendation letters for your academic/college/career dreams?

20. What do you want teachers/school counselors to say about you and your academic/career/college goals in your recommendation letters?

21. How would you summarize your academic, career, and college readiness accomplishments in one sentence?

Source: Chen-Hayes (2013).

Solution Success Stories

Story 1

Danielle, a K–8 school counselor in the mid-Atlantic region, developed a concept called Career Café in which students are invited in small groups to hear community-based speakers on various careers during their lunch times. Danielle begins by targeting a specific grade level or group of students and assesses their career interests. After determining the primary interests, she recruits one or more speakers from related fields. Students receive a special invitation to come to a location during their lunch time for the Career Café, usually the library, media center, a classroom, or other space that can accommodate up to 30 students. Students bring their lunches and engage with the guests, who discuss their unique careers and answer questions. See the Career Café at www .schcounselor.com/2011/03/career-Café.html.

Story 2

Dustin, a counselor in a midwestern suburban high school, tells of working with a student, Katie, for four years. "Every year I met with her numerous times each semester to cover academics and grades," he says. "We talked about her study skills and set realistic short- and long-term goals to monitor her success.

(Continued)

(Continued)

As we neared her junior year, she was very confused on whether she wanted (or could afford) to attend higher education. During our conversations, I discovered she was living with her sister and had no communication with her mother. I realized then that I needed to advocate for Katie and contacted our district homeless liaison and assistant principal. We were able to declare Katie homeless and emancipated her from her mother. We worked together to help find her employment to help her make money and provide her transportation.

"Through our core curriculum on careers, we were able to narrow possible career paths. She stated in our last sophomore-year meeting that she might want to pursue a career in the medical field or business, so for registration for junior year, we signed her up for numerous electives to help her narrow her career path. We selected college accounting, psychology, human growth and development, and chemistry. After junior year, we were able to view grades and talk about ups and downs of each class. I recommended [she] attend some of our career treks (career field trips) in the business and medical field[s]. After numerous conversations about course selection, core curriculum presentations, and setting goals, Katie decided to attend a state university [to study] business focusing on accounting. I assisted her in the application process and helped her identify a major by relying on our conversations and work on course selection and career treks.

"After deciding which school she wanted to go to, we helped her apply for admission and financial aid. Once her application and financial aid were approved, the counseling department took up a collection so that we could help her purchase the essentials for her to take to school. Start to finish, we worked on a plan to identify a school, help her apply, and find her the means to be able to attend the school of her choice. She just finished her first semester and earned all As and Bs, making a quick connection with her Accounting 101 teacher. She wants to pursue an internship during second semester and [is] really excited to return back to school after winter break. I believe through working with her on course selection, our core curriculum on careers, and social/emotional support, Katie was able to be successful and will be a great member [of] the business community."

Story 3

New York City school counselor educator Stuart Chen-Hayes created a planning tool to help all school counselors close opportunity and future attainment gaps, especially with elementary and middle school students and more intensively with high school freshmen and sophomores. Every school counselor is mandated by the ASCA ethical code (ASCA, 2010) to provide annual planning for every student. ACCESS/Accomplishments Plans (Chen-Hayes, 2013) help students annually develop and modify goals and share achievements on their

(Continued)

academic, career/college readiness, and personal/social journeys. The ACCESS Plan questions include the nine core ASCA Student Standards (Campbell & Dahir, 1997) and eight NOSCA career and college access competencies (NOSCA, 2010). The Accomplishments Plan is like a brag sheet, but why wait until high school to have students focus on their interests, talents, extracurricular activities, service, and leadership? It makes more sense to start in elementary school to build college and career aspirations. Over the last few years, many CUNY Lehman College graduate students and alumni have used ACCESS/ Accomplishments Plans or modified versions for younger students to help close opportunity gaps in K–12 schools in metro New York City, particularly in schools with challenged budgets and large caseloads of poor and working-class students of color with little access to career and college planning.

Resources

Digital

(NOSCA 2) Academic Planning for College and Career Readiness

The Algebra Project (mathematics as an organizing tool for quality public school education): www.algebra.org

Bright Outlook (occupations expected to grow rapidly in the near future with large numbers of job openings and/or new/emerging fields): www.onetonline.org/find/bright?b=0&g=Go

Career Cluster Search (discover occupational interests and then focus education plan on a career pathway): www.onetonline.org/find/career?c=0&g=Go

Career Key (research-based career and college major information and assessments): www.careerkey.org

Center for the Study of Race and Equity in Education: www.gse.upenn.edu/equity

College Advising Guide for Undocumented Students (NACAC): www.nacacnet.org/research/KnowledgeCenter/Pages/View-by-Subject.aspx?MetaTopic=Undocumented%20Students

College Board: www.collegeboard.org

College Majors 101: www.collegemajors101.com

College Partnerships and Articulation Agreements (transfer-student transitions between two-year community and four-year colleges): www.finaid.org/otheraid/partnerships.phtml

College Planning for Students With Disabilities: www.educationquest.org/swd.asp

College Prep Calendar: Grades 9–12 (NACAC): www.nacacnet.org

Common Core State Standards Initiative (preparing all students for college and careers): www.corestandards.org

Counseling for all students: A response to the Chicago Tribune: http://myisca.blogspot.com/2012/12/counseling-for-all-students-response-to.html

Early College High School Initiative (motivating students by compressing time to complete a high school diploma and first two years of college): www.earlycolleges.org

Employment Projections (information about the USA labor market 10 years in advance): www.bls.gov/emp/home.htm

Graduation Plans (Indiana's academic, career, and college planning docs required for grades 6–12): www.learnmoreindiana.org/K12academics/Requirements/Pages/GradPlan.aspx

High-Quality Decision Making (ACIP model: alternatives, consequences, information, plans): www.careerkey.org/asp/your_decision/high_quality_decisions.html

International Baccalaureate (English, español, français): www.ibo.org

My Child's Future (career development and educational/college planning for K–12 parents and guardians): www.mychildsfuture.org/parents/item.htm?id=0

My Road (College Board career and college planning website): https://myroad.collegeboard.com/myroad/navigator.jsp

Naviance (online course, college, and career planning): www.naviance.com/about

NCAA (National College Athletic Association) Clearinghouse/Eligibility Center: web1.ncaa.org/ECWR2/NCAA_EMS/NCAA.jsp

NOSCA's Eight Components of College and Career Readiness Counseling: www.collegeboard.org/nosca

NOSCA's Own the Turf College Readiness Toolkit: www.collegeboard.org/nosca

Plans of Study (16 career clusters and pathways for student academic course selection in high school and beyond): www.careertech.org/career-clusters/resources/

(NOSCA 8) Transition from High School Graduation to College Enrollment

Campus Compact: www.compact.org

College Completion Agenda: http://completionagenda.collegeboard.org

College Unbound (using peer learning and authentic assessment to increase high school graduation rates for nontraditional college students): www.collegeunbound.org

First in the Family—Your College Years (audio slideshows for first-generation college students transitioning from high school): www.firstinthefamily.org/collegeyears/index.html

First in the Family—Your High School Years (resources on college from first-generation college students): www.firstinthefamily.org/high school/Introduction.html

Gateway to College (empowering high school dropouts and graduation-in-doubt students to earn college diplomas and dual credit): www.gatewaytocollege.org/home.asp

National Academic Advising Association (NACADA): www.nacada.ksu.edu/

National Institute for Learning Outcomes Assessment: www.learning outcomesassessment.org

National Institute for the Study of Transfer Students: http://blog.northgeorgia.edu/transferinstitute

National Survey of Student Engagement (annual report of undergraduates' college experience, benefits, and use of time): http://nsse.iub.edu

StudentTracker for High Schools (Program for high schools to monitor opportunity and attainment gaps based on where students go to college, if they graduate, and how long it takes): www.student clearinghouse.org/high_schools/studenttracker/

Young Men of Color Initiative (Improving educational participation and college completion for young men of color): http://advocacy.collegeboard.org/college-preparation-access/young-men-color-initiative and http://youngmenofcolor.collegeboard.org

Print

College Board. (2012). *College counseling sourcebook: Advice and strategies from school counselors* (7th ed.). New York, NY: Author.

Hines, P., Lemons, R., & Crews, K. (2011). *Poised to lead: How school counselors can drive college and career readiness.* Washington, DC: National Center for Transforming School Counseling.

National Association of College Admission Counseling. (2012). *Fundamentals of college admission counseling* (3rd ed.). Arlington, VA: Author.

Savitz-Romer, M., & Bouffard, S. (2012). *Ready, willing, and able: A developmental approach to college access and success.* MA: Harvard University Educational Press.

8

School-Family-Community Partnership Solutions

School counselors and other school leaders cannot work in isolation to address the multitude of needs facing students. Thus, they must invest time and energy into building mutually beneficial relationships with parents/guardians, caregivers, families, and the surrounding community. While some school counselors cite lack of time as a barrier to forming these relationships, overall school counselors endorse the efficacy of forming partnerships, especially those congruent with their perceived roles and responsibilities (Bryan & Holcomb-McCoy, 2007).

Joyce Epstein, a leader in building school-family-community partnerships, cites many reasons to develop and maintain them, including improved school climate, linking families to needed services, and helping children and adolescents succeed in life and the world of work (Epstein, 1995; Epstein & Associates, 2009). To develop and maintain school-family-community partnerships, school counselors must be strategic in engaging and partnering with others. When working with community agencies and businesses, school counselors must assess both the strengths and needs of their school and how the strengths of those around them can bolster assets and mitigate needs. Bryan and Henry (2008) endorsed two essentials to building a strengths-based partnership: (1) recognize and affirm the strengths inherent in children, their families, and communities regardless of their background, and (2) utilize the strengths in the school, families, and community to create assets, resources, and supports that empower children (p. 150).

Thus, school counselors must first build a personal relationship with community agencies, one based on mutual trust and respect. Doing so allows for school counselors to confidently make a referral to a student, parent/guardian/caregiver, or staff member with the understanding that quality assistance will be received. Conversely, should a student, staff member, or parent/guardian/caregiver be met with a negative referral experience, the school counselor's credibility may be harmed. Making time to visit agencies; learning names of specific points of contact; knowing specifics of the programs offered, fee structures and affordable transportation, and knowing whether or not multiple languages are spoken or translators are available are all important components of working collaboratively and effectively with community partners. As such, school counselors should create community maps either in print or digital formats. These maps highlight mental health, after-school and educational programs, medical facilities, businesses and industries, and legislative offices (see Figure 8.1). At the beginning of the school year, school counselors can update their community maps with new contacts and helpful local agencies.

In challenging times and in a culture that is often not family friendly nor open to family diversity, with few safety nets for new parents/guardians, concerns over health, illness, and disability in families, and constant struggles in assisting younger and older generations, school-family-community partnerships are a critical source of supporting student success. School counselors also must be allies and aware of "the new normal" of family diversity and the complexity

Figure 8.1   Community Mapping

Community Mapping can be done online by using Google Maps and pairing it with a free website platform like http://weebly.com. As seen in the screenshots below, schools can locate agencies in distinct categories (legislative offices, after-school/educational services, religious/spiritual institutions, physical health, social/emotional health, and business and industries).

On the website, clicking on the color-coded tacks displays the agencies with contact information, brief descriptions, and links to their web pages. Because this site is online and free, it's accessible to the entire school community and can be modified and updated at any point during the academic year.

Figure 8.1

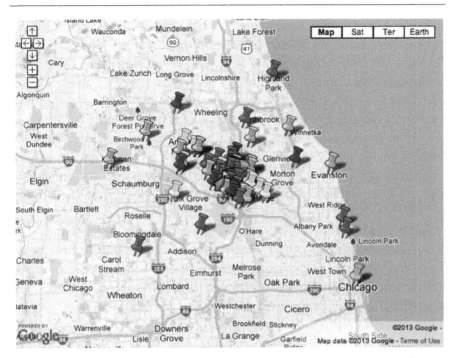

AFTER SCHOOL/EDUCATIONAL SERVICES

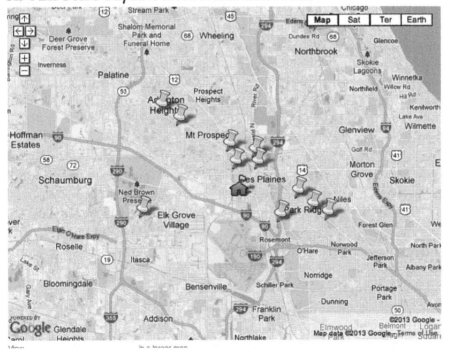

of *family process* or quality of relationships between family members (Solomon, 2012; Walsh, 2012). The model of a two-parent, heterosexual, married couple with one parent staying at home with children is not the average family. However, schools are often built around the inaccurate assumption that one parent will be home or volunteer during the day or that parent/guardian working hours fit the school day. Part of the school counselor's role is to challenge *familyism* (Chen-Hayes, 2009; Holcomb-McCoy & Chen-Hayes, in press)—the idea that traditional family types are best or should receive the greatest access to resources in schools. Instead of focusing on one family type as optimal, school counselors need to affirm the diversity of families as a strength. School counselors can help students find resiliency in their own family types and build strengths in relationships with their own and other diverse family structures, family members, and multiple systems outside the family, including school staff (Solomon, 2012; Walsh, 2012).

From an extended *family life cycle* perspective (McGoldrick, Carter, & Garcia-Prieto, 2011), over the course of a family life cycle, there are normative and unexpected interruptions or stressors experienced by all family members, and school counselors can assist families to normalize the stressors. *Horizontal stressors* occur as predictable transitions over the life cycle (births, marriages, divorces, deaths) and as unexpected events (accidents, disabilities, illnesses, sudden death). *Vertical stressors* include long-standing family patterns such as legacies, myths, secrets, and patterns that influence family processes. School counselors need to have both short-term and long-term group counseling and developmental school counseling core curriculum lessons to address competencies for students dealing with family loss issues, including divorce, death, illness, and disability, as well as family diversity issues such as children of LBGTIQ parents, mixed-race families, single-parent families, adoption and foster-care families, grandparents raising grandchildren, and homeless families. Another key concept for school counselors is the family life cycle and the various stages and developmental tasks that families go through, although they are not necessarily linear (McGoldrick et al., 2011). School counselors benefit from working with students and their families with an understanding of the constant tasks and challenges for each student/family member in the family life cycle: family of origin, leaving home/single adult, dating, coupling/marriage/partnership, parenting young children, parenting adolescents, launching adolescents, and later life (McGoldrick et al., 2011).

Working with parents, guardians, and caregivers also requires special attention, particularly when working with adults who have suffered negative experiences with schools themselves. This chapter will help school counselors understand the theory behind school-family-community partnerships and how best to create them. It offers solutions and ideas for bridging gaps and for building mutually beneficial and synergistic relationships among all parties to benefit all students. The chapter concludes with a list of digital and print resources for empowering diverse family types.

Key Words

Community: A group comprising familial, social, religious, occupational, business, and legislative entities surrounding a school; a sense of belonging to something larger or greater than oneself

Epstein's School-Family–Community-Partnership Model: There are six different types of involvement that promote collaborative relationships: (1) parenting; (2) communicating; (3) volunteering; (4) learning at home; (5) decision-making; and (6) collaboration with the community

Family: The roles and relationships of a domestic unit of people connected by birth, marriage or other legal commitments, or in spirit

Family Life Cycle: The developmental stages over time that include normative tasks whose successful resolution indicates greater likelihood of success in future stages; stages are not necessarily linear and don't necessarily apply to all persons or families

Family Process: The type and quality of roles and relationships between family members that affect family functioning

Family Resilience: Strengths-based perspective on working to build family patterns, interactions, and relationships for optimal functioning

Family System: A unit with complex interactions or processes and subsystems (parental, sibling, child) that mediate interactions between members of the system

Familyism: Prejudice multiplied by power used by persons from traditional family types to deny individual, cultural, and systemic resources based on nondominant family type (single, single-parent, same-gender, multiracial, homeless, adoptive, foster, divorced)

Horizontal and Vertical Stressors: Predictable transitions over the life cycle (births, marriages, divorces, deaths) and unexpected events (accidents, disabilities, illnesses, sudden death); vertical stressors include long-standing family patterns such as legacies, myths, secrets, and patterns that influence family processes

Partnership: Collaborative work on the part of people or institutions to meet a common goal

Key Questions and Solutions

1. How can school counselors use school-family-community partnerships to engage parents and guardians?

Epstein (1987) introduced a model of school-family-community partnerships that placed the child at the center, believing that these partnerships enhance children's success and play an integral role in shaping their future life chances (Epstein, 1995; Epstein & Associates, 2009). Through her research, Epstein formulated a theory of *overlapping spheres of influence*—home, school, and community—that intersect and have the ability to form positive results for students. Within these spheres, Epstein developed six different types of involvement to promote school-family-community partnerships: (1) parenting; (2) communicating; (3) volunteering; (4) learning at home; (5) decision making; and (6) collaborating with the community (Epstein, 1987, 1995; Epstein & Associates, 2009; Epstein & Van Voorhis, 2010).

Griffin and Van Steen (2010) applied these six types of involvement to school counselor practices and added the category of *leadership and advocacy.* They noted that much of the collaborative work school counselors do requires leadership and advocacy skills versus simple participation or coordination. Given that the ASCA National Model (American School Counselor Association, 2012), the NOSCA (2010) *Eight Essential Elements of College and Career Counseling,* and the Transforming School Counseling Initiative (House & Sears, 2002) call for these skill sets, school counselors can harness their leadership and advocacy roles into spearheading and developing collaborative programs and supporting these programs through the use of data (Griffin & Van Steen, 2010).

2. How do school counselors involve parents/guardians who have negative experiences with schools and parents/guardians who experience difficulty attending school events?

Previous negative experiences within educational settings, inconvenient times of scheduled school events, transportation, poor communication between the school and home, disparate parent-teacher expectations, and child care issues create barriers to parental involvement in schools. Thus, forming collaborative partnerships with parents has been difficult in many urban settings (Bryan, 2005; Perry, 2000). According to Bryan (2005), schools must undergo a paradigm shift whereby parents are seen as "valuable resources and assets" and as having a "shared responsibility and equal capacity to contribute to the education of their children" (p. 222).

One way to help foster parent/guardian/caregiver ownership is to create and maintain a Parent Involvement Committee (Bryan & Henry, 2008) whereby parents/guardians/caregivers are part of a school-based committee charged with creating and implementing positive school programming. School counselors may also provide workshops for parents who are in need of education, GED, or job-placement skills. Home visits or neighborhood meetings may also be appropriate when trying to bridge the gap between school and home (Epstein, 1995). The goal is to help parents/guardians/caregivers view the school as a resource and a place of assistance, thereby reversing past experiences and breaking the cycle of acrimonious relationships between the two.

3. What types of community agencies can school counselors partner with to promote academic achievement for all students?

Given that school counselors must be partners in ensuring academic achievement for all students (ASCA, 2010, 2012), they must look beyond the walls of the school for additional supports. Oftentimes, this comes in the form of after-school programming that provides homework help to students or tutoring agencies in the surrounding area. Local libraries often have quiet study spaces and after-school programming involving reading enhancement. It is also wise for school counselors to reach out to community supports such as the Urban League that could provide one-on-one mentoring and tutoring for students in need. As cited by Epstein and Van Voorhis (2010), one high school recruited teachers, parents, and college students to provide after-school math tutoring for ninth-grade students resulting in an 18% increase in math scores. Additionally, Sheldon (2003) found that urban low-income elementary schools that have established family and community partnerships and have worked to overcome barriers to involvement and shown increased scores on state-mandated achievement tests.

4. What community agencies can school counselors partner with to promote mental, emotional, and physical wellness for all students?

School counselors know that often what impedes academic success is related to nonacademic barriers. Therefore, it is imperative that school counselors help all students gain necessary supports in mental, emotional, and physical well-being. If a student has a persistent medical condition that goes undiagnosed or untreated, academic performance suffers. Given the shortage of school nurses in schools (often school nurses are asked to service multiple schools in one week), many students' health needs are not met. Thus, linking with local community health clinics and hospitals, dental and eye care offices, and immediate care centers is imperative. Strong connections with runaway and homeless shelters in the community are also necessary. Moreover, creating strong contacts with local utility companies (e.g., gas, electric) and housing authorities will also help serve families in need. Careful attention should be made to ensure sliding fee scales are offered and that bilingual service is provided when working with low-income students, students of color, and bilingual students.

Furthermore, students need physical outlets in which to play and practice sports and teamwork. Local park districts, YMCAs, and fitness centers may offer such programming. Given that the peak time for juvenile crime and experimentation with drugs, alcohol, and sexual behaviors (Snyder & Sickmund, 1999) is during after-school hours (3 pm–7 pm), linking students with healthy and productive after-school activities is an important initiative for school counselors.

In addition, connecting students with positive adult role models also provides a healthy alternative after school. There is much research to support the need for mentoring, especially among oppressed populations (Cunningham, 1999; Ford, 1995; Lee & Bailey, 1997). Reaching out to organizations that offer mentoring, such as Big Brothers, Big Sisters, the Urban League, 100 Black Men, and local community agencies can help meet this need.

Local businesses can also offer needed services, including legal aid, internships, employment opportunities, and donations (food, prizes, or incentives). Local grocery stores will often provide free or reduced baked goods, and pizza parlors may donate pizzas for small-group or after-school activities. School counselors should be vigilant about making connections with local businesses and parlaying their resources for the benefit of their students and families.

Given that school counselors have increasingly large and challenging caseloads, on average of 471 to 1 (ASCA, 2012), school counselors must refer serious or long-term mental and emotional/behavioral health concerns to outside mental health professionals or school-based health clinics. This means strong connections with various agencies, including those that specialize in addictions, mood disorders, abuse, and family counseling, are crucial. School counselors should obtain releases of information to allow them to confer with these professionals to support and maintain open lines of communication regarding ongoing treatment goals.

Some community agencies harness many of the community assets to help youth in the community. Tippecanoe Youth Center, run by school counselor DuShaun Goings, does just that:

Featured Community Organization: Tippecanoe Youth Center (TYC): This program targets at-promise and low-income families throughout Tippecanoe County in Indiana to provide afford-able after-school programming that includes computer programs, board games, educational video games, sports, and field trips through-out the county and state. This helps to build peer-relationship skills, appropriate social skills, and leadership skills to compete in the com-petitive technological world. TYC proudly joins this cause with pro-grams like the Boys and Girls Club to provide a safe haven for youth to stay clear from drugs, alcohol, and gangs. Two premier shuttle companies, Lafayette Limo and Air Coach Express Shuttle, share the same vision. Both companies provide transportation for students throughout Tippecanoe County at no cost indefinitely. Purdue University allows TYC to hire work-study students, and Purdue pays 70% of each worker's wage. Multiple Purdue student organizations will donate time and energy to help provide mentoring for youth dur-ing TYC's after-school programming as well.

---

5. What community agencies can school counselors partner with to promote college and career readiness for all students?

As demonstrated above, accessing local college and university resources can be instrumental for garnering academic success, finan-cial support, and exposure to college life. As many undergraduate education majors are looking for experiences working with children and may require service-learning or field experience hours, school counselors can work with them to form mutually beneficial partner-ships. Often colleges and universities provide summer bridge pro-gramming that offers orientation activities for incoming freshmen and/or summer camps designed to feature specific programs (e.g., computer technology, engineering, journalism) for interested stu-dents. For example, Northwestern University offers academically gifted pre-K through 12th graders a wide range of summer programming through its Center for Talent (www.ctd.northwestern.edu/summer/programs/). Schools can also apply to local community agencies, such as the Washington, DC-based College Bound Program (http://collegebound.publishpath.com), which provides free academic tutoring, mentoring, and enrichment programs geared toward college preparation for students in Grades 8–12.

There are a plethora of national not-for-profit and federally funded organizations that also work with underserved youth to provide access to postsecondary options. Perhaps the most known are the federally funded TRIO programs, eight programs that target low-income and first-generation college students with the goal of increased college completion rates. Another lauded national effort, the Advancement Via Individual Determination (AVID) program, "places academically average students in advanced classes and provides them with an elective class that prepares them to succeed in rigorous curricula, enter mainstream activities in school, and increase their opportunities to enroll in four-year colleges" (www.avid.org). Schools may link with higher educational institutions or state or local education agencies that have received funds from the federally funded Gaining Early Awareness and Readiness for Undergraduate Programs (GEAR UP), a six-year grant to assist low-income students access college (www2.ed.gov/programs/gearup/index.html).

By accessing research-based and proven national and local college readiness programs, school counselors can effectively link these programs to district and school improvement goals. Doing so will allow administrators to understand the value of investing time and energy to create and maintain these partnerships, resulting in increased graduation and college-going rates.

6. How can school counselors engage all parents and guardians in annual academic, career, college access, and personal/social planning with children and adolescents?

Not only must administrators understand how effective sequential academic and career planning can substantially increase students' life chances, so too must parents/guardians/caregivers. As discussed in Chapters 6 and 7, school counselors at all levels must be vigilant about individual annual planning and creating and implementing developmental academic, career/college, and personal/social lessons that link subject matter to relevant career and college goals. These messages must be conveyed to parents/guardians/caregivers in annual meetings that discuss the connection between academic rigor and college completion (Trusty, 2004). The College Board makes three specific recommendations: (1) parents are included in selection of children's courses; (2) districts develop methods to explain/reinforce the educational and postsecondary planning process to parents; and (3) schools assist parents in knowing what types of financial aid are available for postsecondary education (College Board, 2011b).

All parents/guardians/caregivers should know what Advanced Placement (AP) and International Baccalaureate (IB) classes are offered, why they are important, and how students can obtain extra academic support should they need it. Moreover, helping parents/caregivers understand that the most cited reason students give for dropping out is boredom (Metropolitan Life, 2002) will help to motivate and challenge them to engage in school and make connections between subject matter and real-life relevancy.

School counselors must also help parents/guardians/caregivers understand the financial aid process, the challenging FAFSA application, and scholarship opportunities. Effectively teaming with local college financial aid officers and local offices of College Board and ACT can help in creating and implementing workshops on and off school premises. Partnering with local libraries, universities, and community centers where parents/guardians/caregivers without computers can access them for free will help facilitate the college admissions and selection process.

Additionally, school counselors can ask for volunteers from the parent community (particularly alumni of the school) to discuss their current jobs and their academic preparation while addressing how they overcame barriers to their success. This can be particularly powerful if school counselors target parents/guardians/caregivers from traditionally underrepresented groups and those engaged in gender nontraditional careers (e.g., male nurses, female engineers) to help build self-efficacy among students (Savitz-Romer & Bouffard, 2012). That is, children need to have opportunities where they see other people who *look* like them be successful in careers that require advanced education. Parents can also serve as volunteer chaperones on college visits, assist other parents complete the FAFSA if they have successfully done so, and lend their unique talents (organization, technology, etc.) to the school counseling department's efforts. Actively engaging parents/guardians/caregivers to help create a college-going culture will help schools view parents as resources and parents view the school as a partner—with the common goal of help-ing children achieve their college and postsecondary dreams.

7. How do school counselors determine and implement the best means of regular communication with families and community partners?

Maintaining consistent and proactive communication with par-ents/guardians/caregivers is essential in creating mutually beneficial partnerships. Taking advantage of technology is a helpful and inex-pensive way to relay important information, deadlines, and upcom-ing events. Computer programs like Naviance allow school counselors to filter parent e-mails and send relevant information to them (e.g., an e-mail to all senior students' parents/guardians/caregivers). Also, school counselors should create a link to the school counseling department on the school web site. The school counseling depart-ment web page should introduce all school counselors, provide a calendar of upcoming events and counseling initiatives, and provide links to important events, registration, and resources, including col-lege and scholarship information. Additionally, school counselors can utilize newsletter templates (on programs such as Publisher) and dis-seminate monthly newsletters via e-mail and their web pages. In instances where many parents/guardians/caregivers lack access to computers, hard copies of these newsletters should be made available and sent home with school report cards and distributed during orien-tations and parent conference nights.

School counselors have also reported success with initiatives such as "Second Cup of Coffee," where elementary school counsel-ors have tables available during drop-off and pick-up times for children, whereby parents/guardians/caregivers can enjoy a com-plimentary cup of coffee and obtain information about the school counseling department as well as make a personal connection to school counselors in the building.

It is clear that school counselors cannot address the multitude of constantly evolving needs of children and their families by them-selves. Thus, school counselors must actively seek allies who bring different sets of skills and strengths to assist them. Serving as a hub of reliable local community resources and supports in and outside of the school walls will not only aid students but help convince others that school counselors care about the community in which they serve and are team players in the effort to help all kids be healthy, successful, and productive world citizens.

Solution Success Stories

Story 1

A school counseling intern named Sarah was working in a Columbus, Ohio, public high school that served a large African American and low-income population. She worked closely with a young sophomore girl who often came to school unkempt, in dirty, ill-fitting clothing. Embodying the new vision for school counselors (Education Trust, 2003) and the ASCA National Model (ASCA, 2012), Sarah thought about how she might help not only her student but other students in the school who exhibited these needs. Discussing possibilities with the counseling staff, she decided to initiate the Clothing Closet to be housed in an unused storage closet in the school. Starting first within the school, she collaborated with the school nurse, who was able to solicit companies for free samples of hygienic products (including feminine hygiene, soap, deodorant, etc.) to offer to students. She then created a "spring cleaning" campaign among teachers and staff, encouraging them to donate gently used clean clothing. She then contacted a local department store and was able to obtain old clothing racks and a local dry cleaner that donated hangers. Soon, she had a fully functioning clothing closet where students could "shop" during their free period or during lunch and also obtain hygiene products. Because the school was heavily inundated with gangs, wearing the color red (a color associated with the gangs) was strictly prohibited. Prior to Clothing Closet, students were sent home if they violated this code. The Clothing Closet, however, allowed violators of the code to change their clothing and remain in school. During the spring, staff and teachers were encouraged to bring in old prom and bridesmaid dresses, along with shoes, jewelry, and purses. A prom dress campaign was a huge success, and several female students who would have struggled to pay for the expense of the prom were able to obtain clothing and accessories free of charge. Within six months, over 40 students had used the Clothing Closet. This is a prime example of how one person can broker the services of the school and local community to better serve many students' needs and make a positive difference.

Story 2

A middle school in the South received a number of students from Louisiana after Hurricane Katrina in 2005. Most of these students arrived with their families and little else. Damaris, the counselor, worked together with the school social worker and volunteers from the PTA to turn an unused portable building on the school's campus into a "store." Donations were solicited from

(Continued)

(Continued)

the community, the store was stocked, and families were invited in to shop. In the meantime, the school counselor wrote a community-based grant proposal and received $5,000 in gift cards to give to the Katrina families for the holidays. Once the holidays arrived, the "store" was restocked and families were invited to shop again and given the gift cards. The Katrina students were invited to a special event in which they were able to "shop" for gifts for their families while the school counselor and other staff helped with wrapping.

Story 3

A middle school in New England struggled with not having enough time for school counselors to engage in counseling with families. The district entered into a school-family-community partnership agreement to hire a part-time school counselor from a nearby child, adolescent, and family counseling agency to work with students and families during the day to complement the work of the full-time school counselors. Stuart, the school/family counselor, worked with a range of issues always focused on greater academic success for students. Family issues included single parenting, divorce, parent chemical dependency, and parent joblessness. The school counseling consisted of working with students and parental, grandparental, and/or sibling subsystems of first-generation Portuguese immigrant families to increase academic success for students. One year after the interventions, marked improvement was seen in academic performance by 85% of the students who received family-centered school counseling.

Resources

Digital

Active Parenting: www.activeparenting.com
AdoptUsKids (advocating with foster/adoptive families for children in the child welfare system): www.adoptuskids.org
AFS-USA (international and intercultural learning): www.afsusa.org
AVID (Advancement Via Individual Determination): www.avid.org
Bastard Nation (open adoption record advocacy): www.bastards.org
Big Brothers Big Sisters: www.bbbs.org
Bilingual Families Connect: www.bilingualfamiliesconnect.com
Campaign for Better Care: www.nationalpartnership.org/site/Page Server?pagename=cbc_issues_landing
The Center for Effective Discipline: www.stophitting.com
Center for the Improvement of Child Caring: www.ciccparenting.org

Center on School, Family and Community Partnerships: www.csos.jhu
.edu/p2000/center.htm

Children of Lesbians and Gays Everywhere (COLAGE): www.colage.org

CoAbode (single mothers house sharing): www.coabode.org

Coalition for Asian American Children and Families: www.cacf.org

Children Awaiting Parents: www.capbook.org

College Board: www.collegeboard.org

College Bound: http://collegebound.publishpath.com

College Preparation Checklist: http://studentaid.ed.gov/PORTALS
WebApp/students/english/checklist.jsp

College Savings Plan Network: www.collegesavings.org/index.aspx

Council on Contemporary Families: www.contemporaryfamilies.org

FAFSA Completion Guide for LBGTIQ Families: www.finaid.org/
fafsa/lgbtfafsa.phtml

FAFSA FAQs for Students and Families: http://studentaid.ed.gov/
PORTALSWebApp/students/english/faqs.jsp

Families and Advocates Partnership for Education (FAPE) (families
with youth with disabilities): www.fape.org

Families, Counselors, and Communities Working Together for Higher
Education (NACAC): (English/español): www.nacacnet.org

Families and Work Institute: www.familiesandwork.org

Families Like Ours (adoption exchange for prospective LBGTIQ and
non-LBGTIQ parents): www.familieslikeours.org

Family Acceptance Project (evidence-based tools to help traditional
and religious families embrace rather than reject their LBGTIQ children and youth for optimal health and suicide/crisis prevention;
(Chinese, English, español): www.familyproject.sfsu.edu

Family Advocacy and Support Training Project (families with children
with disabilities; English, español): www.fastfamilysupport.org

Family and Community Resources for Infants, Toddlers, Children, and
Adolescents with Disabilities (English, español): http://nichcy
.org/families-community

Family Equality Council (LBGTIQ-parented family advocacy): www
.familyequality.org

Family Involvement Network of Educators (strengthening family-
school-community partnerships): www.hfrp.org

Family Promise (independence for homeless and low income families):
www.familypromise.org

Family Violence Prevention Fund: www.endabuse.org

GEAR UP: www2.ed.gov/programs/gearup/index.html

Gottman Institute (research on couples, parenting, divorce prevention,
and emotion coaching): www.gottman.com

Grandparents Raising Grandchildren: www.raisingyourgrandchildren .com

International Network of Donor Conception Organizations: www .inodco.org

Keep a Child Alive (support for families affected by HIV/AIDS): http://keepachildalive.org

Little People of America (resources and support for people of short stature and their families): www.lpaonline.org

Long-Distance Parenting: http://distanceparent.org

Loving Day Project (celebrating mixed-race, multiethnic, multiracial couples and families): www.lovingday.org

mothers2mothers (care, support, and education for pregnant women and new mothers living with HIV): www.m2m.org

My Child's Future (career development and academic/college planning suggestions for parents and guardians of K–12 students): www.mychildsfuture.org/parents/item.htm?id=0

National Adoption Foundation: www.nafadopt.org

National Alliance for Caregiving: www.caregiving.org

National Center on Family Homelessness: www.familyhomelessness.org

National Child Care Information and Technical Assistance Center: http://nccic.acf.hhs.gov

National Compadres Network (strengthening traditional "compadre" extended family systems supporting the positive involvement of Latinos): www.nationalcompadresnetwork.com

National Family Planning and Reproductive Health Association: www .nfprha.org

National Foster Care Coalition: www.nationalfostercare.org

National Foster Parent Association: www.nfpainc.org

National Latino Fatherhood and Family Institute (strengths-based support for Latinos in families addressing child abuse, domestic violence, gang violence, school failure, illiteracy, teen pregnancy): www.nlffi.org

National Network of Partnership Schools: www.csos.jhu.edu/p2000/

National Partnership for Women and Families: www.nationalpartner ship.org

National Stepfamily Resource Center: www.stepfamilies.info

NOH8 Campaign (promoting marriage, gender, and human equality through education, advocacy, and visual protest): www.noh8cam paign.com

North American Council on Adoptable Children (NACAC): (promoting permanent families for children/youth in foster care): www.nacac .org

Nurse Family Partnerships (transforming the lives of vulnerable first-time moms and their babies): www.nursefamilypartnership.org

Parent Hotline (for families in crisis): 1–800–840–6537

Parent Involvement in Career and Educational Planning and College Access With Elementary, Middle, and High School Age Students (PowerPoint slideshows): http://acrn.ovae.org/counselors/involvingparents.htm

Parents Anonymous (child abuse prevention): www.parentsanony mous.org

Parents, Families, and Friends of Lesbians and Gays (PFLAG): www .pflag.org

Parents' Role in Career Development for Children and Youth: www .careerkey.org/asp/career_development/parents_role.html

Parents Without Partners: www.parentswithoutpartners.org

Project Appleseed (organizing parents, grandparents and caring adults for public school improvement including Parent Pledge and Parent Involvement Day): www.projectappleseed.org/

Proud Parenting (resources for LBGTIQ parents): www.proudparenting .com/

Single Parents Network: http://singleparentsnetwork.com

Stop the Deportations—The DOMA Project (fighting LBGTIQ couple deportation, separation, and exile in the USA): www.stopthedepor tations.com/blog/

Straight Spouse Network (support and information for heterosexual spouses/partners of LBGTIQ mates and mixed-orientation couples): www.straightspouse.org

Systematic training for effective parenting (STEP) (research-based parenting curricula, videos): www.steppublishers.com

TransFamily: www.transfamily.org

TransYouthFamilyAllies: www.imatyfa.org

Unmarried and Single Americans Week: www.sacbee.com/2011/09/12/3903260/unmarried-and-single-americans.html

WeParent (co-parenting): www.weparent.com

What's Your Parenting Style? Quiz: www.activeparenting.com

Wider Opportunities for Women (WOW) (building economic independence for America's families, women, and girls): www.wowonline.org/

Print

Bryan, J., & Henry, L. (2008). Strengths-based partnerships: A school-family-community partnership approach to empowering students. *Professional School Counseling, 12,* 149–156.

Epstein, J. L. (1995). School/family/community partnerships: Caring for the children we share. *Phi Delta Kappan, 76*, 701–712.

Epstein, J. L., & Associates. (2009). *School, family, and community partnerships: Your handbook for action* (3rd ed.). Thousand Oaks, CA: Corwin.

Epstein, J. L., & Sanders, M. G. (2006). Prospects for change: Preparing educators for school, family, and community partnerships. *Peabody Journal of Education, 81*, 81–120.

Epstein, J. L., & Van Voorhis, F. L. (2010). School counselors' roles in developing partnerships with families and communities for student success. *Professional School Counseling, 14*, 1–14.

McGoldrick, M., Carter, B., & Garcia-Prieto, N. (2011). *The expanded family life cycle: Individual, family, and social perspectives* (4th ed.). Boston, MA: Pearson.

Perry, N. S. (2000). Reaching out: Involving parents and community members in the school counseling program. In J. Wittmer (Ed.), *Managing your school counseling program: K–12 developmental strategies* (2nd ed.; pp. 264–269). Minneapolis, MN: Educational Media.

Solomon, A. (2012). *Far from the tree: Parents, children, and the search for identity.* New York, NY: Scribner.

Van Velsor, P., & Orozco, G. L. (2007). Involving low-income parents in the schools: Communitycentric strategies for school counselors. *Professional School Counseling, 11*, 17–24.

Walsh, F. (Ed.). (2012). *Normal family processes: Growing diversity and complexity* (4th ed.). New York, NY: Guilford.

9

Ethics Solutions

School counselors have ethical training invaluable for increasing the academic, career, college readiness, and personal/social success of students, educators, and leaders in school. However, sometimes school counselors get stuck and are not sure what to do and neglect to share the ethics information they possess to help all stakeholders be ethical and legal advocates for all students. For example, school counselors, like school social workers and school psychologists, must keep confidentiality (with exceptions), which can be a challenge for other school leaders and teachers at times as they are not bound by the same codes of ethics (American Counseling Association [ACA], 2005; American School Counselor Association [ASCA], 2010; National Association for College Admission Counseling [NACAC], 2012).

Solutions to ethical challenges include educating all staff on ethical codes and updating legal issues for staff and all stakeholders regularly in consultation with the school district's attorney. It is important to work from and share with all stakeholders digitally (on school counseling program websites, e-counseling newsletters, and e-mail/text blasts) and traditionally on school counseling program bulletin boards and handouts with links to the three major ethical codes that include school counselors:

- American School Counselor Association's *Ethical Code for School Counselors* (ASCA, 2010)

- American Counseling Association's *ACA Code of Ethics* (ACA, 2005)
- National Association for College Admission Counseling's *Statement of Principles of Good Practice (SPGP)* (NACAC, 2012)

These three codes of ethics for school counselors are reviewed every few years and strengthened by members of their respective associations as ethical issues unfold in the profession. Codes of ethics are never static documents and member input is integral for future changes. The three codes of ethics affecting school counselors are significantly larger and greater in depth than educational leader and teacher codes of ethics from the American Association of School Administrators (AASA, 2013), the National Association of Elementary School Principals (NAESP, 1976), the National Association of Secondary School Principals (NASSP, 2001) and the National Education Association (NEA, 1975). The three educational leader codes of ethics are 10 to 12 sentences each; the NEA teacher code consists of two pages of general ethics. In contrast, professional counseling codes of ethics focus on much greater depth and specificity in ethics for all professional counselors (ACA, 2005), school counselors (ASCA, 2010), and college counselors (NACAC, 2012). School counselors have much to share with school leader and teacher colleagues to support the ethical well-being of all school stakeholders, particularly children, adolescents, and their parents/guardians, regarding how all school stakeholders can make the best decisions in promoting equitable student academic, career/college readiness, and personal/social competencies.

Students, families, and staff need to know their rights and responsibilities for ethical and legal issues in schools, and the school counseling program is an ideal agent to teach about ethical codes.

A top ethical issue facing the profession is who has access to a data-driven comprehensive school counseling program and who does not (Lapan, 2012). As Stone (2005) stated after ASCA delegates overwhelming voted to change the ASCA code of ethics in 2004:

> It is our ethical imperative to provide all students with equity of service. The delegates revised the ethical standards to add equity and emphasize that school counselors will survey the school landscape for practices and policies that adversely stratify students' opportunities and we will responsibly tackle those policies to make changes to benefit students. (p. 296)

When school counselors collaborate with other educational leaders and teachers to ensure all students receive an equity-focused, data-driven school counseling program with academic, career, college access, and personal/social competencies in each grade level in every school that helps close achievement, opportunity, and attainment gaps, they have fulfilled a central role of the ethical code for school counselors.

In Figure 9.1, 15 ethical case scenarios are provided to increase school counselor, leader, and other stakeholder ethical decision-making skills.

Key Words

AASA Code of Ethics: Ethical code for building and district leaders who are American Association of School Administrators members

ACA Code of Ethics: Ethical code for counselors of all specialty areas, including school counselors, from the American Counseling Association

ASCA Ethical Code for School Counselors: Ethical code for all school counselors with specificity on K–12 schools for members of the American School Counselor Association

Confidentiality: A practice in which information shared with the school counselor is not revealed to any other person, that is, "What you say here stays here," with exceptions including (1) imminent danger to self or others; (2) consultation/supervision with school counselor, psychologist, or social worker colleagues and school counseling program director; (3) court sub-poenas/orders (but the school counselor/district can challenge them); (4) release of information consent forms, including those signed by parents/guardians for counseling a minor; and (5) confidentiality challenges with more than one client/student in group or family counseling

Do No Harm: Also known as *nonmaleficence,* this covenant ensures that school counseling program policies and practices governing delivery of academic, career and college readiness, and personal/social competencies treat all K–12 students equitably (harm results from not having equitable access to these competencies).

Dual Relationships: Acting in another role or roles in addition to that of school counselor toward students or their families (e.g., also being a teacher or being a dean or dating a student's parent or guardian)—dual roles are to be avoided/minimized at all times

(Continued)

(Continued)

Duty to Warn: School counselors, like other mental health professionals, have a legal and ethical duty to warn those in imminent danger when a student/client threatens harm to self or others.

Educational Equity: Ensuring all children and adolescents have the resources, opportunities, and fair treatment to be successful in K–12 settings

Ethical Decision-Making Model for School Counselors: Developed by Carolyn Stone and included in the 2010 ASCA *Ethical Code for School Counselors* revision "Solutions to Ethical Problems in Schools" or STEPS:

1. Define the problem emotionally and intellectually
2. Apply the ASCA and ACA ethical codes and the law
3. Consider the students' chronological and developmental levels
4. Consider the setting, parental rights, and minors' rights
5. Apply the moral principles
6. Determine your potential courses of action and their consequences
7. Evaluate the selected action
8. Consult
9. Implement the course of action

Family Educational Rights Privacy Act (FERPA): Federal law proscribing who may have access to a student's educational records and when; it states that schools may not divulge educational records without consent and a written release from a parent/guardian or eligible student; students of a certain age may legally access their records and ask to amend incorrect records

Informed Consent: When a minor student's parent/guardian or student of the legal age of consent gives written permission to receive individual or group counseling from the school counselor with an understanding of the techniques to be used, the duration of counseling, the potential benefits and concerns, and the student's/family's right to stop counseling at any time

NACAC Statement of Professional Good Practice (SPGP): Ethical code of conduct updated annually by the National Association for College Admission Counseling for admission counselors in K–12 and college settings

NAESP Code of Ethics: Code of ethics for elementary and middle school building leaders who are members of the National Association of Elementary School Principals

NASSP Code of Ethics: Code of ethics for middle and high school building leaders who are members of the National Association of Secondary School Principals

NEA Code of Ethics: Code of ethics for teachers who are members of the National Education Association

Privacy: The right to keep one's personal information and records from being disclosed to others

Privileged Communication: A right legally held by the student/client to ensure privacy when discussing personal matters with certain professionals. It applies to relationships with medical doctors, clergy, and attorneys but not at the federal level to relationships with most mental health professionals, including school counselors, unless they practice in a state that legally grants them privileged communication.

Release of Information: A legal document giving permission, when signed and dated by a parent/guardian of a minor or by a student of legal age of consent, to share information about the student from one professional to another

Key Questions and Solutions

1. How do school counselors ensure ethical practice by staff in K–12 schools/the district based on the ASCA code of ethics?

First, share the code on the district's website and on each school counseling program's web page. Additionally, implement regular staff development for all staff on ethics. School counselors can take the lead sharing ethics related to student confidentiality and how important it is for all staff to conduct conversations about students privately and never in hallways or other places where students could overhear them, let alone on Facebook, Twitter, e-mail, or any traceable forms of social media where students could see educators' posts. Gossip has no place in schools on the part of school counselors, leaders, and other educators, especially related to student and staff issues. Plus, with the ethical imperative of an equity-focused school counseling program helping to close gaps for all students, it is essential that school counselors take a leadership and advocacy role helping all stakeholders understand the key roles of school counselors as embraced in the ASCA (2010) Ethical Code for School Counselors preamble:

> Professional school counselors are advocates, leaders, collaborators and consultants who create opportunities for equity in access and success in educational opportunities by connecting

their programs to the mission of schools and subscribing to the following tenets of professional responsibility:

Each person has the right to be respected, be treated with dignity and have access to a comprehensive school counseling program that advocates for and affirms all students from diverse populations including: ethnic/racial identity, age, economic status, abilities/disabilities, language, immigration status, sexual orientation, gender, gender identity/expression, family type, religion/spirituality, and appearance.

Each person has the right to receive the information and support needed to move toward self-direction and self-development and affirmation within one's group identities, with special care being given to students who have historically not received adequate educational services, e.g., students of color, students living in a low socioeconomic status, students with disabilities, and students from nondominant language backgrounds. (ASCA, 2010, p. 1)

2. What ethical decision-making model can school counselors use for best practice?

Dr. Carolyn Stone's STEPS model for school counselors (ASCA, 2010; Stone, 2005) was included in the most recent revision of the ASCA ethical code because school counselors need not only a code of ethics but a model of ethical decision making. Many school-based situations are vague in nature and complex in both ethical and legal issues. The No. 1 rule for all school counselors when in doubt is to consult with the school counseling supervisor, other school counselors, school psychologist, or school social work colleagues, and the district's attorney whenever there are doubts about the appropriate legal or ethical actions in a situation. The goal is to always have the student's best interests in mind and deed and to document exactly what has been done in each situation, including consultation and supervision to ensure the best possible outcomes. This especially applies to any incident involving danger to self or others or the threat of such danger or violence (ACA, 2005; ASCA, 2010; Stone, 2005).

For example, in each area of Stone's STEPS model (ASCA, 2010; Stone, 2005) school counselors have specific items to consider:

1. *Define the problem emotionally and intellectually.* This means that school counselors need to focus first on gut emotional and cognitive reactions and look at how emotions and thoughts shape our conceptualizing of the ethical and/or legal issues at hand. Am I reacting as a parent, as a friend, or as a professional school counselor? Similarly, how are emotions and thoughts coloring how decisions are made about the ethical and legal implications of the situation? Sorting through personal first reactions and then consulting with school counseling colleagues are wise moves.

2. *Apply the ASCA and ACA ethical codes and the law.* After carefully noting emotional and intellectual responses to the situation, it is crucial to know how ethical codes and federal, state, and local laws frame the key issues at hand. While ethics are always important, law carries the most weight, so it is critical that if a school counselor is not sure about federal, state, or local laws that the school district's attorney be consulted when legal issues are involved.

3. *Consider the students' chronological and developmental levels.* Just as in the case of counseling 5-years-olds differently from 17-year-olds, school counselors must consider the student's age, grade level, multiple cultural identities, and family, school, and community contexts in making ethical decisions. Failure to focus on developmental stages and the multiple contexts of school, family, community, and cultural identities can harm successful ethical issue resolution.

4. *Consider the setting, parental rights, and minors' rights.* When ethical issues arise related to academic or personal/social issues, parents and guardians have a legal right to agree to or deny a minor child or adolescent's access to individual or group counseling, as well as to know if a child or adolescent is in danger or harm and how the school is responding. At the same time, due to FERPA, any written legal document on the child's or adolescent's academic records must be shared with parents/legal guardians and becomes available to students at age 18, and parents/legal guardians and students legally have the right to have erroneous information corrected in academic records.

5. *Apply the moral principles.* Stone (2005) referred to Kitchener's (1984) five key moral principles that assist in making ethical decisions in school contexts: School counselors work to ensure *autonomy*, a student's right to self-determination and making his or her own choices in school; *beneficence*, promoting what is good for students in school; *nonmaleficence*, avoiding actions or lack of action that puts students in danger of harm in school; *justice*, ensuring fairness and equal treatment

for all students based on multiple cultural identities in schools; and *fidelity*, loyalty to students and regular connections to all students on one's caseload through planning for all students, classroom lessons, e-counseling newsletters, e-mail/text blasts, updated information on bulletin boards and the school counseling web page, and visibility at transition times throughout the day.

6. *Determine potential courses of action and their consequences.* This ethical decision-making step requires creativity and brainstorming. It is recommended to do a cost-benefit analysis of at least two different actions that could be taken to address the issue at hand and then look at what the results would be for various stakeholders. Find a school counseling colleague to critique potential actions and consequences and consult on the wisest action doing the greatest good for all involved.

7. *Evaluate the selected action.* Once the school counselor has selected the action, then consider the best option for action. Stadler (1986) suggested three "test" questions to clarify the wisdom of using the selected ethical action prior to making a decision:

- Justice: Is it fair to all involved and if it were you, would you want to be treated this way?
- Publicity: How would you react to your ethical decision making being covered by the media (including social media)?
- Universality: Would you recommend this way to any other school counselor?

8. *Consult.* There is a wide array of folks ready to assist school counselors. Failure to involve others can land school counselors in legal challenges. School counselors want to consult and document what was said and what they did based on the consultations when serious issues arise. Consultations can occur with other school counselors, school psychologists and social workers, teachers, administrators, children's services staff, district staff, and the school district's attorney. One of the most important reasons for maintaining professional association memberships is that one can always call on professional counseling association staff and leaders to assist in ethical dilemmas. The danger in not consulting is that there may have been better options, and ignorance of the law is never a successful defense in court and may result in a charge of negligence.

9. *Implement the course of action.* If a school counselor has followed the prior eight steps, implementing the action is easier because the

homework has been done. After implementing the action, follow through with evaluating the effects of the decision on all stakeholders and take additional actions if needed.

3. How can school counselors model confidentiality for all K–12 school stakeholders?

School stakeholders can use constant reminders about the importance of keeping student conversations and records confidential. School counselors can use role plays and case studies in staff development meetings and regularly alert stakeholders and colleagues to best practices. In Figure 9.1, CUNY Lehman College counselor education/school counseling adjunct faculty member Debbie Ashley and associate professor Stuart Chen-Hayes created a series of case studies on ethical issues for school counselors and leaders that are ideal for staff development and school counselor and leader learning. In addition, annual needs assessments from students asking about how well schools maintain confidentiality can be a major eye-opener that gives hard data for school personnel to look at how they can change policies and practices to ensure confidentiality is every staff member's concern. School counselors can share the ASCA (2010), ACA (2005), and NACAC (2012) codes of ethics online, on their school counseling program web pages, via e-counseling newsletters, in e-mail and text blasts, and in the school counseling program brochure. They can also post on bulletin boards a basic definition of confidentiality and its major exceptions and ensure that every student receives this information at the beginning of the school year along with parents/guardians in a welcome letter from the school counseling program.

4. How can school counselors and leaders prepare to testify in court?

It is hard for anyone who is not a lawyer to feel fully prepared for a court hearing or testimony. To prepare, the best consultation is with the school district's attorney to review what to say and what not to say and how to ensure documentation to back up testimony. One of the authors was called to testify in a child custody hearing three times in a doctoral internship. While never having to testify, being present in the courtroom on three occasions sparked an interest in pursuing ethical practice in all professional counseling interactions and wariness of writing professional counseling notes other than basic facts and supervision/consultation contacts. In any situation that might involve legal issues, always document issues related to violence, potential violence, suicidal ideation, homicidal ideation, special education placements, and other concerns with the possibility of future legal issues. The best preparation is having accurate notes of what was done and when and how—in addition to noting consultation/supervision sessions and action taken based on the consultation/supervision. Child custody hearings often seek school personnel as potential sources for information, and school counselors can be proactive with the school district's attorney about a plan to move forward.

5. How can school counselors honor the legal rights of noncustodial parents in schools?

FERPA is clear that any parent/legal guardian has the right to see and challenge the accuracy of a student's academic record. A noncustodial parent also has this right. One of the toughest parts of the job for school counselors is maintaining neutrality with parents and guardians going through relationship difficulties, including relocation, separation, divorce, and child custody battles. School counselors are wisest to not take sides and to state such as a policy in writing. This policy should be reinforced when working with couples and families, emphasizing that the school counselors' role is to support what is in the best interest of the child or adolescent at the school. Even if noncustodial parents have been arrested or convicted of crimes, they still have the legal right to see their children's academic records. Every parent/guardian is legally entitled to a child's records regardless of custody status unless a court order bars such contact.

6. How can school counselors ensure informed consent?

Best practice is sending home at the beginning of the year a blanket welcome letter sharing what school counseling is and how it operates. Having a clear statement on informed consent in the school's parent/guardian/student handbook and explaining methods and effectiveness of individual and group counseling on the school counseling program website is also important. The statement, like other school communications, must be written in the diverse languages used by parents/guardians in the school for optimal effectiveness. It also needs to be explained for releases of information to assist the child or adolescent with service providers outside the school. Minor children are not legally able to consent to counseling or releases of information, so parents/guardians need to make that decision. Age of consent (usually between ages 14 and 17) varies by state, so it's important to know the legal age of consent where you practice school counseling. This does not apply, however, to planning and school counseling core curriculum lessons (ASCA, 2012), which are exclusively academic concerns. But what about students who are homeless or travel between multiple residences to and from school? Those students need to bring the consent form to the parent or legal guardian to have it signed and returned to school.

7. How can school counselors publicize school counselor and educational leader roles in upholding ethical and legal standards?

The best way is to share ASCA (2012), ACA (2005), and NACAC (2013) codes of ethics with all stakeholders. Key passages and concepts can be shared digitally on the school's website/school counseling program pages, on traditional and print bulletin boards, and referenced in the school counseling program brochure and annual letters to staff, students, and families at the beginning of the year. In addition, school counselors can promote an annual ethical issue or case study at staff meetings to keep the ethical fires burning (as opposed to getting burned) throughout the year. Some school counselors will add an ethical-issue-of-the-month scenario to e-counseling newsletters sent to all stakeholders or post an ethical dilemma of the month on the school counseling bulletin board or web page to keep everyone on their toes about the importance and benefits of ethical practice in schools and the school counseling program.

8. How can school counselors clarify the difference between confidentiality and privileged communication and "need to know" so staff members know what information school counselors can share and with whom, particularly when school counselors and building leaders disagree?

This is an area of constant ethical challenge for all school stakeholders. *Confidentiality* means what is said in the counseling session stays there, with exceptions that include danger to self or others; court subpoenas; school counselor supervision or consultation with school counselor, school social worker, or school psychologist colleagues; and release of information forms. *Privileged communication* means that what is said is kept private with no exceptions, and school counselors in most states do not have it. The only professions that have privileged communication in all 50 states are attorneys, medical doctors, and clergy. It is meant to protect the privacy of the student's information. But in school settings with minors, school staff including school counselors function in *loco parentis* (i.e., as caretakers of children/adolescents when parents are not present). At the same time, school counselors' No. 1 priority is the well-being of the child or adolescent balanced with other stakeholders' *need to know*. School counselors must constantly balance the right of the child/adolescent to confidentiality with the need to know by other stakeholders. For example, if a parent asks about what is being talked about in counseling sessions, a school counselor could refer generally to it being an academic, career, college readiness, or personal/social issue but not give any further information if there was no danger to self or others. If, however, a child or adolescent threatened immediate danger to self or others and had a plan, method, and imminent time frame for causing harm, then legally the *principal and parents/guardians would have an immediate need to know.*

It gets trickier when administrators or teachers demand confidential information about students from school counselors. Again, the best policy is educating all stakeholders regularly on what school counselors can and cannot ethically disclose and asking the district's attorney for legal assistance and consults to resolve disputes when staff disagree.

9. What are best practices in cases of hot-button topics regarding duty to warn persons in danger?

Rule of thumb is collaboration between school counselors and leaders and, when necessary, school attorneys, following district crisis procedures regarding violence and potential violence while balancing the duty to warn with confidentiality. If students are in imminent danger of harming themselves or others, school counselors are legally required to break confidentiality to ensure safety of all students. Regular reviews and collaboration with local safety and mental health advocates and agencies are equally important to be prepared. All schools face these issues, and the ones that are successful have plans in place that are regularly reviewed and updated. States vary on laws for whether parents should be notified, have to give consent, or do not have to be notified or give consent for abortions. School counselors need to know their state laws for how to proceed, and the wisest course of action is always to help students clarify their choices but never give advice or tell students what option to pick. To increase school counselor and leader competencies in ethical practice, Figure 9.1 includes a series of ethical school counseling scenarios to further the skills of leaders and school counselors suitable for staff development, professional development of school counselors, and work with school counseling practicum and internship candidates.

Figure 9.1   School Counselor and Leader Ethical Scenarios

1. School Counselor Role When Personal Views and Professional Ethics Differ

James is a student whom you have known for two years and the son of traditional first-generation Jamaican immigrants. He is a high school junior hoping to become a lawyer. He asks to make an appointment with you and reveals that he thinks he is gay and has felt this way for as long as he can remember. He is distraught and feels his family will reject him, especially his father. He has never told anyone else and has tried to date girls, but it just doesn't feel right. During the session, he says he thinks that if he is really gay he might as well kill himself as his life is over. You are a school counselor in an independent school focusing on career and college readiness for all students, and you have a strong religious belief that it's not OK to be lesbian or gay.

Apply Stone's (2005) STEPS Ethical-Decision Making model and include the specific sections of the ASCA (2010), ACA (2005), and NACAC (2012) codes of ethics that apply. As you use the decision-making model, also consider:

- *What would you do as his school counselor?*
- *What are the correct legal and ethical considerations that should be included in your decision?*
- *Would you contact his parents?*
- *What would you say to them if you did speak with them?*
- *How do you reflect upon and evaluate the success of your ethical decision-making action and results?*

2. School Counselor Balancing Family Rights

Beverly is a successful student with excellent grades planning to go to college. She comes into your office and shares that she is pregnant and very frightened. She begins crying. She is 15 years old and has a boyfriend of six months who has not been informed of the pregnancy. Upon questioning her, she reveals that her family is Catholic and would never let her have an abortion. You gently suggest that she speak with her parents or another adult family member about her possible decisions and the alternatives that she has. She never agrees to speak with another family member but does agree to return to see you next week. The following week she doesn't show up for her appointment.

Apply Stone's (2005) STEPS Ethical-Decision Making model and include the specific sections of the ASCA (2010), ACA (2005), and NACAC (2012) codes of ethics that apply. As you use the decision-making model, also consider:

Figure 9.1

- *What are the legal and ethical responsibilities you have in this situation?*
- *What would you do if she refuses to see you when you seek her out?*
- *What if she is absent and not available?*
- *With whom do you need to speak?*
- *What information would you keep confidential and what information would you reveal to other parties?*
- *Would there be a difference in how you would respond in a public school versus an independent or religious school?*
- *How do you reflect upon and evaluate the success of your ethical decision-making action and results?*

3. School Counselor Obligations

The Gomez-Baez family is in an ugly divorce with a fight over who will have custody of their three children. *This is a two-mom family whose marriage occurred in Canada and was subsequently recognized in New York State.* You are an elementary school counselor and have been counseling their daughter, who is in third grade. You receive a subpoena from one parent's lawyer to testify and provide case notes and school records. The student is being strongly affected by the arguing between her parents and has been seeing you regularly for counseling. Only one parent had signed the parent/guardian permission and release form for her to see you on a regular basis. You really don't want to get in the middle of this, and you know that the student needs support as the divorce has been affecting her school work.

Apply Stone's (2005) STEPS Ethical-Decision Making model and include the specific sections of the ASCA (2010), ACA (2005), and NACAC (2012) codes of ethics that apply. As you use the decision-making model, also consider:

- *What will you do about the subpoena?*
- *If you do release records, which records are mandatory that you release?*
- *Will you release more than is necessary, and why?*
- *What would you reveal about the sessions you have had with the daughter if you testify?*
- *Would you ask for support from others within the school?*
- *Whom would you speak with and what kinds of things would you discuss with them?*

(Continued)

Figure 9.1 Continued

- *What specific areas of additional support and advocacy would you need to provide for a child going through a divorce of a same-gender parented family?*
- *How do you reflect upon and evaluate the success of your ethical decision-making action and results?*

4. School Counselors, Records, and Noncustodial Rights

Mr. Wu is a noncustodial parent whose first language is Mandarin and who speaks little English. He would like to meet at your elementary school counseling office about his son's progress. He mentions that he hasn't seen the first-quarter report and wants to know how his son is doing and whether or not he might need extra tutoring in any classes. (His ex-wife has told you how horribly he had treated her and his children and that they want nothing to do with their father. She reveals that she is still not receiving the child support money he is obligated to pay.)

Apply Stone's (2005) STEPS Ethical-Decision Making model and include the specific sections of the ASCA (2010), ACA (2005), and NACAC (2012) codes of ethics that apply. As you use the decision-making model, also consider:

- *What will you say to the father about meeting with him?*
- *What information will you share if you meet with him?*
- *Do you need to report this information to a supervisor before you speak with the father?*
- *How will you ensure the father understands your communication since his main language is Mandarin?*
- *How do you reflect upon and evaluate the success of your ethical decision-making action and results?*

5. School Counselor Role in Preventing Sexual Harassment

Jessica, who is Italian and English and has a physical disability, age 12, comes to your middle school counseling office to complain that a boy in her class, Jason, whose family recently immigrated from Albania, tried to fondle her at her locker when no one else was around. Jason has an IEP for a learning disability that makes reading especially difficult for him. Jessica wants to make sure that he doesn't do it again but is adamant about wanting anonymity. You ask for more specifics about the incident. She says he never did this before, and she says that he tried to reach inside her blouse. You agree to talk to Jason. When you speak to Jason, you remind him about appropriate behavior and reveal that someone has seen him being inappropriate with girls. He says that he doesn't know what you are talking about, goes home, and complains

Figure 9.1

to his parents. The parents have called you demanding to meet with you about the accusations. They want to know who has slandered their son.

Apply Stone's (2005) STEPS Ethical-Decision Making model and include the specific sections of the ASCA (2010), ACA (2005), and NACAC (2012) codes of ethics that apply. As you use the decision-making model, also consider:

- *What are your ethical and legal obligations in this situation?*
- *Do you reveal the student who made the original complaint?*
- *How would you go about resolving the complaint of harassment?*
- *How do you reflect upon and evaluate the success of your ethical decision-making action and results?*

6. School Counselor Needing Parental Consent to Counsel Minors

Luke signs up to be part of the group and tells you that he really needs the support of other students who are going through what he is experiencing. You send home a letter to receive parental permission for students to be in group counseling for families dealing with chemical dependency as Luke's mother is actively alcoholic. Luke's father is Jewish and his mother is Catholic. Luke's mother fills in the form and says "No." Luke's father calls you on the phone, saying that he spoke with Luke about the group and that he thinks it would be a good idea and gives his permission.

Apply Stone's (2005) STEPS Ethical-Decision Making model and include the specific sections of the ASCA (2010), ACA (2005), and NACAC (2012) codes of ethics that apply. As you use the decision-making model, also consider:

- *Would you allow Luke to be in the group?*
- *Would you do anything before making your decision about Luke being in the group?*
- *What would you say to Luke about your decision?*
- *How would you handle divergent religious belief systems in the family?*
- *What would you say to each of the parents?*

7. School Counselor Duty Regarding Criminal Activity

Matt seems like a well-behaved high school junior who is 16 years old. His family speaks only Spanish; they have been in this country for 10 years. He isn't involved with either of the major gangs in the

(Continued)

Figure 9.1 Continued

school. Teachers like him, and he turns in his homework. He is meeting with you concerning next year's schedule and has not signed a release of information form. During the discussion about next year's class selection he reveals that he has been dealing a small amount of drugs to support paying for college but never anywhere near school grounds.

Apply Stone's (2005) STEPS Ethical-Decision Making model and include the specific sections of the ASCA (2010), ACA (2005), and NACAC (2012) codes of ethics that apply. As you use the decision-making model, also consider:

- *What are your ethical and legal obligations in this situation?*
- *Do you need to report his illegal activity?*
- *Who would you report this activity to?*
- *Do parents need to be informed?*
- *What information is confidential?*
- *What would you say to Matt about what he is doing?*
- *How do you reflect upon and evaluate the success of your ethical decision-making action and results?*

8. Principal-School Counselor-Student Issues

A white male principal hears a rumor that a group of African American boys are having sex with girls of different ethnic/racial identities in your middle school and he names several of the boys specifically. He knows that you are counseling the boys in a group and asks you if the rumor is true because he doesn't want anything to get in the way of all students being career- and college-ready.

Apply Stone's (2005) STEPS Ethical-Decision Making model and include the specific sections of the ASCA (2010), ACA (2005), and NACAC (2012) codes of ethics that apply. As you use the decision-making model, also consider:

- *How do you respond (say, for instance, that some of the boys have said they are sexually active)?*
- *How do you reflect upon and evaluate the success of your ethical decision-making action and results?*

9. School Counselor's Dilemma

In the course of career- and college-access counseling, a working-class, Irish Catholic, 14-year-old freshman discloses a lot of anger, that he has been teased regularly by his classmates, and that he doesn't have any close friends. He says he hates the school and

Figure 9.1

thinks about revenge toward the kids who have picked on him and that he hates them so much that he could shoot them. His fantasy job is to go into the Marines and become a combat soldier and then let the military pay for college.

Apply Stone's (2005) STEPS Ethical-Decision Making model and include the specific sections of the ASCA (2010), ACA (2005), and NACAC (2012) codes of ethics that apply. As you use the decision-making model, also consider:

- *How do you respond?*
- *What other information do you need before making a decision?*
- *How do you reflect upon and evaluate the success of your ethical decision-making action and results?*

10. School Counselors and Dual Relationships

You are a Latina counselor in a small high school that is 100% Dominican, Puerto Rican, Mexican, and Central American in student and staff ethnic/national identities. You work with many homeless adolescents on improving grades, staying in school, and applying to and succeeding in college. One adolescent becomes very attached to you, often stating, "You are my best friend and I don't know what I would do without you!" and you feel close to her. When she has a crisis and gets kicked out of her house, you recommend that she go into foster care and especially recommend one of your close relatives who specializes in short-term placements at her home.

Apply Stone's (2005) STEPS Ethical-Decision Making model and include the specific sections of the ASCA (2010), ACA (2005), and NACAC (2012) codes of ethics that apply. As you use the decision-making model, also consider:

- *What are the alternatives for resolution of this situation?*
- *How do you reflect upon and evaluate the success of your ethical decision-making action and results?*

11. Equitable Access to School Counseling Program Services

Students with disabilities (mostly African American and Latino/a) at your middle school are mandated to see you for individual counseling due to their Individualized Educational Plans to increase their academic and career success. You have no time to work with students who don't have disabilities because there are not enough hours in the day and your caseload is large. Everyone laughs when

(Continued)

Figure 9.1 Continued

you say you'd like to clear some time for college readiness counseling as most students are from families who have had no adults who have gone to college.

Apply Stone's (2005) STEPS Ethical-Decision Making model and include the specific sections of the ASCA (2010), ACA (2005), and NACAC (2012) codes of ethics that apply. As you use the decision-making model, also consider:

- *How can you work as a change agent for equity here and deliver academic, career, and college readiness skills for every student?*
- *With whom would you need to team and collaborate?*
- *How could you use data to make change?*
- *How do you reflect upon and evaluate the success of your ethical decision-making action and results?*

12. Confidentiality in Schools

You work as an elementary school counselor in an old building and your office is the broom closet, but it has high ceilings and there are no partitions at the tops of the closet, so it is easy to hear others outside your office and for others to hear inside your office. In addition, the culture of this school is for adults to come into your office whenever they choose as the principal stores things there and the parent coordinator keeps her lunch in your refrigerator, and she's got low blood sugar so she's always looking for a snack. Plus, teachers often take their breaks in the hallway in front of your door and discuss students' concerns publicly.

Apply Stone's (2005) STEPS Ethical-Decision Making model and include the specific sections of the ASCA (2010), ACA (2005), and NACAC (2012) codes of ethics that apply. As you use the decision-making model, also consider:

- *What are the ethical and legal issues?*
- *How can you intervene?*
- *What leadership and advocacy strategies would you need to employ for successful resolution of the situation?*
- *How do you reflect upon and evaluate the success of your ethical decision-making action and results?*

13. Equitable School Counseling Program Services

You have studied and implemented the ASCA (2012) National Model in your practicum and internship, and as a first-year, untenured school counselor in a large, older high school, you seek to provide

Figure 9.1

all students with developmental school counseling core-curriculum lessons on academic, career, and college readiness competenices in your high school as you implement a school counseling program for all students. Yet some of the current school counselors are uncomfortable going into the classroom and say they would do that "over their dead bodies," because they aren't certified teachers, so they are not allowed in the classroom. A small group of "college-bound" students get lessons 9–12 but most students get little in career and college readiness competencies if they have under a 3.0 or B grade point average.

Apply Stone's (2005) STEPS Ethical-Decision Making model and include the specific sections of the ASCA (2010), ACA (2005), and NACAC (2012) codes of ethics that apply. As you use the decision-making model, also consider:

- *What are the ethical and legal issues here?*
- *Could school counselors be sued for not providing services?*
- *What teaming and collaboration, advocacy, leadership, and equity assessment using data strategies will turn this situation around?*
- *How do you reflect upon and evaluate the success of your ethical decision-making action and results?*

14. School Counselors Closing Achievement and Opportunity Gaps

You have been on the job for a year when you discover that African American and Latino/a students are being placed in classes based on wherever the assistant principal can find openings versus students' academic performance. There are only two Advanced Placement courses taught at your high school, and few students have access to them. There has never been career and college readiness competency development for students until the second semester of their junior year.

Apply Stone's (2005) STEPS Ethical-Decision Making model and include the specific sections of the ASCA (2010), ACA (2005), and NACAC (2012) codes of ethics that apply. As you use the decision-making model, also consider:

- *What are the ethical and legal issues at stake here?*
- *What can you do to turn this around?*

(Continued)

Figure 9.1 Continued

- *What specific advocacy, leadership, teaming and collaboration, and equity assessment using data strategies will you use?*
- *How do you reflect upon and evaluate the success of your ethical decision-making action and results?*

15. School Counselor Cultural Competency and Systemic Racism/Classism

A school counselor in a public middle school saw an overwhelming number of referrals to his office for boys of African descent. They are sent to the office by mostly White teachers for disciplinary reasons. Yet when they come to the office, they are gentle, kind, and respectful boys from poor and often single-mother families. With class sizes skyrocketing, more pressure on teachers to show results in the classroom, and fewer dollars for school counseling services including career and college readiness programs, everyone is being crunched, but these young male students of color are in danger of losing their interest in school and dropping out if the flood of discipline referrals isn't stopped—and quickly. The school counselor, who is White, has a good relationship with the principal, who is a person of color known to be a penny pincher. The school counselor has multicultural counseling training and is able to show success with the boys in group and individual counseling settings but finds them repeating their journeys to his office multiple times in a semester.

Apply Stone's (2005) STEPS Ethical-Decision Making model and include the specific sections of the ASCA (2010), ACA (2005), and NACAC (2012) codes of ethics that apply. As you use the decision-making model, also consider:

- *What professional development is needed for the school counselor and the teachers and administrators?*
- *What would be the risks of addressing the real issues in this school and for which stakeholders?*
- *If the school counselor was not tenured, how would this change your response to the scenario?*
- *How could the school counselor use data to show how boys of African descent are being unfairly targeted?*
- *How could the school counselor lessen school suspensions and educate staff instead about restorative justice as an ethical best practice?*
- *How do you reflect upon and evaluate the success of your ethical decision-making action and results?*

Created by Stuart Chen-Hayes and Debbie Ashley.

Solution Success Stories

Story 1

Change can happen in unique circumstances. An urban northeastern elementary school in an old building had no privacy for students and school counselors. The school counselors were stuck in an old classroom with an attendance teacher and the parent coordinator and no barriers for sound—not even cubicles to separate conversations. All individual counseling occurred in this space, which was not to CACREP 2009 Standards (Council for Accreditation of Counseling and Related Educational Programs, 2009) or ASCA ethical codes (ASCA, 2010). Leverage from a Counselor Educator site visit that deemed the site unacceptable allowed the school counselor, Enrique, to petition and rally the principal to install fully soundproofed barriers in the room so that privacy could be allowed for the school counselor and other school personnel in working with students successfully and ethically.

Story 2

Flor, a Bronx high school counselor, encountered colleagues who spread students' private information publicly on a regular basis. Due to not being tenured, the school counselor chose to work with students and encouraged them *not* to share personal business with persons whom they could not trust. She didn't speak badly of colleagues but helped students to see how she was trustworthy and kept confidentiality to model appropriate ethical behavior for all stakeholders.

Story 3

I-Li, a male urban/suburban East coast high school counselor, thought it was ethical to keep windows and doors open so all could see inside his office to ensure no sexual abuse was occurring. Although France uses a system of guilty until proven innocent, the United States does not. When it was pointed out by a site supervisor that this did not provide privacy for students and families, he worked to ensure the door and windows were closed and covered with opaque materials so that students' privacy was protected at all times during counseling and advising in his office.

Resources

Digital

American Association of School Administrators: www.aasa.org
American Counseling Association: www.counseling.org/resources/codeofethics/TP/home/ct2.aspx

American School Counselor Association: www.schoolcounselor.org/files/EthicalStandards2010.pdf

National Association for College Admission Counseling: www.nacacnet.org/about/Governance/Policies/Documents/SPGP.pdf

National Association of Elementary School Principals: www.naesp.org/what-we-believe-1

National Association of Secondary School Principals: www.nassp.org/Content.aspx?topic=47104

National Education Association: www.nea.org/home/30442.htm

Print

Lapan, R. T. (2012). Comprehensive school counseling programs: In some schools for some students but not in all schools for all students. *Professional School Counseling, 16,* 84–88.

Moyer, M. S., & Sullivan, J. R. (2008). Student risk-taking behaviors: When do school counselors break confidentiality? *Professional School Counseling, 11,* 236–245.

Moyer, M. S., Sullivan, J. R., & Growcock, D. (2012). When is it ethical to inform administrators about student risk-taking behaviors? Perceptions of school counselors. *Professional School Counseling, 15,* 98–109.

Stone, C. B. (2005). *School counseling principles: Ethics and law.* Alexandria, VA: American School Counselor Association.

Stone, C. B., & Zirkel, P. A. (2010). School counselor advocacy: When law and ethics may collide. *Professional School Counseling, 13,* 244–247.

10

Cultural Identity and Language Solutions

School counselors and other leaders are in an excellent position to affirm the multiple cultural and language identities of students and stakeholders in K–12 schools. Nieto and Bode (2011) used the term *affirming diversity* in their work showcasing multiple case studies of how educators can empower culturally and linguistically diverse students in K–12 classrooms. But school counselors often aren't sure how to begin or how to show our efforts connect to academic achievement and career and college readiness for every student. For example, what is *culture?* There are hundreds of definitions. K–12 schools have their own culture, and within that culture every stakeholder has a host of cultural identities—particularly students and their families—with some identities more salient than others. The challenge and opportunity for school counselors and other leaders in the school is to focus on equity: How are all students and their families affirmed in their multiple cultural and linguistic identities to be successful (American School Counselor Association [ASCA], 2010; Chen-Hayes, 2007; Chen-Hayes, 2013; Holcomb-McCoy & Chen-Hayes, in press)? What does the data show for which groups of students receive the best resources (challenging classes, best teachers, intensive career/college counseling, personal/social resources)? How can school counselors and other leaders guarantee equity for every student to reach his or her hopes and dreams?

One of the most powerful solutions is to focus on data-driven awareness of policies and patterns affecting and empowering (or disempowering) multiple cultural identities of students (ASCA, 2010, 2012; Chen-Hayes, 2007; National Office for School Counselor Advocacy [NOSCA], 2010). Data for some cultural identities, although not always disaggregated nor accurate, are often found in demographic sections of three public documents in most U.S. states:

1. Public all-school report cards
2. Standardized achievement score data
3. School improvement plans

The cultural identities that are most often reported in public school data are

- ability/disability (percentage of students with IEPs but rarely are data released on percentage of gifted/talented students),
- age (grade level, although not always an accurate measure for overage and underage students),
- ethnicity/race (although data often confuses the two with no specificity for ethnicity or mixed-race students),
- gender,
- language background (students whose first language is not English in bilingual classes or programs), and
- social class (students eligible for free/reduced lunch).

But there are a range of other student cultural identities harder to collect data on in either public or independent schools that may be as salient as, if not more so than, ability/disability, age, ethnicity/race, gender, language, and social class. Those identities include

- appearance,
- family type,
- gender identity/expression,
- immigration status,
- sexual orientation, and
- religion/spirituality/meaning-making system.

School counselors who graduated from Council for Accreditation of Counseling and Related Educational Programs [CACREP]-accredited programs (www.cacrep.org) received some course content and learning experiences in multicultural counseling and/or cultural foundations of education (CACREP, 2009). Other school counselors and leaders may have received nothing. Plus, most educational leaders and school counselors in the United States are monolingual or may have a few years of high school or college language study in a European romance language but lack fluency. However, current and future K–12 public school demographics indicate school counselors and other leaders who are culturally and linguistically competent are more likely to be successful leading the way to the best achievement, career and college readiness, and behavioral outcomes for all K–12 students (Schellenberg & Grothaus, 2011).

The United States is rare among developed countries for not promoting study of two or more languages to fluency in K–12 schools starting in early elementary grades. It is behind as most countries expect students to be fluent in two languages by high school graduation with the concomitant cultural competence and cognitive benefits that accompany bilingual fluency in an interconnected world. This chapter gives best solutions and print and digital resources for school counselor and other leader development to empower all stakeholders to affirm student and family multiple cultural identities including language in school counseling programs.

So whether the data is easy to access or more obscure, school counselors and other leaders must be culturally competent in specific multicultural awareness, knowledge, and skills (Sue, Arredondo, & McDavis, 1992) to affirm students' multiple cultural and language identities in K–12 school counseling programs and support their success. We must challenge various *oppressions* including *ableism, ageism, beautyism, classism, familyism, genderism, heterosexism, immigrationism, linguicism, racism, religionism, sexism,* and other barriers to learning (ASCA, 2010; Burnes et al., 2010; Chen-Hayes, 2007; Chen-Hayes, 2009; Chen-Hayes, 2013; Harper et al., n.d.; Holcomb-McCoy & Chen-Hayes, in press) to ensure *equity* for all students whether data points are easy to access or not. School/community/family partnerships and challenging familyism are covered separately in Chapter 8, and challenging ableism and ability, disability, and gifted/talented solutions are covered separately in Chapter 16.

Key Words

Ableism: Prejudice multiplied by power used by persons without disabilities to restrict individual, cultural, and systemic resources to persons with developmental, emotional, intellectual, learning, or physical disabilities

ACA Competencies for Counseling Transgender Clients: Best practices in counseling transgender persons from the American Counseling Association

(Continued)

(Continued)

Acculturation: A balancing of one's cultures/languages; the ability to appreciate the strengths and concerns of one's original and host cultures

Ageism: Prejudice multiplied by power used by persons 18–49 to deny individual, cultural, and systemic resources based on nondominant age (affects children, adolescents, persons age 50-plus)

ALGBTIC Competencies for Counseling with Lesbian, Gay, Bisexual, Queer, Questioning, Intersex, and Ally (LGBQQIA) Individuals: Best practices in counseling persons with nondominant sexual orientations or those who are questioning their sexual orientation from the Association for Lesbian, Gay, Bisexual, and Transgender Issues in Counseling

ASCA (Personal/Social) Student Standards: The three original ASCA personal/social student standards are (1) understanding and respecting self and others, (2) decision-making and achieving goals, and (3) safety and survival skills

Assimilation: Valuing one's new or host culture/language as better than one's prior culture or language and denigrating one's prior culture/language as negative or inferior; it can be chosen or coerced

Beautyism: Prejudice multiplied by power used by persons with culturally valued appearances to deny individual, cultural, and systemic resources based on nondominant appearance

Bilingual Education: Using two languages to teach and learn academic subjects in K–12 schools

Classism: Prejudice multiplied by power used by persons with dominant social class resources (wealthy and upper middle class) to deny individual, cultural, and systemic resources to persons of nondominant social classes (poor, working class, lower middle class)

Cultural Identity Development Models: Human developmental models based on cultural variables including ethnicity, gender, race, sexual orientation, social class, religion/spirituality, and others that emphasize integrating and valuing one's cultural identity(-ies) over time. Understanding and affirming identity development has been shown to mitigate against stress from oppression and promote feelings of pride in one's identity(-ies) and the history of challenging oppression.

Dual Language Immersion or Two-Way Education: Classroom instruction in both the native and the target language, usually at the elementary level, that takes place primarily in the target language (i.e., 90–10 model) until fluency is gained and then shifts to equal proportions of both languages. Only one language is used in the classroom at a time, which moves students toward greater proficiency faster, and students learn about all subjects in both languages. This approach increases students' skills in both languages and fosters high levels of cognitive complexity.

Equity Assistance Centers: Ten regional offices around the United States that deliver resource assistance for K–12 school and district staff to promote equity and equal opportunities based on race, gender, and national origin; funded by the U.S. Department of Education and Title IV of the 1964 Civil Rights Act

Familyism: Prejudice multiplied by power used by persons from traditional family types to deny individual, cultural, and systemic resources based on nondominant family type (single, single-parent, same-gender, multiracial, homeless, adoptive, foster, divorced)

Genderism: Prejudice multiplied by power used by traditionally gendered persons to deny individual, cultural, and systemic resources to gender-variant and transgender persons

Heritage Language: Language spoken at home that is the original language of some or all family members but not the main language of instruction in a K–12 school

Heterosexism: Prejudice multiplied by power used by heterosexuals to deny individual, cultural, and systemic resources to lesbian, bisexual, and gay persons

Immigrationism: Prejudice multiplied by power used by persons of legal citizenship status to deny individual, cultural, and systemic resources to persons of nondominant citizenship status

Language Immersion: Instruction given exclusively in a target language for a sustained period to promote fluency

Linguicism: Prejudice multiplied by power used by persons of a dominant language denying individual, cultural, and systemic resources to persons of a nondominant language background

Multicultural Competencies: Specific cultural awareness, knowledge, and skills that professional counselors use to effectively counsel culturally diverse clients/students

Multicultural Education: A discipline in education focused on creating educational equity for all students focused on both content about diverse groups and how educational processes are conducted regarding multiple cultural identities for students K–12

Oppressions: Prejudice multiplied by power that dominant cultural groups use to restrict access to individual, cultural, and systemic resources by nondominant cultural group members; examples include ableism, ageism, beautyism, classism, familyism, genderism, heterosexism, immigrationism, linguicism, racism, religionism, and sexism

(Continued)

(Continued)

Racism: Prejudice multiplied by power used by persons of a dominant racial group (in the United States, Whites) to deny persons of color and mixed-race persons individual, cultural, and systemic resources

Religionism: Prejudice multiplied by power used by persons of a dominant religion to deny individual, cultural, and systemic resources based on nondominant religion, spirituality, or meaning-making system

Sexism: Prejudice multiplied by power used by persons of a dominant gender (men and boys) to deny individual, cultural, and systemic resources to women and girls

Social Justice: Equity in access to resources including human and civil rights movements that challenge oppression

Transitional Bilingual Education: Courses taught in school for up to three years in the native language with the goal of students then shifting exclusively to the target language; often used to promote the target language as the primary goal for future instruction

World View: A cultural group's set of values and beliefs passed on over time that can include cosmology and epistemology

Young Men of Color Initiative: Young men of color often face some of the most dire outcomes in society and K–12 schools; this initiative is designed by the College Board Advocacy and Policy Office to help school counselors, leaders, and all educators turn around that data with effective policies and practices that empower all young men of color to successfully reach their career and college dreams.

Key Questions and Solutions

1. How can school counselors and other leaders promote cultural identity and language solutions across multiple identities?

The first step in multicultural competency is to examine one's own ethnic/racial/cultural identities (Sue et al., 1992). How salient or important are ethnic and racial identities to you, family, friends, school colleagues, and the children, adolescents, and families who attend school? How do you work with others who find the salience of their identities different from yours? How do you define the difference between ethnicity (similar across all cultures) and race (a more recent term whose meaning varies around the world)? How do students, families, and staff at your school identify in terms of ethnic, racial, and cultural/linguistic identities? How does the school counseling program acknowledge and affirm multiple cultural and language identities in school counseling core curriculum lessons, planning for all students, and group and individual counseling? How do school counseling program needs assessments survey all school stakeholders about their multiple cultural identities and languages and how they feel affirmed or disrespected in your school? Knowledge is power and some of the words in everyday language, on forms, and in surveys for data collection can include or disempower stakeholders as follows:

- Alien ("immigrant" has fewer negative connotations)
- At-risk ("at-promise" focuses on strengths)
- Disabled ("person with a disability" or "a child with ADHD" focuses on the person first)
- Homosexual ("gay" and "lesbian" are self-determined terms from the LBGTIQ community without negative connotations)
- Illegal ("undocumented" lacks negative connotations)
- Minority (people of color, i.e., folks descended from African, Asian and indigenous racial/ethnic groups, are the largest racial groups internationally and will be in the United States by 2040; minority, therefore, is an inaccurate term for people of color)
- Mom and dad ("parent/guardian" includes all caregivers and family types without assuming two parents or heterosexual parents)

While language is always shifting, it's wise to ask students and families what they prefer to be called and make sure that language is inclusive, welcoming, and focused on strengths throughout the school culture.

Language is a perfect place to be proactive in schools. Culturally competent school counselors and leaders assess personal values and beliefs about culture and cultural and linguistic identities. School counselors and other leaders examine personal beliefs and values prior to developing knowledge and skills in working with others, and this chapter gives key places to make culturally and linguistically responsive changes with stakeholders of multiple cultural and linguistic identities in schools.

Key areas of intervention and learning for staff professional development include the concepts of *oppression, cultural identity development models,* and *world view* (Holcomb-McCoy & Chen-Hayes, in press; Sue et al., 1992). Savvy school counselors and leaders tailor their interventions, including school counseling core curriculum lessons and group and individual counseling interventions, to empower students and families of diverse cultural and linguistic identities K–12.

Too many schools, however, do little in depth that targets cultural and linguistic competency for staff and students. Schools often feature examples of the "tourist approach"—a focus on food, costumes, and travel pictures, all of which are external artifacts that may not represent any deep cultural values or beliefs. But culture is primarily internal. Culture is found in the core beliefs and values of a group of people over time. That is where school counselors and leaders can make a huge difference—by working on our student/family competencies in learning, understanding, and celebrating diverse values and beliefs as they manifest in school counseling program interventions, activities, and whole-school policies and practices. Cultural festivals and celebrating holidays and feasts can open a door toward the larger work of policy and practice affirmation for all groups. But festivals and holidays alone rarely push the needed buttons to assess equity and how power, privilege, and oppressions operate in schools and how school resources (or lack thereof for some students) shape students' futures in public and independent schools (E. Lee, Menkart, & Okazawa-Rey, 1998).

2. What policies, practices, and resources support academic, career/college access, and personal/social success in terms of ethnicity and race, particularly for students of color (African descent, Asian, Latino/a, Native American Indian, mixed race)?

Race and social class are central organizers of K–12 schools in the United States. Most poor students of all ethnic/racial identities and most students of African, Latino/a, and indigenous ethnic/racial identities are found in public schools. The history of racism and classism in K–12 schools and colleges has been to exclude those without access to resources on many levels (Duncan & Murnane, 2011; Sacks, 2007;). For years, U.S. educational policy was focused on *assimilation*—that students should give up any prior ethnic/racial, linguistic, and national identities to solely adopt American cultural ideals using only English. However, certain oppressed groups have resisted and challenged oppression and forced assimilation (Zinn, 2005). A legacy of inequitable access to resources in housing, job opportunities, immigration status, access to quality public schools, and other oppressive practices continue. Where poor persons live and the inequities in school funding found in most states determine how poor students are educated. The public schools that poor Whites and children of color attend often do not receive the same funding compared to the schools where children of wealthier persons reside, usually wealthier suburbs and magnet schools in urban communities (Duncan & Murnane, 2011; Sacks, 2007). Schools with the most students in poverty and students of color often have large school counselor-to-student ratios and lack fully implemented school counseling programs (Lapan, 2012).

With that said, there are initiatives that school counselors and other leaders can access inside and outside their schools to broker services challenging a legacy of classism and racism. One key step is working toward the ethical imperative of fully implementing school counseling programs reaching every student with demonstrable results in closing achievement and opportunity gaps (ASCA, 2010, 2012). To do so, school counselors need to be aware of data for poor and working-class students and students of color, mixed race, and White students in schools and challenge patterns of inequities in resources as they directly affect achievement, opportunity, and attainment gaps (see Chapters 4 and 5). Once patterns are located, school counselors can shift school counseling program and other leadership and advocacy interventions to close the gaps (ASCA, 2010, 2012).

One excellent resource focused on ethnicity/race, gender, and national origin fairness in K–12 schools is equity assistance centers, grouped around the United States with the specific mission of assisting all school staff in ensuring equitable opportunities. In addition, school counselor educators have developed specific programs and models for students of various backgrounds: Empowered youth programs (Bailey & Bradbury-Bailey, 2013) and the "brotherhood" for African American adolescents (Wyatt, 2009); using the ASCA National Model (Villalba, Akos, Keeter, & Amers, 2007); Spanish-speaking school counselors sought to lessen Spanish-dominant Latino/a isolation in schools (Smith-Adcock, Daniels, Lee, Villalba, & Indelicato, 2006); and models empowering Native American adolescents (Turner, Conkel, Reich, Trotter, & Slewart, 2006). Missing in the literature are programs specific to mixed-race students and Asian and Pacific Islander students; Shen and Lowing (2007) published a study looking at school counselors' self-perceptions of competency in counseling Asian Americans.

In policy and practice for challenging racism, school counselors can join data, leadership, and inquiry teams to be front and center in looking at data related to ethnicity and race in terms of outcomes in all aspects of academics and career and college readiness opportunities, as well as personal/social issues. Similar to the community maps from Chapter 8, cultural audits can survey the visuals used in the school and how the curriculum includes persons of color and mixed-race persons. Do the images in the school and in the curricular offerings affirm the ethnic and racial identities of students in the school and outside the school? Next, staffing is a key issue—what are the ethnic/racial identities of staff stakeholders and how do they mirror student stakeholders? School counselors can spearhead hiring decisions advocating for increasing ethnic/racial diversity of school staff. The College Board's Young Men of Color website is full of data and resources to challenge the racism/classism affecting young men of color's chances in schools. Mixed-race issues can be facilitated through use of materials from the Mavin Foundation, and multiple websites specific to empowering persons of color and challenging racism can be found in the racism-challenging digital resources at the end of this chapter.

3. What policies, practices, and resources provide for the academic, career/college access, and personal/ social success of students by social class, particularly poor, working-class, and lower-middle-class students?

Amatea and West-Olatunji (2007) encouraged school counselors to examine how to challenge poverty in schools. As Duncan and Murnane (2011) demonstrated, schools are full of inequalities that disproportionately harm poor and working-class children and youth. Lapan, Gysbers, Bragg, and Pierce (2012) found in a statewide study of Missouri comprehensive school counseling programs that big school counselor-to-student ratios disproportionately occurred in schools with high poverty rates, and lessening those ratios challenges classism toward students in need of the greatest school counseling program resources. Data, inquiry, and school counseling program advisory council teams all need to disaggregate school outcomes in academics and career/college access based on free/reduced lunch to find the outcomes of school policies and practices for poor and working-class students versus wealthier students. Websites to

empower poor and working class students include http://classism
.org, and NOSCA's (2010) website on the eight career and college
readiness counseling components to give away the social capital
needed to build poor and working-class students' capacity for career
and college readiness. Additional digital resources for challenging
classism appear at the end of the chapter.

4. What policies, practices, and resources can school counselors and other leaders provide for the academic, career/college access, and personal/social success of boys and girls?

The paradox of gender in schools is that girls are targets of sexism and exclusion in sports and funding, yet they excel and in
many cases do better academically and are more likely to enroll in
and graduate from college than boys (Chen-Hayes, 2013). Again,
school counselors must disaggregate data patterns in academic,
career, and college access, and personal/social issues, and target
gender to challenge sexism that traditionally has kept girls from
thriving in STEM fields as well as the challenges of empowering
boys' success in school and college completion. Multiple resources
for challenging sexism are listed in the digital resources at the end
of this chapter.

5. What policies, practices, and resources promote the academic, career/college access, and personal/social success of bilingual students including recent immigrant and undocumented students?

The key is the diversity and complexity of language learners
and bilingual language programs in the United States (compared
to other nations and curriculum frameworks such as International
Baccalaureate) and connecting students to the best learning experiences based on varied language-learning backgrounds and
resources.

Bilingual education has been controversial in many communities
and a cherished resource in other U.S. schools. Effective bilingual
education has many benefits for students, including increased cognitive complexity and the ability to negotiate the world in two languages building cultural and linguistic competency. School counselors
and other leaders need to know how bilingual education is done in

schools for the best possible learner outcomes. Advocating for *dual language immersion programs* is an excellent step. Immersion programs are the fastest way to fluency, including *90–10 models* in elementary schools where content is taught in early elementary grades for 90% of the day and then in middle elementary grades the ratio is moved up to even amounts in both languages. The key is that academic content is taught in both languages so that students learn material in both languages. The federal government sponsors multiple language development centers such as the Center for Applied Linguistics (CAL) and The Center for Applied Research in Language Acquisition (CARLA) (see challenging-linguicism resources at the end of the chapter) that assist in implementation and evaluation research on effective bilingual education. *Heritage language learners* are a unique population whose needs are often underserved in schools—an original language in the family is spoken at home but is not the primary language of instruction in the school. Checking in with bilingual and heritage language students and families and having all school communication translated and available in a family's original language, as well as ensuring translators are available, are helpful practices to challenge *linguicism* in schools. Encouraging schools to increase world language offerings, such as implanting language-based AP and IB programs, is another important policy that school counselors can advocate. One example of challenging linguicism by school counselor educators was when Shi and Steen (2012) developed a school counseling program to support the academic and personal/social needs of bilingual students. Additional challenging linguicism digital resources are found at the end of the chapter.

6. What policies, practices, and resources encourage the academic, career/college access, and personal/social success of lesbian, bisexual, gay, transgender, intersex, queer, and questioning students?

Most important is to recognize that all schools have LBGTIQ (lesbian, bisexual, gay, transgender, intersex, queer, and questioning) students, whether they are out of the closet or not. By making that assumption, school counselors can promote a climate of equity and information in the building for all students to help end heterosexism and genderism. Chen-Hayes (2001) wrote on specific policies that schools can use to support transgender and gender-variant students. Burnes et al. (2010) developed ACA transgender counseling competencies for the American Counseling Association. Harper et al. (n.d.) developed Association for Lesbian, Gay, Bisexual, Transgender Issues in Counseling (ALGBTIC) competencies for counseling with lesbian, gay, bisexual, queer, questioning, intersex, and ally individuals. Smith and Chen-Hayes (2004) wrote multiple lesson plans and group counseling outlines on LBGTIQ knowledge issues for K–12 students to be used by school counselors; DePaul, Walsh, and Dam (2009) wrote on school counselors' roles in addressing sexual orientation in schools, as did Goodrich and Luke (2009) on school counselors being responsive to LBGTIQ youth. All of these authors stressed the importance of helping stakeholders clarify the difference between sexual orientation and gender identity/expression as a baseline and that neither sexual orientation nor gender identity is a choice. They stated the importance of helping students with the coming out process and that school counselors and other leaders are not to tell students when to come out. In addition, ethical codes are clear that LBGTIQ students need to be safe and affirmed and schools need to have clear policies in place for safety and nonviolence toward LBGTIQ students. Many online resources in the challenging heterosexism and genderism sections at the end of the chapter include the work of Dr. Caitlin Ryan at the Family Acceptance Project: the world's first evidence-based practice assessment tool to prevent LBGTIQ youth suicide and a series of research-based tools to help conservative and religious families embrace LBGTIQ youth rather than shunning them from the family (Ryan & Chen-Hayes, 2013). GLSEN sponsors multiple resources for empowering LBGTIQ students and has done a series of research studies showing how LBGTIQ students are subject to abuse and violence in schools (Ryan & Chen-Hayes, 2013). It also supports No Name Calling Week, Day of Silence, Ally Week, and other programs to empower LBGTIQ youth and allies, which school counselors and other leaders can use in schools. Starting and advising Gay Straight Alliances (GSAs) is another key tool; many high schools and some middle schools in progressive areas have them, but conservative areas still challenge their existence (which is illegal in public schools unless all school clubs are disavowed). SIECUS has comprehensive sexuality education guidelines K–12 that give educators and school counselors specific tools in how to address sexual orientation and gender identity; *Live Out Loud* is a program designed to bring out LBGTIQ high school alumni back to their schools to support current students; and *Welcoming Schools* is a curriculum from the Human Rights Campaign designed to promote family diversity, oppose bullying, and support

LBGTIQ youth in elementary schools. These and other resources on challenging genderism and challenging heterosexism are found in the digital resources at the end of the chapter.

7. What policies, practices, and resources empower students with nondominant age (overage, under-credited, or accelerated), appearance, and religious/spiritual identities?

Schools need to monitor the academic and social experiences of both accelerated students (see Chapter 16) and overage, under-credited students in unique aspects of *ageism*. The key is to ensure supports are available for academic success early on, and school counselors and other leaders need to push for academic intervention services by monitoring grades every marking period and intervening as early as possible. Dropping out is more likely for over-age students who fall further behind in needed course credits and watch similar-age peers graduate without them. Additional digital resources for challenging ageism are listed at the end of the chapter.

As for challenging *beautyism*, students who are overweight or who have otherwise nondominant appearances are often targeted for abuse and bullying, and school counselors and other leaders need to model how to challenge beautyism. Web pages like Adios Barbie have a fun twist to challenging appearance-related bias and media images that often influence who/what is attractive or not. Schools need to be safe zones for all students, regardless of appearance, to achieve academic success. More digital resources for challenging beautyism are located at the end of the chapter.

Finally, public schools often are leery of addressing anything related to religion, spirituality, or belief systems. Yet many students are subject to *religionism* (targeting students from nondominant religions or students who are not religious or spiritual). In public schools, this is usually not addressed other than student clubs being legal for religious/spiritual purposes and for students who are not religious (i.e., atheist or agnostic) and certain religious holidays (usually Christian Christmas, Easter, and Good Friday) often coinciding with public school breaks. School counselors constantly need to monitor policies and practices crossing belief systems from an annual review of holidays (why are some religious holidays for some groups privileged and others not?), and equally affirm students who have no religious/spiritual identities or interest in them. Additional digital religionism-challenging resources are listed at the end of the chapter.

Solution Success Stories

Story 1

Franklin, a middle school principal in a large northeastern city, created a new small school based on the International Baccalaureate curriculum framework to jump-start the academic success of his 100% Latino/a student population. He sought to hire school counselors to support the mission of IB but was stopped due to budget cuts. Once his budgets recover, he wants equity-focused school counselors to assist him in his mission of ensuring all his first-generation Mexican, South, and Central American students graduate from high school with fluency in two world languages and career and college readiness skills. Many small urban high schools (and some middle and elementary schools) with large populations of poor and working-class students of color, many of whom are recent immigrants and bilingual, have adopted International Baccalaureate programs to support students in academic, career, and college readiness because study of at least two languages is expected, with results showing bilingual students of color can thrive in challenging international curricula frameworks where being bilingual is an asset.

Story 2

Jose, a school counseling program district director in a large Texas urban district, encouraged bilingual recent immigrant freshmen and sophomores to take AP Spanish courses for credit, especially Spanish-speaking students early in their high school careers to boost academic, career, and college access among Latino/as. While the teaching staff at some schools were highly skeptical, as were some school counselors, when word got around to students and their families about the option, teachers and school counselors agreed to see what would happen. Not only did Latino/a participation surge in AP Spanish courses, but students thrived in the courses, and the excitement of receiving strong grades by 80% of the students on the exams (i.e., eligible to receive college credit in their first two years of high school) was an excellent motivator pushing district high schools to higher graduation rates for Latino/as and increased college admission for first-generation Latino/a students.

Story 3

Kai, a private religious high school counselor on the East Coast, is known by students as the LBGTIQ ally. In his religion, he could be ostracized for being an LBGTIQ ally. Instead, students know that he is safe to talk to in advising and during individual and group counseling sessions about coming out as

(Continued)

(Continued)

LBGTIQ. In his advising and counseling presence, students can be all of who they are without fear of being kicked out of school or their religion. The school counselor upholds ACA and ASCA ethical code expectations for affirming LBGTIQ students effectively. While he can't start a GSA or waive a rainbow flag overtly, he has figured out within the cultural constraints of the religious organization employing him how to be an ethical heterosexual ally for students at the school.

Resources

Digital

Ableism-Challenging Resources

(See Chapter 16 digital resources)

Ageism-Challenging Resources

Advocates for Youth: www.advocatesforyouth.org

Agediscrimination.info: www.agediscrimination.infohttp://pubs .niaaa.nih.gov/publications/Practitioner/YouthGuide/ YouthGuideOrderFrom.htm

Alliance for Retired Americans: www.retiredamericans.org

Alzheimer's Association 24-hour helpline, 800–272–3900: www.alz.org

Campaign for Better Care: www.nationalpartnership.org/site/PageServer? pagename=cbc_issues_landing

Campaign for a Commercial-Free Childhood: www.commercialexploi- tation.com

Campaign for Youth: www.campaignforyouth.org

Campaign for Youth Justice: www.campaignforyouthjustice.org/

Caring Across Generations: http://caringacrossgenerations.org/

Center for Effective Discipline: www.stophitting.com/

Center for Young Women's Health: www.youngwomenshealth.org

Child Abuse Hotline: 800-4-A-CHILD (800–422–4453) or 800-2- A-CHILD (222-4453, TDD)

Child Labor Coalition: http://clc.designannexe.com

Children of Lesbians and Gays Everywhere (COLAGE): www.colage.org

Children's Defense Fund: www.childrensdefense.org

Children's Environmental Health Network: www.cehn.org

Children's Rights: www.childrensrights.org

Children's Rights Information Network: www.crin.org

Coming of Age: http://comingofage.org

Compassion and Choices (end of life care): www.compassionand
    choices.org

Developmental Assets: www.search-institute.org/

Do Something.org: www.dosomething.org

Elder Abuse Hotline: 800-252-8966

Elder Maltreatment Prevention: www.cdc.gov/ViolencePrevention/elder-
    maltreatment/index.html

Every Child Matters Education Fund: www.everychildmatters.org

Family and Community Resources for Infants, Toddlers, Children, and
    Adolescents with Disabilities (English, español): http://nichcy.org/
    families-community

First Star: www.firststar.org

The FreeChild Project: www.freechild.org

Free the Children: www.freethechildren.com

Generations United: www.gu.org

GirlsInc.: www.girlsinc.org

Global Fund for Children: www.globalfundforchildren.org

Global Youth Action Network: www.youthlink.org

Global Youth Connect: www.globalyouthconnect.org

Homeless/Runaway Youth Helpline/The Nine Line, 800-999-9999:
    www.covenanthouse.org

Indykids! (progressive newspaper focused on social justice by/for
    grades 4–8): www.indykids.net

International Day of Older Persons (October 1): http://www.un.org/
    en/events/olderpersonsday/

International Youth Day (August 12): www.un.org/en/events/youth
    day/

International Youth Foundation: www.iyfnet.org

Invisible Children (ending child soldiers): www2.invisiblechildren.com

It Gets Better Project (empowering LBGTIQ youth via videos): www
    .itgetsbetter.org/

Justice for Children: www.jfcadvocacy.org

KidsCamps.com: www.kidscamps.com/

Kids Helping Kids (catastrophic illness/mobility needs): www
    .kidshelping.org

My Child's Future: www.mychildsfuture.org/parents/item.htm?id=0

National Association for the Education of African American Children
    With Learning Disabilities (AACLD): www.aacld.org/

National Center for Children in Poverty: www.nccp.org

National Center for Youth Law: www.youthlaw.org

National Dissemination Center for Children With Disabilities: http://
    nichcy.org

National Network for Youth: www.nn4youth.org

National Resource Center for Youth Development: www.nrcyd.ou
.edu

National Resource Center on LGBT Aging: www.lgbtagingcenter.org

National Runaway Switchboard 1-800-Run-Away: www.1800runaway
.org/

National Senior Citizens Law Center (protecting the rights of
low-income older adults): www.nsclc.org

National Youth Advocacy Coalition: www.nyac.org

SafeKids.com: www.safekids.com

Safe Kids USA: www.safekids.org

Save the Children: www.savethechildren.org

Services and Advocacy for GLBT Elders (SAGE): www.sage.org

Share Our Strength (ending child hunger): www.strength.org

Stand for Children: www.stand.org

Stand Up for Kids (homeless and street youth): www.standupforkids
.org

Support Kids Now (child support payment enforcement): www
.supportkidsnow.org

Taking It Global (youth online): www.tigweb.org

Teen Angels (cybersafety): www.teenangels.org

Teen Voices (empowering girls via media): www.teenvoices.com

Tween Angels (cybersafety): www.tweenangels.org

UNICEF: www.unicef.org

United Nations Convention on the Rights of the Child (1989): www
.hrweb.org.

United We Dream (equitable youth access to higher education): www
.unitedwedream.org

Voices for America's Children: www.voices.org

What Kids Can Do: www.whatkidscando.org

Women's College Coalition: www.womenscolleges.org

Worldwide Orphans Foundation: www.wwo.org

Youth and Gender Media Project: www.youthandgendermediaproject
.org/

Youth for Environmental Sanity: www.yesworld.org

Youth on Board: www.youthonboard.org

Youth Service America: www.ysa.org

Youth Venture: www.genv.net

Beautyism-Challenging Resources

About-Face: www.about-face.org

Adios Barbie: www.adiosbarbie.com

Body Positive: www.bodypositive.com

Council on Size and Weight Discrimination: www.cswd.org

Eating Disorders (National Institute of Mental Health): www.nimh.nih
.gov

FAT!SO? (size empowerment): http://fatso.com

International Size Acceptance Association: www.size-acceptance.org

Love Your Body Day: http://loveyourbody.nowfoundation.org

National Association to Advance Fat Acceptance: www.naafaonline
.com

National Organization for Albinism and Hypopigmentation: www
.albinism.org

Classism-Challenging Resources

5 Ways Ed Pays: http://advocacy.collegeboard.org/five-ways-ed-
pays/home

99% Power: www.the99power.org

Accion (English, español): www.accion.org

Action Against Hunger/ACF International: www.actionagainsthun
ger.org

Alliance for Democracy: www.thealliancefordemocracy.org

America Saves Week.org: www.americasavesweek.org/

American Rights at Work: www.americanrightsatwork.org/

Bankruptcy and Student Loans: www1.salliemae.com/after_gradua
tion/manage_your_loans/borrower_responsibility/managing_
debt/bankruptcy.htm

Behindthelabel.org (textile worker rights): www.behindthelabel.org

Buy Nothing Day: www.adbusters.org

Center for Community Change: http://www.communitychange.org/

Center for Economic and Policy Research (English, español, additional
languages): www.cepr.net

Center for Law and Social Policy: www.clasp.org

Center for New American Dream: www.newdream.org

Center for Responsive Politics (challenging money in politics): www
.opensecrets.org

Center for Study of Working Class Life: www.stonybrook.edu/work
ingclass/

Class Action: www.classism.org

Clean Clothes Campaign: www.cleancothes.org

Coalition of Immokalee Workers: www.ciw-online.org/

Coalition on Human Needs: www.chn.org/

College Savings Calculator: studentaid2.ed.gov/getmoney/save_for_
college/save_calculator.html

College Savings Initiative: www.collegesavingsinitiative.org/content/
about-initiative

College Savings Plan Network: www.collegesavings.org/index
.aspx

Common Security Club: www.commonsecurityclub.org

Community Voice Mail: www.cvm.org/

Confront Corporate Power: http://confrontcorporatepower.org

Consumer Financial Protection Bureau Student Loan Complaint
System: https://help.consumerfinance.gov/app/studentloan/ask

Corporate Accountability International: http://stopcorporateabuse.org

CorpWatch: www.corpwatch.org

Dollars&Sense: www.dollarsandsense.org

Dollars for Docs: http://projects.propublica.org/docdollars

Early College High School Initiative: www.earlycolleges.org

Economic Policy Institute: www.epi.org

Education Sector: www.educationsector.org

Fair Labor Association: www.fairlabor.org

Fair Trade Federation: www.fairtradefederation.com

Fair Trade USA: www.fairtradeusa.org

Farm Land Grab: www.farmlandgrab.org

Federal Aid First: www.federalstudentaid.ed.gov/federalaidfirst/

Federal Student Aid Ombudsman Group: www.studentaid.ed.gov/
repay-loans/disputes/prepare

Feed Our Vets: www.feedourvets.org/index/home

Feeding America (English, español): www.feedingamerica.org

Food First/Institute for Food and Development Policy: www.foodfirst
.org

Food Not Bombs: www.foodnotbombs.net

Food Research and Action Center (FRAC): www.frac.org

Free the Slaves: www.freetheslaves.org

Freedom From Hunger: www.freedomfromhunger.org

FreeRice.com: www.freerice.com

Global Exchange: www.globalexchange.org

Global Stewards: www.globalstewards.org

Global Water: www.lobalwater.org

Goodweave (ending child labor in rug industry): www.goodweave
.org;

GRAIN (supporting international small farmers and social movements
in their struggles for community-controlled and biodiversity-based
food systems; English, español, other languages): www.grain.org

Green America's Ending Sweatshops Program: www.greenamerica.org

Green America's Fair Trade Program: www.greenamerica.org

Green Belt Movement: www.greenbeltmovement.org

Green for All: www.greenforall.org

Gynunity Health Projects: www.gynunity.org

Heifer International: www.heifer.org

Help the Afghan Children: www.helptheafghanchildren.org/pages.aspx?
content=6

Hotel Workers Rising: www.hotelworkersrising.org

Hunger Project: www.thp.org

Hunger Site: www.thehungersite.com

Institute for Research on Poverty: www.irp.wisc.edu;

International Forum on Globalization: www.ifg.org/

International Labor Organization: www.ilo.org

International Labor Rights Forum: www.laborrights.org

International Society for Ecology and Culture: www.localfutures.org

International Trade Union Confederation: www.ituc-csi.org

Jobs With Justice: www.jwj.org

Jubilee USA Network: www.jubileeusa.org

Kiva (microloans): www.kiva.org

La Via Campesina (English, español): www.viacampesina.org

Labor History Curriculum (USA): www.kentlaw.edu

Lambdi Fund of Haiti: www.lambifund.org/

Let Justice Roll (living wage campaign): http://letjusticeroll.org

Managing Student Loans: www1.salliemae.com/after_graduation/
manage_your_loans/

Maquila Solidarity Network (labor and women's rights): www.en
.maquilasolidarity.org

MercyCorps: www.mercycorps.org

Millenium Promise Alliance: www.aidforafrica.org

ModestNeeds.org: www.modestneeds.org

Money as You Grow: http://moneyasyougrow.org

National Alliance to End Homelessness: www.endhomelessness.org

National Center for Children in Poverty: www.nccp.org

National Coalition for the Homeless: www.nationalhomeless.org

National Coalition for Homeless Veterans: www.nchv.org

National Guestworker Alliance: www.guestworkeralliance.org

National Labor Committee: www.nlcnet.org

National Law Center on Homelessness and Poverty: www.nlchp.org

National Low Income Housing Coalition: www.nlihc.org

National Student Campaign Against Hunger and Homelessness:
www.studentsagainsthunger.org

National Student Loan Data System: www.nslds.ed.gov/nslds_SA/

New American Dream: www.newdream.org

New Bottom Line (fighting for struggling and middle-class communities): www.newbottomline.com

Occupy Wall Street: https://occupywallst.org/

One International: www.one.org

One Laptop Per Child: www.11aptop.org

Organisation for Economic Co-operation and Development (OECD): www.oecd.org

Our World Is Not For Sale: www.ourworldisnotforsale.org

Over Fifty and Out of Work: www.overfiftyandoutofwork.com/

Oxfam America: http://oxfamamerica.org/

PharmedOut: www.pharmedout.org/

Physicians for a National Health Program: www.pnhp.org

Poor People's Economic Human Rights Campaign: http://old.economichumanrights.org/

PreventObesity.net: www.preventobesity.net/

Public Campaign (clean elections): www.publicampaign.org

Rebuild the Dream: www.rebuildthedream.com

Results (ending poverty): www.results.org

Reverend Billy and the Church of Life After Shopping: www.revbilly.com

Share the World's Resources: www.stwr.org;

Solart Cookers: www.solarcookers.org/

Solidaridad Network (empowering poor workers): www.solidaridadnetwork.org

Solidarity Center: www.solidaritycenter.org

Stanford Center for the Study of Poverty and Inequality: www.stanford.edu

Student Labor Action Project (SLAP): www.studentlabor.org

Student Loan Borrower Assistance Program: www.studentloanborrowerassistance.org

Supplemental Nutrition Assistance Program (SNAP): www.cbpp.org/cms/index.cfm?fa=view&id=2226

Sweatfree Communities: www.sweatfree.org

Tax Justice Network USA: www.tjn-usa.org

Tax.com (education about the tax system): www.tax.com

Trickle Up (ending poverty): www.trickleup.org

Union Songs: http://unionsong.com/

Unions.org: www.unions.org

United Farm Workers: www.ufw.org

United for a Fair Economy: www.faireconomy.org

United Nations International Covenant on Economic, Social, and Cultural Rights (1966, yet to be ratified): www.hrweb.org

United Students Against Sweatshops: www.usas.org

US Uncut: (ending public service cuts): www.usuncut.org

Wealth for the Common Good: http://wealthforcommongood.org/

Why Hunger: www.whyhunger.org

Wider Opportunities for Women: www.wowonline.org/

Working Class Studies Association: www.wcstudies.org

Working Group on Extreme Inequality: www.extremeinequality.org

World Bicycle Relief: www.worldbicyclerelief.org

World Hunger Year: www.whyhunger.org

World Social Forum: www.forumsocialmundial.org;

WTF Where's the Funding?/Student Labor Action Project: www.stu
   dentlabor.org

YouthBuild International: www.youthbuildinternational.org

Yummy Pizza Company (labor studies curriculum for elementary
   schools): www.cft.org/index.php?option=com_content&view=arti
   cle&id=215%3Athe-yummy-pizza-company&catid=40%3Auncate
   gorized&Itemid=8

Familyism-Challenging Resources

See Chapter 7 digital resources.

Genderism-Challenging Resources

Athlete Ally (encouraging athletes, coaches, families, and fans to
   respect all persons involved in sports of all sexual orientations and
   gender identities/expression): www.athleteally.com

Campus Pride (LBGTIQ student leaders): www.campuspride.org

FAFSA Completion Guide for LBGTIQ Families: www.finaid.org/
   fafsa/lgbtfafsa.phtml

Financial Aid for LBGTIQ Students: www.finaid.org/otheraid/lgbt
   .phtml/

Gender Education and Advocacy: www.gender.org

Gender Spectrum: http://genderspectrum.org

GLBT National Help Center and Peer-Support Chat: www.glbtnation
   alhelpcenter.org

GLBT National Hotline: 1-888-843-4564

GLBT Youth Talkline: 1-800-246-PRIDE

International Foundation for Gender Education: www.ifge.org

International Transgender Day of Remembrance—Memorializing
   Those Killed by Anti-Trans Hate or Violence: www.transgenderdor
   .org

Intersex Society of North America (devoted to systemic change to
   end shame, secrecy, and unwanted genital surgeries for people

born with an anatomy not standard for male or female): www
.isna.org

LBGTIQ-Friendly Campus Climate Index (national listing of LBGTIQ-
friendly campuses): www.campusprideindex.org

LGBTQArchitect (grass-roots, open-content project providing resources
for creating and improving programs supporting lesbian, gay,
bisexual, transgender, queer, and ally [LGBTQA] people on campus): www.architect.lgbtcampus.org

Live Out Loud (LBGTIQ youth connecting with LBGTIQ adults): www
.liveoutloud.info

National Center for Transgender Equality: www.transequality.org

NOH8 Campaign: (promoting marriage, gender, and human equality
through education, advocacy, social media, and visual protest):
www.noh8campaign.com

OUTSERV (association of actively serving LBGTIQ military personnel):
www.outserve.org

TransActive (education and advocacy for trans children and youth):
www.transactiveonline.org

TransFamily: www.transfamily.org

Transgender Basics (educational video clip on transgender and gender
variance issues): www.gaycenter.org/gip/transbasics/video

Transgender Law and Policy Institute: www.transgenderlaw.org

TransYouthFamilyAllies: www.imatyfa.org

True Child: www.truechild.org

Wild Gender (celebrating gender-variant persons): www.wildgender
.com

Youth and Gender Media Project (films about social change for and
about gender nonconforming youth): www.youthandgendermedi
aproject.org/

Heterosexism-Challenging Resources

Ali Forney Center (housing for homeless LBGTIQ youth): www.alifor-
ney center.org/

All Out (bringing people of every identity together—LBGTIQ and
straight—to build equality; English, español, français, português):
www.all out.org/

Ally Week (students organizing events in schools against anti-LBGTIQ
language, bullying, and harassment): www.allyweek.org

Ambiente Joven (servicios para la communidad LBGTIQ; español):
www.ambientejoven.org

Amplify Your Voice.org (LBGTIQ young people's website on holistic
sexual health): www.amplifyyourvoice.org

Athlete Ally (encouraging athletes, coaches, families, and fans to respect all persons involved in sports of all sexual orientations and gender identities/expression): www.athleteally.com

Campus Pride (LBGTIQ student leaders): www.campuspride.org/

Children of Lesbians and Gays Everywhere (COLAGE): www.colage .org

Day of Silence (ending violence, harassment, and abuse of LBGTIQ youth): www.dayofsilence.org

eQuality Giving (for LBGTIQ equality): www.equalitygiving.org

FAFSA Completion Guide for LBGTIQ Families: www.finaid.org/ fafsa/lgbtfafsa.phtml

Faith in America (ending religion-based bigotry toward LBGTIQ people): www.faithinamerica.org/

FIERCE (building the leadership and power of LBGTIQ youth of color): www.fiercenyc.org

Financial Aid for LBGTIQ Students: www.finaid.org/otheraid/lgbt .phtml/

Freedom to Marry: www.freedomtomarry.org

Gay, Lesbian, Straight Education Network: www.glsen.org

Gay and Lesbian Alliance Against Defamation: www.glaad.org

Gay and Lesbian National Hotline (M–F, 6–11 p.m. EST): 1-888-843-4564

Gay Men's Domestic Violence Project: 1-800-832-1901 www.gmdvp .org

Gay Straight Alliance Network: www.gsanetwork.org

Gay Straight Alliance Network International: www.gsani.org

GetEqual (empowering LBGTIQ community and allies to take bold action to demand full legal and social equality): www.getequal.org

Give A Damn Campaign (LBGTIQ equality): www.wegiveadamn.org

GLBT National Help Center and Peer-Support Chat: www.glbtnation alhelpcenter.org

GLBT National Hotline: 1-888-843-4564

GLBT Youth Talkline: 1-800-246-PRIDE

Human Rights Campaign (LBGTIQ equal rights): www.hrc.org

Immigration Equality (LBGTIQ and HIV+ community): www.immigra tionequality.org

International Gay and Lesbian Human Rights Commission: www.igl hrc.org

International Lesbian and Gay Association: www.ilga.org

It Gets Better Project (LBGTIQ youth): www.itgetsbetter.org/

Lambda Legal (LBGTIQ civil rights): www.lambdalegal.org

LBGTIQ-Friendly Campus Climate Index: www.campusprideindex.org

LGBTQArchitect (LGBTQA campus resources): http://architect.lgbt
     campus.org

Live Out Loud (LBGTIQ youth connecting with LBGTIQ adults): www
     .liveoutloud.info

Make It Better Project (LBGTIQ youth): www.makeitbetterproject.org

Marriage Equality: www.marriageequality.org

Matthew Shepard Foundation/Matthew's Place (LBGTIQ youth
     safety): www.matthewshepard.org/

National Gay and Lesbian Task Force (NGLTF): www.thetaskforce.org

National Safe Schools Roundtable (LBGTIQ youth): www.safeschool
     sroundtable.org

The Network/La Red (ending LBGTIQ partner abuse; English, español):
     www.tnlr.org

NOH8 Campaign (marriage equality visual protest): www.noh8cam
     paign.com

Out 4 Immigration (LBGTIQ and HIV+ immigration rights): www
     .out4immigration.org

OUTSERV (active-duty LBGTIQ military personnel): www.outserve.org

Parents, Families, and Friends of Lesbians and Gays (PFLAG): www
     .pflag.org

Point Foundation (LBGTIQ college scholarships): www.pointfoundation
     .org

Proud Parenting (resources for LBGTIQ parents): www.proudparenting
     .com/

Queer Rising (equality advocacy): www.queerrising.wordpress.com

Racial Equity (funders for LBGTIQ issues): www.lgbtracialequity.org

Service Members Legal Defense Network: www.sldn.org

Services and Advocacy for LBGTIQ Elders (SAGE): www.sage.org

Sexualidades Latinas! (español): www.sexualidadeslatinas.org/

Soulforce (LBGTIQ nonviolent resistance): www.soulforce.org

Stop the Deportations—The DOMA Project: www.stopthedeportations
     .com/blog/

The Trevor Lifeline (24-hour confidential free LBGTIQ/questioning
     crisis/suicide prevention hotline): 866-4-U-TREVOR (866-488-7386)

The Trevor Project (LBGTIQ youth crisis and suicide prevention): www
     .thetrevorproject.org

True Colors Fund: www.truecolorsfund.org

Truth Wins Out (fighting anti-gay lies and ex-gay myth): www.truth
     winsout.org/

Unid@s (LBGTIQ voices in the United States and Puerto Rico): http://
     unidoslgbt.blogspot.com/

Welcoming Schools Project (LBGTIQ-inclusive K–5 curriculum): www
.welcomingschools.org

Immigrationism-Challenging Resources

Advising Undocumented Students for College Admission: http://pro
fessionals.collegeboard.com/guidance/financial-aid/undocu
mented-students

Equity Assistance Centers: www.equityassistancecenters.org

Immigrant Solidarity Network: www.immigrantsolidarity.org

Immigration Equality (advancing equal immigration rights for the
LBGTIQ and HIV+ community): www.immigrationequality.org

In Motion—The African American Migration Experience: www.inmo
tionaame.org

International Migrants Day: http://www.un.org/en/events/migrants
day/

International Organization for Migration: www.iom.int

National Guestworker Alliance (empowering guest workers and
expanding the right to organize for all excluded workers, reversing
retaliation against workers of color who organize): www.guestwor
keralliance.org

National Immigration Forum (creating vision, consensus, strategy for a
welcoming United States treating all newcomers fairly): www
.immigrationforum.org

National Immigration Law Center (defending and advancing the
rights and opportunities of low-income immigrants and family
members): www.nilc.org

National Immigration Project: www.nationalimmigrationproject.org

No More Deaths/No Mas Muertes (ending death and suffering on the
U.S./Mexico border through civil initiative): www.nomoredeaths
.org/

Out 4 Immigration (united by love, divided by law; addressing the
discriminatory impact of U.S. immigration laws on LBGTIQ and
HIV+ people and families): www.out4immigration.org

Stop the Deportations—The DOMA Project (gay and lesbian bi-national
couples fighting deportation, separation, and exile in the United
States): www.stopthedeportations.com/blog/

United We Dream (network of youth-led immigration organizations in
the United States focused on equitable access to higher education for
all students without regard to immigration status led by undocumented immigrant youth and allies): www.unitedwedream.org

Unrepresented Nations and Peoples Organizations: www.unpo.org

We Are America (stories of today's immigrants; English, español): www.weareamericastories.org/

World Refugee Day: www.worldrefugeeday.us/site/c.arKKI1MLIjI0E/b .8092105/k.B369/World_Refugee_Day.htm

Young Lives on Hold (college dreams of undocumented students): http://professionals.collegeboard.com/guidance/financial-aid/ undocumented-students

Linguicism-Challenging Resources

American Sign Language (ASL): www.handspeak.com

Bilingual Families Connect: www.bilingualfamiliesconnect.com

Center for Advanced Language Proficiency Education and Research (CALPER): http://calper.la.psu.edu

Center for Advanced Research on Language Acquisition (CARLA): www.carla.unm.edu

Center for Applied Linguistics (CAL): www.cal.org/

Center for Applied Second Language Studies (CASLS): http://casls .uoregon.edu

Center for Educational Resources in Culture, Language and Literacy (CERCLL): http://cercll.arizona.edu

Center for Language Education and Research (CLEAR): http://clear .msu.edu

Center for Languages of the Central Asian Region (CeLCAR): www .indiana.edu/~celcar

Center for Open Educational Resources and Language Learning (COERLL): www.coerll.utexas.edu

International Mother Language Day (promoting education and instruction in heritage languages): www.unesco.org/new/en/education/ themes/strengthening-education-systems/languages-in-educa tion/international-mother-language-day/

Language Acquisition Resource Center (LARC): http://larcnet.sdsu .eduhttp://www.carla.unm.edu/

Multilingual Living: www.multilingualliving.com

National Association for Bilingual Education: www.nabe.org

National Capital Language Resource Center (NCLRC): www.nclrc.org

National Clearinghouse for English Language Acquisition and Language Instruction Educational Programs: www.ncela.gwu.edu

National Foreign Language Center: www.nflc.org

National Foreign Language Resource Center (NFLRC): http://nflrc .hawaii.edu

National Heritage Language Resource Center (NHLRC): www.nhlrc
.ucla.edu

National Middle East Language Resource Center (NMELRC): http://
nmelrc.org

Native Languages of the Americas (native language preservation):
www.native-languages.org

Omniglot (world languages and writing systems): www.omniglot
.com

Slavic and East European Language Research Center (SEELRC): www
.seelrc.org

Terralingua (bio/cultural/linguistic diversity): www.terralingua.org

Racism-Challenging Resources

Advancement Project (working for just democracy/racial justice):
www.advancementproject.org

Allianza—National Latino Alliance for the Elimination of Domestic
Violence: www.dvalianza.org

Amazon Watch (supporting indigenous peoples in the Amazon): www
.amazonwatch.org

American-Arab Anti-Discrimination Committee: www.adc.org

American Indian and Indigenous Peoples Resource Directory: www
.indians.org

American Indian Heritage Foundation: www.indians.org

American Indian Tribal Listings (federally recognized): www.indians
.org

Applied Research Center (fighting for racial justice): www.arc.org

Arab American Institute: www.aaiusa.org/

Asian American Center for Advancing Justice: www.advancingjustice
.org

Asian American Legal Defense and Education Fund: www.aaldef
.org

Asian American Net: www.asianamerican.net

Asian Nation: www.asian-nation.org

Association of MultiEthnic Americans: www.ameasite.org

Black AIDS Institute: www.blackaids.org

Black Excel (college help network for Black students and other students
of color): www.blackexcel.org

Black History Pages: www.blackhistory pages.com

Center for the Study of Race and Equity in Education: www.gse.upenn.
edu/equity/

Center for World Indigenous Studies: http://cwis.org

The Civil Rights Project/Proyecto Derecho Civiles (research on ethnicity/race equity in schools): www.civilrightsproject.ucla.edu

Color of Change: www.colorofchange.org

Cuentame (Latino advocacy): www.mycuentame.org

Cultural Survival (partnering with indigenous peoples): www.culturalsurvival.org

DNA Ancestry Project (discovering ancestral roots): www.genebase.com

Equal Justice Society (race equity issues): www.equaljusticesociety.org

Equity Assistance Centers (providing assistance in race, gender, and national origin equity to public schools to promote equal educational opportunities): www.equityassistancecenters.org

Evaluation Tools for Racial Equity: www.evaluationtoolsforracialequity.org

FIERCE (building LBGTIQ youth of color leadership): www.fiercenyc.org

First Voices Indigenous Radio (First Nations): www.firstvoicesindigenousradio.org

Gender, Race, and Inclusive Education Project (Peggy McIntosh/Wellesley Centers for Women): www.wcwonline.org

Global Black Experience Radio: www.wbai.org

Hapa Project (advocacy for mixed race persons of Asian Pacific Islander descent): http://seaweedproductions.com/the-hapa-project/hapa-about/

Hawai'i (Hawai'ian sovereignty): www.hawaii-nation.org

Honor the Earth (resources for survival of sustainable Native communities): www.honorearth.org

Idle No More (indigenous sovereignty): www.idlenomore1.blogspot.com

Indian Country Today: www.indiancountrytoday.com

Indigenous Environmental Network: www.ienearth.org

International Indian Treaty Council/Consejo Internacional de Tratados Indios: www.treatycouncil.org

International Work Group for Indigenous Affairs: www.iwgia.org

Latino USA: www.latinousa.org

League of United Latin American Citizens (English, español): www.lulac.org

Loving Day Project (celebrating mixed-race, multiethnic, multiracial couples and families): www.lovingday.org/

Mavin Foundation (advocacy for persons of mixed race experience): www.mavin.org

NAACP: www.naacp.org

National Association for the Education of African American Children With Learning Disabilities: www.aacld.org/

National Black Justice Coalition: www.nbjc.org

National Boys and Men of Color Institute: www.nationalboysandme
nofcolorinstitute.org

National Compadres Network (strengthening traditional "compadre"
extended family systems supporting positive involvement of
Latinos): www.nationalcompadresnetwork.com

National Congress of American Indians: www.ncai.org

National Council of La Raza: www.nclr.org

National Guestworker Alliance: www.guestworkeralliance.org

National Latino Children's Institute: www.ncli.org

National Latino Fatherhood and Family Institute: www.nlffi.org

Native American Facts for Kids: www.native-languages.org

Native American Rights Fund: www.narf.org

NativeWeb: www.nativeweb.org

OCA (Asian Pacific American advocacy): www.ocanational.org

Presente.org (Latino advocacy): www.presente.org

Project RACE (organizing for multiracial classification): www.projec
trace.com

RACE (are we so different?): www.understandingrace.org

Racism. No way. (anti-racism education): www.racismnoway.com.au

Racism Review: www.racismreview.com

Stand Against Racism: www.standagainstracism.org

Survival International (tribal peoples advocacy): www.survivalinterna
tional.org

Trace American Indian/Native Alaskan Ancestry: www.doi.gov

Transafrica (advocacy for persons of African descent): www.transaf
rica.org

United Confederation of Taino People: www.uctp.org

United National Indian Tribal Youth (UNITY): http://unityinc.org

United Nations Declaration on the Rights of Indigenous Peoples: www
.un.org

Young Men of Color Initiative (increasing college access, readiness, and
completion): http://advocacy.collegeboard.org/college-prepara
tion-access/young-men-color-initiative and http://youngmenof
color.collegeboard.org/

Religionism-Challenging Resources

Americans United for Separation of Church and State: www.au.org

Center for Inquiry (fostering science, reason, freedom of inquiry, and
humanism): www.centerforinquiry.net

Faith in America (ending religion-based bigotry toward LBGTIQ people): www.faithinamerica.org/

Freedom From Religion: www.ffrf.org

Interfaith Alliance (protecting faith and freedom): www.interfaithal
liance.org

Military Association of Atheists and Freethinkers: www.militaryatheists
.org

National Center for Science Education (defending public schools teaching evolution): http://ncse.com

Religious Institute (changing sexuality and religion views for social
justice): www.religiousinstitute.org

Secular Coalition for America: www.secular.org

Soulforce (LBGTIQ nonviolent resistance): www.soulforce.org

United Nations Declarations on Religious Intolerance (1981, 1993):
www.religioustolerance.org

Sexism-Challenging Resources

American Association of University Women (advancing equity for
women and girls): www.aauw.org/

Association for Women's Rights in Development: www.awid.org

Center for Reproductive Rights (advancing reproductive freedom):
http://reproductiverights.org

Equal Rights Advocates (expanding economic and educational access
and opportunities for women and girls): www.equalrights.org

Equality Now: www.equalitynow.org

Equity Assistance Centers (providing federal assistance in race, gender,
and national origin equity to public schools for equal educational
opportunities): www.equityassistancecenters.org

Gender, Race, and Inclusive Education Project (Peggy McIntosh/
Wellesley Centers for Women): www.wcwonline.org

GirlsInc.: www.girlsinc.org

Global Fund for Women: www.globalfundforwomen.org

Guerrilla Girls: www.guerrillagirls.com

Gynunity Health Projects (ensuring reproductive health technologies
are widely available at reasonable cost): http://gynunity.org

Institute for Women's Policy Research: www.iwpr.org

International Women's Day (March 7): www.internationalwomensday
.com

Madre (international women's human rights; English, español): www
.madre.org

National Abortion and Reproductive Rights Action League (NARAL)
(protecting a woman's right to choose): www.naral.org

National Abortion Federation (supporting reproductive choice): www
.prochoice.org

National Boys and Men of Color Institute: www.nationalboysandme nofcolorinstitute.org

National Compadres Network (strengthening traditional "compadre" extended family systems, supporting Latinos in families and communities): www.nationalcompadresnetwork.com

National Council for Research on Women: www.ncrw.org

National Organization for Women (NOW): www.now.org

National Organization of Men Against Sexism (NOMAS) (pro-feminist men): www.nomas.org

National Partnership for Women and Families: www.nationalpartner ship.org

National Women's Law Center: www.nwlc.org

Nobel Women's Initiative: www.nobelwomensinitiative.org

Third Wave Foundation: www.thirdwavefoundation.org

United Nations Convention on Discrimination Against Women (1979): www.hrweb.org

Wider Opportunities for Women (economic independence for families, women, and girls): www.wowonline.org/

Women for Women International: www.womenforwomen.org

Women in World History: www.womeninworldhistory.com

Women's College Coalition: www.womenscolleges.org

Women's Initiatives for Gender Justice: www.iccwomen.org

Women's Institute for Financial Education: www.wife.org

Women's International League for Peace and Freedom: www.wilpf.org

WomensLaw.org (challenging domestic violence): www.womenslaw .org

Women's Law Project: www.womenslawproject.org

Women's Voices (empowering unmarried women voters): www.wvwv .org

XY (men, masculinities, and gender politics): www.xyonline.net

Young Men of Color Initiative (improving educational participation and college completion for young men of color): http://advocacy. collegeboard.org/college-preparation-access/young-men-color-initiative and http://youngmenofcolor.collegeboard.org/

Print

Amatea, E. S., & West-Olatunji, C. A. (2007). Joining the conversation about educating our poorest children: Emerging leadership roles for school counselors in high-poverty schools *Professional School Counseling, 11,* 81–89.

Bidell, M. P. (2005). The Sexual Orientation Counselor Competency Scale: Assessing attitudes, skills, and knowledge of counselors working with lesbian/gay/bisexual clients. *Counselor Education and Supervision, 44,* 267–279.

Buser, J. K. (2010). American Indian adolescents and disordered eating. *Professional School Counseling, 14,* 146–155.

Chen-Hayes, S. F., & Haley-Banez, L. (2000). *Lesbian, bisexual, gay, and transgendered counseling in schools and families (1, 2)* [DVDs]. Hanover, MA: Microtraining Associates.

Day-Vines, N. L., & Day-Hairston, B. O. (2005). Culturally congruent strategies for addressing the behavioral needs of urban African American male adolescents. *Professional School Counseling, 8,* 236–243.

Day-Vines, N., Patton, J., & Baytops, J. (2003). African American adolescents: The impact of race and middle class status on the counseling process. *Professional School Counseling, 7,* 40–51.

Gizir, C. A., & Aydin, G. (2009). Protective factors contributing to the academic resilience of students living in poverty in Turkey. *Professional School Counseling, 13,* 38–49.

Goodrich, K. M., & Luke, M. (2010). The experiences of school counselors-in-training in group work with LGBTQ adolescents. *Journal for Specialists in Group Work, 35,* 143–159.

Goodrich, K. M., & Luke, M. (2011). The LGBTQ Responsive Model for group supervision of group work. *Journal for Specialists in Group Work, 36,* 22–39.

Grothaus, T., Lorelle, S., Anderson, K., & Knight, J. (2011). Answering the call: Facilitating responsive services for students experiencing homelessness. *Professional School Counseling, 14,* 191–201.

Holcomb-McCoy, C., & Chen-Hayes, S. F. (in press). Culturally competent school counselors: Affirming diversity by challenging oppression. In B. T. Erford (Ed.), *Transforming the school counseling profession* (4th ed.). Boston, MA: Pearson.

Lapan, R. T. (2012). Comprehensive school counseling programs: In some schools for some students but not in all schools for all students. *Professional School Counseling 16,* 84–88.

Lapan, R. T., Gysbers, N. C., Bragg, S., & Pierce, M. E. (2012). Missouri professional school counselors: Ratios matter, especially in high-poverty schools. *Professional School Counseling, 16,* 117–124.

Lara-Alecio, R. (2005). A model for training bilingual school counselors. In J. Tinajero & V. Gonzales (Eds.), *Review of research and practice* (pp. 145–161). Mahwah, NJ: Lawrence Erlbaum.

Luke, M., Goodrich, K. M., & Scarborough, J. L. (2011). Integration of K–12 LGBTQI student population into school counselor education curricula: The current state of affairs. *The Journal of LGBT Issues in Counseling, 5,* 80–101. doi:10.1080/15538605.2011.574530

Malott, K. M., Alessandria, K. P., Kirkpatrick, M., & Carandang, J. (2009). Ethnic labeling in Mexican-origin youth: A qualitative assessment. *Professional School Counseling, 12,* 352–364.

Maxwell, M. J., & Henriksen, R. C. (2012). Counseling multiple heritage adolescents: A phenomenological study of experiences and practices of middle school counselors. *Professional School Counseling, 16,* 18–28.

McFarland, W. P. (2001). The legal duty to protect gay and lesbian students from violence in school. *Professional School Counseling, 4,* 171–179.

McGoldrick, M., Giordano, J., Garcia-Prieto, N. (Eds.). (2005). *Ethnicity and family therapy* (3rd ed.). New York, NY: Guilford.

Portman, T. A. A. (2009). Faces of the future: School counselors as cultural mediators. *Journal of Counseling & Development, 87,* 21–27.

Satcher, J., & Leggett, M. (2005). What to say when your student may be gay? A primer for school counselors. *Alabama Counseling Association Journal, 31,* 44–52.

Satcher, J., & Leggett, M. (2007). Homonegativity among professional school counselors: An exploratory study. *Professional School Counseling, 11,* 10–16.

Schellenberg, R., & Grothaus, T. (2009). Promoting cultural responsiveness and closing the achievement gap with standards blending. *Professional School Counseling, 12,* 440–449.

Seo, M., Sink, C. A., & Cho, H.-I. (2011). Korean version of the Life Perspectives Inventory: Psychometric properties and implications for high school counseling. *Professional School Counseling, 15,* 15–33.

Shen, Y.-J., & Lowing, R. J. (2007). School counselors' self-perceived Asian American counseling competence. *Professional School Counseling, 11,* 69–71.

Shi, Q., & Steen, S. (2012). Using the Achieving Success Everyday (ASE) group model to promote self-esteem and academic achievement for English as a second language (ESL) students. *Professional School Counseling, 16,* 63–70.

Shin, R. Q., Daly, B. P., & Vera, E. M. (2007). The relationships of peer norms, ethnic identity, and peer support to school engagement in urban youth. *Professional School Counseling, 10,* 379–388.

Suh, S., & Satcher, J. (2005). Understanding at-risk Korean American youth. *Professional School Counseling, 8,* 428–435.

Trusty, J. (2002). African Americans' educational expectations: Longitudinal causal models for women and men. *Journal of Counseling & Development, 80,* 332–345.

Turner, S. L., Conkel, J. L., Reich, A. N., Trotter, M. J., & Slewart, J. J. (2006). Social skills efficacy and proactivity among Native American adolescents. *Professional School Counseling, 10,* 189–194.

Van Velsor, P., & Orozco, G. L. (2007). Involving low-income parents in the schools: Communitycentric strategies for school counselors. *Professional School Counseling, 11,* 17–24.

Varjas, K., Graybill, E., Mahan, W., Dew, B., Marshall, M., & Singh, A. (2007). Urban service providers' perspectives on school responses to gay, lesbian, and questioning students: An exploratory study. *Professional School Counseling, 11,* 113–119.

Vera, E. M., Vacek, K., Coyle, L. D., Stinson, J., Mull, M., Buchheit, C., & Langrehr, K. J. (2011). An examination of culturally relevant stressors, coping, ethnic identity, and subjective well-being in urban ethnic minority adolescents. *Professional School Counseling, 15,* 55–66.

Walsh, F. (Ed.). (2012). *Normal family processes: Growing diversity and complexity* (4th ed.). New York, NY: Guilford.

Whitman, J. S., Horn, S. S., & Boyd, C. J. (2007). Activism in the schools: Providing LGBTQ affirmative training to school counselors. *Journal of Gay & Lesbian Mental Health, 11,* 143–154.

Wyatt, S. (2009). The brotherhood: Empowering adolescent African American males toward excellence. *Professional School Counseling, 12,* 463–470.

11

Technology
Solutions

Are you tech-savvy or tech-phobic? Either way, school counselors and other leaders have a wealth of solutions that they can use to reach the needs of all stakeholders in schools. However, the use of technology, particularly Web 2.0 tools and social media, in the practice of school counseling remains sparse as does research on this topic (Perera-Diltz & Mason, 2012; Sabella & Booker, 2003). Rockinson-Szapkiw and Walker (2009) offered this definition of Web 2.0:

> Web 2.0 refers to the second generation of the Internet that utilizes the Web as a platform to facilitate collective intelligence, contribution, and collaboration (O'Reilly, 2005), and it is defined by its technological components, including content management systems (CMS), podcasts, vodcasts, 3-D virtual worlds and simulations, collaborative conferencing software, blogs, and wikis. Web 2.0 technologies provide users with an opportunity to interact online both synchronously (real-time) and asynchronously (different time) via text, audio, video, and graphics.

Some literature examines the use of Web 2.0 tools in counseling practice but mostly in reference to interfacing with individual clients or in how it is used to train counseling students, through virtual means, on the use of basic counseling skills (Trepal, 2007). There is a slow but growing body of research on the use of technology specific to school counseling.

As professionals working in school settings, school counselors are charged with serving all students (American School Counselor Association, 2012; Paisley & McMahon, 2001). Given the unwieldy student-to-school counselor ratios that exist in many school districts (e.g., the national average is 457:1) providing quality services to students is a challenge (ASCA, 2012; Barstow & Terrazas, 2012). Additionally, the constantly changing nature and often immediately needed types of information and expertise school counselors provide (e.g., crisis response, graduation requirements, and college and financial aid application requirements) benefit students and families most with broad, efficient, engaging, and timely dissemination. Furthermore, some school counselors are the only school counselors in their schools or are serving in remote, rural areas with minimal access to colleagues or in-person professional development opportunities. Technology is a powerful tool for furthering students' success and for furthering school counselor professional development. The digital resources at the end of the chapter include technology and media literacy resources.

Key Words

ASCA SCENE: A professional networking platform that is part of the American School Counselor Association

Asynchronous: Interacting with technology sources at one's own convenience and not in real time

Blogs: Journal entries or short personal or professional opinion pieces found on the Internet

Cloud Computing: The use of a web-based tool, site, or platform for storing documents, photos, or music so that the user has access to the most updated version. It reduces or eliminates use of computer hard drives for file storage and allows easier file sharing.

Collaborative Conferencing Software: Specialized software applications that allow for multiple participants to interact with one another despite being in different geographic locations

Content Management Systems: Educationally driven websites designed to deliver content to participants who have access to the system, commonly used in colleges and universities for managing courses and communication between students and instructors

Digital School Counseling Brochure: A brochure from the school counseling program that exists in digital form instead of or in addition to print format

Digital School Counseling Bulletin Board: A picture of the school counseling program bulletin board posted on the school counseling program web pages

E-Newsletters: Newsletters that are delivered in graphic form via e-mail or an Internet link

Massive Open Online Courseware (MOOC): An Internet-based platform for providing education and/or training to large and broad audiences

Online Instruction: A means of using the Internet as a source of instruction in concert with or in lieu of face-to-face instruction

Podcasts: Audio recordings of lectures or presentations that can be listened to online or through accessible applications for mobile devices

School Counseling Program Website: Website designed to educate readers about the school counseling program with information such as services provided, upcoming events, and contact information for school counselors

Social Media Sites: Web-based tools or locations that allow for social and/or professional interaction

Synchronous: Interacting with technology sources in real time or "live"

Virtual Worlds/Simulation: Virtual spaces, games, or scenarios in which persons can engage online or through specialized software

Vlogs: Video-based journal entries or short personal or professional opinion pieces that can be found on the Internet

Vodcasts: Video-based recordings of lectures or presentations that can be viewed online or through accessible applications for mobile devices

Webinars: Interactive or noninteractive lectures and presentations that are typically "live" or synchronous and presented through the Internet

Wikis: Collaboratively constructed websites that allow multiple users to add and edit information

Key Questions and Solutions

1. What are school counselors expected to know and do with technology?

Even by national standards this is a growing area, however, the ASCA published School Counselor Competencies (2007), identifying a few skills related to use of technology:

III-B-1f. Knows, understands and uses a variety of technology in the delivery of guidance (school counseling core) curriculum activities

V-B-1f. Uses technology in conducting research and program evaluation

I-B-1g. Uses technology effectively and efficiently to plan, organize, implement, and evaluate the comprehensive school counseling program

Additionally, the ASCA (2010) Code of Ethics offers ethical obligations to school counselors in relation to technology:

A.10. Technology

Professional School Counselors:

A. Promote the benefits of and clarify the limitations of various appropriate technological applications. Professional school counselors promote technological applications (1) that are appropriate for students' individual needs, (2) that students understand how to use, and (3) for which follow-up counseling assistance is provided.

B. Advocate for equal access to technology for all students, especially those historically underserved.

C. Take appropriate and reasonable measures for maintaining confidentiality of student information and educational records stored or transmitted through the use of computers, facsimile machines, telephones, voicemail, answering machines, and other electronic or computer technology.

D. Understand the intent of FERPA and its impact on sharing electronic student records.

E. Consider the extent to which cyberbullying is interfering with students' educational process and base guidance (school counseling core) curriculum and intervention programming for this pervasive and potentially dangerous problem on research-based and best practices.

2. Why should school counselors bother with technology?

Given the increasing use of technology in society in general but especially among school-aged populations, it is imperative that school counselors understand how technology can assist them in their work. Furthermore, as new technologies emerge and are used, they are often noted for their detrimental or potentially detrimental effects on children and adolescents; there is great concern about the misuse of technology by parents and educators (Barreto & Adams, 2011).

School counselors who are well versed in available Web 2.0 tools can help ease concerns among families and staff with whom they work, and they can model safe, fun, and engaging technology practices for all. Given the perpetually increasing technological savvy of P–12 education students (i.e., "digital natives") and their families (Zur & Zur, 2011; Prensky, 2010), there is a need for all educators, including school counselors, to stay current with technology tools that engage these audiences.

3. What can school counselors use technology for?

Not only do Web 2.0 tools change the way students and families communicate with school staff, they also continue to change the way students at all levels learn about relevant content. K–12 students show preferences for learning core subjects with digital devices and Web 2.0 tools (Jensen, Boschee, & Whitehead, 2002). Greater parent/guardian involvement and information accessibility can also be achieved with Web 2.0 tools (Luckin et al., 2008). Furthermore, technology has also changed the way that school counselors, and educators in general, engage in professional development, work-related tasks, professional networking, and communication.

Technology provides school counselors with tools to reach more students and families in a more appealing, proficient, opportune, and often economical way than through conventional means of delivery (e.g., costly printed materials, multiple phone calls and e-mails to provide repetitive answers to questions, a standard classroom lecture).

4. How do school counselors get started with technology when it is intimidating?

Getting started with technology can seem daunting, given that it is always changing. Embracing the ever-evolving nature of technology is part of the adoption process. Far more important than trying to keep up with *all* of the new tools and gadgets is to know well those tools that help school counselors make work engaging and efficient. When one can share the "what" and "how" with others about these tools, school counselors generate confidence in others who may also be reluctant to try technology. The best way to get started with technology is to try out just a few sites or tools of interest that come recommended by trusted professionals. School counselors can also start by considering the tasks or role that could be improved by technology; these may include file storage and organization, communication, or presentations.

5. How does technology lessen school counselor overload and free up time for student planning, school counseling core curriculum lessons, and counseling?

The simple act of going "paperless," as much as possible, by utilizing web-based, cloud computing for forms, lesson plans, and other documents, can help tidy up the administrative side of the job so that school counselors have time to invest in more important tasks like meeting with students. Cloud storage (Dropbox, Google Drive, etc.) allows users to share files more easily and to be more environmentally and economically conscious.

Data collection tools and specialized software programs that focus on time-tracking can allow for a clearer perspective on where time actually goes at school (ASCA, 2012). An audit of school counselor time, even one week per month, will help in identifying direct and indirect service and making recommendations to shift, adjust, minimize, or eliminate indirect responsibilities.

Additionally, digital presentation tools and hardware can enhance the breadth of delivery of core curriculum and professional development. Not only can these tools make standard classroom presentations more engaging and creative but they can easily be shared electronically. Those students, families, and staff who may miss a face-to-face presentation can view and, in some cases, interact with, the information if e-mailed via a link or embedded onto a web page. Pre-prepared presentations from school counselors can be run by teachers in classrooms or viewed independently by recipients to reinforce information.

6. How can school counselors use technology to share school counseling program mission, goals, resources, and outcomes?

Technology provides a wealth of tools for presenting information and data collection. With cloud computing, there is the capacity for multiple members of a team to work from and edit the same document, saving the hassle of multiple versions being shared back and forth. Many educators also use online document presentation tools that some can edit and all can view. Additionally, the Internet is a key place to showcase school counseling program information, whether it is a connected page to the school's website or a stand-alone website or blog for the school counseling program. Technology allows for much broader and more engaging dissemination of program information and is more easily edited and updated than traditional print materials. A growing number of school counselor bloggers capitalize on their blogs to share nonconfidential reflections, activities, program highlights, and outcomes.

7. How can school counselors encourage appropriate and creative uses of technology within the school community?

Students are the early adopters of technology and have less fear than adults because they have grown up in a digital world; they are "digital natives." Often, they are the ones to pave the way for use of technology in schools. As educators, we need to be open to their ideas while presenting and problem solving the challenges alongside them. Paying attention to what other schools and districts are using by being a step behind the curve can help schools plan to implement new tools by learning from what others have experienced. For example, more schools are implementing "1-to-1" programs, which provide every student with a school-issued device such as a tablet or laptop while others are using "BYOD" or "bring your own device" programs so that students can actively use technology in the classroom.

8. How can school counselors develop technology and social media policies that promote positive, fair, and safe use?

Each school community is unique, and the factors to consider in using technology in schools grow more complex. A school-level technology team or committee, if not already established, is a valuable and inclusive way to develop policy, assess needs, and examine tools for adoption. A technology team can be composed of school staff and those with technological skill and/or interest, and with valuable community business partners, parents/guardians, and students.

The significance of following ethical mandates within the profession, including those technology-related standards mentioned in the introduction, is paramount. Consulting key resources that provide guidance on these issues can help uphold ethical and legal guidelines while promoting positive student engagement. The American School Counselor Association and iKeepSafe.org (2012) collaborated to provide *Facebook for School Counselors* to offer guidelines about dealing with students' technology use inside and outside school walls. This document recommends specific ways in which school counselors help create a climate of digital citizenship and safety (p. 2):

1. Helping develop school policies
2. Responding to online incidents that impact conditions for learning
3. Assisting the community in detecting at-risk behavior
4. Addressing digital citizenship: technology literacy, privacy, reputation, and social awareness

Another helpful source for school counselors and leaders is a recent article, "Ethically Assisting Students via Social Media," (Froeschle, Crews, & Li, 2013). The article authors offer the following concrete, practical suggestions for ethically based practices:

- Seek approval for posted content from appropriate department chairs and/or administration.
- Consult other professionals as ethical concerns related to social media and students or families arise.
- If creating "page" or social media sites to deliver information to students and families about the school counseling program, ensure that it is a separate professional, not personal, account designed as a one-way delivery vehicle. Create and distribute accompanying print materials containing the same information as the page or site (brochures, newsletters, etc.).
- Be knowledgeable about social media accounts' privacy disclosures and ensure that the school community is also informed.
- Utilize settings on the page or site that prohibit others from making posts or comments or allow page or site managers to monitor them before posting.
- Provide an informed consent statement that the site is not a substitute for counseling services. In no way should it be used for posting crisis or emergency needs, and any such posts or comments of this type should be hidden or deleted.

- Provide on the page or site a clear process for requesting appointments from the counseling department.
- Provide information about limitations to confidentiality on the page or site.
- Do not post personal, sensitive information about individual students on the page or site.
- Do not "follow" or "friend" students or families from the page or site or use personal accounts to connect with students or families.
- As students and families "like" or follow the page or site, do not inspect their personal accounts.

We offer a few additional recommended practices in using social media:

- Before sharing personal information about students, provide a voluntary procedure with written consent for parents and guardians who may wish for information to be shared about their child on the page or site such as awards, scholarships, honors, and artistic, academic, or sporting competitions or events.
- School counselors and other leaders should utilize settings on their personal accounts that offer the highest security and privacy so as to minimize the risk of students or families accessing personal information, posts, and photos.
- School counselors and other leaders should engage with social media, personally and professionally, in a way that models integrity and positive digital citizenship for students and the school community.
- Especially in small communities or communities in which the probability of dual relationships may be greater, school counselors and leaders should consider carefully when choosing whether or not to "friend" others, accept friend requests, or follow other accounts.
- Unfriend or unfollow any accounts that have or may create dual relationships or ethical issues while providing those individuals with a professional, ethical rationale for doing so (e.g., friends or work colleagues whose children are temporarily students on the school counselor's caseload).

9. How can school counselors utilize social media to keep students, families, and community partners informed?

The use of social media can help with communication by reaching school communities more broadly and quickly. In 2012, Mason and Schultz documented more than 150 Twitter accounts managed by school counseling departments. These accounts are used for sharing announcements, reminders, and events with school communities. Social media allows recipients to get important information without filling up e-mail inboxes. Additionally, these vehicles allow school counselors to share information without creating lengthy e-mails or flyers.

10. Where can school counselors learn more about technology tools and how they can work for the school counseling program?

Counselor educator and former school counselor Erin Mason manages a site called SCOPE, which stands for "School Counselors' Online Professional Exchange." SCOPE addresses the need to teach school counselor educators and school counseling graduate students, as well as school counselors in the field, about current Web 2.0 tools. SCOPE provides those in the profession with a central and continuously updated clearinghouse of resources related to the incorporation of technology into school counseling practice. SCOPE also encourages interaction among all the professional audiences it targets so that there is a dynamic mechanism for theory-to-practice learning. SCOPE already has more than 300 members, most practicing school counselors, and has sustained slow but regular growth since its establishment in August 2011.

SCOPE operates as a collaborative socio-technological innovation so that members may both consume and contribute within its environment. SCOPE is arranged categorically by function, and then within those categories, alphabetically by Web 2.0 tool. Each tool is showcased with multiple, real examples of the tool as it has been or is being used by someone in the field of school counseling. All tools highlighted by SCOPE are free, and membership in SCOPE is free. SCOPE will evolve and grow, adding new tools that emerge and removing tools that become obsolete.

11. Where can school counselors find the best source for websites with academic, career, college-access, and personal/social competency resources for school counseling programs?

School counselor educator Stuart Chen-Hayes compiled 1,500-plus website links for school counseling programs on a Digication e-portfolio website in alphabetical order color-coded by academic/career/college access sites in red and personal/social sites in multiple additional colors (https://lehmanedu.digication.com/stuartchen-hayes/Change_the_World). The same website links are also grouped with similar color-coding by ASCA student standards and the NOSCA eight career and college readiness components (https://lehmanedu.digication.com/stuartchen-hayes/Academic_Development_Competencies/published). Click on the left sidebar career and college readiness components and the personal/social competencies to reveal the full list of additional link categories.

Solution Success Stories

Story 1

Sometimes a simple solution has a big impact. A high school counseling department in Georgia uses Google Drive to manage sign-ups for several significant events. For example, the scheduling of advising sessions for juniors and their families had become a logistical nightmare and meeting with each student is a state mandate. The school counselors determined how many days were needed to meet with the juniors on their caseloads and created the needed number of appointment slots, plus a few extra for rescheduling, in a spreadsheet. The spreadsheet was uploaded to Google Drive and mailed out as a link to all junior families for signing up. Once the schedule was finalized, a mail merge function was used to send confirmation letters to families and to create passes to the school counseling office for students at their scheduled time. The department has used a similar system for its holiday toy drive. A relatively small, simple use of technology such as this saves endless amounts of time, phone calls, and clerical work.

Story 2

Marissa, a Midwest elementary school counselor, says, "I use technology throughout every aspect of my school counseling program." When the school has a special event, videos and pictures are taken and she compiles them into 12–15-minute movies. These movies are shown on a loop during lunch times so that students can enjoy commemorating the event. Marissa says these movies also help create a calmer lunchroom!

Marissa also likes to use a SMARTboard during her school counseling core curriculum lessons and specifically likes the "keyword dice." She uses the digital dice by specifying one dye with feeling words and the other dye with animals.

(Continued)

(Continued)

Students come to the board, tap the dice, and then act out the feeling words and animals they get. Marissa says, "It's fun and pretty funny for the students ... and, of course, educational too!"

Story 3

Technology makes data collection a snap, so no more tallying paper and pencil surveys. Rick, an elementary school counselor in Oregon, uses Google Forms to create short, web-based surveys for students in order to assess the learned concepts from his school counseling core curriculum lessons in the classroom. Rick says, "I'm instantly able to see the results. Exciting stuff."

Story 4

In addition to using e-mail templates and a shared drive for storing documents in his department, Jeremy, a high school counselor in the Mid-Atlantic, uses spreadsheets to streamline normally time-consuming tasks like registration for Advanced Placement courses and the PSAT. Jeremy also uses spreadsheets to collect, filter, and sort student data from multiple sources, including needs assessment responses, making it quick and easy to identify students with particular needs and to target them for specific interventions.

Additionally, Jeremy uses a screen-recording tool called Screen-Cast-O-Matic to create narrated, visual tutorials that walk students through the complicated process of requesting transcripts. Not only can these tutorials be shown in classrooms but they can also be embedded on websites or e-mailed out as links for continuous reference.

Of using Twitter, Jeremy says, "And Twitter!? Twitter! How awesome is this technology that allows me to filter information that supports my students' academic, career, and personal/social development, and retweet, directly from the source, that information to my students and their parents!" Jeremy manages multiple Twitter accounts, one for his school counseling department, which he uses to share information and announcements with students and families, and another for himself for engaging with other educators on Twitter and for professional development on the go.

Resources

Digital

Admitted—the National Association for College Admission Counseling (NACAC) Blog: www.nacacnet.org/learning/com munities/admitted/default.aspx

ASCA Podcasts: http://ascaway.podbean.com

ASCA Scene: https://schoolcounselor.groupsite.com/main/summary

ASCA Webinars: www.schoolcounselor.org/content.asp?pl=325 &sl=129&contentid=609

Campaign for a Commercial-Free Childhood: www.commercialexploi tation.com

Caring Bridge (making health journeys easier with free patient web-sites): www.caringbridge.org

Center for Digital Democracy: www.democraticmedia.org

Center for Media and Democracy's PR Watch: www.prwatch.org/cmd

Center for Media Literacy (helping young citizens develop critical thinking and media production skills): www.medialit.org

College Bound Blog: http://blogs.edweek.org/edweek/college_bound/

The College Solution Blog (college affordability and admissions tips): www.thecollegesolution.com/tag/college-blog

Common Sense Media (family media and technology information): www.commonsensemedia.org

Connect Safely (social media safety tips for youth): www.connectsafely .org/

Counselors' Corner Blog: hscw-counselorscorner.blogspot.com

CrossRef.org (collaborative reference linking service through Digital Object Identifiers [DOIs] for ease of article access): www.crossref.org

Democracy Now: www.democracynow.org/

Digital Learning Environments (tools and technologies for effective classrooms): www.guide2digitallearning.com/

Education Week: www.edweek.org

Edudemic (open access college courses): http://edudemic.com/

Electronic Frontier Foundation (defending rights in the digital world): www.eff.org

Electronic Privacy Information Center (protecting privacy, open gov-ernment, free speech): http://epic.org

Eric Sheninger, Digital Principal: http://ericsheninger.com/

EZAnalyze and Time Tracker—Data Tools for Educators (free, Excel-based tools to enhance the data-driven work of school counselors and other educators): www.ezanalyze.com

FreeSpeech.org: www.freespeech.org/

From the Counselor's Office Blog: http://counselorsoffice.blogspot.com

Groundspark (igniting change through film): www.groundspark.org

Guarding Kids: www.guardingkids.com

iKeepSafe.org: www.ikeepsafe.org

Independent Media Center: www.indymedia.org

Indykids! (students in grades 4–8 reporting in print and online on social justice issues and media): www.indykids.net

International Society for Technology in Education (ISTE): www.iste.org

Jitsi (free encrypted video calls, messaging, and document sharing): www.jitsiproject.org

Kleinspiration (connecting tradition and technology): www.kleinspiration.com/

Leading Success (online toolkit for educators from College Board): www.leadingsuccess.org

Media Education Foundation: www.mediaed.org

New Media Literacies (play, performance, simulation, appropriation, multitasking, distributed cognition, collective intelligence, judgment, transmedia navigation, networking, negotiation, and visualization): www.newmedialiteracies.org/

NOSCA Webinars: http://nosca.collegeboard.org/tools-resources/webinars

ProPublica: www.propublica.org/

SchoolCounselor.com: www.schoolcounselor.com

School Counselor Blog: www.schcounselor.com

School Counselors' Online Professional Exchange (SCOPE): http://sconlineprofessionalexchange.wikispaces.com/

Storybird (artful storytelling): http://storybird.com

Teach-nology (free support for educators incorporating technology): www.teach-nology.com

TedEd: http://ed.ted.com

TedTalks: www.ted.com

Tor (free software improving Internet privacy and security): http://torproject.org

Upside Down World: http://upsidedownworld.org/

Voki (free speaking avatars as a learning tool in 25 languages): www.voki.com

What Kids Can Do (using media to show what young people can accomplish, especially youth marginalized by poverty, race, and language): www.whatkidscando.org

Wired Safety (internet safety, help, and education): wiredsafety.org

The Young People's Project (math literacy and social change): www.typp.org/

The Youth and Gender Media Project: www.youthandgendermediaproject.org/

Youtube.edu (educational videos): www.youtube.com/education

Print

Abney, P. C., & Maddux, C. D. (2004). Counseling and technology: Some thoughts about the controversy. *Journal of Technology in Human Services, 22*, 1–24. doi:10.1300/J017v22n03_01

American School Counselor Association. (2012). *The ASCA national model: A framework for comprehensive school counseling programs* (3rd ed.). Alexandria, VA: Author.

Aspy, D. N., Aspy, C. B., Russel, G., & Wedel, M. (2000). Carkhuff's human technology: A verification and extension of Kelly's (1997) suggestion to integrate the humanistic and technical components of counseling. *Journal of Counseling & Development, 78*, 29–37.

Barreto, S., & Adams, S. K. (2011). Digital technology and youth: Developmental approach. *Brown University Child & Adolescent Behavior Letter, 27*, 1–6.

Barstow, S., & Terrazas, A. (2012). Department of Education to accept new round of ESSCP application. Retrieved from http://ct.counseling.org/2012/03/department-of-education-to-accept-new-round-of-esscp-applications/

boyd, d. m., & Ellison, N. B. (2007), Social network sites: Definition, history, and scholarship. *Journal of Computer-Mediated Communication, 13*, 210–230. doi:10.1111/j.1083–6101.2007.00393.x

Elleven, R. K., & Allen, J. (2004). Applying technology to online counseling: Suggestions for the beginning e-therapist. *Journal of Instructional Psychology, 31*, 223–226.

Froeschle, J. G., Crews, C. R., & Li, J. (2013). Ethically assisting students via social media. Retrieved from http://counselingoutfitters.com/vistas/vistas13/Article_13.pdf

Hartig, N. A., Terry, K. P., & Turman, A. M. (2011). Social networking websites and counselors-in-training: Ethical and professional issues. Retrieved from http://counselingoutfitters.com/ vistas/vistas11/Article_64.pdf

iKeepSafe.org & American School Counselor Association. (2012). Facebook for school counselors. Retrieved from http://www.ikeepsafe.org/wp-content/uploads/2012/04/Facebook-For-School-Counselors-Final-Revision1.pdf

Lundberg, D. J. (2000). Integrating on-line technology into counseling curricula: Emerging humanistic factors. *Journal of Humanistic Counseling, Education & Development, 38*, 142–151.

Mell, P., & Grance, T. (2011). The NIST definition of cloud computing. Retrieved from http://csrc.nist.gov/publications/nistpubs/800–145/SP800–145.pdf

Milsom, A., & Bryant, J. (2006). School counseling departmental websites: What message do we send? *Professional School Counseling, 10*, 210–216.

Perera-Diltz, D. M., & Mason, K. L. (2012). A national survey of school counselor supervision practices: Administrative, clinical, peer, and technology mediated supervision. *Journal of School Counseling, 10*. Retrieved from http://www.jsc.montana.edu/articles/v10n4.pdf

Prensky, M. (2010). *Teaching digital natives: Partnering for real learning.* Thousand Oaks, CA: Corwin.

Renfro-Michel, E. L., O'Halloran, K. C., & Delaney, M. E. (2010). Using technology to enhance adult learning in the counselor education classroom. *Adultspan: Theory Research & Practice, 9*, 14–25.

Rockinson-Szapkiw, A. J., & Walker, V. L. (2009). Web 2.0 technologies: Facilitating interaction in an online human services counseling skills course. *Journal of Technology in Human Services, 27,* 175–193. doi:10.1080/15228830903093031

Sabella, R. (2003). *SchoolCounselor.com: A friendly and practical guide to the World Wide Web* (2nd ed.). Minneapolis, MN: Educational Media.

Sabella, R. (2004). *Counseling in the 21st century: Using technology to improve practice.* Alexandria, VA: American Counseling Association.

Sabella, R. (2008). *GuardingKids.com: A practical guide to keeping kids out of high-tech trouble.* Minneapolis, MN: Educational Media.

Sabella, R., & Booker, B. L. (2003). Using technology to promote your guidance and counseling program among stakeholders. *Professional School Counseling, 6,* 206.

Van Horn, S. M., & Myrick, R. D. (2001). Computer technology and the 21st century school counselor. *Professional School Counseling, 5,* 124.

Williams, J. L. (2005). Technology in counseling and psychotherapy: A practitioner's guide. *Social Science Computer Review, 23,* 389–391. doi:10.1177/0894439305275918

12

School-Wide and Multi-Systemic Intervention Solutions

Historically, the school counseling profession has included some well meaning but burned out professionals content with providing individual services for some students without understanding the significance of a school counseling program to the whole school system (Baker & Gerler, 2008; Herr, 2002; Paisley & Borders, 1995; Schimmel, 2008). The tradition of school counselors waiting idly in their offices waiting for individual students to visit with no school counseling program focus was challenged with the work of Norman Gysbers and the proliferation of comprehensive developmental school counseling programs. The notion was further disputed when, in the late 1990s, the Education Trust teamed up with a grant from the Dewitt Wallace-Reader's Digest Fund to transform the role of school counselors. This five-year multistage national project, the Transforming School Counseling Initiative, was designed to transform the education and training of school counselors through fostering *systemic change.* Trish Hatch and Judy Bowers co–authored the original American School Counselor Association (ASCA) National Model school counseling program framework, which underscored this need by deeming systemic change as one of the four essential themes fundamental to the framework of the ASCA

National Model (ASCA, 2012). The National Office for School Counselor Advocacy (NOSCA, 2010) further promoted the idea of multi-systemic change through the intentional use of strategic planning for college and career readiness counseling. Progressive school counselors know and understand the tenets for creating systemic change and how to position their school counseling programs into school-wide transformation movements that focus on equity for all students.

Key Words

Change Agent: An individual who works for justice for all groups and persons by identifying gaps and needs and then taking productive action

Data-Driven: Decisions concerning future action that are based on survey reports, assessments, statistics, or other forms of data

RAMP: Recognized ASCA Model Program is an award given to school counseling programs for their data-driven outcomes in fully implementing a school counseling program including closing achievement and/or opportunity gaps in their schools.

Response to Intervention: Schools identify students facing poor learning outcomes, monitor student progress, provide evidence-based interventions, and adjust the interventions depending on a student's responsiveness.

School Climate: The overall feelings, attitudes, and expectations prevalent in a school

School Culture: The institutionalized atmosphere or "feel" of a school on a day-to-day basis

System: A collection of parts joined together by multiple relationships that are interrelated and interdependent

Systemic Change: Change that occurs within and between the multiple spheres of influence that shape educational processes and policies, including (but not limited to) students, parents/guardians, teachers, administrators, and community members

Key Questions and Solutions

1. What is systemic change and how do school counselors create it in schools and districts?

When examining systems theory and systemic change, there are many interconnected systems (i.e., school, family, community) and subsystems (i.e., classroom, parents/guardians/caregivers, political institutions) impacting the complex nature of a student's academic, career/college, and emotional concerns (Keys & Lockhart, 1999; Kraus, 1998). To be successful, therefore, change in one system necessitates modifications in other related subsystems (Reigleuth & Garfinkle, 1994), yet systems are prone to maintain the status quo (Keys & Lockhart, 1999). V. V. Lee and Goodnough (2011) noted that working systemically—understanding all of the subsystems and interrelationships that affect the individual—allows school counselors to address barriers in policy and procedures that will serve every student, thereby maximizing the effectiveness of a school counselor.

As such, the ASCA (2012) National Model promotes systemic change as one of its four skill themes. When school counselors engage in data-driven leadership, advocacy, and collaboration, barriers to students' academic success can be overcome as school counselors create systemic, long-lasting positive changes. As cited by ASCA (2012), Anderson (1993) highlighted the stages of systemic change:

A. *Maintenance of the old system:* Similar to Prochaska and Norcross's (2001), pre-contemplation stage in this initial stage people in the system are unaware that the system is not working and have yet to recognize the need for necessary modifications and adaptations to become more current and effective.
B. *Awareness:* In this stage, the notion of change begins to take shape but clear steps to foster change have yet to be established.
C. *Exploration:* During the exploratory stage, educators and administrative leaders begin trying new ways of doing things and seek examples of similar systems that have successfully made strides fostering change.
D. *Transition:* It is during this critical time that key players, including administrators, team leaders, and policy makers, commit to making integral changes within the system.
E. *Emergence of a new infrastructure:* During this stage, new system elements are enacted and accepted within the new system.
F. *Predominance of the new system:* The major elements of the system are in place and the new system is established. In a highly functioning new system, leaders understand the system will evolve to keep up with the needs of those served.

2. What are potential barriers to systemic change in schools and districts and how do school counselors mediate them?

Barriers to long-term systemic change include (1) lack of data-driven decision making; (2) inability to secure key stakeholders' support and participation; and (3) collaborative ineptness whereby school counselors misjudge or misinterpret existing political structures and cannot harness the collaborative strengths of their peers. Each of these potential barriers is addressed below.

Utilizing Data. To promote systemic change, a school counselor must review and analyze data with a sharp eye for inequities. Systemic change cannot be enacted if data is not disaggregated, if inequitable trends are not identified, and if data is used only for monitoring and reporting time-on-task (V. V. Lee & Goodnough, 2011). School counselors must be proficient in collecting, analyzing, and sharing data that examines rigorous course enrollment trends, discipline records, achievement patterns, and college-going rates, and then ask difficult questions about what is discovered. Once these questions are placed at the forefront of conversations, without falling prey to the blame game, equitable practices and systemic change can begin.

Mobilizing Key Stakeholders' Support and Participation. Arming oneself with numbers—the language building and district leaders and policy makers speak—greases the wheels for change and provides an entree for constructive conversations. School counselors must be savvy about providing a clear data picture of problems while presenting solution-focused ideas for remedying them. For example, discussing statistics regarding the underenrollment of poor and working-class youth of color in advanced courses must be linked to graduation and college-going/success rates within the district so that a clear picture of what needs to be done can emerge. Thus, making connections between data and district goals is paramount in securing the support of key players when asking them to shift system-wide practices to equitable outcomes for all students. School counselors must understand that this shift may take time and that tenacity and perseverance are necessary to accomplish it.

Collaboration and Political Savviness. All systems are held together by those in power and many persons in power seek to keep their power. Therefore, if school counselors are careless in their quest for change, they may offend the very leaders needed to enact it.

As discussed in Chapter 2, harnessing one's collaborative skills is imperative to creating a healthy school environment and for creating systemic change. Finding allies such as department chairs, trusted community leaders, and involved parents/guardians who have historical political clout within the system is a first step toward reaching others. Once convinced that systemic change is necessary to serve *all* students and that their opinions are heard and respected, these "ambassadors" can help champion the cause. Hastily moving about without recognizing the inherent power structures can doom even the best and most well-intentioned plans for change.

3. How do school counselors enact multi-system interventions?

NOSCA is a visionary in viewing the school counseling process as multi-systemic. Given its strong stance that "strategic planning is an essential tool for school counselors to drive positive change in schools" (NOSCA, 2010), leaders at NOSCA created the School Counselor Strategic Planning Tool, which includes various systems that affect college and career readiness counseling for all students. The six steps outlined in the tool are as follows:

- Collect, analyze, and interpret data to identify gaps in student outcomes.
- Develop and prioritize measurable, data-driven goals aligned with school, district, state, and national goals.
- Develop strategies and interventions to meet goals.
- Develop and implement the plans for each goal, including benchmarks to monitor progress.
- Collect and report outcome data to all stakeholders, and adjust strategies and interventions based on results.
- Institutionalize policies, practices, and procedures to sustain gains in equity.

Following these steps allows school counselors to create meaningful school counseling programs inclusive of local, district, state, and national mandates. This creates the foundation to sustain a systemic college-going culture and equitable college and career readiness practices that permeate the school, reaching every student and family.

4. How can school counselors leverage federal mandates such as Response to Intervention to serve all students through school-wide initiatives?

With the reauthorization of the IDEA in 2004, Response to Intervention (RTI) employs multilevel, researched-based interventions aimed at determining learning disability eligibility for successful academic and behavioral outcomes (Gruman & Hoelzen, 2011; Ockerman, Mason, & Hollenbeck, 2012). Given that 14 states have legal requirements or concrete guidelines for RTI (Zirkel & Thomas, 2010), school counselors must learn how to embrace it and skillfully establish themselves as key contributors to this systemic educational reform. In fact, school counselors' expertise in advocacy, leadership, counseling, collaboration, and utilizing data for systemic change positions them as indispensable in this movement (Ockerman et al., 2012). Specifically, school counselors who employ a comprehensive developmental school counseling program (CDSCP) can connect their existing interventions with RTI's tiered delivery system (see Figure 12.1). In other words, school counselors can use school-wide interventions through their annual school counseling core curriculum (ASCA, 2012) to deliver Tier 1 interventions. School counselors can contribute to Tier 2 interventions by offering more targeted interventions via small-group counseling and mentoring and tutoring programs. Finally, school counselors can employ Tier 3 interventions through solution-focused brief individual counseling. It is crucial that professional school counselors make the link between what they contribute to student success transparent to other educational professionals, as many educators do not understand school counseling services, school counseling programs, and their alignment with student learning and achievement outcomes (Ockerman et al., 2012).

School counselors' competence in collecting, analyzing, and interpreting data is paramount within the RTI framework. School counselors are indispensable members of the RTI team by helping to monitor progress, interpret results, and evaluate effectiveness of interventions implemented. School counselors should also use evidenced-based counseling interventions to align with the tenets of RTI and evaluate their efforts on a consistent basis (Dimmitt, Carey, & Hatch, 2007; Ockerman et al., 2012).

The historical social justice underpinnings of RTI, which aimed to eliminate the overidentification of students of color in special education settings (Newell & Kratochwill, 2007),

Figure 12.1   Aligning RTI and School Counseling Interventions

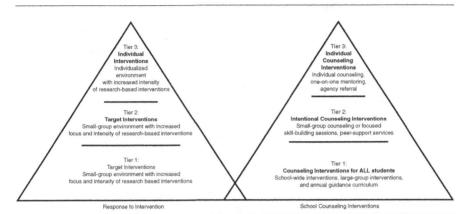

Source: Adopted from Smith, Kinard and Lozo, 2008.

complements school counselors' advocacy role. Given the transformative movements in school counseling and the ASCA (2010) Ethical Code for School Counselors, it is a professional and ethical responsibility to ensure that all students are treated equitably and that biases within the system are eradicated. Thus, school counselors must take a proactive role using data to ensure that RTI is implemented with fidelity to its foundational tenets (Ockerman et al., 2012). Successfully aligning school counseling programs to federal school-wide mandates, such as RTI, places school counselors in leadership roles and ensures their work is valued (see Figure 12.2).

5. What levels of intervention must occur to make systemic school-wide and district change successful?

RTI lends itself to a school-wide, multitier intervention strategy. However, wise and effective school counselors reach beyond the school walls to ensure systemic change is realized (Mason, Ockerman, & Chen-Hayes, 2013). Beyond large-group/classroom, group, and individual counseling, school counselors must be purveyors of community resources and actively broker community partnerships that bolster positive changes within the school system. For instance, school counselors working in schools where budgetary limitations impede access to technology could establish strong relationships with technological firms and local computer technology programs (e.g., ITT Technical Institute) to help mitigate need and advance technological

Figure 12.2 School Counselor's Role and Program Element as a Response to RTI

		School Counselor Role	
		Supporter	**Intervener**
School counseling program element	**Tiered model**	Highlight at RTI team meetings the evidence-based counseling interventions at various settings that already serve the goals of the team and the needs of identified students, as well as those that could contribute	Provide evidence-based counseling interventions in school-wide, classroom, small-group, and individual settings to address academic and/or behavioral concerns
	Data	Share data collected from counseling interventions with the RTI team to document student movement through the tiers	Collect and analyze data regarding all interventions used to meet the goals of the RTI team and to serve students identified by the team
	Social advocacy	Highlight specific data from needs assessments that demonstrate academic and/or behavioral issues identified by students, staff and/or parents; bring to the team's attention issues of social justice and the needs of marginalized populations while connecting these issues to the RTI team's goals.	Design and implement needs assessments for students, staff, and/or parents to give them a voice in identifying needed academic and/or behavioral supports; create and deliver specific counseling interventions based upon the needs of underserved populations

competence among students. School counselors must also be persistent about family communication and, in many instances, offer educational and informational workshops to family members to ensure changes within the school are maintained and encouraged in the home setting. V. V. Lee and Goodnough (2011) reminded school counselors that district-wide efforts between and among grade levels help to maximize resources and ensure consistency in reaching district goals. For example, they noted that school counselors at elementary, middle, and high school levels can contribute to increasing the college-going rate of students by employing strategic interventions that build upon the developmental levels of students at all ages.

Moreover, school counselors must understand the institutional and policy changes that have to occur to make systemic change persist. School counselors need to ensure that changes in practices are reflected in school policy and that this policy is made known to stakeholders. Advocating for needed changes with local, state, and national policy makers is also necessary for sustained systemic change (see Chapter 14). Evaluating multilevel changes and measuring their impact upon student achievement will help to ensure that forward momentum continues and that the system becomes responsive and adaptive to the evolving needs of students and their families.

Solution Success Stories

Story 1

A school counseling district supervisor in the Southeast, Gail, saw the need to empower school counselors to position themselves as credible, valuable professionals in their schools because their positions were often on the chopping block. She sought out several progressive and influential school counselors within the district and created a School Counseling Program advisory team, a group whose role would be to discuss major issues facing school counselors in the district and to guide her in taking action. Meetings with the advisory team highlighted the need for more school counselors and administrators to be trained in the ASCA National Model. Thus, the supervisor set out with a pilot group of several school counselors and their administrators and trained them in the model with the promise that each would

(Continued)

(Continued)

complete a data project highlighting how they had worked to close an achievement gap in their schools by the end of the year. As a result of this work, one district school counselor was recognized as the ASCA School Counselor of the Year and several schools went on to receive RAMP recognition. Over the course of the next few years, the initial work of the pilot group grew and became the foundation for district-wide training on the ASCA National Model for counselors and administrators.

Story 2

As part of the RTI process, Michele, a high school counselor in a Midwestern suburb, is part of the Early Intervention Team (EIT). They meet each week to discuss students that they have been on the D/F grade list.

"Sarah, now a senior, would often show up on the D/F list. First, I called her into our EIT meeting to check in with her and find out what the problems/concerns were regarding her keeping up her grades. Upon talking with her, three factors seemed to stand out as those hindering her success: (1) her attendance; (2) she didn't have a rapport and didn't really like some of her teachers; (3) no follow-through on homework. These three factors needed to be addressed, and the team needed to come up with a plan to help her in these areas.

"First, every student, including Sarah, received a letter (sent home) that suggested groups, academic resources, and supports that are available at our high school. The team then called in the students to discuss which of these supports they were willing to try. Sarah chose to participate in 'Saturday Success' and go for tutoring." As Michelle discussed with Sarah how to better the relationship with teachers, they also needed to address the connection between *not* being in class and how it affects a teacher's view of a student. Basically, Sarah needed to be in school more consistently.

Each week, Sarah would come into Michele's office and give her an update on how she was doing, not only in her classes, but also with all of the supports they had chosen. Often, the conversation would go back to her attendance issue—that's when they needed to have the dean host a parent/student meeting. Michele also attended, reminding Sarah of her goal to graduate from high school. This reminder to her was especially important because she would be the only high school graduate in her family.

Michele reported that Sarah met all of the graduation requirements and participated in the graduation ceremony!

(Continued)

Story 3

Funded by a large federal grant, three elementary school counselors and one social worker in a Southern California school district set out to increase social and emotional competencies and academic achievement for all students. Under the tutelage of Dr. Trish Hatch, this team designed, implemented, and evaluated school-wide programming, including school counseling core curriculum lessons, social- and academic-skills small groups, ancillary programs (e.g., peace patrols, recess programming), and parent/guardian/caregiver workshops. In all three schools, the impact of these interventions was astonishing: significant decreases in truancy and discipline referrals and improvement on state achievement tests. But the team also knew that sharing their work was essential to keeping the monies that funded them. Using the Flashlight Approach to creating a school board presentation, the team was able to effectively present the highlights of their work to key central office and school board members and to gain recognition for the data-driven results they achieved. Impressed with the undeniable impact of this team, the school board moved to sustain funding for the elementary team and expanded the program to district middle schools. Through commitment and hard work, thoughtful and intentional programming, and strong evaluation measures, systemic change is indeed possible (Hatch, 2014).

Resources

Digital

Center for School Counseling and Leadership (CESCAL): www.cescal.org

Center for School Counseling Outcome Research and Evaluation (CSCORE): http://www.umass.edu/schoolcounseling/

National Center for Culturally Responsive Educational Systems (NCCRESt): www.nccrest.org/professional/culturally_responsive_response_to_intervention.html

National Center for Transforming School Counseling: www.edtrust.org/dc/tsc

National Center on Response to Intervention: www.Rti4sucess.org

NOSCA's Eight Components of College and Career Readiness Counseling: www.collegeboard.org/nosca

NOSCA's Own the Turf College Readiness Toolkit: www.collegeboard
.org/nosca

NOSCA School Counselor Strategic Planning Tool: http://media
.collegeboard.com/digitalServices/pdf/nosca/11b_4393_counseling_
page_WEB_111107.pdf

RTI Action Network: http://RTInetwork.org

Print

American School Counselor Association. (2012). *The ASCA national model: A framework for school counseling programs* (3rd ed.). Alexandria, VA: Author.

Education Trust. (2003). *A new core curriculum for all: Aiming high for other people's children.* Retrieved from http://www2.edtrust.org/NR/rdonlyres/26923A64-4266-444B-99ED-2A6D5F14061F/0/k16_winter2003.pdf

King, S. A., Lemons, C. J., & Hill, D. R. (2012). Response to intervention in secondary schools: Considerations for administrators. *NASSP Bulletin, 96,* 5–22.

Lee, V. V., & Goodnough, G. E. (2011). Systemic data-driven school counseling practices and programming for equity. In B. T. Erford (Ed.), *Transforming the school counseling profession* (3rd ed., pp. 129–153). Boston, MA: Pearson Merrill Prentice-Hall.

Mason, E., Ockerman, M. S., & Chen-Hayes, S. F. (2013). Change-Agent-for-Equity (CAFÈ) model: A framework for school counselor identity. *Journal of School Counseling, 11.* Retrieved from http://www.jsc.montana.edu/articles/v11n4.pdf

Ockerman, M. S., Mason, E. C. M., & Hollenbeck, A. F. (2012). Integrating RTI with school counseling programs: Being a proactive professional school counselor. *Journal of School Counseling, 10.*

Ryan, T., Kaffenberger, C. J., & Gleason Carroll, A. (2011). Response to intervention: An opportunity for school counselor leadership. *Professional School Counseling, 14,* 211–221.

Schimmel, C. (2008). *School counseling: A brief historical overview.* West Virginia Department of Education. Retrieved from http://wvde.state.wv.us/counselors/history.html

Sink, C. (2011). School-wide responsive services and the value of collaboration. *Professional School Counseling, 14,* II–IV.

13

Administrative, Operational, and Supervision Solutions

School counselors can take a major leadership role in school functioning with a focus on the operational, organizational, administrative, and supervision structures and processes of schools. School counselors often have the most global and systemic view of an entire school of any staff member (McMahon, Mason, Daluga-Guenther, & Ruiz, in press). But to evaluate school counselors based on teacher standards with teacher evaluation tools makes no sense and is in part why we created the CAFÉ School Counselor Evaluation (see Chapter 1). Schools vary in how they are organized and in how staff are supervised due to the aspects and practices of leadership in the building and district (see Chapter 1) and the ways in which staff collaborate (see Chapter 2). School counselors must play an educational role in informing others of the professional ethics, competencies, and standards to which they are held at the national, state, and local levels.

For example, the size of a school or the number of grade levels may generate a need for more creative divisions of the student body. Schwartz, Stiefel, Rubenstein, and Zabel (2011) found that K–4, 5–8, and K–8 schools have positive effects on student performance. Also, for students who change schools more often, the later the grade in which the first transition is made, the larger the cohort in the school, or the less stable the peer group, the worse effect on student performance. For school staff, including school counselors, various administrative, organizational, and supervisory arrangements, both physical (office space, location, etc.) and task-related (caseload size, assignment, etc.), influence operations and effectiveness of both the individual professional and the multiple systems within a school.

Key Words

Administrative Supervision: Supervision of school counselors or other staff by a principal, dean, or assistant principal; it may be evaluative in nature and/or revolve around logistical concerns

ASCA School Counselor Competencies: The professional expectations of every school counselor in implementing a school counseling program that provides academic, career, and personal/social competencies to all students K–12

Budgeting: The process of appropriation of funds to staff and support the school according to federal mandates, state requirements, and local needs

Caseload Assignments: The portion of a school's student body assigned to a school counselor; often determined by dividing up students' names alphabetically or by grade level or other unit

Child Study Team: A team of school staff members including the school counselor who discuss and plan for students with academic and/or behavioral concerns

Data Team: A team of school staff members including the school counselor who discuss national, state, district, and/or schoolwide data sets to determine areas of strength and improvement

Efficiency: The effectiveness of school operations and organization to meet the goals of the school and to facilitate student success

Integrative Developmental Model: A model of counselor supervision that centers on the counselor's professional development in the areas of awareness of self and others, motivation, and autonomy

Leadership Team: A team of school staff members including the school counselor that discusses relevant issues of the school

Operations: The day-to-day management of a school inclusive of facility use, master schedules, traffic flow patterns, budgetary practices, staffing, policies, and procedures

Organization: The structure of groupings or assigning tasks and responsibilities to certain persons within schools such as teams, grade levels, departments, and committees

School Counselor Performance Standards: District or state standards used to evaluate school counselor effectiveness

School Counselor Performance Tool: District or state template, rubric, or form used to evaluate school counselor effectiveness

Teams/Houses/Units/Clusters: Organizational units used to divide a school's student body based on geographical layout, efficiency, or convenience

Use of Time Analysis Assessment: An ASCA National Model form that allows school counselors to enter their daily activities and tasks to analyze where time is spent and where it is not

Key Questions and Solutions

1. What organizational, administrative, and supervision structures work best for school counseling programs?

The organizational structures for teams in schools including school counseling departments vary. In schools that have more than one school counselor, it is common for them to be assigned to a student caseload according to grade level or a portion of the alphabet. Where there are school counseling departments, as in high schools or schools with more than one school counselor, an administrator may be assigned to be the supervisor for the full department rather than school counselors split between various administrators for supervision and evaluation.

However, there are other organizational structures for school counselors. Some schools utilize the concept of "houses" or "teams" to create schools within schools. With this approach, some students of each grade level make up a house or team and a school may consist of three, four, or five houses or teams. Often in these arrangements, a school counselor may be assigned to a particular house or team and paired with an administrator. This means the school counselor deals with a cross-section of the student population, inclusive of multiple grades, rather than a particular segment of the population. Other schools have "academies" for certain grade levels, often freshmen, to ease the transition to high school. When determining the best organizational structure for school counseling departments, there are multiple factors to consider, such as the developmental and learning needs of students, size of school population, building layout, and experience of the school counselors.

2. How can school counselors guarantee they are evaluated according to their unique skill and knowledge sets?

Too often school counselors are evaluated by administrators who have little or no training in the current role of the school counselor, experience as a school counselor, or experience in the supervision of school counselors. Additionally, school counselors often are evaluated in their schools and districts using a teacher evaluation tool, which is an inadequate and inappropriate evaluation. At the time of this writing, the Danielson model (www.danielsongroup.org) has increased in popularity for the purpose of evaluating teachers, but there is, as of yet, little research to support the model (McClellan, Atkinson, & Danielson, 2012). It is only an updated version of an earlier model that addressed a few pages for school counselors and other school personnel without depth or specifics to the uniqueness of school counselor roles and how they differ from those of other educators. While some districts that have taken the lead or are developing and using school counseling–specific evaluation tools for their school counselors, some are working to transform teacher evaluation tools like the Danielson model into school counselor–friendly versions. Many districts, however, are not there yet. Until everyone catches up, the implementation of an equitable supervision and evaluation process is a point of leadership and advocacy for school counselors. Creation and use of the CAFÉ School Counselor Evaluation (see Chapter 1) is our contribution to strengthening the equity-focused evaluation process for school counselors K–12.

Key to demonstrating that school counselors need a unique evaluation is the practice of visibility. School counselors and their school counseling programs need to be highly visible for others to understand and appreciate the comprehensiveness of the school counselor's role, especially administrators. Consider that if others don't know what school counselors are doing, they will be more suspicious or assume that they can be assigned any responsibilities at any time. Visibility includes practices recommended by the American School Counselor Association, including ASCA National Model school counseling program components (ASCA, 2012) also discussed in Chapter 14:

- Post and circulate weekly, monthly, and annual school counseling program calendars highlighting key activities.
- Position yourself in key spots during the morning, afternoon, and lunch as well as during class change as often as possible.
- Complete periodic time analyses and share them with building and district leaders and other key stakeholders; simplify the information into easy-to-read graphs and charts.
- Utilize bulletin boards, websites, newsletters, or morning announcements to spotlight key data, activities, or commendations.
- Periodically send building and district administrators and supervisors key literature about school counseling as suggested reading.
- Investigate and discuss with stakeholders what school counselors do at other schools and in other districts that is working for the academic, career, college readiness, and personal/social success of every student in their school counseling programs.
- Gather support from others and advocate that the district develop a school counselor–specific evaluation tool and provide training for all building and district leaders educating them about school counselor ethics, competencies, and standards.

3. What is the organizational structure that best suits the core values and beliefs of a school community?

The core values and beliefs, if they are evident in the school's mission statement, should also be reflected in the organizational structure of school staff and the building. In large schools that aim to honor a greater sense of belonging for each student, then a model of schools within schools that house their own school counselor may be more aligned with the mission. In this case, housing a school counselor office physically on a hallway or in a space where students pass makes them more accessible. School counselors can be instrumental in helping administrators and stakeholders consider the social, emotional, and developmental aspects of school functioning because of their training. By using tools like needs assessments, school counselors can gauge the school climate and determine specific gaps that could be addressed through changes in organizational structures of the school.

4. Where are the gaps in school operational/supervision structure and budgets/resource allocation?

Unfortunately, everything does not proceed smoothly all the time in schools. Schools are complex ecological systems with multiple sub-systems and feedback loops (McMahon et al., in press). Operational efficiency in a school requires that each system is functioning as intended and functioning with other subsystems as intended. However, schools, like most systems and their subsystems, don't always run the way they are supposed to, and functioning is inter-rupted. Leaders in the school, inclusive of but not limited to the prin-cipal, must periodically assess the operational efficiency of a school and determine what processes must be changed to improve. Sometimes these assessments will call for a change (small or large) in procedure, a change in resource allocation, or a change in personnel when the status quo is not consistent with desired outcomes and/or the school mission.

5. How can school counselors determine strengths and improvements needed for organizational structure and operational procedures from community stakeholders and school staff?

Because school climate and operations often go hand in hand, needs assessments are key tools for determining school strengths and areas for improvement as they relate to operations and efficiency. School counselors are appropriate personnel to examine issues of school climate to develop needs assessments and analyze resulting data because they often have a broad knowledge of the school culture and are attuned to systemic issues. In addition to assessing the needs of students or staff, school counselors can also seek a more com-prehensive perspective of needs by assessing parents/guardians/caregivers, community members, and other stakeholders.

Solution Success Stories

Story 1

An elementary school counselor in an urban district in the Midwest took the lead to simplify the process for teachers to refer students for support services in her school. In addition to the school counselor, the school also had two full-time

(Continued)

social workers. Rather than having a separate referral processes for teachers to understand, the school counselor created a single referral form and process for all three of the support service staff. The form was streamlined for teachers with checkboxes rather than open-ended questions for easier and quicker completion. Once forms were received, the school counselor and the two social workers met together to assign referrals based on their unique availability, expertise, and current caseloads.

Story 2

A middle school counseling program in an urban setting in the Northeast was doing constant reactive crisis management responding to every behavioral issue that arose in every classroom and every stakeholder concern by phone or in person, leaving zero time to focus on counseling, planning, or school counseling core curriculum for the four school counselors. A consultation from a school counselor educator resulted in creating a crisis-of-the-day on-duty school counselor so that the other three could work exclusively on preventive counseling, school counseling core curriculum, and planning initiatives. This group of school counselors learned how to systemically say no, set limits, and organize their time as professionals so that they could deliver academic, career, college-readiness, and personal/social competencies to all students rather than monitor "drama club" all day long.

Story 3

A high school counseling department in a suburban Midwest school houses a "drop-in center" as part of its services to students. Each day of the week, specific school counselors staff the center to run personal/social groups and to provide responsive services such as crisis management or individual counseling. Other school counselors are utilized for providing the school counseling core curriculum—academic, college, and career-related services.

Resources

Digital

Indiana School Counselor Evaluation Tool: www.indianaschool counselor.org/Default.aspx?pageId=1116338

National Office of School Counselor Advocacy's Principal Counselor Relationship Toolkit: http://nosca.collegeboard.org/research-policies/principal-counselor-toolkit

Texas School Counselor Evaluation Tool: www.tea.state.tx.us/ couseling_job_desc.html

West Virginia School Counselor Evaluation Tool: http://wvde.state .wv.us/counselors/administrators/documents/wvevaluation_ counselorguideOct29_2012.pdf

Print

American School Counselor Association. (2010). *Ethical code for school counselors.* Alexandria, VA: Author.

American School Counselor Association. (2012). *The ASCA national model: A framework for school counseling programs* (3rd ed.). Alexandria, VA: Author.

Beesley, D., & Frey, L. L. (2001). Principals' perceptions of school counselor roles and satisfaction with school counseling services. *Journal of School Counseling, 4,* 1–27.

Bifulco, R., & Bretschneider, S. (2001). Estimating school efficiency: A comparison of methods using simulated data. *Economics of Education Review, 20,* 417–429.

Chata, C. C., & Loesch, L. C. (2007). Future school principals' views of the role of professional school counselors. *Professional School Counseling, 11,* 35–41.

Clark, M., & Stone, C. (2001). School counselors and principals: Partners in support of academic achievement. *National Association of Secondary Principals Bulletin, 85,* 46–53.

Clemens, E. V., Milsom, A., & Cashwell, C. S. (2009). Using leader-member exchange theory to examine principal-school counselor relationships, school counselors' roles, job satisfaction, and turnover intentions. *Professional School Counseling, 13,* 75–85.

DeVoss, J. A., & Andrews, M. F. (2006). *School counselors as educational leaders.* Boston, MA: Houghton Mifflin.

Dodson, T. (2009). Advocacy and impact: A comparison of administrators' perceptions of the high school counselor role. *Professional School Counseling, 12,* 480–487.

Dollarhide, C. T., Smith, A. T., & Lemberger, M. E. (2007). Critical incidents in the development of supportive principals: Facilitating school counselor-principal relationships. *Professional School Counseling, 10,* 360–369.

Herr, E. L., Heitzmann, D. E., & Rayman, J. R. (2006). *The professional counselor as administrator.* Mahwah, NJ: Lawrence Erlbaum.

Leuwerke, W. C., Walker, J., & Shi, Q. (2009). Informing principals: The impact of different types of information on principals' perceptions of professional school counselors. *Professional School Counseling, 12,* 263–271.

Levin, H. M. (2001). *Privatizing education: Can the marketplace deliver choice, efficiency, equity, and social cohesion?* Boulder, CO: Westview Press.

McMahon, H. G., Mason, E. C. M., Daluga-Guenther, N., & Ruiz, A. (in press). Towards an ecological model of school counseling. *Journal of Counseling and Development.*

Ockerman, M. S., Mason, E. C. M., & Chen-Hayes, S. F. (2013). School counseling supervision in challenging times: The CAFÉ supervisor model. *Journal of Counselor Preparation and Supervision, 5(2), Article 4.* doi:http://dx.doi.org/10.7729/51.0024

Schwartz, A. E., Stiefel, L., Rubenstein, R., & Zabel, J. (2011). The path not taken: How does school organization affect eighth-grade achievement? *Educational Evaluation and Policy Analysis, 33,* 293–317.

Stiefel, L., Schwartz, A. E., Rubenstein, R., & Zabel, J. (2005). *Measuring school performance and efficiency: Implications for practice and research.* Larchmont, NY: Eye on Education.

Stoltenberg, C. D., & McNeill, B. W. (2010). *IDM supervision: An integrated developmental model for supervising counselors and therapists* (3rd ed.). San Francisco, CA: Jossey-Bass.

Stone, C. B., & Dahir, C. A. (2011). *School counselor accountability: A MEASURE of student success* (3rd ed.). Upper Saddle River, NJ: Pearson.

Yoep Kim, D., Zabel, J. E., Stiefel, L., & Schwartz, A. E. (2006). School efficiency and student subgroups: Is a good school good for everyone? *Peabody Journal of Education, 81,* 95–117.

14

Advocacy and Public Relations Solutions

For many educators, school counselors, and other leaders, the idea of advocacy may seem daunting and outside one's skill set. Many educators were not taught about advocacy or public relations in college. However, given the public and political nature of education issues, including funding, class sizes, overuse of standardized testing, corporate influence, teacher and leader evaluation, and constant pressure on school budgets and funding for public, charter, and independent schools, knowledge of advocacy and public relations are crucial aspects of educators' positions including school counselors and leaders. Much like other school leaders, school counselors must be advocates in equity-focused roles for students, school counseling programs, and school counselor positions. At the same time, school counselors can use advocacy to increase stakeholder knowledge of school counseling program benefits and outcomes to gain greater staffing, funding, and support for school counselors and school counseling programs focused on equitable academic, career, college-access, and personal/social competencies for every student.

Key Words

Activism: Publicly campaigning for a topic, cause, need, person, or group of persons

Advocacy: Creating positive change where change is needed; supporting, in word and deed, a topic, cause, need, person, or group of persons

External Public Relations: Explaining the school counseling program and the larger school context to stakeholders outside the building: parents/guardians, community organizations, businesses, places of worship, and voters

Internal Public Relations: Explaining the school counseling program to all internal stakeholders including students, educators, staff, and building leaders

Public Relations: Marketing school counseling programs and positions by investing time and energy in building relationships with stakeholders and sharing news, updates, and outcomes in both digital and traditional formats

Tenacity: Strong persistence

Key Questions and Solutions

1. What does it mean to advocate in schools?

Advocacy in schools can happen on varied levels in a systemic fashion (C. C. Lee & Rodgers, 2009). For example, a school counselor can advocate with teachers on behalf of a student who needs additional time completing assignments due to a recent family tragedy. Or a group of teachers may advocate to administration for a change in the master schedule to shorten passing times and increase instructional time. At larger levels, educators may engage in policy advocacy by being involved in district or state organizations or groups for increased education funding and to challenge the misuse of high-stakes testing or mass closings of public schools and layoffs of employees in urban communities. Other examples include a group of principals lobbying the school board to create a change in the district's anti-bullying policy that protects LBGTIQ students and leaders of the state school counseling organization lobbying a state appropriations board to stress the significance and impact of lowering the ratio in schools.

2. How do school counselors leverage success with students to advocate for their needs?

Data is one of the most powerful tools for advocacy and public relations, especially with less informed or skeptical stakeholders. The ASCA National Model (ASCA, 2012), Dimmit, Carey, and Hatch (2007), and Young and Kaffenberger (2011) emphasized the importance of collecting process, perception and outcome data from student interventions. Having multiple types of data strengthens the message sent to stakeholders. For example, an assessment of a five-session (process data) small-group counseling intervention focused on study skills development can demonstrate that the involved students not only believed the intervention was helpful (perception data) but that they each improved their overall grade point average (outcome data).

3. In what types of outlets should school counselors publicize the school counseling program's goals, activities, and outcomes?

Multiple, repeated, and simple displays of school counseling program goals, activities, and outcomes are best in reaching a broad range of stakeholders via e-mails, websites, live presentations, videos, fliers, brochures, and so on. In a technological age, both print and digital communications are necessary, and in schools even bulletin boards can showcase what school counselors are doing. Perhaps the most important approaches are to use more than one outlet to communicate the same information and to represent key data points with easy-to-understand graphs and charts. In addition, regular press releases to local newspapers and participation in press conferences are critical to assist with highlighting the school counseling program's value and success in the local community for bettering students' lives and helping them achieve their academic, career, college readiness, and personal/social goals.

4. How do school counselors toot their horns without being self-serving?

Given that school counselors see themselves in a helpful and supportive role, rather than vying for the spotlight, it is no wonder that many do not toot their own horns. But not teaching others about the school counselor and school counseling program inside and outside of schools has kept other educators and the public questioning, "What do school counselors do?"

There is nothing self-serving about having professional pride and confidence in one's work, particularly when concrete results are demonstrated, that is, student academic and behavioral improvement, career and college readiness successes, school climate change, increased satisfaction ratings from families, and so on. Reporting, sharing, and celebrating success is well worth it and well deserved. A perfect time to do so is during National School Counseling Week in early February, when special events can be held to demonstrate and recognize the hard work of school counselors. Additionally, RAMP, the Recognized ASCA Model Program, nationally recognizes the excellence of school counseling programs and brings attention to the hard work of school counselors. NOSCA and the College Board also sponsor "Inspiration Awards" for school counselors leading the way in creating equitable college and career readiness counseling success in K–12 schools.

5. What communication styles and strategies work best for sharing critical issues with various stakeholders (e.g., legislators, families, school board members)?

Knowing the audience is key in discussing issues of concern with others. It is important to know what kind of information is compelling to stakeholders. For example, families, the media, and community members are often moved by anecdotal information or stories while building and district leaders, school board members, and legislators find numerical data more persuasive. In addition, when presenting information to the media or other stakeholders, it is important to be prepared, especially because you may not have a great deal of time to present. Talking "off the cuff" or in an aggressive style can turn others off to the message. Brief talking points and simple handouts or presentations created ahead of time can help keep the message brief, effective, and on track. If school counselors don't know an answer to a question, they can volunteer to get back to those who ask it and then make sure to follow through to build trust and credibility.

6. How does it benefit the school, community, and district when school counselors share school counseling program successes?

The benefits of sharing successes with stakeholders are many. Not only does this spotlight the school counseling program role but it clarifies the sometimes misused or misunderstood role of school counselors. Moreover, it helps to leverage allies who may assist in either promoting or funding future school counseling initiatives. Another key benefit is to highlight the unique mission and vision of the school counseling program and how they complement the mission and vision of the entire school. Sharing student success stories regarding academics, college and career readiness, and personal/social triumphs also shows the positive effects of school counseling programs and demonstrates a solution-focused approach to school counseling when some stakeholders still attempt to keep us in a reactive or problem-focused mode. But sharing stories of success and proactive building of student competencies is the essential tool to bring around skeptics who inaccurately see school counselors only as the "guiders" and "drama-control" people in schools.

7. How do school counselors engage in political conversations and issues?

Recognizing the political aspects of education and working in a school is essential for school counselors and other leaders. The political context of education is unwise to ignore. Similar to leadership, advocacy and public relations come in many styles and forms and should draw on school counselor strengths and skills. What is most important is to be personally and professionally driven by a cause such as equity for all students. There are huge political forces at work in all schools but especially public schools in challenging times, for example, budget cuts, vouchers, corporate influence, high-stakes testing, No Child Left Behind, and Race to The Top federal education initiatives. It is critical that school counselors and leaders educate themselves and all stakeholders as to who has the power, the money, and the ideological rationales behind "reform" movements in K–12 schools and which students are most harmed by which "reformers."

Advocacy and activism are not the same. Advocacy is an ongoing process, for example, the advocacy movement to ensure all students receive publicly funded pre-school and all-day kindergarten to boost successful early and later learning in K–12 schools. Activism is associated with specific events such as picketing, striking, or rallies related to a particular cause such as challenging public school closures in primarily poor and working class, people of color neighborhoods in US cities or large-scale layoffs of public education workers in Detroit, New Orleans, Philadelphia, and Washington, D.C. Each educator must find their own place on the continuum of advocacy and use activism activities to support the school counseling program and issues that affect student, family, and staff success in delivering academic, career, college readiness, and personal/social competencies to every student.

8. What are common obstacles or challenges with advocacy or public relations?

Fear of change is a prevalent barrier facing school counselors and other leaders engaged in advocacy or public relations. In fact, fear of change, which appears as resistance, creates the need for advocacy. Resistance can come from many points such as a lack of information, incorrect information, staunch beliefs, or fear of change. Finding allies who support the school counselor's position increases the persuasiveness of the argument and builds confidence among the hesitant to advocate the cause.

School counselors and other leaders who use advocacy effectively influence a change in school policy or implement a needed program by empowering themselves, the school community, and the students. For example, Oceanside, California schools had no elementary school counseling program and the district applied for and was awarded an elementary and secondary school grant to hire multiple elementary school counselors in multiple schools. The school counselors were so successful at demonstrating their results in improving student academics, lessening behavioral and attendance issues, and increasing career and college readiness that the school system found the money to not only keep them after the grant ended but to increase funding for more school counselors due to their success. Katzenmeyer and Moller (2001) have suggested these six steps for gaining influence (p. 96):

1. Clearly and confidently state your own position.
2. Use data to support the position taken.
3. Seek out and understand the perspective of others.
4. Identify what is at stake for both parties.
5. Generate options for a specific situation or problem resolution.
6. Reach agreement.

9. How do school counselors get started with advocacy and public relations?

Educators have natural advocacy and public relations tools such as instructing, explaining, and engaging others in discussion. They are experienced presenters in front of large groups of people. English and language arts teachers are skilled in the persuasive writing instrumental in reaching board members or legislators. Math and science teachers are skilled with collecting facts and data that can support causes for advocacy. Building and district leaders have the knowledge of budget constraints and operational issues that help determine the viability of creating change on an issue. School counselors are skilled in listening and being attuned to the school climate and can synthesize concerns of groups of students, parents, or staff. As the late counselor educator Dr. Reese House, former director of the National Center for Transforming School Counseling, often said, "School counselors are the eyes and the ears of the school." Therefore, school counselors can harness strengths from educators within the school to create a strong and well-articulated advocacy and activism message on behalf of students and the school community on a variety of issues.

10. How do school counselors advocate on state and national levels for school counseling?

All professional educators represent the students in our schools, ourselves, and colleagues in the district, state, and nation; they represent the profession at large. Being involved in advocacy and public relations and activism at a state or national level may seem intimidating, especially for new professionals, but it is imperative. It is important to connect with others at all levels to share successes and challenges in school counseling and leadership and to build on the collective voice as stronger than a singular one.

The following are suggestions for getting involved in state- or national-level advocacy:

1. Join professional organizations including unions as these will connect you to other colleagues and keep you up to date with advocacy and public relations issues including your local and state branches of ACA, ASCA, and NACAC. Regularly follow the work of advocacy organizations such as NOSCA.

2. Identify those who are involved in state or national education and school counseling advocacy. Use them as mentors and consultants; ask them how they became involved and how they suggest you get started and what the most pressing issues are currently.

3. Research the most challenging issues relevant in terms of education "reform," funding for public schools, standardized test

overuse, and school vouchers, and identify at least one you are passionate about.

4. Find others who are also passionate and committed to the issues chosen and develop action plans together in person and using technology. The Internet, Skype, Google Chat, Facebook, Twitter, other social media, and free phone conference lines have revolutionized the speed and effectiveness of advocacy and activism for multiple issues in education.

11. How do school counselors stay motivated when advocating?

Tenacity, leadership, and advocacy go hand in hand when confronting outdated school policies and inequitable practices. Tenacity is a professional responsibility for educators if they are to address inequity found in achievement, opportunity, and attainment gaps and be integral participants in equitable school reform. However, for many educators, particularly school counselors, tenacity is an intimidating notion as it may appear to contradict other "soft skills" of the profession, such as listening, flexibility, and impartiality. However, the educator's job requires interacting with varied stakeholders, many of whom do not understand complex needs of students. Tenacity is the tool for persuasion and influence. For example, the Transforming School Counseling Initiative (Martin, 2002) and the ASCA (2012) National Model call for school counselors to be advocates and leaders for students, especially for marginalized and underserved populations such as young men of color, students with disabilities, bilingual students, poor and working-class students, and LBGTIQ students. Tenacity requires courage, risk-taking, and assertiveness that takes educators out of their comfort zones. Those trained in older models of professional preparation may not see themselves as capable of tenacity. However, many school counselors have strong convictions about their work, their role, and what is equitable for students.

Misused or *unused* tenacity is passive and often shows when educators feel strongly that a situation is unjust but do not take action. *Misdirected* tenacity is aggressive and occurs when educators go to stakeholders to address an injustice but the approach is inflexible, uncompromising, one-sided, and blaming. Too often inappropriate uses of tenacity drives a wedge between educators and stakeholders, leaving others to perceive them as complacent or petulant. The effective use of tenacity rests not on power and control but on empowerment and influence. "Diplomatic tenacity" (Mason, 2009) is the goal—in which issues are well presented and invite collaboration when obstacles are encountered. At a time when education and students depend on educators for social justice and systemic change, no one can afford to neglect effective tenacity.

Solution Success Stories

Story 1

Bob, a high school counselor in the Northeast, combines his leadership and advocacy skills to maximize impact in his district and state. By becoming part of his school's district leadership team and with the use of critical data, he has been able to secure funding to maintain and even add school counselor positions so as to directly reduce ratios and caseloads to more manageable numbers. As the advocacy chair of his state school counseling association he has also been active in introducing bills that would mandate elementary school counselors across the state. According to Bob, school counselors have the necessary skills needed to advocate to administrators, district leaders, and state officials but must make this type of advocating for the profession just as much of a priority as advocating for students.

Story 2

Each year, on a winter day, a busload of counseling graduate students from Chicago's DePaul University join practitioners in the field and the lobbyist for Illinois counseling organizations at the state capitol. By design, the purpose of the trip is for the students to learn hands on about the significance and process of connecting with state legislators. For many on the trip, it is their first time engaging in this type of advocacy activity. They are provided with training, information, and materials so that they feel more prepared, but despite that, it is an intimidating process. For some of the practitioners, professors, and certainly for the lobbyist, the process is more familiar, so they are able to guide and mentor the "newbies," in vivo, as they pull their legislators from the floor to discuss key issues and advocate change.

Story 3

At Lehman College of the City University of New York, graduate school counselor candidates in Stuart Chen-Hayes's EDG 733 Developmental School Counseling class create a school counseling bulletin board (traditional and digital), a school counseling brochure (traditional and digital), and a school

(Continued)

(Continued)

counseling program website with specific links for students, educators, and families that showcase the school counseling program's role in delivering academic, career, college access, and personal/social competencies to all students through a fully implemented school counseling program, including achievement and opportunity gaps, interventions, and results, as well as ASCA model assessments and program tools and use of the NOSCA eight components in college and career readiness counseling. While not an easy assignment, it is done concurrently with internship and allows the school counseling site supervisor and the school counselor candidate to work closely in assessing, creating, implementing, evaluating, and publicizing the school counseling program. But the biggest benefit for some candidates has been that it has sealed the deal on their being hired as school counselors by principals in challenging budgetary times. The ability of school counselor candidates to articulate their work and then demonstrate it in digital and traditional print ways increases school counselor credibility and demonstrates connections to the academic mission of the school. Lisa, as a school counselor at the Computer School, a middle school in Manhattan, created and maintained the school counseling program website linked prominently on the school's homepage as Counseling: www .computerschoolcounselors.org/.

Story 4

Students in core school counseling courses in The DePaul University school counseling graduate program spend approximately six months in advocacy work with area schools and their school counselors. Prior to practicum and internship, graduate school counseling students are assigned to a school in a small team. These teams, in collaboration with the school counselor, develop and administer a needs assessment. From the needs assessment, the students analyze and disaggregate the data and present it to the school. Next, the students develop interventions to address gaps and needs from the data. At the end of the project, the school counselor has a comprehensive set of interventions and accompanying materials ready for implementation.

Resources

Digital

ACA Advocacy Competencies: www.counseling.org/resources/ competencies/advocacy_competencies.pdf

ASCA RAMP Award: www.ascanationalmodel.org/content.asp?contentid=11

ASCA School Counselor Competencies: www.schoolcounselor.org/files/SCCompetencies.pdf

The Extraordinary School Counselor: http://extraordinaryschcounselor.blogspot.com/

From the Counselor's Office: http://counselorsoffice.blogspot.com/

National Office for School Counselor Advocacy: http://nosca.collegeboard.org/

National Office of School Counselor Advocacy's Principal Counselor Relationship Toolkit: http://nosca.collegeboard.org/research-policies/principal-counselor-toolkit

The Savvy School Counselor: http://savvyschoolcounselor.com/

School Counselor Blog: www.schcounselor.com/

Vote-smart.org: http://votesmart.org/

Print

American School Counselor Association. (2010). *ASCA ethical code for school counselors.* Alexandria, VA: Author.

Chen-Hayes, S. F., & Getch, Y. Q. (in press). Leadership and advocacy for every student's achievement and opportunity. In B. T. Erford (Ed.), *Transforming the school counseling profession* (4th ed.). Boston, MA: Pearson.

Eagle, J. (2013, January). Counselor, educator, advocate: School counselors making a difference. *Counseling Today,* pp. 10–11.

Lee, C. C., & Rodgers, R. A. (2009). Counselor advocacy: Affecting systemic change in the public arena. *Journal of Counseling and Development, 8,* 284–287.

Martin, P. J. (2002). Transforming school counseling: A national perspective. *Theory Into Practice, 41,* 148–153.

Mueller-Ackerman, B. (2002). *Public relations toolbox.* Chapin, SC: Youthlight.

National Office for School Counselor Advocacy. (2010). *Eight components of college and career readiness counseling.* Washington, DC: Author.

Pérusse, R., & Goodnough, G. E. (2004). *Leadership, advocacy, and direct service strategies for professional school counselors.* Belmont, CA: Brooks/Cole.

Ratts, M., DeKruyf, L., & Chen-Hayes, S. F. (2007). The ACA advocacy competencies: A social justice advocacy framework for professional school counselors. *Professional School Counseling, 11,* 90–97.

Ratts, M. J., & Hutchins, A. M. (2009). ACA advocacy competencies: Social justice advocacy at the client/student level. *Journal of Counseling and Development, 87,* 269–275. doi:10.1002/j.1556–6678.2009.tb00106.x

Ratts, M. J., Toporek, R. L., & Lewis, J. A. (Eds.). (2010). *ACA advocacy competencies: A social justice framework for counselors.* Alexandria, VA: American Counseling Association.

Stone, C. B., & Dahir, C. A. (2011). *School counselor accountability: A MEASURE of student success* (3rd ed.). Boston, MA: Pearson.

Trusty, J., & Brown, D. (2005). Advocacy competencies for professional school counselors. *Professional School Counseling, 8,* 259–265.

15

Anti-Violence, Bullying, and Safety Solutions

School counselors and other leaders are key role models and advocates to end violence and bullying in schools. But too often they are not sure where to turn or what to do first. The epidemic of traditional bullying (verbal, physical, and social) and the newer phenomenon of cyberbullying are pervasive in many schools. In fact, over 30% of students report frequent involvement in traditional bullying (Nansel et al., 2001; Wang, Iannotti, & Nansel, 2009). While some reports indicate bullying beginning as early as first grade, research indicates it tends to peak in middle school. The myriad of harmful consequences experienced by bullying victims include the following:

- Withdrawing from friends and activities
- Lower levels of self-esteem
- Higher levels of depression, anxiety, and anger
- Academic disengagement and decreased academic performance

Also alarming are the long-term effects bullying has on both the victim and the aggressor. Students who feel unsafe at school are less likely than their peers to have postsecondary plans, and they are more likely to carry a weapon to school and receive injuries requiring hospitalization (*Illinois School Bullying Prevention Task Force Report*, 2011). And students who bully also are affected adversely. For example, students who engage in bullying behavior are more likely to engage in criminal behavior as adults. In fact, nearly 60% of boys classified as bullies in Grades 6–9 were convicted of at least one crime by age 24 and 40% had three or more convictions (Fight Crime: Invest in Kids, 2003). In addition, some students have been subject to violence including sexual abuse, rape, incest, and intimate partner violence, and schools need to provide appropriate support and referrals for students who have survived sexual and relationship trauma. Clearly, school counselors and building and district leaders must proactively create, implement, and evaluate comprehensive anti-violence and anti-bullying programs for all students to feel safe to learn in K–12 schools.

Key Words

Acceptable Use Policy: A written policy describing expectations regarding student and staff use of technology and mobile devices

Bullying: Intentionally and repeatedly inflicting unwanted emotional, verbal, physical, and/or social harm on another person that involves a disparity of power between the bully and the victim

Crisis Intervention: A form of counseling that focuses on critical immediate situations

Cyberbullying: The use of technological devices and software (e.g., computers, tablets, cell phones, Internet chat rooms, website posts, Twitter, Facebook, Instagram, other social media) to intentionally inflict unwanted emotional harm on another person repeatedly

Cyberstalking: Repeated threats or intimidating messages or images sent via electronic devices to monitor another person with unwanted attention or electronic interactions

Digital Citizenship: Behaving online in an ethical and responsible way

Emotional Abuse: Abuse that includes but is not limited to constant criticism, intimidation, manipulation, name-calling, threats, and invalidation

Flaming: Sending spiteful or vulgar messages about someone to a person or group online or via text messaging

Incest: Illegal sexual relations between people who are closely related

Intimate Partner Violence: Emotional, physical, and/or sexual violence and/or threats thereof inflicted on an intimate partner; formerly known as domestic violence

Masquerading: Sending or posting potentially harmful information via snail mail, chatrooms, websites, or Facebook posts under an assumed identity

Neglect: Refusal or delay in timely and appropriate health care, permitted chronic truancy, or inattention to special education needs without reasonable cause; inadequate nurturance or affection; encouraging or permitting drug or alcohol use by children or adolescents; or refusal to allow needed medical treatment for a child or adolescent's emotional or psychological care

Netiquette: Appropriate behavior using digital network communications

Online Harassment: Persistent, offensive messaging from one or more persons who send unwanted messages or images that may include threats of emotional or physical harm to the recipient or others close to the recipient

Outing or Trickery: Tricking an individual into providing confidential information with the intention of making it public to others via chatrooms, e-mail, Facebook, snail mail, Twitter, texting, or websites

Physical Abuse: Acts including hitting with hand, stick, strap, or other object; punching; kicking; shaking; throwing; burning; stabbing; or choking

Pseudonym: A false identity created to hide the identity of a bully while making fun of, harassing, threatening, or intimidating others or instigating fights online

Rape: The act of forced sexual activity with an unwilling or nonconsenting person

Sexting: Sending sexual images of oneself or of one's target through electronic means to others

Sexual Abuse: Oral, vaginal, or anal intrusion or penetration using the genitals or touching genitals with body parts or other objects, enacted on a child or adolescent; may include adult nudity, genital exposure, or inappropriate observation of a child or adolescent while nude (e.g., undressing, bathing)

Sexual Harassment: Unwelcome and unsolicited advances, teasing, and/ or comments of a sexual nature

Social Exclusion: Intentionally prohibiting or limiting an individual's participation in an online group, social network, e-mail list, or chat room

Key Questions and Solutions

1. What are definitions of bullying and cyberbullying?

Bullying is repeated behavior intended to harm another person that involves a disparity of power; that is, the aggressor has more power than his or her target (Nansel et al., 2001; Wang et al., 2009). Typically, traditional forms of bullying have fallen into three categories: physical (hitting, kicking), verbal (name-calling, teasing), and social (ignoring or isolating). *Cyberbullying*, as Hinduja and Patchin (2008) have characterized it, is "willful and repeated harm inflicted through the use of computers, cell phones and other electronic devices" (p. 5). This means that no longer is a bully the big student at recess or in the lunchroom; it is now a technologically savvy boy or girl using the Internet (Dooley, Pyzalski, & Cross, 2009). Cyberbullying, therefore, becomes even more complex because now students may or may not know who is bullying them and the audience is not limited to those on the playground or in the cafeteria—it can spread like wildfire on the Internet (Bauman, 2011; Hinduja & Patchin, 2008). Also alarming is the anonymity that technology permits, and because students may not know the identity of the bully, they may feel more hopelessness and powerlessness. This could result in heightened anxiety in school, prompting victims to live in chronic fear of being humiliated or embarrassed (Bauman, 2011; Dooley et al., 2009; Hinduja & Patchin, 2008; Kowalski & Limber, 2007). Because of the anonymity, potential for widespread public transmission, and instantaneous nature of cyberbullying, some researchers believe, "The effect of the cyber group far surpasses the schoolyard group" (Dooley et al., 2009, p. 187). Therefore, school counselors cannot create effective comprehensive bullying programs without addressing cyberbullying (Ockerman, Kramer, & Bruno, in press).

2. How can school counselors focus less on individual bullying and violence issues and increase focus on academics and career/college access?

Cultivating a positive school environment is critical to moving from solely remediating bullying to a proactive stance. Literature consistently promotes a holistic, multidimensional solution to bullying in schools involving multiple stakeholders. In fact, the most effective anti-violence interventions in schools harness the strengths of school leaders, school counselors, teachers, parents/guardians/caregivers, students, and all staff members. All members of the school community must understand and implement policies related to bullying and other forms of violence including neglect and emotional, physical, and sexual abuse; how to report it; and how to combat it. A paradigm shift occurs in schools when the focus promotes a respectful environment that embraces diversity rather than a punitive environment that punishes offenders. When children and adolescents are rewarded for positive interactions and use social skills that promote healthy relationships and peaceful conflict resolution, the whole school thrives. By creating whole-school assemblies and classroom school counseling lessons as well as having anti-violence materials linked on school counseling web pages, school counselors can free up time for academics and career/college readiness by proactively deveoping anti-violence school cultures.

3. How can school counselors and other leaders address gun violence in schools?

Schools and communities in urban, suburban, and rural areas continue to face a proliferation of guns in schools and react with alarm when mass shootings occur around the country. From the mass shootings at Columbine High School in Colorado to Sandy Hook Elementary School in Connecticut and rampant daily shootings in large cities, schools must have plans in place to protect children, adolescents, and staff from gun violence. The National Association of Secondary School Principals offers insights in how to prevent gun violence in schools: (1) be prepared and have a plan; (2) quickly gather information; (3) evaluate resources and liabilities; (4) call for help; and then, based on the data gathered, (5) act immediately through predetermined methods or monitor closely the suspected offender until help arrives. Among a plethora of school safety resources, the National Association for School Psychologists suggests these questions to guide violence prevention efforts:

- Which problems are we likely to face at *our* school?
- What are the primary short-term and long-term objectives of *our* school violence prevention efforts?
- Who are the targets of the violence prevention efforts?
- How is the prevention effort tied to broader community-level violence prevention efforts?
- Five years from now, how will the school know if the violence prevention program worked? (Furlong, Felix, Sharkey, & Larson, 2005, p. 14)

As noted by these researchers, "Garnering parent and community support in developing and maintaining an efficient and responsive violence prevention program is necessary to intervention success" (p. 14). By ensuring preventive efforts, including regular enactments of lock-downs, updating the school crisis plan, and an annual review of both efforts by multiple key school stakeholders, the safety and security of all children and staff will be increased.

4. How can school counselors reduce social media–induced cyber harassment and fallout?

Researchers agree that efforts to address cyberbullying should be developed within a comprehensive anti-bullying program (Beran & Li, 2007; Pearce, Cross, Monks, Waters, & Falconer, 2011; Ttofi &

Farrington, 2011) as many victims who suffer traditional forms of bullying also experience cyberbullying. In fact, a research study in Australia reported 87% of those victimized by technology also indicated that they had been bullied in other ways (Cross et al., 2009).

Therefore, school counselors can lead the charge for a multi-pronged, whole-school, systemic anti-bullying and anti-cyberbullying program. To begin, clear school policies need to be created specifying that all forms of bullying, including cyberbullying, will not be tolerated in the school community. These policies, called Acceptable Use Policies (AUP; Willard, 2007), should be designed by stakeholders, including community members, parents, and educators (Bauman, 2011; Beale & Hall, 2007), to promote buy-in and to ensure the expertise of all members. A committee should update the policy annually to keep current. Moreover, all students should sign the AUP, indicating they have read, understood, and will abide by the policy. School counselors can lead conversations about the policies and about the need for respect and appreciation of diversity and healthy conflict resolution through the use of school counseling core curriculum lessons and groups. They can also model digital citizenship to students and staff in their use of e-mail, Facebook, websites, and Twitter. The policy should be prominently displayed, distributed in counseling e-newsletters and the school's website, and be accessible via login pages of school computers (Bauman, 2011). This ensures that each time a member of the school community (students, staff, and building and district leaders) uses a computer on school grounds he or she is reminded about proper *netiquette* (i.e., Internet etiquette, the rules surrounding safe use of technology in schools online), the respect and dignity the school upholds, and the consequences for breaking the rules (Ockerman, Kramer, & Bruno, in press).

5. How can school counselors stop verbal and physical abuse of LBGTIQ students?

Given that students report hearing anti-gay slurs 25 times each day and 61% of LBGTIQ students report that they feel unsafe in their schools because of their sexual orientation (*GLSEN* National School Climate Survey, 2009), it is imperative that professional school counselors make concerted efforts on behalf of LBGTIQ students and allies. One of the most effective ways to do so is to first understand the laws related to the rights of all students. Lambda Legal (www.lambdalegal.org/) is an excellent source for understanding federal, state, and local laws and policies that protect LBGTIQ students. Armed with this knowledge, school counselors and leaders can effectively advocate for the rights of LBGTIQ students. Moreover, presenting facts such as those listed below about the pervasiveness of maltreatment and bullying of LBGTIQ students needs to be shared with everyone in the school to work to promote the safety of *all* students:

- 29.1% of LBGTIQ youth report missing one or more days of school in the past month because they felt unsafe due to their sexual orientation. (*GLSEN* National School Climate Survey, 2009)
- 84.6% of students report being verbally harassed by peers in the past school year. (*GLSEN* National School Climate Survey, 2009)
- 40.1% of LBGTIQ youth report experiencing physical harassment at school in the past year (*GLSEN* National School Climate Survey, 2009).
- LBGTIQ youth are four times as likely to have attempted suicide in the last year as their heterosexual peers (National Youth Association [NYA], 2010).

Based on this need, school counselors and leaders must provide a comprehensive approach to stopping violence against LBGTIQ students. Strategies include (1) advocating for and providing staff training regarding the laws and statistics about LBGTIQ students; (2) providing school counseling core curriculum classroom instruction to students aimed at increasing positive interactions and acceptance; (3) advocating for clear policies related to harassment on not only sexual orientation and gender identity but other cultural identities, including ethnicity/race, social class, ability/disability, immigration status, appearance, family type, age, gender, and religious/spirituality/meaning-making system; (4) working with parents/guardians/caregivers and community members to understand and embrace diversity; (5) garnering support from local, state, and national LBGTIQ and anti-violence organizations; and (6) attending professional development for continued education and support, such as the annual Supporting Students/Saving Lives National Educator Conference Focused on LBGTIQ Youth, hosted by the Center for Excellence in School Counseling and Leadership in San Diego, California.

School administrators and school counselors must lead the charge in broadening the conversation about universal respect and values. They must help others understand the impact of violence and harassment in their schools affects students of all sexual orientations. In fact, for every LBGTIQ student who reports being bullied or harassed, four heterosexual students report being bullied or harassed for being perceived as gay or lesbian (National Mental Health Association, 2002). When denigration of any student is perpetuated, all students suffer.

6. What evidence-based curricula and programming are effective in addressing violence and bullying?

Pearce et al.'s (2011) research validated the importance of a systematic whole-school approach to effectively prevent and manage all forms of bullying behaviors in schools. Specifically, researchers found six broad whole-school indicators that were well supported and necessary to thwart bullying in schools. Briefly, these factors are engaged principal leadership; a supportive school culture; proactive school policies, procedures, and practices; school-community training and education; a protective school environment; and making cyberbullying a responsibility of the whole school and surrounding community. Ttofi and Farrington's (2011) meta-analytic study of 89 reports detailing evaluations of 53 different anti-bullying programs found the most effective programs were intensive and long-lasting, included parent/guardian meetings, upheld strict discipline for infractions, and heightened playground supervision.

Additionally, several researchers made recommendations for the role of educational professionals to prevent and remediate bullying and cyberbullying behavior. Feinberg and Robey (2008) advocated that principals co-create anti-bullying policies and protocols with staff and that students, staff, and parents/guardians/caregivers receive education and training about bullying and cyberbullying prevention and intervention. Furthermore, Bhat (2008) recommended that school counselors offer character education and social skills training emphasizing empathy and positive peer conflict resolution, including the *Second Step: A Violence Prevention Program* and the *Steps to Respect: A Bullying Prevention Program* to all students. She also encouraged school counselors to become knowledgeable about resources designed to educate others about online safety (Ockerman, Kramer, & Bruno, in press).

7. How can school counselors assist parents/guardians/caregivers in the fight against bullying and cyberbullying?

Feinberg and Roby (2008) noted that much of cyberbullying activity is initiated at home. Conversely, positive parental behaviors protect adolescents not only from bullying others but from being bullied

(Wang et al., 2009). Given the tremendous influence of parents/ guardians/caregivers, schools must be vigilant about working with them through educational workshops and information sessions. School counselors can conduct parent outreach workshops around positive parenting skill sets, including setting limitations and expectations of their children's Internet use. Moreover, they can ask parents/guardians/caregivers to have honest conversations with their children about netiquette and their subsequent rules for abiding by it (see Commonsensemedia.org for examples of free family media agreements). It is also recommended that parents teach their children empathy through talking about their feelings, praising empathetic behavior, teaching basic rules of politeness, and setting positive examples (www.stopbullying.gov). Often, school counselors can work with local law enforcement officers to provide educational information sessions for parents and students regarding anti-bullying and anti-cyberbullying laws and regulations.

School counselors can also utilize readily available websites, featuring videos, PowerPoint presentations, and resources for student, staff, and parent workshops about the topic (for a more exhaustive list of helpful websites, see Bauman, 2011). It is essential that school counselors be diligent about communicating that they are open and willing to talk about bullying and cyberbullying (a topic that is sometimes taboo among students, teachers, and parents) and make every effort to publicly speak about it to students, parents/caregivers, and staff (Bauman, 2011; Bhat, 2008). Doing so creates an open, proactive school climate, where all students, staff, and administrators feel valued and can begin to work together to promote dignity and respect for all members of the school community (Ockerman, Kramer, & Bruno, in press).

Solution Success Stories

Story 1

Brea is an urban midwestern high school counselor. Using data, she identified a need within the school and implemented an intervention in order to address this need and help close the identified gap. Through individual interaction and observation, it felt obvious to her that bullying needed to be addressed. Further, she analyzed 9th- and 10th-grade needs assessment data and determined students were inconsistent in their self-reporting of bullying

(Continued)

(Continued)

behaviors; 18% of students said they witnessed bullying every day while 35% said they never witnessed it occur. Additionally, almost 80% of students reported that if they saw bullying occur, they would ignore it or do nothing. Because of these inconsistencies and the apparent lack of bystander intervention, Brea decided to target students who wanted to make a difference. She believed any large-scale bullying intervention needed to come from students themselves, and she wanted students to recognize their ability to make a difference.

Because of the inconsistency in students' reporting of bullying behavior, she believed it necessary to define bullying and provide examples. So she embarked on a three-week campaign to spread awareness and create consistent language around bullying behaviors, hanging up colorful signs around school complete with definitions, nationwide and school-specific data, and finally a call to action, urging students to attend an after-school meeting if they wanted to help address this problem. A nine-member task force emerged, and they spent five weeks as the year drew to a close discussing the school climate. Several common themes appeared, most notably, the lack of skills around communication and conflict resolution. They used their meeting time to practice skill-building activities, and Brea facilitated discussion focused on perspective-taking and becoming more self-aware. Students worked on these skills in their own interactions and on a school-wide level tried to help defuse conflict and model effective patterns of communication.

Based on pre/post-test data, the most heartening statistic to emerge involved students' self-efficacy; after five weeks of skill-building and peer modeling, students were 68% less likely to agree with the statement "I'm only one person . . . how can I make a difference?" As counselors, we can come up with all the interventions in the world to solve a problem, and many of them will undoubtedly prove effective. However, by giving students a voice in how to address bullying, not only will the problem itself become easier to clarify, conceptualize, and conquer, but the students themselves may gain something immeasurable—an internal locus of control, a belief that they can create change.

Story 2

The principal at a small Catholic middle school in the Midwest was concerned about the level of disrespect among students at his school. So three interns and a school counseling professor were asked to help formulate a plan to help create a positive school climate. Here's what they did:

- Met with the principal and vice principal to better understand the problem from their perspective

(Continued)

- Created an online survey on Google administered to middle school students to better understand their perspective
- Developed a school counseling core curriculum instruction lesson that highlighted the needs expressed; during the lesson, students participated in various activities and role plays representative of the issues students had indicated were problematic in the surveys

After the activities, the interns and professor led the students in self-reflection small groups and each student was asked to create a SMART goal (specific, measurable, attainable, results-oriented, and time-bound) in relation to how they could create a safe, more respectful school climate

When the large group reconvened, some students then offered their goals as examples to the rest of the group. A survey was given to determine if students believed the session was helpful, if they learned any new ways of coping with conflict, and if they had met their goals. Results indicated the session was successful at meeting its objectives and follow-up sessions were scheduled.

Story 3

Felipe, an elementary school counselor in the Southwest, notes that bullying is a prevalent topic in schools today. Repeated harassment with intent to create a power imbalance (bullying) has risen to the awareness of local and national leaders as an important issue. He stated "Our elementary school reviewed referral, process, and anecdotal data from students, parents, and teachers and found it was a problem that was not dealt with. In response, the counselor and administration reviewed the research on how to respond to bully issues in schools. The research suggested that all players—bullies, henchmen, bystanders, and victims—need to learn key social skills in order for students to engage in a safe and positive school environment (Bolton & Graeve, 2005). In response, over the course of two months, our school launched a massive "Stop Bullying Now" campaign that was centered on the instruction of social skills to stop bullying. These skills included but are not limited to stopping negative thoughts, peer reporting, showing empathy, and making an apology. Students took ownership of the skills by demonstrating them through videos shared daily with the whole school. This was done in concert with school counseling classroom core curriculum lessons on bullying. Preliminary results have actually produced more office referrals claiming bullying; however, our school does not necessarily view it as negative but rather as a more realistic number that the campus community is able to respond to. Our student support personnel team is now looking at next steps and reviewing long-term data to analyze the impact of the campaign."

(Continued)

(Continued)

Story 4

Elissa, an elementary school counselor from the West Coast, stated that when she arrived at the school the number of referrals involving aggression was high. "We realized that a change in our school culture was needed if we were going to change the behavior of our students. My principal and I reviewed the literature, examined the statistics and bullying trends at our school, and came up with a plan. The following is how we went about creating a bully prevention program at our school.

"After assessing the school culture, we had to face the hard facts—students felt that adults at our school ignored bullying incidents, and that there were very few staff members the students felt they could talk to about being bullied. My principal also noticed that students did not have the vocabulary necessary to solve problems.

"We already had a school-wide positive behavior program in place that needed some revamping. Next, we instituted a conflict management program that the entire staff used consistently with the students in order to empower students with the vocabulary, concepts, and behaviors for solving problems, reporting problems, and knowing the difference.

"The next thing we did was conduct a training workshop to promote consistency and commitment with the entire staff. The training included the following:

- Sharing the results of our assessment: We came to terms with how the students felt and made a commitment to change our behavior.
- Designing/implementing school policy: This took some planning. There was already a district policy in place, but we needed to create a policy and program that was specific to our school. I presented the staff with the following concept: the PLC—Peaceful Learning Community. Based on the Professional Learning Community, our PLC would be similar in goals and vision. Each class developed the following:
  - Norms/values, such as class rules and a mission statement or pledge
  - SMART goals: specific, measurable, attainable, realistic, timely
  - Class meetings were essential to creating a safe learning environment
  - Cooperative Learning Structures to build increase student engagement and cooperation
  - Supplementing with guidance lessons as well as individual and group counseling
- Once the school and classroom PLCs were established, I was able to incorporate classroom lessons, individual counseling, and group counseling as part of the school's comprehensive counseling program, which was directly related to the goals and vision of the PLC.

(Continued)

- Establishing procedures for dealing with bullying: The staff agreed that with a procedure in place, students (and staff) knew that all of us were accountable to each other—students knew that they could talk to adults they trusted and that problems reported would be handled by the adults on campus.
- Reporting results: From time to time, either during grade-level PLCs or staff in-services, we celebrated successes and reevaluated parts of our PLC for improvement.

"Within the first year of implementing our PLC, bus referrals decreased by more than half. Student referrals decreased by half as well. Parents, students, and staff members saw a definite change, and everyone involved knew that issues could be easily managed in a positive way, ensuring safety for the victim, accountability for the offender, and consistency from the staff. Most rewarding was the change in the children. More poignant was the change in the grown-ups."

Resources

Digital

Ally Week (students organizing events in schools against anti-LBGTIQ language, bullying, and harassment): www.allyweek.org

American Association of Suicidology: www.suicidology.org

American Foundation for Suicide Prevention: www.afsp.org

BullyBust (anti-bullying campaign teaching all stakeholders to be upstanders): www.schoolclimate.org

Center for the Prevention of School Violence: www.ncdjjdp.org/cpsv/about_center.html

Conflict Resolution Education Connection: www.creducation.org

Day of Silence (ending violence, harassment, and abuse of LBGTIQ youth): www.dayofsilence.org

Electronic Aggression (technology and youth violence prevention): www.cdc.gov/ViolencePrevention/youthviolence/electronic-aggression/index.html

Facing History and Ourselves: www.facing.org

GLSEN: www.glsen.org

iKeepSafe (Internet safety coalition for children and youth): www.ikeepsafe.org

iKeepSafe (Facebook guide for school counselors): www.ikeepsafe
.org/wp-content/uploads/2012/04/Facebook-For-School-
Counselors-Final-Revision1.pdf

It Gets Better Project (giving hope to LBGTIQ youth): www.itgetsbetter
.org

Lambda Legal: www.lambdalegal.org

Make It Better Project: www.makeitbetterproject.org

Matthew Shepard Foundation/Matthew's Place (encouraging respect
for human dignity and difference/safe Internet space for LBGTIQ
youth): www.matthewshepard.org

National School Climate Center (promoting a positive and sustained
school climate including a safe, supportive environment nurturing social and emotional, ethical, and academic skills): www
.schoolclimate.org

National Suicide Prevention Lifeline 1–800–273-TALK (8255): www
.suicidepreventionlifeline.org

No Name-Calling Week (challenging bullying of LBGTIQ students and
other oppressed persons in schools): www.nonamecallingweek
.org

Olweus (bullying prevention program and curriculum): www.olweus
.org

Preventing Gun Violence in Schools (tools for assessment and action
from school building leaders): www.nassp.org/Content.aspx?
topic=55496

Rape, Abuse, and Incest National Network (RAINN): www.rainn.org/

Red Cross Disaster Management, Psychological First Aid: www
.redcross.org/ma/boston/take-a-class/emergency-service-
courses

Research Summaries and Fact Sheets on Cyberbullying: www
.cyberbullying.us/publications.php#fs15

SafeKids.com (promoting online safety and civility skills): www
.safekids.com

School Safety and Crisis Resources (NASP; English, español): www
.nasponline.org/resources/crisis_safety/

Second Step Social Skills for Grades K-8 and Bully Prevention
Curriculum: www.cfchildren.org/second-step.aspx

Steps to Respect—Bullying Prevention for Elementary School
Curriculum: www.cfchildren.org/steps-to-respect.aspx

Stop Bullying.gov: www.stopbullying.gov/

Stop Cyberbullying (how to deal with cyberbullies): www
.stopcyberbullying.org

Supporting Students/Saving Lives—The National Educator Conference on LBGTIQ Youth: www.cescal.org

Teaching Tolerance: www.tolerance.org

A Thin Line (identifying, responding to, and stopping digital abuse): www.athinline.org

Think Before You Speak (ending use of "that's so gay" and verbal abuse toward LBGTIQ youth): www.thinkb4youspeak.com

Tips for Reinforcing School Safety (for building leaders, educators, parents/guardians, and students): www.nasponline.org/resources/crisis_safety/schoolsafety_admin.aspx

Print

Bauman, S. (2011). *Cyberbullying: What counselors need to know.* Alexandria, VA: American Counseling Association.

Beale, A. V., & Hall, K. R. (2007). Cyberbullying: What school administrators (and parents) can do. *The Clearing House: A Journal of Educational Strategies, Issues and Ideas, 81*, 8–12. doi:10.3200/TCHS.81.1.8–12

Bhat, C. S. (2008). Cyber bullying: Overview and strategies for school counsellors, guidance officers, and all school personnel. *Australian Journal of Guidance and Counseling, 18*, 53–66. doi:10.1375/ajgc.18.1.53

Common Sense Media. (2012). *Family media agreement.* Retrieved from http://www.commonsensemedia.org/educators/parent-media-education/family-media-agreements

Hinduja, S., & Patchin, J. (2008). *Bullying beyond the schoolyard: Preventing and responding to cyberbullying.* Thousand Oaks, CA: Corwin.

Ttofi, M. M., & Farrington, D. P. (2011). Effectiveness of school-based programs to reduce bullying: A systematic and meta-analytic review. *Journal of Experimental Criminology, 7*, 27–56. doi:10.1007/s11292–010–9109–1

Wang, J., Iannotti, R. J., & Nansel, T. R. (2009). School bullying among U.S. adolescents: Physical, verbal, relational, and cyber. *Journal of Adolescent Health, 45*, 368–375. Retrieved from http://jahonline.org/

Willard, N. E. (2007). *Cyber-safe kids, cyber-savvy teens: Helping young people learn to use the Internet safely and responsibly.* San Francisco, CA: Jossey-Bass.

16

Ability, Disability, and Gifted/Talented Solutions

School counselors and other leaders are responsible for assisting students with *developmental, emotional/behavioral, intellectual, learning, and physical disabilities* with academic, career and college readiness, and personal/social competencies. Similarly, school counselors and other leaders are responsible for ensuring students with unique gifts and talents receive academic, career and college readiness, and personal/social competencies. Students with disabilities have often faced barriers in schools (Marshak, Dandeneau, Prezant, & L'Amoreaux, 2009; Rock & Leff, 2011; Trolley, Haas, & Patti, 2009) and gifted/talented students often report boredom, personal/social challenges, and/or behavioral incidents when their needs are not met. School counselors have often had inadequate training in how to be effective advocates for students in special education with disabilities or with gifted/talented students (Rock & Leff, 2011; Trolley et al., 2009).

The challenges are great for school counselors and other leaders who wish to empower students of all abilities and disabilities by challenging *ableism*, prejudice multiplied by power used by persons without disabilities to keep resources away from persons with disabilities on individual, cultural, and systemic levels (Chen-Hayes, 2009; Holcomb-McCoy & Chen-Hayes, in press).

Too many school counselors received little or no pre-service education about exceptional students and the range of abilities, disabilities, gifts, and talents, let alone how to challenge ableism unless they chose elective coursework or have prior personal experience. The national accreditation group for school counseling, the Council for the Accreditation of Counseling and Related Educational Programs (CACREP), requires no specific knowledge or fieldwork in working with ability/disability for master's or doctoral-level school counselors or school counselor educators (CACREP, 2009; Trolley et al., 2009). It is essential that school counselors only practice within their professional competency and seek additional consultation, supervision, and professional development to work effectively and affirmatively with students with disabilities and gifts/talents.

Although there has been a dearth of information for school counselors about effective practice with students with varied abilities and disabilities, the last decade has seen increased information about the importance of school counselors assisting students with varied abilities and disabilities (Baumberger & Harper, 2007; Krell & Pèrusse, 2012; Marshak et al., 2009; Mason, 2002; Milsom, 2006, 2007; Rock & Leff, 2011), gifted/talented students (Wood, 2009, 2010a, 2010b; Wood, Portman, Cigrand, & Colangelo, 2010) and in the school counselor's role in special education (Trolley et al., 2009). That information is essential to support the success of all students.

In light of insufficient information, this chapter gives basic keywords and interventions for the full range of abilities and disabilities. The need is great in challenging times where a majority of students who have emotional disabilities go through K–12 schools with mild disabilities but too often drop out or receive inadequate services (Rock & Leff, 2011). This chapter presents specific solutions that school counselors and leaders can use immediately to make a difference for students with exceptionalities.

Ongoing professional development to affirm and encourage the full range of student abilities and disabilities including gifts/talents is important to ensure that school counselors are comfortable advocating for all learners' success with appropriate *accommodations*, regularly reviewed 504 Plans and IEPs, high standards, rigorous curriculum, appropriate *assessment*, including the *Diagnostic and Statistical Manual for Mental and Emotional Disorders* (DSM-5; American Psychiatric Association [APA], 2013) and *International Statistical Classification of Diseases and Health-Related Problems*, 10th edition

(*ICD-10*), engaging extracurricular experiences including *acceleration* and *enrichment* for gifted and talented students, and appropriate supports to help every student reach their academic, career/college, and interpersonal dreams.

Key Words

504 Plan: Legally mandated accommodations in learning specified for students with particular disabilities

Abilities: Focusing on what students in schools can do (versus what they can't do) using a strengths-based perspective

Acceleration: Moving students into more challenging material at the same grade level or advancing to a higher grade level

Accommodations: Changes to a classroom or policy that allow students with disabilities to fully participate; examples include extended time for assignments, extra visual and verbal cues/prompts, frequent breaks, graphic organizers, large-print text, testing format alterations, visual/written daily schedules, daily homework logs, assistive technology, speech-activated software, wheelchairs, and classroom changes such as preferred seating or altered seating arrangements

Assessment: Determining needs for intervention and determining effectiveness of interventions over time

Autism Spectrum: The range of pervasive developmental disorders where the person experiences impairments in social interaction and communication and evidences repetitive and restricted behaviors

Developmental Disabilities: Chronic impairments appearing prior to adulthood that can be physical, cognitive, and/or learning that limit functioning in at least three areas of living: self-care, language (receptive/expressive), learning, mobility, self-direction, independent living, and ability to be economically independent

Differentiation: Using varied instructional methods and assessments to enhance learning for every student

DSM-5: Classification system used by mental health professionals for diagnosis and treatment of mental and emotional/behavioral disorders; contains research- and evidence-based decision-making tools for diagnosis and dimensional assessments

Eligibility: The identified classification of the particular special needs of a student that qualifies the student for services

Emotional/Behavioral Disabilities: Conditions over time that harm a child or adolescent's academic abilities, including at least one of the following: an inability to learn not explained by other factors; poor peer and teacher interpersonal relationships; inappropriate behaviors or feelings; pervasive unhappiness or depressed mood; and physical symptoms or fears related to school or personal factors

Enrichment: For gifted/talented students, staying at grade level but learning more in depth at particular periods during the day and outside of school compared to peers

Gifted/Talented: K–12 students with outstanding aptitude/capabilities in intellectual, artistic, creative, and leadership domains or specific academic disciplines needing specialized activities/services to develop full capabilities

Goals/Objectives: Specified target levels of performance for the student to reach as identified by the IEP team

ICD-10: *International Statistical Classification of Diseases and Health-Related Problems,* 10th edition, an international medical disease classification system

Inclusion: Placing students with disabilities in general education classrooms with appropriate support services and staffing

Individualized Educational Plan (IEP): Written statement, updated regularly, outlining specific academic/social services, service providers, goals, and objectives for a child or adolescent with one or more disabilities

Intellectual Disabilities: Below-average cognitive functioning in two or more behaviors first appearing in childhood or adolescence

Learning Disabilities: Learning and cognition challenges in particular academic subjects, including reading (*dyslexia*), writing (*dysgraphia*), and mathematics (*dyscalculia*), where learners need varied approaches to learn material successfully

Learning Styles: Learning varies by individuals, and all persons have preferred ways of learning, including aural, visual, and tactile-kinesthetic; lesson planning and delivery is enhanced when school counselors provide content and experiences suited to diverse learning styles

Least Restrictive Environment: Ensuring maximum interaction with the general school environment for students with disabilities

Physical Disabilities: Bodily impairments that can occur prior to, during, or after birth that affect physical functioning and/or limit daily functioning; examples include impaired hearing or vision, epilepsy, and respiratory disorders

Positive Behavior Support (PBS): A form of Applied Behavioral Analysis (ABA) using functional behavioral assessments (FBA) to get a baseline of data about a student's behavior, contexts, and consequences and then create goals, interventions, and monitoring of changes pre- and post-intervention

Scaffolding: Temporary instructional supports that assist learners in creating new knowledge that gives added structure to ensure success

Transition Planning: Students with IEPs by age 14 are required to have a plan in place for transition from high school to the world of work and/or college, and it is mandated in IEPs for students age 16 and older

Twice Exceptional Students: Students identified as gifted/talented and having learning and/or emotional/behavioral disabilities

Universal Design for Learning: Creating and implementing curriculum that is effective with the widest range of learners and learning styles

Key Questions and Solutions

1. How can school counselors affirm the academic, career, college-access, and interpersonal needs of students with disabilities and gifted/talented students?

Assisting all school counselors and leaders to be allies to students with disabilities and students with gifted/talented issues means ensuring students receive academic, career, college-access, and personal/social competencies in equitable amounts compared to students who do not have disabilities or gifts/talents. It also means making appropriate referrals, helping with in-school and out-of-school services, questioning inappropriate diagnosis and eligibility, confirming that interventions for IEPs are appropriately implemented and 504 plan accommodations regularly reviewed, and challenging inappropriate ableism (Kaffenberger, 2011). It means engaging with parents and guardians and all educators in focusing on strengths and including students in the school culture as fully as possible and listening for family resilience and strengths in working with difference (Baumberger & Harper, 2007; Solomon, 2012; Walsh, 2012). It means constantly monitoring the data in school report cards, assessments, and standardized tests to see how students with disabilities are performing academically, in career and college assessments, and in personal/social planning. The goal is guaranteeing students in all cultural groups have equitable access to gifted/talented student experiences (or the entire school instead if only certain students), and that students with disabilities do not disproportionately represent only certain cultural groups.

School counselors must learn how to use multiple skills to assist diverse students with various disabilities and gifts/talents in the classroom:

- *Differentiation* in school counseling core curriculum lessons (ASCA, 2012) as well as collaborating with other educators, particularly special educators, on which differentiation strategies are most successful with diverse abilities and disabilities in the school.
- *Learning styles* are a key part of school counseling core curriculum delivery success; educators including school counselors seek to design lessons that have visual, auditory, and tactile-kinesthetic elements to enhance the three major learning styles and promote effective classroom learning.
- *Scaffolding* is used as a bridging device that helps learners figure out how to use prior knowledge as they make new connections with new assignments and materials.
- *Transition planning* is a critical skill for all school counselors to have for students with disabilities as it sets a specific plan in motion for the skills students will need to be career- and college-ready upon leaving high school and how to ensure those skills are in place prior to graduation
- *Universal design for learning* is a concept that originally started in architecture—how to build buildings for one's life span so that as persons age the buildings we live in are adaptable with grab bars, walk-in showers, and one-level access to all household essentials without having to climb stairs. Applied to classrooms, the idea is similar in providing lessons that universally appeal to multiple learning styles all at once to ensure the greatest ease for all learners as teachers and school counselors deliver content.

2. How do school counselors reach all students when mandated students with IEPs constitute a majority of some school counselors' days?

Students with IEPs are often assigned individual counseling. While some students may benefit, the literature demonstrates group counseling reaches more students more effectively and frees up time for school counselors to focus on school counseling core curriculum classroom lessons (ASCA, 2012) for all students, not only students who are mandated for counseling because it is written into their IEPs.

Shifting to a six- to eight-student group focus is a better use of school counselor time and allows for students to interact with each other—and sometimes their peers without IEPs—in addition to addressing their academic, career/college, and personal/social competencies. Additionally, when facilitating lessons from the school counseling core curriculum, students who are in more restrictive environments can be brought in to join general education classes, often to the benefit of both student groups, and this is an excellent way to promote inclusion.

3. What are the most important ways to affirm gifted/ talented students for academic, career/college readiness, and interpersonal success?

There is controversy about who is gifted/talented, and no one definition or assessment is definitive. What is important is to see all students as having gifts/talents and knowing that some students who are exceptional in their speed and creativity in learning benefit from *acceleration* and/or *enrichment* in their studies. Those students often benefit from additional opportunities and specialized counseling attention to their unique interpersonal skills as well. Budget cuts often harm gifted/ talented programs, or they have been used primarily to keep upper-middle-class and wealthy White parents in cities and often found to exclude poor students, students of color, and students with disabilities. See the digital resources at the end of the chapter for best practices and research in gifted/talented education, including the Belin-Blank Center at the University of Iowa, the Johns Hopkins Center for Gifted and Talented Youth, and the Neag Center for Gifted and Talented at the University of Connecticut (including the Best-of-the-Best enrichment materials database), focused on assessing, affirming, and researching the needs of gifted/talented students and their families.

4. With unwieldy school counselor-to-student ratios, what are effective assessment practices to reach students with learning and emotional/behavioral disabilities?

With learning and behavioral/emotional disabilities the most common in K–12 schools, school counselors need to have savvy strategies for effective practice, including the following:

- Monitor the data and disaggregate for patterns that indicate which students from what cultural identities have IEPs for learning and emotional disabilities. Assess for patterns of some groups being overrepresented and what is causing that overrepresentation. Also, check whether the IEPs are accurate, implemented with integrity, and regularly updated.

- Create group work opportunities wherever possible to lessen isolation, and replace individual counseling time with group counseling to reach more students and free up time for school counseling core curriculum lessons for all students.

- Monitor social interactions and extracurricular activity rates of participation by cultural identity. Encourage more students with IEPs to engage in extracurriculars as both an academic strategy for career and college readiness and as a personal/ social skills strategy, and monitor/disaggregate rates of participation.

Many school counselors have had an assessment course, but often little or no training on assessments specific to working with the range of student abilities, disabilities, gifts, and talents. For many emotional/behavioral disabilities, school counselors may have had little or no education in diagnosis and treatment. While no school counselor has time to do intensive individual mental health counseling, all school counselors benefit from knowing the DSM-5 classification system, and the politics behind it (it is evidence- and research-based, but there have always been controversies around how the diagnoses are formulated for certain disorders, and how certain disorders are added or removed). School counselors must ask who formulated the IEP and monitor the accuracy of both the IEP and the students' effectiveness in reaching IEP goals, especially toward poor and working-class boys, boys of color, and African American, Latino, and Native American Indian boys, who are disproportionately receiving disability diagnoses and IEPs and not nearly enough gifted/talented assessments, let alone placements. Finally, because the DSM-5 (APA, 2013) is only a classification system, school counselors must monitor effective behavioral/emotional disability treatment inside and outside the school and observe carefully when diagnostic criteria no longer match a student's behavior or emotional issues. Seligman and Reichenberg's (2012, p. 8) DOACLIENTMAP is an exemplary treatment planning system that is easy to learn and use for school counselors to work effectively with students with emotional/behavioral disabilities:

Diagnosis
Objectives of Treatment
Assessments
Clinician Characteristics

Location of Treatment

Interventions to be Used

Emphasis of Treatment (directive/nondirective, supportive, cognitive/ behavioral/affect emphasis)

Numbers (individual, group, family)

Timing (frequency, pacing, duration)

Medications (if needed)

Adjunct Services

Prognosis

Seligman and Reichberg's (2012) treatment planning model reflects an excellent understanding of evidence-based treatment for major disorders that school counselors can follow easily to monitor success with IEPs and to challenge inappropriate diagnoses when they occur. However, while the current edition needs to be updated based on the DSM-5 (APA, 2013), Seligman and Reichberg's research and clarity with DOACLIENTMAP makes it an important tool for school counselors working with emotional and behavioral disabilities.

5. What are the needs of parents and guardians of students with disabilities and gifts/talents, and how can school counselors collaborate as allies?

Parents and guardians of students with diverse abilities and disabilities need school counselors to be allies for students with diverse abilities and disabilities as evidenced in the following examples:

- Teach advocacy skills and the importance of how to advocate for the best services for one's child or adolescent in the school system. No parent or guardian should rely on the school alone to do what's best for his or her child or adolescent. Parent/ guardian/caregiver involvement is critical to ensure a successful partnership with the school and community for students with disabilities and with gifts/talents.
- Help leverage multiple systems inside the school and in the community with disability and gifted/talented advocacy organizations, and help families find outside second opinions/ consultants if a parent/guardian/caregiver disagrees with an IEP or 504 recommendation.
- Ensure high expectations for all students with varied abilities and disabilities but not unrealistic expectations.
- Help foster independence for each child and adolescent and assist parents/guardians/caregivers in how to help students be more independent.

- Plan for transitions between grades and the strengths and challenges for all students with disabilities and gifts/talents as they move between grade levels.
- Plan for transition into the world of work and college from elementary school through high school by delivering academic and career and college readiness competencies annually to all students.
- Use technology to find the best resources online and online support for parents, guardians, caregivers, and families of persons with disabilities and students who are gifted/talented.

Solution Success Stories

Story 1

Valerie, an East Coast urban public elementary school counselor assigned to work exclusively with students with emotional/behavioral disabilities individually, has shifted to doing group work and less individual counseling to focus more on planning and school counseling core curriculum lessons for all students at the school, a stronger focus on career and college access and readiness for students. She has families at the elementary level using NOSCA's elementary school career and college readiness implementation guide. She draws on her prior experience as a college access/readiness counselor for high school students. This is the first time this school has had an elementary school counselor closing opportunity gaps for students with disabilities with a focus on their career and college readiness needs in addition to academic and personal/social/mental health issues. She is the only school counselor at the school with a student population that is Latino/a, African, and African American students on free and reduced lunch, and she is the first school counselor to work with all students at the school instead of only students with disabilities. By freeing her time by switching from individual counseling to group counseling with students with disabilities, she implements school counseling core curriculum lessons and planning with students in the classroom to reach the needs of all students.

Story 2

Derek, a middle school counselor in a rural southeastern school with 4,000 sixth, seventh, and eighth graders and three school counselors proposed a new

(Continued)

school counseling model and job description to serve the school's 250–300 special needs students. The school housed the district's newly implemented program for students with Asperger syndrome, multiple separate self-contained classrooms each for students with emotional behavior disorders; severe learning disabilities; mild, moderate, and severe intellectual disabilities; severe physical disabilities; and resourced students who were part of an inclusion model with general education classrooms. The school counseling team often reported that these students were denied adequate and equitable services because of the large caseloads of all school counselors even though these students were divided among the counselors as part of their caseloads. The students with special needs had unique needs (e.g., crises, transition planning, academic and career development, social skills development) that were not being addressed; their special education teachers were in many ways expected to handle these needs. The newly hired school counselor proposed that she serve as the sole school counselor for all of the students with special needs, and the school counseling team and administration approved. Given the specific circumstances of this school, the re-assigning of a school counselor to this role, which had never been done before, proved successful. The special education teachers and their students had a single school counselor to serve them who was a part of all IEP team meetings. School counseling programs and interventions were tailored to their unique needs, including school counseling core curriculum lessons, and greater rapport was built between the students, teachers, and the school counselor due to more consistency and frequency of interactions.

Story 3

Jen, a suburban school counseling intern in the northeastern United States, analyzed school report card data with her school counseling site supervisor and saw that most students with learning disabilities in the high school were not using Naviance and not receiving systematic career/college readiness help. She shifted her focus to close an opportunity gap by ensuring all students with IEPs on her caseload did multiple career and college planning assessments in Naviance and had full career/college access/readiness counseling, planning, and advocacy with her in individual, group counseling, and classroom school counseling core curriculum lessons. She demonstrated 100% of the students with IEPs she worked with completed college and career assessments and continued on to college applications at a higher rate than in prior years, in large part due to her making college/career readiness a priority focus for students with learning disabilities with IEPs.

Resources

Digital

ADA (Americans with Disabilities Act) National Network: 1-800-949-4232 and www.adata.org

Alcohol Screening and Brief Intervention for Youth (a practitioner's guide): http://pubs.niaaa.nih.gov/publications/Practitioner/YouthGuide/YouthGuideOrderFrom.htm

Alzheimer's Association (24-hour helpline; multiple languages): 1-800-272-3900

American Association of People With Disabilities: www.aapd.com

American School Counselor Association (special needs position statement): www.schoolcounselor.org/files/PS_SpecialNeeds.pdf

American Sign Language (ASL): www.handspeak.com

Anxiety Disorders (National Institute of Mental Health): www.nimh.nih.gov

Anxiety Disorders Association of America: www.adaa.org

The Arc (intellectual and developmental disabilities): www.thearc.org

The Association for the Gifted (TAG): www.cectag.org

Autism Speaks: www.autismspeaks.org

Belin-Blank Center for Gifted Education and Talent Development: www.education.uiowa.edu/belinblank/

Best-of-the-Best Enrichment Materials Database: www.gifted.uconn.edu/sem/enrichment/typeii_enrichment.cfm

Black AIDS Institute: www.blackaids.org

Braille Institute: www.brailleinstitute.org

The Cancer Project: www.cancerproject.org

Caring Bridge: www.caringbridge.org

Center for an Accessible Society: www.accessiblesociety.org

Center for Mental Health in Schools: http://smhp.psych.ucla.edu

Cleft Palate Foundation: www.cleftline.org

College Funding/Scholarships for Students With Disabilities: www.washington.edu/doit/Brochures/Academics/financial-aid.html

College Planning for Students With Disabilities: www.educationquest.org/swd.asp

Council for Exceptional Children (CEC) (voice and vision of special education): www.cec.sped.org

Deaf Resource Library: www.deaflibrary.org

Depression (National Institute of Mental Health): www.nimh.nih.gov

Disability Rights Advocates: www.dralegal.org

Disability Rights Education and Defense Fund: www.dredf.org

Disability World: www.videos.disabled-world.com

Disabled Peoples International: www.dpi.org

Donate Life America (organ donation and transplants community): www.donate.life.net

Eating Disorders (National Institute of Mental Health): www.nimh.nih .gov

Families and Advocates Partnership for Education (FAPE): www.fape .org

Family and Community Resources for Infants, Toddlers, Children, and Adolescents with Disabilities (English, español): http://nichcy .org/families-community

Global and Regional Asperger Syndrome Partnership (GRASP) (English/español): www.grasp.org

Going to College (for persons with a disability): www.going-to-college .org/overview/index.html

Icarus Project (challenging psychiatric ableism): http://theicarusproject .net/

Institute for Research and Policy on Acceleration: www.accelerationinstitute .org

International Day of Persons With Disabilities (December 3): www .un.org/disabilities/default.asp?id=111

International Early Psychosis Association: www.iepa.org.au

Iris Center (school counselors facilitating transitions for students with disabilities from high school to post-school settings): http://iris .peabody.vanderbilt.edu/cou2/chalcycle.htm

Johns Hopkins Center for Talented Youth (identifies and develops the talents of advanced K–12 learners including Talent Search program for grades 2–8): www.cty.jhu.edu

Join Together (alcohol and drug policy, prevention, and treatment): www.jointogether.org

Kids Helping Kids (catastrophic illness/mobility needs): www .kidshelping.org

Little People of America (people of short stature and families): www .lpaonline.org

Mental Health America: www.nmha.org

Mobility International USA: www.miusa.org

mothers2mothers (women living with HIV): www.m2m.org

NADD (persons with developmental, emotional, and/or intellectual disabilities): www.thenadd.org

National Alliance on Mental Illness (NAMI): www.nami.org

National Association for Down Syndrome: www.nads.org

National Association for the Education of African American Children With Learning Disabilities (AACLD): www.aacld.org

National Association for Gifted Children: www.nagc.org

National Association of People With AIDS: www.napwa.org

National Center for Learning Disabilities: www.ld.org

National Center on Response to Intervention (RTI) (integrating data-based instruction and assessment into an academic and behavioral issues prevention system): www.rti4success.org

National Child Traumatic Stress Network: www.nctsnet.org

National Disability Rights Network: www.ndrn.org

National Dissemination Center for Children With Disabilities: www.nichcy.org

National Down Syndrome Society: www.ndss.org

National Institute for Mental Health: www.nimh.nih.gov

National Institute on Drug Abuse: www.drugabuse.gov

National Organization for Albinism and Hypopigmentation: www.albinism.org

National Research Center on the Gifted and Talented: www.gifted.uconn.edu

Neag Center for Gifted Education and Talent Development (assessing, screening, and supporting best practices in gifted and talented education; schoolwide enrichment model): www.gifted.uconn.edu

OASIS (online Asperger syndrome information and support): www.aspergersyndrome.org/

Parent to Parent USA (support for families of children with special needs): www.p2usa.org/

A Ragged Edge Online: www.ragged-edge-mag.com

School Mental Health.org: www.schoolmentalhealth.org

Screening for Mental Health: www.mentalhealthscreening.org/

The Sparkle Effect (students with disabilities in school-based cheerleading and dance): www.thesparkleeffect.org

Students With Disabilities Preparing for College/Post-Secondary Education (know your rights and responsibilities): www2.ed.gov/about/offices/list/ocr/transition.html

Substance Abuse and Mental Health Services Administration: www.samhsa.gov

TASH (equity, opportunity, and inclusion for people with disabilities): www.tash.org

Teaching for Diverse Abilities and Learning Styles: www.celt.iastate.edu/teaching/udl.html

Treatment Advocacy Center (reason in treating severe mental illness): www.treatmentadvocacycenter.org

United Network for Organ Sharing: www.unos.org

Universal Design for Learning: www.celt.iastate.edu/teaching/udl .html

Wrightslaw Special Education Law and Advocacy: www.wrightslaw .com/

WrongPlanet.net (online resources and community for autism): www .wrongplanet.net

Print

Bauman, S. M. (2010). School counselors and survivors of childhood cancer: Reconceptualizing and advancing the cure. *Professional School Counseling, 14,* 156–164.

Baumberger, J. P., & Harper, R. E. (2007). *Assisting students with disabilities: A handbook for school counselors.* Thousand Oaks, CA: Corwin.

Davis, G. A., Rimm, S. B., & Siegle, D. (2010). *Education of the gifted and talented* (6th ed.). Boston, MA: Pearson.

Erford, B. T., Lattanzi, G., Weller, J., Schein, H., Wolf, E., Hughes, M., . . . Peacock, E. (2011). Counseling outcomes from 1990 to 2008 for school-age youth with depression: A meta-analysis. *Journal of Counseling & Development, 89,* 439–458.

Hamlet, H. S., Gergar, P. G., & Shaefer, B. A. (2011). Students living with chronic illness: The school counselor's role. *Professional School Counseling, 14,* 202–210.

Krell, M., & Pèrusse, R. (2012). Providing college readiness counseling for students with autism spectrum disorders: A Delphi study to guide school counselors. *Professional School Counseling, 16,* 29–39.

Marshak, L. E., Dandeneau, C. J., Prezant, F. P., & L'Amoreaux, N. A. (2009). *The school counselor's guide to helping students with disabilities.* San Francisco, CA: Jossey-Bass.

Mason, E. C. M. (2002). Facing the challenge: School counselors and special needs students. *Georgia School Counselors Association Journal, 2,* 14–21.

Milsom, A. (2006). Creating positive school experiences for students with disabilities. *Professional School Counseling, 10,* 66–72.

Milsom, A. (2007). Interventions to assist students with disabilities through school transitions. *Professional School Counseling, 10,* 273–278.

Milsom, A., & Dietz, L. (2009). Defining college readiness for students with learning disabilities: A Delphi study. *Professional School Counseling, 12,* 315–323.

Peterson, J. S. (2006). Addressing counseling needs of gifted students. *Professional School Counseling, 10,* 43–51.

Seligman, L., & Reichenberg, L. W. (2012). *Selecting effective treatments: A comprehensive guide to treating mental disorders* (4th ed.). Hoboken, NJ: Wiley.

Siegel, L. M. (2011). *The complete IEP guide: How to advocate for your special ed child* (7th ed.). Berkeley, CA: Nolo.

Solomon, A. (2012). *Far from the tree: Parents, children, and the search for identity.* New York, NY: Scribner.

Trolley, B. C., Haas, H. S., & Patti, D. C. (2009). *The school counselor's guide to special education.* Thousand Oaks, CA: Corwin.

Wood, S. M. (2009). Counseling concerns of gifted and talented adolescents: Implications for school counselors. *Journal of School Counseling, 7.*

Wood, S. M. (2010). Best practices in counseling the gifted in schools: What's really happening. *Gifted Child Quarterly, 54,* 42–58.

Wood, S. M. (2010). Nurturing a garden: A qualitative investigation into school counselors' experiences with gifted students. *Journal for the Education of the Gifted, 34,* 261–302.

Wood, S. M., Portman, T., Cigrand, D. L., & Colangelo, N. (2010). School counselors' perceptions and experience with acceleration as a program option for gifted and talented students. *Gifted Child Quarterly, 54,* 168–178.

Wright, P. W. D., & Wright, P. (2006). *Wrightslaw: From emotions to advocacy: The special education survival guide.* Hartfield, VA: Harbor House Law Press.

Wright, P. W. D., & Wright, P. D. (2007). *Wrightslaw: Special education law* (2nd ed.). Hartfield, VA: Harbor House Law Press.

References

Abney, P. C., & Maddux, C. D. (2004). Counseling and technology: Some thoughts about the controversy. *Journal of Technology in Human Services, 22,* 1–24. doi:10.1300/J017v22n03_01

Achieve. (2012). *Implementing the Common Core standards: The role of the school counselor action brief.* Available from www.achieve.org

Adelman, C. (2006). *The toolbox revisited.* Washington, DC: U.S. Department of Education.

Amatea, E. S., & West-Olatunji, C. A. (2007). Joining the conversation about educating our poorest children: Emerging leadership roles for school counselors in high-poverty schools *Professional School Counseling, 11,* 81–89.

American Association of School Administrators. (2013). *Statement of ethics for school leaders.* Alexandria, VA: Author. Available from www.aasa.org

American Counseling Association. (2005). *ACA code of ethics.* Alexandria: VA: Author. Retrieved from http://www.counseling.org/resources/aca-code-of-ethics.pdf

American Psychiatric Association. (2013). *Diagnostic and statistical manual of mental disorders (DSM-5).* Arlington, VA: Author.

American School Counselor Association. (2007). *School Counselor Competencies.* Alexandria, VA: Author. Retrieved from www.schoolcounselor.org/files/SCCompetencies.pdf

American School Counselor Association. (2010). *ASCA ethical code for school counselors.* Alexandria, VA: Author. Retrieved from www.schoolcounselor.org/files/EthicalStandards2010.pdf

American School Counselor Association. (2012). *The ASCA national model: A framework for comprehensive school counseling programs* (3rd ed.). Alexandria, VA: Author.

Anderson, B. (1993). The stages of systemic change. *Educational Leadership, 51,* 14–17.

Aspy, D. N., Aspy, C. B., Russel, G., & Wedel, M. (2000). Carkhuff's human technology: A verification and extension of Kelly's (1997) suggestion to integrate the humanistic and technical components of counseling. *Journal of Counseling & Development, 78,* 29–37.

Bailey, D. F., & Bradbury-Bailey, M. (2013). *Project Gentlemen on the Move: Nurturing excellence in African-American youth.* New York: Routledge.

Baker, S. B., & Gerler, E. R. (2008). *School counseling for the 21st century* (5th ed.). New York, NY: Merrill.

Barreto, S., & Adams, S. K. (2011). Digital technology and youth: Developmental approach. *Brown University Child & Adolescent Behavior Letter, 27,* 1–6.

Barstow, S., & Terrazas, A. (2012). Department of Education to accept new round of ESSCP application. Retrieved from http://ct.counseling.org/2012/03/department-of-education-to-accept-new-round-of-esscp-applications/

Bauman, S. (2011). *Cyberbullying: What counselors need to know.* Alexandria, VA: American Counseling Association.

Baumberger, J. P., & Harper, R. E. (2007). *Assisting students with disabilities: A handbook for school counselors.* Thousand Oaks, CA: Corwin.

Beale, A. V., & Hall, K. R. (2007). Cyberbullying: What school administrators (and parents) can do. *The Clearing House: A Journal of Educational Strategies, Issues and Ideas, 81,* 8–12. doi:10.3200/TCHS.81.1.8-12

Bennis, W. G. (1994). *On becoming a leader.* Cambridge, MA: Perseus.

Bennis, W. G., & Nanus, B. (1997). *Leaders: Strategies for taking charge.* New York, NY: HarperBusiness.

Beran, T., & Li, Q. (2007). The relationship between cyberbullying and school bullying. *Journal of Student Wellbeing, 1,* 15–33. Retrieved from http://www.ojs.unisa.edu.au/index.php/JSW

Bhat, C. S. (2008). Cyberbullying: Overview and strategies for school counsellors, guidance officers, and all school personnel. *Australian Journal of Guidance and Counseling, 18,* 53–66. doi:10.1375/ajgc.18.1.53

Bolman, L. G., & Deal, T. E. (1991). Leadership management and effectiveness: A multi-frame, multi-factor analysis. *Human Resource Management, 30,* 509–533.

Bolton, J., & Graeve, S. (2005). *No room for bullies.* Boys Town, NE: Boys Town Press.

Bottoms, G., Spence, D., & Young, M. (2009). The next generation of school accountability: A blueprint for raising high school achievement and graduation rates in SREB states. Atlanta, GA: Southern Region Educational Board.

boyd, d. m., & Ellison, N. B. (2007), Social network sites: Definition, history, and scholarship. *Journal of Computer-Mediated Communication, 13,* 210–230. doi:10.1111/j.1083–6101.2007.00393.x

Brigman, G. A., & Campbell, C. (2003). Helping students improve academic achievement and school success behavior. *Professional School Counseling, 7,* 91–98.

Brigman, G. A., Webb, L. D., & Campbell, C. (2007). Building skills for school success: Improving the academic and social competence of students. *Professional School Counseling, 10,* 279–288.

Bryan, J. (2005). Fostering educational resilience and achievement in urban schools through school-family-community partnerships. *Professional School Counseling, 8,* 219–227.

Bryan, J., & Henry, L. (2008). Strengths-based partnerships: A school-family-community partnership approach to empowering students. *Professional School Counseling, 12,* 149–156.

Bryan, J., & Holcomb-McCoy, C. (2007). An examination of school counselor involvement in school-family-community partnerships. *Professional School Counseling, 10,* 441–454.

Burkhard, A. W., Gillen, M., Martinez, M. J., & Skytte, S. (2012). Implementation challenges and training needs for comprehensive school counseling programs in Wisconsin high schools. *Professional School Counseling, 16,* 136–145.

Burnes, T. R., Singh, A. A., Harper, A. J., Harper, B., Maxon-Kann, W., Pickering, D. L, & Hosea, J. (2010). American Counseling Association competencies for counseling with transgender clients. *Journal of LGBT Issues in Counseling, 4,* 135–159.

Bush T. (2003). Theories of educational management (3rd ed). London, UK: Sage.

Campbell, C. A., & Dahir, C. A. (1997). *Sharing the vision: The national standards for school counseling programs.* Alexandria, VA: American School Counselor Association.

Carey, J., & Dimmitt, C. (2012). School counseling and student outcomes: Summary of six statewide studies. *Professional School Counseling, 16,* 146–153.

Carey, J. C., & Elsner, D. (2006). School counseling program implementation scale. Amherst, MA: Center for School Counseling Outcome Research, University of Massachusetts at Amherst Center.

Carey, J., Harrington, K., Martin, I., & Hoffman, D. (2012). A statewide evaluation of the outcomes of the implementation of ASCA National Model school counseling programs in rural and suburban Nebraska high schools. *Professional School Counseling, 16,* 89–107.

Carey, J., Harrington, K., Martin, I., & Stevenson, D. (2012). A statewide evaluation of the outcomes of the implementation of ASCA National Model school counseling programs in Utah high schools. *Professional School Counseling, 16,* 89–99.

Chen-Hayes, S. F. (2001). Counseling and advocacy with transgendered and gender-variant persons in schools and families. *Journal of Humanistic Counseling, Education, and Development, 40,* 34–48.

Chen-Hayes, S. F. (2007). The ACCESS Questionnaire: Assessing K–12 school counseling programs and interventions to ensure equity and success for every student. *Counseling and Human Development, 39,* 1–10.

Chen-Hayes, S. F. (2009). Types of oppression. In American Counseling Association (Ed.), *American Counseling Association encyclopedia of counseling* (pp. 383–84). Alexandria, VA: Author.

Chen-Hayes, S. F. (2013). Empowering multiple cultural identities in college readiness and admission. In National Association for College Admission Counseling (Ed.), *Fundamentals of college admission counseling* (3rd ed.), (pp. 150–174). Arlington, VA: Author.

Chen-Hayes, S. F., & Getch, Y. Q. (in press). Leadership and advocacy for every student's achievement and opportunity. In B. T. Erford (Ed.), *Transforming the school counseling profession* (4th ed). Boston, MA: Pearson.

Chen-Hayes, S. F., & Ockerman, M. S. (in press). Academic development planning for and college and career readiness K–12. In B. T. Erford (Ed.), *Transforming the school counseling profession* (4th ed.). Boston, MA: Pearson.

College Board National Office for School Counselor Advocacy. (2010). *School counselor strategic planning* tool. Retrieved from http://advocacy.college board.org/sitesdefault/files/NOSCA%20Strategic%20planning%20 tool.pdf

College Board. (2011a). *2011 national survey of school counselors: Counseling at a crossroads.* Washington, DC: Author.

College Board. (2011b). *Involving parents and guardians in college planning.* Retrieved from http://media.collegeboard.com/digitalServices/pdf/ advocacy/preparate/Involving-Parents-and-Guardians-in-College-Planning.pdf

College Board. (2012a). *2012 national survey of school counselors—True north: Charting the course to career and college readiness.* Washington, DC: Author.

College Board. (2012b). *College counseling sourcebook: Advice and strategies from experienced school counselors* (7th ed.). New York, NY: Author.

Conley, D. T. (2010). *College and career ready: Helping all students succeed beyond high school.* San Francisco, CA: Jossey-Bass.

Council for Accreditation of Counseling and Related Educational Programs. (2009). *CACREP 2009 standards.* Available from www.cacrep.org

Cross, D., Shaw, T., Hearn, L., Epstein, M., Monks, H., Lester, L., & Thomas, L. (2009). *Australian covert bullying prevalence study* (ACBPS). Retrieved from http://foi.deewr.gov.au/documents/australian-covert-bullying-prevalence-study-executive-summary

Cunningham, M. (1999). African American adolescent males' perceptions of their community resources and constraints: A longitudinal analysis. *Journal of Community Psychology, 27,* 569–588.

Dahir, C. A., & Stone, C. B. (2012). *The transformed school counselor* (2nd ed.). Belmont, CA: Brooks/Cole.

Danielson, C. (2007). *Enhancing professional practice: A framework for teaching* (2nd ed.). Alexandria, VA: Association for Supervision and Curriculum Development.

Depaul, J., Walsh, M. E., & Dam, U. C. (2009). The role of school counselors in addressing sexual orientation in schools. *Professional School Counseling, 12,* 300–308.

DeVoss, J. A., & Andrews, M. F. (2006). *School counselors as educational leaders.* Boston, MA: Houghton Mifflin.

Dimmit, C. (2009). Why evaluation matters: Determining effective school counseling practices. *Professional School Counseling, 12,* 395–399. doi:10.5330/PSC.n.2010–12.395

Dimmit, C., Carey, J., & Hatch, T. (2007). *Evidence-based school counseling: Making a difference with data-driven practices.* Thousand Oaks, CA: Corwin.

Dimmit, C., & Wilkerson, B. (2012). Comprehensive school counseling in Rhode Island: Access to services and student outcomes. *Professional School Counseling, 16,* 125–135.

Dollarhide, C. T. (2003). School counselors as program leaders: Applying leadership contexts to school counseling. *Professional School Counseling, 6,* 304–308.

Dooley, J. J., Pyzalski, J., & Cross, D. (2009). Cyberbullying versus face-to-face bullying: A theoretical and conceptual review. *Journal of Psychology, 217,* 182–188. doi:10.1027/0044–3409.217.4.182

Duncan, G. J., & Murnane, R. J., (Eds.). (2011). *Whither opportunity? Rising inequality, schools, and children's life chances.* New York, NY: Russell Sage Foundation.

Education Trust. (2003). *A new core curriculum for all: Aiming high for other people's children.* Retrieved from http://www.edtrust.org/dc/publication/a-new-core-curriculum-for-all-aiming-high-for-other-peoples-children-0

Epstein, J. L. (1995). School/family/community partnerships: Caring for the children we share. *Phi Delta Kappan, 76,* 701–712.

Epstein, J. L., & Van Voorhis, F. L. (2010). School counselors' roles in developing partnerships with families and communities for student success. *Professional School Counseling, 14,* 1–14.

Epstein, J. L., and Associates. (2009). *School, family, and community partnerships: Your handbook for action* (3rd ed.). Thousand Oaks, CA: Corwin.

Erford, B. T, Lee, V. V., Newsome, D. W., & Rock, E. (2011). Systemic approaches to counseling students experiencing complex and specialized programs. In B. T. Erford (Ed.), *Transforming the school counseling profession* (3rd ed., pp. 288–313). Boston, MA: Pearson Merrill Prentice-Hall.

Feinberg, T., & Robey, N. (2008, September). Cyberbullying. *Principal leadership.* Retrieved from http://www.nasponline.org/resources/principals/Cyberbulling%20NASSP%209-08.pdf

Fight crime: Invest in Kids. (2003, September). *Bullying prevention* is *crime prevention.* Washington, DC: Author. Retrieved from http://www.fightcrime.org/wp-content/uploads/sites/default/files/reports/BullyingReport.pdf

Ford, D. Y. (1995). *Counseling gifted African American students: Promoting achievement, identity, and social and emotional well-being.* Retrieved from http://www.gifted.uconn.edu/nrcgt/ford2.html

Froeschle, J. G., Crews, C. R., & Li, J. (2013). *Ethically assisting students via social media.* Retrieved from http://counselingoutfitters.com/vistas/vistas13/Article_13.pdf

Furlong, M. J., Felix E. D., Sharkey, J. D., & Larson, J. (2005). *Preventing school violence: A plan for safe and engaging schools.* Retrieved from http://www.nasponline.org/resources/principals/Student%20Counseling%20Violence%20Prevention.pdf

GLSEN National School Climate Survey. (2009). Retrieved from http://www.glsen.org/nscs

Goodrich, K. M., & Luke, M. (2009). LGBTQ responsive school counseling. *Journal of LGBT Issues in Counseling, 3*, 113–127.

Greene, J. P. (2003). *Public high school graduation and college readiness rates in the United States.* New York, NY: Manhattan Institute.

Griffin, D., & Van Steen, S. (2010). School-family-community partnerships: Applying Epstein's theory of the six types of involvement to school counselor practice. *Professional School Counseling, 13*, 218–226.

Gruman, D. H., & Hoelzen, B. (2011). Determining responsiveness to school counseling interventions using behavioral observations. *Professional School Counseling, 14*, 183–190.

Harper, A., Finnerty, P., Martinez, M., Brace, A., Crethar, H., Loos, B., & Lambert, S. (n.d.). *Association for Lesbian, Gay, Bisexual, and Transgender Issues in Counseling (ALGBTIC) competencies for counseling with lesbian, gay, bisexual, queer, questioning, intersex and ally individuals.* Washington, DC: ALGBTIC. Retrieved from http://www.algbtic.org/resources/competencies

Hartline, J., & Cobia, D. (2012). School counselors: Closing achievement gaps and writing results reports. *Professional School Counseling, 16*, 71–79.

Hatch, T. (2012). Advocacy and social justice. In American School Counselor Association (Ed.), *The ASCA national model: A framework for school counseling programs* (3rd ed., pp. 14–16). Alexandria, VA: Author.

Hatch, T. (2014). *The use of data in school counseling: Hatching results for students, programs, and the profession.* Thousand Oaks, CA: Corwin.

Herr, E. L. (2002). School reform and perspectives on the role of school counselors: A century of proposals for change. *Professional School Counseling, 5*, 220–234.

Hinduja, S., & Patchin, J. (2008). *Bullying beyond the schoolyard: Preventing and responding to cyberbullying.* Thousand Oaks, CA: Corwin.

Hines, P., Lemons, R., & Crews, K. (2011). *Poised to lead: How school counselors can drive college and career readiness.* Washington, DC: National Center for Transforming School Counseling.

Holcomb-McCoy, C. (2007). *School counseling to close the achievement gap: A social justice framework for success.* Thousand Oaks, CA: Corwin.

Holcomb-McCoy, C., & Chen-Hayes, S. F. (in press). Culturally competent school counselors: Affirming diversity by challenging oppression. In B. T. Erford (Ed.), *Transforming the school counseling profession* (4th ed.). Boston, MA: Pearson.

House, R. M., & Sears, S. J. (2002). Preparing school counselors to be leaders and advocates: A critical need in the new millennium. *Theory Into Practice, 41*, 154–162. Retrieved from http://www.jstor.org/table/1477236

iKeepSafe.org & American School Counselor Association. (2012). *Facebook for school counselors.* Retrieved from http://www.ikeepsafe.org/wp-content/uploads/2012/04/Facebook-For-School-Counselors-Final-Revision1.pdf

Illinois School Bullying Prevention Task Force Report. (2011). Retrieved from http://www.isbe.state.il.us/SBPTF/pdf/sbptf_rec_exec_smry0511.pdf

Isaacs, M. L. (2003). Data-driven decision making: The engine of accountability. *Professional School Counseling, 6*, 288–95.

Janson, C. (2009). High school counselors' views of their leadership behaviors: A Q methodology study. *Professional School Counseling, 13*, 86–97.

Jenson, D. F. N., Boschee, F., & Whitehead, B. M. (2002). *Planning for technology: A guide for school administrators, technology coordinators, and curriculum leaders.* Thousand Oaks, CA: Corwin.

Johnson, B. (2003). Teacher collaboration: Good for some, not so good for others. *Educational Studies, 29*, 337–350.

Johnson, R. S. (2002). *Using data to close the achievement gap: How to measure equity in our schools.* Thousand Oaks, CA: Corwin.

Kaffenberger, C. J. (2011). Helping students with mental and emotional disorders. In B. T. Erford (Ed.), *Transforming the school counseling profession* (3rd ed., pp. 342–370). Boston, MA: Pearson.

Katzenmeyer, M., & Moller, G. (2001). *Awakening the sleeping giant.* Thousand Oaks, CA: Corwin.

Kelly, F. R., & Ferguson, D. G. (1984). Elementary school guidance needs assessment: A field-tested model. *Elementary School Guidance and Counseling, 18*, 176–180.

Keys, S. G., & Lockhart, E. J. (1999). The school counselor's role in facilitating multisystemic change. *Professional School Counseling, 3*, 101–107.

Kitchener, K. S. (1984). Intuition, critical evaluation, and ethical principles: The foundation for ethical decisions in counseling psychology. *The Counseling Psychologist, 12*, 43–55.

Kouzes, J. M., & Posner, B. Z. (2002). *The leadership challenge* (3rd ed.). San Francisco, CA: Jossey-Bass.

Kowalski, R. M., & Limber, S. P. (2007). Electronic bullying among middle school students. *Journal of Adolescent Health, 41*, S22–S30.

Kraus, I. (1998). A fresh look at school counseling: A family-systems approach. *Professional School Counseling, 1*, 12–17.

Krell, M., & Pèrusse, R. (2012). Providing college readiness counseling for students with autism spectrum disorders: A Delphi study to guide school counselors. *Professional School Counseling, 16*, 29–39.

Lapan, R. T. (2012). Comprehensive school counseling programs: In some schools for some students but not in all schools for all students. *Professional School Counseling, 16*, 84–88.

Lapan, R. T., Gysbers, N. C., Bragg, S., & Pierce, M. E. (2012). Missouri professional school counselors: Ratios matter, especially in high-poverty schools. *Professional School Counseling, 16*, 117–124.

Lapan, R. T., Whitcomb, S. A., & Aleman, N. M. (2012). Connecticut professional school counselors: College and career counseling and smaller ratios benefit students. *Professional School Counseling, 16*, 117–124.

Lee, C. C., & Bailey, D. F. (1997). Counseling African American male youth and men. In C. C. Lee (Ed.), *Multicultural issues in counseling: New approaches to diversity* (pp. 123–154). Alexandria, VA: American Counseling Association.

Lee, C. C., & Rodgers, R. A. (2009). Counselor advocacy: Affecting systemic change in the public arena. *Journal of Counseling and Development, 8*, 284–287.

Lee, E., Menkart, D., & Okazawa-Rey, M. (Eds.). (1998). *Beyond heroes and holidays: A practical guide to K–12 anti-racist multicultural education and staff development.* Washington, DC: Teaching for Change.

Lee, V. V., & Goodnough, G. E. (2011). Systemic data-driven school counseling practices and programming for equity. In B. T. Erford (Ed.), *Transforming the school counseling profession* (3rd ed., pp. 129–153). Boston, MA: Pearson Merrill Prentice-Hall.

Leithwood, K., Louis, K. S., Anderson, S., & Wahlstrom, K. (2004). *How leadership influences student learning.* New York, NY: Wallace Foundation.

Levine, T. H., & Marcus, A. (2008). Closing the achievement gap through teacher collaboration: Facilitating multiple trajectories of teacher learning. *Journal of Advanced Academics, 19,* 116–138.

Lippe, J., Brener, N. D., McManus, T., Kann, L., & Speicher, N. (2005). *Youth risk behavior survey 2005: Commonwealth of the Northern Mariana Islands, Republic of Palau, Commonwealth of Puerto Rico.* Atlanta, GA: Centers for Disease Control and Prevention.

Luckin, R., Logan, K., Clark, W., Graber, R., Oliver, M., & Mee, A. (2008). *Learners' use of Web 2.0 technologies in and out of school in key stages 3 and 4.* Coventry, UK: Becta.

Marks, H. M., & Printy, S. M. (2003). Principal leadership and school performance: An integration of transformational and instructional leadership. *Educational Administration Quarterly, 39,* 370–397.

Marlow, L., Bloss, K., & Bloss, D. (2000). Promoting social and emotional competency through teacher/counselor collaboration. *Education, 120,* 668–674.

Marshak, L. E., Dandeneau, C. J., Prezant, F. P., & L'Amoreaux, N. A. (2009). *The school counselor's guide to helping students with disabilities.* San Francisco, CA: Jossey-Bass.

Martin, P. J. (2002). Transforming school counseling: A national perspective. *Theory Into Practice, 41,* 148–153.

Martin, P. J., & Robinson, S. G. (2011). Transforming the school counseling profession. In B. T. Erford (Ed.), *Transforming the school counseling profession* (3rd ed., pp. 1–18). Boston, MA: Pearson.

Mason, E. C. M. (2002). Facing the challenge: School counselors and special needs students. *Georgia School Counselors Association Journal, 2,* 14–21.

Mason, E. C. M. (2009). The capacity for tenacity. *Chi Sigma Iota Exemplar, 24,* 5.

Mason, E. C. M. (2010a). Leadership practices of school counselors and counseling program implementation. *National Association of Secondary School Principals (NASSP) Bulletin, 94,* 274–285.

Mason, E. C. M. (2010b, July/August). Leveraging classroom time. *ASCA School Counselor,* 27–29.

Mason, E. C. M., & McMahon, H. G. (2009). Supporting academic improvement among 8th graders at risk of retention: A study using action research. *Research in Middle Level Education Online, 33.*

Mason, E. C. M., Ockerman, M. S., & Chen-Hayes, S. F. (2013). The Change Agent for Equity School Counselor (CAFÉ) model: Uniting professional identity and practice. *Journal of School Counseling, 11.* Retrieved from http://www.jsc.montana.edu

Mason, E. C. M., & Schultz, D. *An exploratory study of school counselor use of twitter for professional purposes.* (Unpublished manuscript).

McClellan, C., Atkinson, M., & Danielson, C. (2012). *Teacher evaluator training and certification.* Retrieved from http://www.teachscape.com/resources/teacher-effectiveness-research/2012/02/teacher-evaluator-training-and-certification.html

McGoldrick, M., Carter, B., & Garcia-Prieto, N. (2011). *The expanded family life cycle: Individual, family, and social perspectives* (4th ed.). Boston, MA: Pearson.

McMahon, H. G., Mason, E. C. M., Daluga-Guenther, N., & Ruiz, A. (in press). Towards an ecological model of school counseling. *Journal of Counseling and Development.*

McMahon, H. G., Mason, E. C. M., & Paisley, P. O. (2009). School counselor educators as educational leaders promoting systemic change. *Professional School Counseling, 13,* 116–124.

Mell, P., & Grance, T. (2011). The NIST definition of cloud computing. http://csrc.nist.gov/publications/nistpubs/800-145/SP800-145.pdf

Metropolitan Life. (2002). *Survey of the American teacher 2002: Student life: school, home and community.* Retrieved from http://www.metlife.com/assets/cao/contributions/foundation/american-teacher/MetLife_Teacher_Survey_2010.pdf

Milsom, A. (2006). Creating positive school experiences for students with disabilities. *Professional School Counseling, 10,* 66–72.

Milsom, A. (2007). Interventions to assist students with disabilities through school transitions. *Professional School Counseling, 10,* 273–278.

Murray, L. (2011). *Diploma matters: A field guide for college and career readiness.* San Francisco, CA: Wiley.

Nansel, T. R., Overpeck, M., Pilla, R. S., Ruan, W. J., Simons-Morton, B., & Scheidt, P. (2001). Bullying behaviors among U.S. youth: Prevalence and association with psychological adjustment. *Journal of the American Medical Association, 306,* 2094–2100. doi:10.1001/jama.285.16.2094

National Association for College Admission Counseling. (2012). *Statement of principles of good practice. (SPGP).* Arlington, VA: Author. Retrieved from http://www.nacacnet.org/about/Governance/Policies/Documents/SPGP.pdf

National Association of Elementary School Principals. (1976). *Code of ethics.* Washington, DC: Author. Retrieved from http://www.naesp.org/what-we-believe-1

National Association of School Psychologists. (2012). *School violence prevention and response.* Retrieved from http://www.nasponline.org/resources/crisis_safety/school-violence-prevention.aspx

National Association of Secondary School Principals. (2001). *Ethics for school administrators.* Reston, VA: Author. Retrieved from http://www.nassp.org/Content.aspx?topic=47104

National Education Association. (1975). *Code of ethics.* Washington, DC: Author. Retrieved from http://www.nea.org/home/30442.htm

National Mental Health Association. (2002). *Annual report.* Retrieved from http://www.nmha.net/files/NMHA2002Annual_Report.pdf

National Office for School Counselor Advocacy. (2010). *Eight components of college and career readiness counseling.* Retrieved from http://advocacy.collegeboard.org/sites/default/files/10b_2217_EightComponents_WEB_100625.pdf

National Office for School Counselor Advocacy. (2013). http://nosca.collegeboard.org/

National Youth Association. (2010). *Gay bullying.* Retrieved from http://www.nyaamerica.org/2010/11/07/gay-bullyin/

Newell, M., & Kratochwill, T. R. (2007). The integration of response to intervention and critical race theory-disability studies: A robust approach to reducing racial discrimination in evaluation decisions. In S. R. Jimerson, M. K. Burns, & A. M. VanDerHeyden (Eds.), *Handbook of response to intervention: The science and practice of assessment and intervention.* New York, NY: Springer.

Nieto, S., & Bode, P. (2011). *Affirming diversity: The sociopolitical context of multicultural education* (6th ed.). Boston, MA: Pearson.

Northouse, P. G. (2004). *Leadership theory and practice* (3rd ed.). Thousand Oaks, CA: Sage.

Ockerman, M. S., Kramer, C., & Bruno, M. (in press). From the school yard to cyber space: A pilot study of bullying behaviors amongst middle school students. *Research in Middle Level Education.*

Ockerman, M. S., Mason, E. C. M., & Chen-Hayes, S. F. (2013). School counseling supervision in challenging times: The CAFÉ Supervisor Model. *Journal of Counselor Preparation and Supervision, 5 (2), Article 4.* doi:http://dx.doi.org/10.7729/51.0024

Ockerman, M. S., Mason, E. C. M., & Hollenbeck, A. F. (2012). Integrating RTI with school counseling programs: Being a proactive professional school counselor. *Journal of School Counseling, 10.*

OECD. (2013), *Education at a glance 2013: OECD indicators.* Paris, France: OECD. http://dx.doi.org/10.1787/eag-2013-en

O'Reilly, T. (2005). *What is Web 2.0?* http://oreilly.com/web2/archive/what-is-web-20.html?page=5

O'Shaughnessy, L. (2012). *The college solution: A guide for everyone looking for the right school at the right price.* Upper Saddle River, NJ: FT Press.

Paisley, P. O., & Borders, L. D. (1995). School counseling: An evolving specialty. *Journal of Counseling and Development, 74,* 150–153.

Paisley, P. O., & McMahon, H. G. (2001). School counseling for the twenty-first century: Challenges and opportunities. *Professional School Counseling, 5,* 106–115.

Pearce, N., Cross, D., Monks, H., Waters, S., & Falconer, S. (2011). Current evidence of best practices in whole-school bullying intervention and its potential to inform cyberbullying interventions. *Australian Journal of Guidance and Counselling, 21*, 1–21. doi:10.1375/ajgc.21.1.1/

Perera-Diltz, D. M., & Mason, K. L. (2012). A national survey of school counselor supervision practices: Administrative, clinical, peer, and technology mediated supervision. *Journal of School Counseling, 10.* Retrieved from http://www.jsc.montana.edu/

Perry, N. S. (2000). Reaching out: Involving parents and community members in the school counseling program. In J. Wittmer (Ed.), *Managing your school counseling program: K–12 developmental strategies* (2nd ed., pp. 264–269). Minneapolis, MN: Educational Media.

Prensky, M. (2010). *Teaching digital natives: Partnering for real learning.* Thousand Oaks, CA: Corwin.

Prochaska, J. O., & Norcross, J. C. (2001). Stage of change. *Psychotherapy, 38,* 443–448.

Reardon, R. (2011). Elementary school principals' learning-centered leadership and educational outcomes: Implications for principals' professional development. *Leadership & Policy in Schools, 10,* 63–83. doi:10.1080/15700760903511798

Reigeluth, C. M., & Garfinkle, R. J. (1994). *Change in education.* Englewood Cliffs, NJ: Educational Technology Publications.

Rock, E., & Leff, E. H. (2011). The professional school counselor and students with disabilities. In B. T. Erford (Ed.), *Transforming the school counseling profession* (3rd ed., pp. 314–341). Boston, MA: Pearson.

Rockinson-Szapkiw, A. J., & Walker, V. L. (2009). Web 2.0 technologies: Facilitating interaction in an online human services counseling skills course. *Journal of Technology In Human Services, 27,* 175–193. doi:10.1080/15228830903093031

Roderick, M., Nagaoka, J., & Coca, V. (2009). College readiness for all: The challenge for urban high schools. *The Future of Children, 19,* 185–210. 10.1353/foc.0.0024

Ryan, C., & Chen-Hayes, S. F. (2013). Educating and empowering families of lesbian, gay, bisexual, transgender, and questioning students. In E. S. Fisher & K. Komosa-Hawkins (Eds.), *Creating safe and supportive learning environments: A guide for working with lesbian, gay, bisexual, transgender, and questioning youth and families* (pp. 209–229). New York, NY: Routledge.

Sabella, R. A., & Booker, B. L. (2003). Using technology to promote your guidance and counseling program among stakeholders. *Professional School Counseling, 6,* 206–213.

Sacks, P. (2007). *Tearing down the gates: Confronting the class divide in American education.* Berkeley, CA: University of California Press.

Savitz-Romer, M., & Bouffard, S. (2012). *Ready, willing, and able: A developmental approach to college access and success.* Cambridge, MA: Harvard Educational Press.

Scarborough, J. L. (2005). The School Counselor Activity Rating Scale: An instrument for gathering process data. *Professional School Counseling, 8,* 3, 274–283.

Schellenberg, R. (2007). Standards blending: Aligning school counseling programs with school academic achievement missions. *Virginia Counselors Journal, 29,* 13–20.

Schellenberg, R. (2008). *The new school counselor: Strategies for universal academic achievement.* Lanham, MD: Rowman & Littlefield Education.

Schellenberg, R., & Grothaus, T. (2009). Promoting cultural responsiveness and closing the achievement gap with standards blending. *Professional School Counseling, 12,* 440–449.

Schellenberg, R., & Grothaus, T. (2011). Using culturally competent responsive services to improve student achievement and behavior. *Professional School Counseling, 14,* 222–230.

Schimmel, C. (2008). *School counseling: A brief historical overview.* West Virginia Department of Education. Retrieved from http://wvde.state .wv.us/counselors/history.html

Schwartz, A. E., Stiefel, L., Rubenstein, R., & Zabel, J. (2011). The path not taken: How does school organization affect eighth-grade achievement? *Educational Evaluation and Policy Analysis, 33,* 293–317.

Seligman, L., & Reichenberg, L. W. (2012). *Selecting effective treatments: A comprehensive guide to treating mental disorders* (4th ed.). Hoboken, NJ: Wiley.

Sergiovanni, T. J. (2000). *Leadership for the schoolhouse: How is it different? Why is it important?* San Francisco, CA: Jossey-Bass.

Sheldon, S. (2003). Linking school-family-community partnerships in urban elementary schools to student achievement on state tests. *The Urban Review, 35,* 149–165.

Shen, Y.-J., & Lowing, R. J. (2007). School counselors' self-perceived Asian American counseling competence. *Professional School Counseling, 11,* 69–71.

Shi, Q., & Steen, S. (2012). Using the Achieving Success Everyday (ASE) group model to promote self-esteem and academic achievement for English as a Second Language (ESL) students. *Professional School Counseling, 16,* 63–70.

Sink, C. A., Akos, P., Turnbull, R. J., & Mvududu, N. (2008). An investigation of comprehensive school counseling programs and academic achievement in Washington State middle schools. *Professional School Counseling, 12,* 43–53.

Sink, C. A., & Stroh, H. R. (2003). Raising achievement test scores of early elementary school students through comprehensive school counseling programs. *Professional School Counseling, 6,* 352–364.

Smith, S. D., & Chen-Hayes, S. F. (2004). Leadership and advocacy strategies for lesbian, bisexual, gay, transgendered, and questioning (LBGTIQ) students: Academic, career, and interpersonal success. In R. Pèrusse & G. E. Goodnough (Eds.), *Leadership, advocacy, and direct service strategies for professional school counselors* (pp. 187–221). Belmont, CA: Brooks/Cole/Cengage.

Smith-Adcock, S., Daniels, M. H., Lee, S. M., Villalba, J. A., & Indelicato, N. A. (2006). Culturally responsive school counseling for Hispanic/Latino students and families: The need for bilingual school counselors. *Professional School Counseling, 10*, 92–101.

Snyder, H. N., & Sickmund, M. (1999). *Juvenile offenders and victims: 1999 national report.* Washington, DC: Office of Juvenile Justice and Delinquency Programs.

Solomon, A. (2012). *Far from the tree: Parents, children, and the search for identity.* New York, NY: Scribner.

Springer, S. P., Reider, J., & Franck, M. R. (2009). *Admission matters: What students and parents need to know about getting into college* (2nd ed.). San Francisco, CA: Jossey-Bass.

Stadler, H. A. (1986). Making hard choices: Clarifying controversial ethical issues. *Counseling & Human Development, 19*, 1–10.

Stone, C. B. (2005). *School counseling principles: Ethics and law.* Alexandria, VA: American School Counselor Association.

Stone, C. B., & Dahir, C. A. (2011). *School counselor accountability: A MEASURE of student success* (3rd ed.). Boston, MA: Pearson.

Stringer, S. J., Reynolds, G. P., & Simpson, F. M. (2003). Collaboration between classroom teachers and a school counselor through literature circles building self-esteem. *Journal of Instructional Psychology, 30*, 69–76.

Sue, D. W., Arredondo, P., & McDavis, R. J. (1992). Multicultural counseling competencies and standards: A call to the profession. *Journal of Counseling & Development, 70*, 477–486.

Thornberg, R. (2012). A grounded theory of collaborative synchronizing in relation to challenging students. *Urban Education, 47*, 312–342. doi: 10.1177/0042085911427735

Trepal, H. (2007). Considerations and strategies for teaching online counseling skills: Establishing relationships in cyberspace. *Counselor Education & Supervision, 46*, 266–279.

Trolley, B. C., Haas, H. S., & Patti, D. C. (2009). *The school counselor's guide to special education.* Thousand Oaks, CA: Corwin.

Trusty, J. (2004). *Effects of students' middle-school and high-school experiences on completion of the bachelor's degree* (Research Monograph No. 1). Amherst, MA: Center for School Counseling Outcome Research.

Ttofi, M. M., & Farrington, D. P. (2011). Effectiveness of school-based programs to reduce bullying: A systematic and meta-analytic review. *Journal of Experimental Criminology, 7*, 27–56. doi:10.1007/s11292–010–9109–1

Turner, S. L., Conkel, J. L., Reich, A. N., Trotter, M. J., & Slewart, J. J. (2006). Social skills efficacy and proactivity among Native American adolescents. *Professional School Counseling, 10*, 189–194.

Villalba, J. A., Akos, P., Keeter, K., & Ames, A. (2007). Promoting Latino student achievement and development through the ASCA National Model. *Professional School Counseling, 12*, 272–279.

Walsh, F. (Ed.). (2012). *Normal family processes: Growing diversity and complexity* (4th ed.). New York, NY: Guilford.

Wang, J., Iannotti, R. J., & Nansel, T. R. (2009). School bullying among U.S. adolescents: Physical, verbal, relational, and cyber. *Journal of Adolescent Health, 45,* 368–375. Retrieved from http://jahonline.org/

Weiner, R., & Hall, D. (2004). Accountability under No Child Left Behind. *The Clearinghouse, 78,* 17–21.

West Virginia Community and Technical College System. (2013). *Advanced training and education required for future jobs.* Retrieved from http://wvctcs.org/state-council/chancellors-page/180-advanced-training-and-education-required-for-future-jobs

Whiston, S. C. (2002). Response to the past, present, and future of school counseling: Raising some issues. *Professional School Counseling, 5,* 148–157.

Willard, N. E. (2007). *Cyber-safe kids, cyber-savvy teens: Helping young people learn to use the Internet safely and responsibly.* San Francisco, CA: Jossey-Bass.

Williams, A., Prestage, S., & Bedward, J. (2001). Individualism to collaboration: The significance of teacher culture to the induction of newly qualified teachers. *Journal of Education for Teaching, 27,* 253–267.

Wood, S. M. (2009). Counseling concerns of gifted and talented adolescents: Implications for school counselors. *Journal of School Counseling, 7.*

Wood, S. M. (2010a). Best practices in counseling the gifted in schools: What's really happening. *Gifted Child Quarterly, 54,* 42–58.

Wood, S. M. (2010b). Nurturing a garden: A qualitative investigation into school counselors' experiences with gifted students. *Journal for the Education of the Gifted, 34,* 261–302.

Wood, S. M. (2012). Rivers' confluence: A qualitative investigation into gifted educators' experiences with collaboration with school counselors. *Roeper Review, 34,* 261–274. doi:10.1080/02783193.2012.715337

Wood, S. M., Portman, T., Cigrand, D. L., & Colangelo, N. (2010). School counselors' perceptions and experience with acceleration as a program option for gifted and talented students. *Gifted Child Quarterly, 54,* 168–178.

Wyatt, S. (2009). The brotherhood: Empowering adolescent African-American males toward excellence. *Professional School Counseling, 12,* 463–470.

Young, A., & Kaffenberger, C. (2013). *Making data work* (3rd ed.). Alexandria, VA: American School Counselor Association.

Young, A., & Kaffenberger, C. (2011). The beliefs and practices of school counselors who use data to implement comprehensive school counseling programs. *Professional School Counseling, 15,* 67–76.

Zinn, H. (2005). *A people's history of the United States.* New York, NY: Harper Perennial.

Zirkel, P. A., & Thomas, L. B. (2010). State laws and guidelines for implementing RTI. *Teaching Exceptional Children, 43,* 60–73.

Zur, O. & Zur, A. (2011). *On digital immigrants and digital natives: How the digital divide affects families, educational institutions, and the workplace.* Zur Institute. Retrieved from http://www.zurinstitute.com

Glossary

504 Plan: Legally mandated accommodations in learning specified for students with particular disabilities

AASA Code of Ethics: Ethical code for building and district leaders who are American Association of School Administrators members

Abilities: Focusing on what students in schools can do (versus what they can't do) using a strengths-based perspective

Ableism: Prejudice multiplied by power used by persons without disabilities to restrict individual, cultural, and systemic resources to persons with developmental, emotional, intellectual, learning, or physical disabilities

ACA Code of Ethics: Ethical code for counselors of all specialty areas, including school counselors, from the American Counseling Association

ACA Competencies for Counseling Transgender Clients: Best practices in counseling transgender persons from the American Counseling Association

Acceleration: Moving students into more challenging material at the same grade level or advancing to a higher grade level

Acceptable Use Policy: A written policy describing expectations regarding student and staff use of technology and mobile devices

ACCESS and Accomplishments Plans: Planning tool to help school counselors and school counseling programs close opportunity and attainment gaps by ensuring K–12 students get annual planning focused on academic, career, college-access, and personal/social competencies using the National Office for School Counselor Advocacy (NOSCA) 8 college and career readiness components and ASCA 9 student standards

Accommodations: Changes to a classroom or policy that allow students with disabilities to fully participate; examples include extended time for assignments, extra visual and verbal cues/prompts, frequent breaks, graphic organizers, large-print text, testing format alterations, visual/written daily schedules, daily homework logs, assistive technology, speech-activated software, wheelchairs, and classroom changes such as preferred seating or altered seating arrangements

Accountability: Being held responsible for one's work and the impact it has on stakeholders

Acculturation: A balancing of one's cultures/languages; the ability to appreciate the strengths and concerns of one's original and host cultures

Achievement Data: Academic performance information about K–12 students derived from school report cards, school improvement plans, standardized testing, grades, career and college assessments, and state and national databases

Achievement Gap: The difference in academic performance between and across diverse cultural groups by ethnicity/race, gender, ability/disability, social class, language, and other cultural variables

Action Plan: A document that sets forth the objectives, resources needed, and persons responsible for enacting a desired outcome, such as the ASCA model tool to plan interventions to close gaps

Action Research: Research that is specific to a local school and is aimed at generating solutions not necessarily generalizable to larger populations

Activism: Publicly campaigning for a topic, cause, need, person, or group of persons

Administrative Supervision: Supervision of school counselors or other staff by a principal, dean, or assistant principal; it may be evaluative in nature and/or revolve around logistical concerns

Advanced Placement (AP): College-level course material taught in high school courses that offer the possibility of advanced standing in college courses and/or college credit if an exam is taken and passed with a certain score

Advocacy: Creating positive change where change is needed; supporting, in word and deed, a topic, cause, need, person, or group of persons

Ageism: Prejudice multiplied by power used by persons 18–49 to deny individual, cultural, and systemic resources based on nondominant age (affects children, adolescents, persons age 50-plus)

ALGBTIC Competencies for Counseling with Lesbian, Gay, Bisexual, Queer, Questioning, Intersex, and Ally (LGBQQIA) Individuals: Best practices in counseling persons with nondominant sexual orientations or those who are questioning their sexual orientation from the Association for Lesbian, Gay, Bisexual, and Transgender Issues in Counseling

Annual Agreement: The ASCA National Model tool that delineates the school counselor's time spent in various tasks and the major function of the school counseling department; the agreement is to be co-constructed and agreed upon by school counselors and administrators

ASCA Ethical Code for School Counselors: Ethical code for all school counselors with specificity on K–12 schools for members of the American School Counselor Association

ASCA SCENE: A professional networking platform that is part of the American School Counselor Association

ASCA School Counselor Competencies: The professional expectations of every school counselor in implementing a school counseling program that provides academic, career, and personal/social competencies to all students K–12

ASCA Student Standards: Originally called national standards, these were developed to outline the academic, career, and personal/social competencies each student is expected to learn from a school counseling program

ASCA Student Standards (Academic): The original three elements of what students should learn from a school counseling program in the academic domain are effective learning, academic preparation for postsecondary options, and relating academics to careers

ASCA Student Standards (Careers): The original three ASCA student standards for career development are (1) Career Exploration; (2) Achieve Future Career Goals; and (3) Personal Qualities, Education, and Career Relationship

ASCA Student Standards (Personal/Social): The three original ASCA personal/social student standards are (1) understanding and respecting self and others, (2) decision-making and achieving goals, and (3) safety and survival skills

Assessment: Determining needs for intervention and determining effectiveness of interventions over time

Assimilation: Valuing one's new or host culture/language as better than one's prior culture or language and denigrating one's prior culture/language as negative or inferior; it can be chosen or coerced

Asynchronous: Interacting with technology sources at one's own convenience and not in real time

Attainment Data: Information showing which students are graduating from undergraduate two-year and four-year colleges and universities with a diploma within four, five, or six years after enrollment, disaggregated by cultural group/identities

Attainment Gap: The difference in rates of students graduating with a college diploma (two-year or four-year) across different cultural groups when data is disaggregated by ethnicity/race, social class, ability/disability, language background, and gender

Authoritarian Leadership: Leadership that comes from one person who dictates what others are to do

Autism Spectrum: The range of pervasive developmental disorders where the person experiences impairments in social interaction and communication and evidences repetitive and restricted behaviors

Beautyism: Prejudice multiplied by power used by persons with culturally valued appearances to deny individual, cultural, and systemic resources based on nondominant appearance

Bilingual Education: Using two languages to teach and learn academic subjects in K–12 schools

Blogs: Journal entries or short personal or professional opinion pieces found on the Internet

Budgeting: The process of appropriation of funds to staff and support the school according to federal mandates, state requirements, and local needs

Bullying: Intentionally and repeatedly inflicting unwanted emotional, verbal, physical, and/or social harm on another person that involves a disparity of power between the bully and the victim

Career and Technical Education: The goal of CTE is to prepare students to gain entry-level employment in high-skill, high-wage jobs and/or to continue their education in their chosen career field.

Career Development: Understanding interests, skills, and personality strengths in the process of making successful transitions between grade levels to postsecondary options and the world of work

Carnegie Unit: A measure for the amount of time a student has studied a subject. Instruction that lasts 40–60 minutes 4–5 times a week, for 36–40 weeks, for a total of 120 hours annually, is one "unit" of high school credit.

Caseload Assignments: The portion of a school's student body assigned to a school counselor; often determined by dividing up students' names alphabetically or by grade level or other unit

Change Agent: An individual who works for justice for all groups and persons by identifying gaps and needs and then taking productive action

Child Study Team: A team of school staff members including the school counselor who discuss and plan for students with academic and/or behavioral concerns

Classism: Prejudice multiplied by power used by persons with dominant social class resources (wealthy and upper middle class) to deny individual, cultural, and systemic resources to persons of nondominant social classes (poor, working class, lower middle class)

Closing-the-Gap Action Plan: The ASCA Model planning tool to help close achievement (and opportunity and attainment) gaps

Closing-the-Gap Results Report: The ASCA Model planning tool that shows process, perception, and outcome data in closing achievement (and opportunity and attainment) gaps

Cloud Computing: The use of a web-based tool, site, or platform for storing documents, photos, or music so that the user has access to the most updated version. It reduces or eliminates use of computer hard drives for file storage and allows easier file sharing.

Collaboration: The process by which school staff from various fields, disciplines, and roles come together to create solutions for issues that arise in their buildings

Collaborative Conferencing Software: Specialized software applications that allow for multiple participants to interact with one another despite being in different geographic locations

College Access: The activities engaged in by students, educators, and students' families that ensure students have the social capital and other resources to successfully pursue a college education

College and Career Readiness: The activities engaged in by students, educators, and students' families that ensure students have the academic, social, and career- and college-planning skills to successfully pursue a college education and/or career of their choice; *college ready* means the ability to begin college with the necessary skills and knowledge to be successful without having to take remedial coursework; *career ready* means one is able to enter the workforce with the requisite skills to be successful and advance in one's chosen profession

College Best Fit: The college that best suits each student on multiple variables—academic major(s), affordability, graduation rate, housing options, location, public/private, two-year or four-year, student activities/services, and so forth

College Knowledge: The ability to navigate the college search and application process

College Results Online: The Education Trust's annually updated website that monitors college graduation rates with disaggregated data for all U.S. four-year colleges and universities

Common Career Technical Core Standards: The academic standards designed to ensure student success in postsecondary career and technical education (including college), which are focused on 16 career clusters and the academic pathways to reach them successfully

Common Core State Standards: Learning standards common across 45 of 50 states aligned with assessments attempting to ensure greater depth in teaching and learning with the outcome that every K–12 student is career and college ready

Common Data Set Initiative: Annual report by colleges and universities compiled by major educational publishers to ensure quality and accurate college information for informed decision making for students, families, and other stakeholders involved in high school to college transition

Community: A group comprising familial, social, religious, occupational, business, and legislative entities surrounding a school; a sense of belonging to something larger or greater than oneself

Confidentiality: A practice in which information shared with the school counselor is not revealed to any other person, that is, "What you say here stays here," with exceptions including (1) imminent danger to self or others; (2) consultation/supervision with school counselor, psychologist, or social worker colleagues and school counseling program director; (3) court subpoenas/orders (but the school counselor/district can challenge them); (4) release of information consent forms, including those signed by parents/guardians for counseling a minor; and (5) confidentiality challenges with more than one client/student in group or family counseling

Content Management Systems: Educationally driven websites designed to deliver content to participants who have access to the system, commonly used in colleges and universities for managing courses and communication between students and instructors

Core Academic Skills: Skills such as critical thinking, writing, and reading comprehension that transcend subject matter and allow students to be successful in a variety of fields

Crisis Intervention: A form of counseling that focuses on critical immediate situations

Cultural Identity Development Models: Human developmental models based on cultural variables including ethnicity, gender, race, sexual orientation, social class, religion/spirituality, and others that emphasize integrating and valuing one's cultural identity(-ies) over time. Understanding and affirming identity development has been shown to mitigate against stress from oppression and promote feelings of pride in one's identity(-ies) and the history of challenging oppression.

Cyberbullying: The use of technological devices and software (e.g., computers, tablets, cell phones, Internet chat rooms, website posts, Twitter, Facebook, Instagram, other social media) to intentionally inflict unwanted emotional harm on another person repeatedly

Cyberstalking: Repeated threats or intimidating messages or images sent via electronic devices to monitor another person with unwanted attention or electronic interactions

Data Team: A team of school staff members including the school counselor who discuss national, state, district, and/or schoolwide data sets to determine areas of strength and improvement

Data-Based Decision Making: Decision making that is accomplished by reviewing critical data elements associated with the problem at hand, such as graduation rates, test scores, grades, and disciplinary or attendance rates

Data-Based Decision-Making Models: Conceptual frameworks that assist school counselors in using information to make successful interventions K–12 that help to close achievement, opportunity, and attainment gaps

Data-Driven: Decisions concerning future action that are based on survey reports, assessments, statistics, or other forms of data

Democratic Leadership: Leadership that involves seeking the perspectives and feedback of those who are led

Developmental Disabilities: Chronic impairments appearing prior to adulthood that can be physical, cognitive, and/or learning that limit functioning in at least three areas of living: self-care, language (receptive/expressive), learning, mobility, self-direction, independent living, and ability to be economically independent

Differentiation: Using varied instructional methods and assessments to enhance learning for every student

Digital Citizenship: Behaving online in an ethical and responsible way

Digital School Counseling Brochure: A brochure from the school counseling program that exists in digital form instead of or in addition to print format

Digital School Counseling Bulletin Board: A picture of the school counseling program bulletin board posted on the school counseling program web pages

Disaggregated Data: Data that is pulled apart to look at differences by group, including grade level, gender, age, ability/disability, ethnicity/race, language, and social class (free and reduced lunch), and is used to identify inequitable policies and practices that can close gaps

Disaggregated Opportunity and Attainment Data: K–12 college/career readiness and college graduation information categorized by cultural group that can indicate inequitable patterns across multiple data points that make the difference in college and career/technical program admission and graduation

Distributed/Shared Leadership: Leadership that is shared within a group that makes decisions together with input from stakeholders

Do No Harm: Also known as *nonmaleficence*, this covenant ensures that school counseling program policies and practices governing delivery of academic, career and college readiness, and personal/social competencies treat all K–12 students equitably (harm results from not having equitable access to these competencies).

DSM-5: Classification system used by mental health professionals for diagnosis and treatment of mental and emotional/behavioral disorders; contains research- and evidence-based decision-making tools for diagnosis and dimensional assessments

Dual Language Immersion or Two-Way Education: Classroom instruction in both the native and the target language, usually at the elementary level, that takes place primarily in the target language (i.e., 90–10 model) until fluency is gained and then shifts to equal proportions of both languages. Only one language is used in the classroom at a time, which moves students toward greater proficiency faster, and students learn about all subjects in both languages. This approach increases students' skills in both languages and fosters high levels of cognitive complexity.

Dual Relationships: Acting in another role or roles in addition to that of school counselor toward students or their families (e.g., also being a teacher or being a dean or dating a student's parent or guardian)—dual roles are to be avoided/minimized at all times

Duty to Warn: School counselors, like other mental health professionals, have a legal and ethical duty to warn those in imminent danger when a student/client threatens harm to self or others.

Educational Equity: Ensuring all children and adolescents have the resources, opportunities, and fair treatment to be successful in K–12 settings

Efficiency: The effectiveness of school operations and organization to meet the goals of the school and to facilitate student success

Eligibility: The identified classification of the particular special needs of a student that qualifies the student for services

Emotional Abuse: Abuse that includes but is not limited to constant criticism, intimidation, manipulation, name-calling, threats, and invalidation

Emotional/Behavioral Disabilities: Conditions over time that harm a child or adolescent's academic abilities, including at least one of the following: an inability to learn not explained by other factors; poor peer and teacher interpersonal relationships; inappropriate behaviors or feelings; pervasive unhappiness or depressed mood; and physical symptoms or fears related to school or personal factors

E-Newsletters: Newsletters that are delivered in graphic form via e-mail or an Internet link

Enrichment: For gifted/talented students, staying at grade level but learning more in depth at particular periods during the day and outside of school compared to peers

Epstein's School-Family–Community-Partnership Model: There are six different types of involvement that promote collaborative relationships: (1) parenting; (2) communicating; (3) volunteering; (4) learning at home; (5) decision-making; and (6) collaboration with the community

Equity: Fairness, justice, and ensuring that all students have the social capital and academic, career and college readiness, and personal/social competencies to reach their career/college dreams, facilitated by a school counseling program; some students need greater resources than others

Equity Assistance Centers: Ten regional offices around the United States that deliver resource assistance for K–12 school and district staff to promote equity and equal opportunities based on race, gender, and national origin; funded by the U.S. Department of Education and Title IV of the 1964 Civil Rights Act

Equity Audit: An assessment of all of a school's policies and practices and their effect on diverse cultural groups/identities within the school; this includes the master schedule, who takes rigorous courses, who receives career and college readiness counseling and planning, who graduates on time, who is over-credited and under-credited, and how school counselors and school counseling program resources are deployed for all students

Ethical Decision-Making Model for School Counselors: Developed by Carolyn Stone and included in the 2010 *ASCA Ethical Code for School Counselors* revision "Solutions to Ethical Problems in Schools" or STEPS:

1. Define the problem emotionally and intellectually
2. Apply the ASCA and ACA ethical codes and the law
3. Consider the students' chronological and developmental levels
4. Consider the setting, parental rights, and minors' rights
5. Apply the moral principles
6. Determine your potential courses of action and their consequences
7. Evaluate the selected action
8. Consult
9. Implement the course of action

Evaluation: A process used by an individual or group to determine progress or quality; evaluation is a key element in any improvement process

Evidence-Based Practices: Interventions or strategies that are grounded in research and have publicly available data

External Public Relations: Explaining the school counseling program and the larger school context to stakeholders outside the building: parents/guardians, community organizations, businesses, places of worship, and voters

EZAnalyze: Free software, developed by Dr. Tim Poynton for school counselors and leaders to use to collect, study, and disseminate data for school counselors, school counseling programs, and educators, that can easily be used to help close achievement gaps

Family Educational Rights Privacy Act (FERPA): Federal law proscribing who may have access to a student's educational records and when; it states that schools may not divulge educational records without consent and a written release from a parent/guardian or eligible student; students of a certain age may legally access their records and ask to amend incorrect records

Family: The roles and relationships of a domestic unit of people connected by birth, marriage or other legal commitments, or in spirit

Family Life Cycle: The developmental stages over time that include normative tasks whose successful resolution indicates greater likelihood of success in future stages; stages are not necessarily linear and don't necessarily apply to all persons or families

Family Process: The type and quality of roles and relationships between family members that affect family functioning

Family Resilience: Strengths-based perspective on working to build family patterns, interactions, and relationships for optimal functioning

Family System: A unit with complex interactions or processes and subsystems (parental, sibling, child) that mediate interactions between members of the system

Familyism: Prejudice multiplied by power used by persons from traditional family types to deny individual, cultural, and systemic resources based on nondominant family type (single, single-parent, same-gender, multiracial, homeless, adoptive, foster, divorced)

Flaming: Sending spiteful or vulgar messages about someone to a person or group online or via text messaging

Free Application for Federal Student Aid (FAFSA): An application required by the federal government that determines the amount of federal financial assistance for which a student qualifies; used by many universities/colleges to determine scholarship and grant contributions.

Genderism: Prejudice multiplied by power used by traditionally gendered persons to deny individual, cultural, and systemic resources to gender-variant and transgender persons

Gifted/Talented: K–12 students with outstanding aptitude/capabilities in intellectual, artistic, creative, and leadership domains or specific academic disciplines needing specialized activities/services to develop full capabilities

Goals/Objectives: Specified target levels of performance for the student to reach as identified by the IEP team

Heritage Language: Language spoken at home that is the original language of some or all family members but not the main language of instruction in a K–12 school

Heterosexism: Prejudice multiplied by power used by heterosexuals to deny individual, cultural, and systemic resources to lesbian, bisexual, and gay persons

Horizontal and Vertical Stressors: Predictable transitions over the life cycle (births, marriages, divorces, deaths) and unexpected events (accidents, disabilities, illnesses, sudden death); vertical stressors include long-standing family patterns such as legacies, myths, secrets, and patterns that influence family processes

ICD-10: *International Statistical Classification of Diseases and Health-Related Problems,* 10th edition, an international medical disease classification system

Immigrationism: Prejudice multiplied by power used by persons of legal citizenship status to deny individual, cultural, and systemic resources to persons of nondominant citizenship status

Incest: Illegal sexual relations between people who are closely related

Inclusion: Placing students with disabilities in general education classrooms with appropriate support services and staffing

Individual Student Planning: Ongoing systemic activities assisting the individual student in establishing personal goals and developing future plans, such as individual learning, graduation, and ACCESS/Accomplishments plans

Individualized Educational Plan (IEP): Written statement, updated regularly, outlining specific academic/social services, service providers, goals, and objectives for a child or adolescent with one or more disabilities

Informed Consent: When a minor student's parent/guardian or student of the legal age of consent gives written permission to receive individual or group counseling from the school counselor with an understanding of the techniques to be used, the duration of counseling, the potential benefits and concerns, and the student's/family's right to stop counseling at any time

Integrative Developmental Model: A model of counselor supervision that centers on the counselor's professional development in the areas of awareness of self and others, motivation, and autonomy

Intellectual Disabilities: Below-average cognitive functioning in two or more behaviors first appearing in childhood or adolescence

Internal Public Relations: Explaining the school counseling program to all internal stakeholders including students, educators, staff, and building leaders

International Baccalaureate: Pre-K–12 course curriculum framework offered for elementary, middle, intensive IB, and high school students focused on depth and breadth of learning using units of inquiry, theme-based learning permeating all course subjects throughout the year, and inquiry-based learning. The last two years of the high school program are known as the IB Diploma and passing intensive IB, college-level content courses, based on essay exams, allows some students to enter college with course credit and/or advanced standing. The IB curriculum framework is taught worldwide and recognized internationally for developing critical thinking and international-mindedness. All students are expected to study at least one world language in addition to the language of instruction in the IB model with a focus on international learning.

Intimate Partner Violence: Emotional, physical, and/or sexual violence and/or threats thereof inflicted on an intimate partner; formerly known as domestic violence

Laissez-Faire Leadership: A leadership style in which leaders are vague and seemingly aimless, hands-off, and/or uninvolved

Language Immersion: Instruction given exclusively in a target language for a sustained period to promote fluency

Leadership: Taking initiative to create positive change

Leadership Practices: Practices, either innate or learned, that create positive change

Leadership Team: A team of school staff members including the school counselor that discusses relevant issues of the school

Learning Disabilities: Learning and cognition challenges in particular academic subjects, including reading (*dyslexia*), writing (*dysgraphia*), and mathematics (*dyscalculia*), where learners need varied approaches to learn material successfully

Learning Styles: Learning varies by individuals, and all persons have preferred ways of learning, including aural, visual, and tactile-kinesthetic; lesson planning and delivery is enhanced when school counselors provide content and experiences suited to diverse learning styles

Least Restrictive Environment: Ensuring maximum interaction with the general school environment for students with disabilities

Linguicism: Prejudice multiplied by power used by persons of a dominant language denying individual, cultural, and systemic resources to persons of a nondominant language background

Masquerading: Sending or posting potentially harmful information via snail mail, chatrooms, websites, or Facebook posts under an assumed identity

Massive Open Online Courseware (MOOC): An Internet-based platform for providing education and/or training to large and broad audiences

Multicultural Competencies: Specific cultural awareness, knowledge, and skills that professional counselors use to effectively counsel culturally diverse clients/students

Multicultural Education: A discipline in education focused on creating educational equity for all students focused on both content about diverse groups and how educational processes are conducted regarding multiple cultural identities for students K–12

NACAC Statement of Professional Good Practice (SPGP): Ethical code of conduct updated annually by the National Association for College Admission Counseling for admission counselors in K–12 and college settings

NAESP Code of Ethics: Code of ethics for elementary and middle school building leaders who are members of the National Association of Elementary School Principals

NASSP Code of Ethics: Code of ethics for middle and high school building leaders who are members of the National Association of Secondary School Principals

NEA Code of Ethics: Code of ethics for teachers who are members of the National Education Association

Needs Assessment: Activities designed to acquire information about stakeholder needs

Neglect: Refusal or delay in timely and appropriate health care, permitted chronic truancy, or inattention to special education needs without reasonable cause; inadequate nurturance or affection; encouraging or permitting drug or alcohol use by children or adolescents; or refusal to allow needed medical treatment for a child or adolescent's emotional or psychological care

Netiquette: Appropriate behavior using digital network communications

NOSCA Eight Components of College and Career Readiness Counseling: The essential tools that all elementary, middle, and high school counselors use to ensure college and career readiness skills by high school graduation

Online Harassment: Persistent, offensive messaging from one or more persons who send unwanted messages or images that may include threats of emotional or physical harm to the recipient or others close to the recipient

Online Instruction: A means of using the Internet as a source of instruction in concert with or in lieu of face-to-face instruction

Operations: The day-to-day management of a school inclusive of facility use, master schedules, traffic flow patterns, budgetary practices, staffing, policies, and procedures

Opportunity Data: Data points that indicate which students K–12 are given the social capital and college and career readiness competencies needed to successfully enter and complete four-year and two-year college, university, and career/technical programs

Opportunity Gap: The difference between disaggregated student cultural group/identities in access to annual career and college readiness planning and counseling interventions, challenging coursework (including Advanced Placement courses, International Baccalaureate curriculum framework courses, and intensive honors courses), the strongest teachers (teaching in-subject with longevity), and other experience and social capital that boosts success in college and career with measurable outcomes

Oppressions: Prejudice multiplied by power that dominant cultural groups use to restrict access to individual, cultural, and systemic resources by non-dominant cultural group members; examples include ableism, ageism, beautyism, classism, familyism, genderism, heterosexism, immigrationism, linguicism, racism, religionism, and sexism

Organization: The structure of groupings or assigning tasks and responsibilities to certain persons within schools such as teams, grade levels, departments, and committees

Outcome Research: Research that demonstrates the effectiveness of an intervention or program and suggests generalizability to larger populations

Outing or Trickery: Tricking an individual into providing confidential information with the intention of making it public to others via chatrooms, e-mail, Facebook, snail mail, Twitter, texting, or websites

Partnership: Collaborative work on the part of people or institutions to meet a common goal

Physical Abuse: Acts including hitting with hand, stick, strap, or other object; punching; kicking; shaking; throwing; burning; stabbing; or choking

Physical Disabilities: Bodily impairments that can occur prior to, during, or after birth that affect physical functioning and/or limit daily functioning; examples include impaired hearing or vision, epilepsy, and respiratory disorders

Podcasts: Audio recordings of lectures or presentations that can be listened to online or through accessible applications for mobile devices

Positive Behavior Support (PBS): A form of Applied Behavioral Analysis (ABA) using functional behavioral assessments (FBA) to get a baseline of data about a student's behavior, contexts, and consequences and then create goals, interventions, and monitoring of changes pre- and post-intervention

Privacy: The right to keep one's personal information and records from being disclosed to others

Privileged Communication: A right legally held by the student/client to ensure privacy when discussing personal matters with certain professionals. It applies to relationships with medical doctors, clergy, and attorneys but not at the federal level to relationships with most mental health professionals, including school counselors, unless they practice in a state that legally grants them privileged communication.

Process, Perception, and Outcome Data for Opportunity and Attainment Gaps: The impact of a school counseling program intervention on moving an opportunity or attainment data point—such as increased attendance, fewer tardies, more students in challenging courses, more students graduating from two-year and four-year colleges and career/technical programs, higher grades, fewer behavioral incidents, every student completing a college/career/academic plan, all students taking PSAT and PLAN, and so forth

Professional Learning Communities: Formalized groups of school staff members, often across disciplines, engaged in ongoing, intentional, organized learning together for the benefit of understanding the needs of students and the school community

Program Assessment: The process of measuring a school counseling program's effectiveness, including process, perception, and outcome results; it typically includes regular pre- and post-tests, needs assessments, surveys, and questionnaires for various stakeholders including students, staff, families, and/or community members

Pseudonym: A false identity created to hide the identity of a bully while making fun of, harassing, threatening, or intimidating others or instigating fights online

Public Relations: Marketing school counseling programs and positions by investing time and energy in building relationships with stakeholders and sharing news, updates, and outcomes in both digital and traditional formats

Racism: Prejudice multiplied by power used by persons of a dominant racial group (in the United States, Whites) to deny persons of color and mixed-race persons individual, cultural, and systemic resources

RAMP: Recognized ASCA Model Program is an award given to school counseling programs for their data-driven outcomes in fully implementing a school counseling program including closing achievement and/or opportunity gaps in their schools.

Rape: The act of forced sexual activity with an unwilling or nonconsenting person

Release of Information: A legal document giving permission, when signed and dated by a parent/guardian of a minor or by a student of legal age of consent, to share information about the student from one professional to another

Religionism: Prejudice multiplied by power used by persons of a dominant religion to deny individual, cultural, and systemic resources based on non-dominant religion, spirituality, or meaning-making system

Response to Intervention: Schools identify students facing poor learning outcomes, monitor student progress, provide evidence-based interventions, and adjust the interventions depending on a student's responsiveness.

Results Report: An ASCA Model tool that helps school counselors monitor the effectiveness of their interventions by documenting outcomes

Scaffolding: Temporary instructional supports that assist learners in creating new knowledge that gives added structure to ensure success

School Climate: The overall feelings, attitudes, and expectations prevalent in a school

School Counseling Core Curriculum: The developmental classroom lessons school counselors plan, create, implement, and evaluate to deliver academic, career/college access, and personal/social competencies to all students K–12 in collaboration with teachers and other school leaders

School Counseling Program Advisory Council: A leadership group comprising stakeholders to include a teacher, school building leader, student, parent/guardian, and community member that advises school counselors on the goals, data, implementation, and evaluation of the school counseling program

School Counseling Program Website: Website designed to educate readers about the school counseling program with information such as services provided, upcoming events, and contact information for school counselors

School Counselor Performance Evaluation: Evaluating school counselors on their school counseling practices in personal/social, college/career, and academic domains and the impact that work has on their students and school community

School Counselor Performance Standards: District or state standards used to evaluate school counselor effectiveness

School Counselor Performance Tool: District or state template, rubric, or form used to evaluate school counselor effectiveness

School Culture: The institutionalized atmosphere or "feel" of a school on a day-to-day basis

School Improvement Plan: School annual goals for improvement that should address achievement, opportunity, and attainment gap performance

School Profile: An overview of the school, including demographics, size, population, location, academic achievement strengths and gaps, and special programs

Servant Leadership: Leadership that has service as a core value and is carried out as a means to serve the greater good

Sexism: Prejudice multiplied by power used by persons of a dominant gender (men and boys) to deny individual, cultural, and systemic resources to women and girls

Sexting: Sending sexual images of oneself or of one's target through electronic means to others

Sexual Abuse: Oral, vaginal, or anal intrusion or penetration using the genitals or touching genitals with body parts or other objects, enacted on a child or adolescent; may include adult nudity, genital exposure, or inappropriate observation of a child or adolescent while nude (e.g., undressing, bathing)

Sexual Harassment: Unwelcome and unsolicited advances, teasing, and/or comments of a sexual nature

Social Exclusion: Intentionally prohibiting or limiting an individual's participation in an online group, social network, e-mail list, or chat room

Social Justice: Equity in access to resources including human and civil rights movements that challenge oppression

Social Media Sites: Web-based tools or locations that allow for social and/ or professional interaction

Standards Blending: Demonstrating the school counseling program's effectiveness in academic success and closing achievement gaps by combining school counseling student standards delivered in school counseling core curriculum lessons with academic standards such as the Common Core State Standards for career and college readiness

Strategic Planning: Planning that is conducted in response to identified needs in a school and as a means to address those needs

StudentTracker: A software program designed to monitor college attainment rates for high school cohorts

Synchronous: Interacting with technology sources in real time or "live"

System: A collection of parts joined together by multiple relationships that are interrelated and interdependent

Systemic Change: Change that occurs within and between the multiple spheres of influence that shape educational processes and policies, including (but not limited to) students, parents/guardians, teachers, administrators, and community members

Teams/Houses/Units/Clusters: Organizational units used to divide a school's student body based on geographical layout, efficiency, or convenience

Tenacity: Strong persistence

Transformational Leadership: A type of leadership that empowers the leadership of others

Transition Planning: Students with IEPs by age 14 are required to have a plan in place for transition from high school to the world of work and/or college, and it is mandated in IEPs for students age 16 and older

Transitional Bilingual Education: Courses taught in school for up to three years in the native language with the goal of students then shifting exclusively to the target language; often used to promote the target language as the primary goal for future instruction

Twice Exceptional Students: Students identified as gifted/talented and having learning and/or emotional/behavioral disabilities

Universal Design for Learning: Creating and implementing curriculum that is effective with the widest range of learners and learning styles

Use of Time Analysis Assessment: An ASCA National Model form that allows school counselors to enter their daily activities and tasks to analyze where time is spent and where it is not

Vertical Teaming: Staffing by educators within specific disciplines and districts or states to develop curricula, programs, and/or procedures sharing continuity and intentionality from one student level (elementary, middle school, high school) to another to ensure student academic success

Virtual Worlds/Simulation: Virtual spaces, games, or scenarios in which persons can engage online or through specialized software

Vlogs: Video-based journal entries or short personal or professional opinion pieces that can be found on the Internet

Vodcasts: Video-based recordings of lectures or presentations that can be viewed online or through accessible applications for mobile devices

Webinars: Interactive or noninteractive lectures and presentations that are typically "live" or synchronous and presented through the Internet

Wikis: Collaboratively constructed websites that allow multiple users to add and edit information

World View: A cultural group's set of values and beliefs passed on over time that can include cosmology and epistemology

Young Men of Color Initiative: Young men of color often face some of the most dire outcomes in society and K–12 schools; this initiative is designed by the College Board Advocacy and Policy Office to help school counselors, leaders, and all educators turn around that data with effective policies and practices that empower all young men of color to successfully reach their career and college dreams.

Index

CORWIN

A SAGE Company

The Corwin logo—a raven striding across an open book—represents the union of courage and learning. Corwin is committed to improving education for all learners by publishing books and other professional development resources for those serving the field of PreK–12 education. By providing practical, hands-on materials, Corwin continues to carry out the promise of its motto: **"Helping Educators Do Their Work Better."**

Made in the USA
Las Vegas, NV
23 February 2023